2002 SUPPLEMENT

FEDERAL COURTS AND THE LAW OF FEDERAL–STATE RELATIONS

FOURTH EDITION

by

PETER W. LOW
Hardy Cross Dillard Professor of Law
University of Virginia

JOHN C. JEFFRIES, JR.
Emerson Spies Professor of Law
Arnold H. Leon Professor and Dean of the Law School
University of Virginia

NEW YORK, NEW YORK
FOUNDATION PRESS
2002

Foundation Press, a division of West Group has created this publication to provide you with accurate and authoritative information concerning the subject matter covered. However, this publication was not necessarily prepared by persons licensed to practice law in a particular jurisdiction. Foundation Press is not engaged in rendering legal or other professional advice, and this publication is not a substitute for the advice of an attorney. If you require legal or other expert advice, you should seek the services of a competent attorney or other professional.

COPYRIGHT © 1998–2001 FOUNDATION PRESS
COPYRIGHT © 2002 By FOUNDATION PRESS
                        395 Hudson Street
                        New York, NY 10014
                        Phone Toll Free 1–877–888–1330
                        Fax (212)3670–6799
                        fdpress.com

All rights reserved
Printed in the United States of America

ISBN 1–58778–362–2

TEXT IS PRINTED ON 10% POST CONSUMER RECYCLED PAPER

PREFACE

In the years since 1998, when the fourth edition of Federal Courts and the Law of Federal-State Relations was published, the Supreme Court has decided a great many cases of relevance to the field. In our coverage of those decisions, we have decided to err on the side of inclusion rather than exclusion. We have therefore included generous treatment of recent decisions because they are recent, even if we expect more summary treatment in the casebook's next edition. Coverage of all these decisions is certainly not essential, but we thought that others would appreciate, as we do, the opportunity to teach recent decisions and thereby to keep abreast of developments in the field.

An example of this policy is **Lee v. Kemna** (2002), which concerned the adequacy of a state court procedural default to bar federal habeas review. Speaking through Justice Ginsburg, the Court found that a Missouri appellate court's insistence on a state rule requiring motions for continuance to be supported by written statement and affidavit was, under the circumstances of the case, an empty ritual. Justice Kennedy, joined by Justices Scalia and Thomas, dissented, objecting to the majority's "contextual approach" to the adequacy of state procedural requirements.

On the same theory, the 2002 Supplement also carries forward the 2001 decision in **Bush v. Gore** as a main case. The case raised a federal courts issue to the extent that three members of the Court relied on a supposed manipulation of state law as the justification for halting the Florida recount. On this understanding, *Bush v. Gore* follows Martin v. Hunter's Lessee (1816) and Indiana ex rel. *Anderson v. Brand* (1938). We have therefore continued *Bush v. Gore* as a main case at that point, together with notes sampling academic reaction.

Also included are two main cases on "implied" private rights of action, plus note treatment of other recent decisions in the field. **Alexander v. Sandoval** (2001) held that the "implied" right of action to enforce Title VI of the 1964 Civil Rights Act, created by *Cannon v. University* of Chicago (1979), did not extend to disparate-impact regulations promulgated by the Department of Justice to enforce that provision. **Gebser v. Lago Vista Independent School District** (1998) involved a Title IX damages action against a school district for sexual harassment by a teacher. The Court ruled that the district could be held liable only if the supervisor actually knew of, or was deliberately indifferent to, the teacher's misconduct. Both decisions were decided five-four, and both providing interesting and controversial contexts in which to discuss the current law on "implied" rights of action.

Other recent decisions included as main cases deal with the Congress's power to preclude judicial review of certain legal claims raised by aliens subject to deportation, ***Calcano-Martinez v. INS*** (2001) and ***INS v. St. Cyr*** (2001); standing, ***Federal Election Commission v. Akins*** (1998); restrictions on federal habeas corpus imposed by the Antiterrorism and Effective Death Penalty Act of 1996, ***Duncan v. Walker*** (2001), ***Tyler v. Cain*** (2001), ***Terry Williams v. Taylor*** (2000), and ***Michael Wayne Williams v. Taylor*** (2000); and of course the continuing saga of the Eleventh Amendment and state sovereign immunity, ***Alden v. Maine*** (1999), ***College Savings Bank v. Fla. Prepaid Postsecondary Educational Expense Board*** (and vice versa) (1999), and ***Board of Trustees of the University of Alabama v. Garrett*** (2001).

In addition to these main cases, many other recent decisions are included in notes, and secondary literature published since the casebook went to press is noted where appropriate.

PERMISSION TO DUPLICATE

There are many intersections between Federal Courts and the Law of Federal-State Relations (4th ed. 1998) and Civil Rights Actions: Enforcing the Constitution (2000). Occasionally, a teacher using one book may wish to use material from the other or its annual supplement. To facilitate such borrowings, we authorize teachers who have adopted either book to duplicate limited portions of the other or its supplement for distribution to their students. We are grateful to Foundation Press for agreeing to make this option available.

PWL
JCJJR

Charlottesville, Virginia
July 2002

TABLE OF CONTENTS

	Supplement Page
PREFACE	iii
TABLE OF CASES	xiii
TABLE OF SECONDARY AUTHORITIES	xxi

PART I. FEDERALISM AND SEPARATION OF POWERS: THE BASIC STRUCTURE

CHAPTER I: CHOICE OF LAW IN THE FEDERAL SYSTEM

Casebook Page		Supplement Page
	Section 1: State Law in Federal Court	
9	Additional Citation	1
12	Additional Citation	1
13	Additional Citation	1
14	Additional Citation	1
15	Additional Citations	1
15	Additional Citations	1
17	***Semteck International Inc. v. Lockheed Martin Corp.***	2
18	Additional Citation	3
22	Revision and Additional Citations	3
22	*Fiore v. White*	3
	Section 2: Federal Law In State Court	
50	***Printz v. United States***	3
62	Additional Citation	4
	Section 3: Supreme Court Review of State Court Decisions	
84	***BUSH v. GORE***	4
	Notes on *Bush v. Gore*	34
	1. Equal Protection	34
	2. Article II	36
92	Additional Citation	37

v

Casebook Page		Supplement Page

CHAPTER II: THE POWER OF THE FEDERAL COURTS TO CREATE FEDERAL LAW

Section 2: Implied Rights of Action to Enforce Federal Statutes

Casebook Page		Supplement Page
175	Additional Citation	38
175	***GEBSER v. LAGO VISTA INDEPENDENT SCHOOL DISTRICT***	38
	Note on *Gebser v. Lago Vista*	47
212	***ALEXANDER v. SANDOVAL***	48
	Note on *Alexander* v. *Sandoval*	65
212	***Correctional Services Corp. v. Malesko***	66

CHAPTER III: CONGRESSIONAL CONTROL OF THE FEDERAL COURTS

Section 1: The Power to Limit Federal Jurisdiction

Casebook Page		Supplement Page
215	Additional Citation	68
218	Additional Citation	68
218	Additional Citation	68
224	Additional Citations	68
232	Additional Citation	68
232	Additional Citation	68
232	Additional Citation	68
232	Additional Citation	68
235	Additional Citations	68
236	Additional Citation	68
238	Additional Citation	69
239	***CALCANO–MARTINEZ v. IMMIGRATION AND NATURALIZATION SERVICE***	70
	IMMIGRATION AND NATURALIZATION SERVICE v. ST. CYR	72

Section 3: The Power to Create Non-Article III Court

Casebook Page		Supplement Page
298	Additional Citation	94

Section 4: The Power to Reopen Final Judgments

Casebook Page		Supplement Page
330	*Miller v. French*	94

CHAPTER IV: JUSTICIABILITY

Casebook Page		Supplement Page
	Section 1: Standing	
357	Additional Citation	97
382	Additional Citation	97
382	*Friends of the Earth v. Laidlaw*	97
383	**FEDERAL ELECTION COMMISSION v. AKINS**	100
388	Additional Citation	108
	Section 2: Related Doctrines	
414	Additional Citation	108
418	*City of Erie v. Pap's "Kandyland"*	109
448	Additional Citation	109

PART II: THE JURISDICTION OF THE FEDERAL COURTS

CHAPTER V: SUBJECT MATTER JURISDICTION

	Section 1: Federal Question Jurisdiction	
451	*The Holmes Group, Inc. v. Vornado Air Circulation Systems, Inc.*	110
459	Add New Notes:	
	7a. *City of Chicago v. International College of Surgeons*	110
	7b. The Primacy of Subject Matter Jurisdiction	111
	(i) Hypothetical Jurisdiction: **Steel Co. v. Citizens for a Better Environment**	112
	(ii) In Personam v. Subject Matter Jurisdiction: **Ruhrgas AG v. Marathon Oil Co.**	114
	Section 2: Diversity Jurisdiction	
485	Additional Citation	115
486	*JPMorgan Chase Bank v. Traffic Stream (BVI) Infrastructure, Ltd.*	115
500	Additional Citations	115
	Section 3: The Substance/Procedure Problem	
518	Additional Citations	116
529	Additional Citation	116
538	**Semtek International Inc. v. Lockheed Martin Corp.**	116
538	Additional Citation	120
	Section 4: Finality and Appellate Review	
552	Additional Citation	120
568	*Jefferson v. City of Tarrant*	120

CHAPTER VI: ABSTENTION

Casebook Page		Supplement Page
	Section 1: General Principles	
590	Additional Citation	121
596	Additional Citation	121
	Section 3: *Younger* Abstention	
629	Additional Citation	121
	Section 4: Anti-Injunction Act	
680	Additional Citations	121
683	*Rivet v. Regions Bank of Louisiana*	122

PART III: FEDERAL COURT ENFORCEMENT OF FEDERAL RIGHTS

CHAPTER VII: HABEAS CORPUS

	Section 1: The Scope of Review	
686	Additional Citation	123
686	Additional Citation	123
709	Additional Citations	123
711	Additional Citations	123
718	Additional Citation	123
722	Additional Citations	124
722	Omit Pages 722–43 and substitute:	
	TERRY WILLIAMS v. TAYLOR	124
	Notes on the 1966 Legislation	146
	1. Questions and Comments on *Terry Williams v. Taylor*	146
	2. ***Bell v. Cone***	147
	3. ***Horn v. Banks***	148
	4. Additional Ambiguities	149
741	Additional Citations	150
742	Additional Citations	150
743	Additional Citations	150
	Section 2: Procedural Foreclosure	
754	*Edwards v. Carpenter*	150
754	***Daniels v. United States and Lackawanna County District Attorney v. Coss***	150
756	*Trest v. Cain*	152
757	Additional Citation	152
763	Omit Pages 763–65 and Substitute:	
	LEE v. KEMNA	152

Casebook Page		Supplement Page
	Notes on Procedural Foreclosure Under the 1996 Legislation	170
	1. Effect of Prior Litigation of the Facts in State Court	170
	2. Effect of Failure to Litigate Claims in State Court	170
	3. *Michael Wayne Williams v. Taylor*	171
	4. Questions and Comments on *Michael Wayne Williams v. Taylor*	175
	5. The New Legislation in Capital Cases	177

Section 3: Exhaustion of State Remedies and Repetitive Applications

Casebook Page		Supplement Page
780	Replace Footnote: *O'Sullivan v. Boerckel*	177
780	Replace Text: *O'Sullivan v. Boerckel*	177
783	*Carey v. Saffold*	177
786	*Slack v. McDaniel*	177
786	Add New Notes and Main Cases:	178
	9. *Stewart v. Martinez-Villareal*	178
	10. Questions and Comments on *Martinez-Villareal*	180
	DUNCAN v. WALKER	180
	TYLER v. CAIN	191

Section 4: Claims of Innocence

Casebook Page		Supplement Page
808	Additional Citations	201
808	BOUSLEY v. UNITED STATES	201

CHAPTER VIII: STATE SOVEREIGN IMMUNITY AND THE 11TH AMENDMENT

Section 1: Nature of the Limitation

Casebook Page		Supplement Page
825	Additional Citations	213

Section 2: Consent and Congressional Abrogation

Casebook Page		Supplement Page
847	*Lapides v. Board of Regents of the University System of Georgia*	214
879	Omit pages 879–80 and Substitute: Note on *Seminole Tribe*	214
880	Add a New Section:	
	Section 2A: The 1999 Decisions	215
	ALDEN v. MAINE	215
	COLLEGE SAVINGS BANK v. FLORIDA PREPAID POSTSECONDARY EDUCATION EXPENSE BOARD	243

Casebook Page		Supplement Page
	FLORIDA PREPAID POSTSECONDARY EDUCATION EXPENSE BOARD v. COLLEGE SAVINGS BANK	255
	Notes on the 1999 Decisions	263
	1. Kimel v. Florida Board of Regents	263
	2. Bibliography	263
	BOARD OF TRUSTEES OF THE UNIVERSITY OF ALABAMA v. GARRETT	266
	Note on Federal Maritime Commission v. South Carolina State Ports Authority	283
	Section 3: Whither *Ex parte Young*	
880	Add Introductory Note on *Coeur d'Alene Tribe*	284
888	Add Note on ***Verizon Maryland Inc. v. Public Service Commission***	285
	Section 4: Constitutionally Required Remedies in State Court	
903	Additional Citation	286

CHAPTER IX: 42 U.S.C. § 1983

	Section 1: "Under Color of" Law	
919	Additional Citation	287
	Section 2: Official Immunities	
937	***Crawford-El v. Britton***	287
940	Additional Citations	288
941	***Wilson v. Layne***; Additional Citations	288
	7a. Unnecessary Merits Adjudication?	288
949	Additional Citations	289
954	Statute	290
	Section 3: Governmental Liability	
1015	Additional Citation	290
1017	Additional Citations	290
	Section 4: For What Wrongs	
1035	Additional Citation	291
1040	***County of Sacramento v. Lewis***	291
1085	*Suter v. Artist M.*; *Blessing v. Firestone*	292
1090	***Gonzaga University v. Doe***	292
	Section 5: Attorney's Fees	
1126	Additional Citations	295

CHAPTER X: REMEDIAL INTERACTIONS

Section 2: Res Judicata

1183   Additional Citation -- 296

APPENDIX B: SELECTED FEDERAL STATUTES

B-33   42 U.S.C. § 1983 -- 297
B-35   42 U.S.C. § 1988(b) -- 297

APPENDIX C: JUDICIAL REVIEW

C-10   Additional Citation -- 299

*

TABLE OF CASES

Principal cases are in bold type. Non-principal cases are in roman type. References are to Pages.

Accardi, United States ex rel. v. Shaughnessy, 347 U.S. 260, 74 S.Ct. 499, 98 L.Ed. 681 (1954), 79, 91, 92
Adams v. Evatt, 511 U.S. 1001, 114 S.Ct. 1365, 128 L.Ed.2d 42 (1994), 195
Alden v. Maine, 527 U.S. 706, 119 S.Ct. 2240, 144 L.Ed.2d 636 (1999), 4, **215,** 243, 250, 252, 261, 263, 264, 265, 266, 275
Alexander v. Choate, 469 U.S. 287, 105 S.Ct. 712, 83 L.Ed.2d 661 (1985), 49, 60
Alexander v. Sandoval, 532 U.S. 275, 121 S.Ct. 1511, 149 L.Ed.2d 517 (2001), **48,** 65, 66, 294
Allen v. Wright, 468 U.S. 737, 104 S.Ct. 3315, 82 L.Ed.2d 556 (1984), 104
Anderson v. Celebrezze, 460 U.S. 780, 103 S.Ct. 1564, 75 L.Ed.2d 547 (1983), 12
Anderson v. Creighton, 483 U.S. 635, 107 S.Ct. 3034, 97 L.Ed.2d 523 (1987), 288
Arizona v. Fulminante, 499 U.S. 279, 111 S.Ct. 1246, 113 L.Ed.2d 302 (1991), 199
ASARCO Inc. v. Kadish, 490 U.S. 605, 109 S.Ct. 2037, 104 L.Ed.2d 696 (1989), 109
Ashwander v. TVA, 297 U.S. 288, 56 S.Ct. 466, 80 L.Ed. 688 (1936), 76
Association of Data Processing Service Organizations, Inc. v. Camp, 397 U.S. 150, 90 S.Ct. 827, 25 L.Ed.2d 184 (1970), 102
Atascadero State Hosp. v. Scanlon, 473 U.S. 234, 105 S.Ct. 3142, 87 L.Ed.2d 171 (1985), 219, 222, 246, 249, 260, 262
Ayers, In re, 123 U.S. 443, 8 S.Ct. 164, 31 L.Ed. 216 (1887), 213, 228, 231

Bailey v. United States, 516 U.S. 137, 116 S.Ct. 501, 133 L.Ed.2d 472 (1995), 202, 203, 204, 205, 206, 207, 211
Beers v. Arkansas, 61 U.S. 527, 20 How. 527, 15 L.Ed. 991 (1857), 246
Bell v. Cone, ___ U.S. ___, 122 S.Ct. 1843 (2002), 147
Bivens v. Six Unknown Named Agents of Federal Bureau of Narcotics, 403 U.S. 388, 91 S.Ct. 1999, 29 L.Ed.2d 619 (1971), 66, 67
Blatchford v. Native Village of Noatak, 501 U.S. 775, 111 S.Ct. 2578, 115 L.Ed.2d 686 (1991), 220, 225

Blessing v. Freestone, 520 U.S. 329, 117 S.Ct. 1353, 137 L.Ed.2d 569 (1997), 292
Boardman v. Esteva, 323 So.2d 259 (Fla. 1975), 15
Board of Pardons v. Allen, 482 U.S. 369, 107 S.Ct. 2415, 96 L.Ed.2d 303 (1987), 93
Board of Trustees of University of Alabama v. Garrett, 531 U.S. 356, 121 S.Ct. 955, 148 L.Ed.2d 866 (2001), **266**
Boerne, City of v. Flores, 521 U.S. 507, 117 S.Ct. 2157, 138 L.Ed.2d 624 (1997), 245, 246, 255, 257, 258, 259, 261, 262, 263, 269, 272, 273, 280, 281
Borden's Farm Products Co. v. Baldwin, 293 U.S. 194, 55 S.Ct. 187, 79 L.Ed. 281 (1934), 279
Bouie v. City of Columbia, 378 U.S. 347, 84 S.Ct. 1697, 12 L.Ed.2d 894 (1964), 14, 25
Bousley v. United States, 523 U.S. 614, 118 S.Ct. 1604, 140 L.Ed.2d 828 (1998), **201**
Brady v. United States, 397 U.S. 742, 90 S.Ct. 1463, 25 L.Ed.2d 747 (1970), 171, 174, 203
Broward County Canvassing Bd. v. Hogan, 607 So.2d 508 (Fla.App. 4 Dist.1992), 17
Brown v. Allen, 344 U.S. 443, 73 S.Ct. 397, 97 L.Ed. 469 (1953), 77
Buck v. Bell, 274 U.S. 200, 47 S.Ct. 584, 71 L.Ed. 1000 (1927), 272
Burlington, City of v. Dague, 505 U.S. 557, 112 S.Ct. 2638, 120 L.Ed.2d 449 (1992), 295
Burroughs v. United States, 290 U.S. 534, 54 S.Ct. 287, 78 L.Ed. 484 (1934), 12
Bush v. Gore, 531 U.S. 98, 121 S.Ct. 525, 148 L.Ed.2d 388 (2000), **4,** 34, 35, 36
Bush v. Palm Beach County Canvassing Bd., 531 U.S. 70, 121 S.Ct. 471, 148 L.Ed.2d 366 (2000), 5, 10, 13, 17, 20, 21, 30
Butler, United States v., 297 U.S. 1, 56 S.Ct. 312, 80 L.Ed. 477 (1936), 34

Cage v. Louisiana, 498 U.S. 39, 111 S.Ct. 328, 112 L.Ed.2d 339 (1990), 191, 192, 193, 194, 195, 196, 198, 199, 200, 201

Calcano–Martinez v. I.N.S., 533 U.S. 348, 121 S.Ct. 2268, 150 L.Ed.2d 392 (2001), **70**, 86, 88

Caldwell v. Mississippi, 472 U.S. 320, 105 S.Ct. 2633, 86 L.Ed.2d 231 (1985), 196

California v. Sierra Club, 451 U.S. 287, 101 S.Ct. 1775, 68 L.Ed.2d 101 (1981), 52, 294

Cannon v. University of Chicago, 441 U.S. 677, 99 S.Ct. 1946, 60 L.Ed.2d 560 (1979), 39, 41, 44, 46, 49, 50, 52, 55, 56, 57, 58, 62, 63, 64, 293

Capron v. Van Noorden, 6 U.S. 126, 2 L.Ed. 229 (1804), 112

Carey v. Saffold, ___ U.S. ___, 122 S.Ct. 2134 (2002), 177

Carter v. Carter Coal Co., 298 U.S. 238, 56 S.Ct. 855, 80 L.Ed. 1160 (1936), 282

Caspari v. Bohlen, 510 U.S. 383, 114 S.Ct. 948, 127 L.Ed.2d 236 (1994), 200

Central Bank of Denver, N.A. v. First Interstate Bank of Denver, N.A., 511 U.S. 164, 114 S.Ct. 1439, 128 L.Ed.2d 119 (1994), 54

Central Union Telephone Co. v. City of Edwardsville, 269 U.S. 190, 46 S.Ct. 90, 70 L.Ed. 229 (1925), 24

Chan v. City of New York, 1 F.3d 96 (2nd Cir.1993), 66

Chevron USA, Inc. v. Natural Resources Defense Council, Inc., 467 U.S. 837, 104 S.Ct. 2778, 81 L.Ed.2d 694 (1984), 24, 61, 62, 133

Chicago, City of v. International College of Surgeons, 522 U.S. 156, 118 S.Ct. 523, 139 L.Ed.2d 525 (1997), 110, 111

Chisholm v. Georgia, 2 U.S. 419, 2 Dall. 419, 1 L.Ed. 440 (1793), 213, 214, 216, 218, 219, 220, 226, 236, 237, 238

Christianson v. Colt Industries Operating Corp., 486 U.S. 800, 108 S.Ct. 2166, 100 L.Ed.2d 811 (1988), 111

City of (see name of city)

Clark v. Barnard, 108 U.S. 436, 2 S.Ct. 878, 27 L.Ed. 780 (1883), 243, 246

Cleburne v. Cleburne Living Center, 473 U.S. 432, 105 S.Ct. 3249, 87 L.Ed.2d 313 (1985), 269, 270, 272, 274, 276, 277, 278, 279, 280

Coleman v. Thompson, 501 U.S. 722, 111 S.Ct. 2546, 115 L.Ed.2d 640 (1991), 158, 163

College Sav. Bank v. Florida Prepaid Postsecondary Educ. Expense Bd., 527 U.S. 666, 119 S.Ct. 2219, 144 L.Ed.2d 605 (1999), 221, 223, **243**, 244, 263

Cooper v. Aaron, 358 U.S. 1, 78 S.Ct. 1401, 3 L.Ed.2d 5, 3 L.Ed.2d 19 (1958), 25

Correctional Services Corp. v. Malesko, 534 U.S. 61, 122 S.Ct. 515, 151 L.Ed.2d 456 (2001), 66, 67

Corrick, United States v., 298 U.S. 435, 56 S.Ct. 829, 80 L.Ed. 1263 (1936), 112

Cort v. Ash, 422 U.S. 66, 95 S.Ct. 2080, 45 L.Ed.2d 26 (1975), 51, 52, 62, 65

County of (see name of county)

Crawford–El v. Britton, 523 U.S. 574, 118 S.Ct. 1584, 140 L.Ed.2d 759 (1998), 287

Crowell v. Benson, 285 U.S. 22, 52 S.Ct. 285, 76 L.Ed. 598 (1932), 76

Cushing v. Cohen, 420 A.2d 919 (Me.1980), 231

Custis v. United States, 511 U.S. 485, 114 S.Ct. 1732, 128 L.Ed.2d 517 (1994), 151, 187

Daniels v. United States, 532 U.S. 374, 121 S.Ct. 1578, 149 L.Ed.2d 590 (2001), 151

Darby, United States v., 312 U.S. 100, 312 U.S. 657, 61 S.Ct. 451, 85 L.Ed. 609 (1941), 282

Davis v. Michigan Dept. of Treasury, 489 U.S. 803, 109 S.Ct. 1500, 103 L.Ed.2d 891 (1989), 193

Davis v. Monroe County Bd. of Educ., 526 U.S. 629, 119 S.Ct. 1661, 143 L.Ed.2d 839 (1999), 55

Davis v. United States, 417 U.S. 333, 94 S.Ct. 2298, 41 L.Ed.2d 109 (1974), 204, 207

Davis v. Wechsler, 263 U.S. 22, 44 S.Ct. 13, 68 L.Ed. 143 (1923), 158

Dellmuth v. Muth, 491 U.S. 223, 109 S.Ct. 2397, 105 L.Ed.2d 181 (1989), 257

Desist v. United States, 394 U.S. 244, 89 S.Ct. 1030, 22 L.Ed.2d 248 (1969), 129

District of Columbia Court of Appeals v. Feldman, 460 U.S. 462, 103 S.Ct. 1303, 75 L.Ed.2d 206 (1983), 121

Douglas v. Alabama, 380 U.S. 415, 85 S.Ct. 1074, 13 L.Ed.2d 934 (1965), 158

Douglas v. New York, N.H. & H.R. Co., 279 U.S. 377, 49 S.Ct. 355, 73 L.Ed. 747 (1929), 239

Duncan v. Walker, 533 U.S. 167, 121 S.Ct. 2120, 150 L.Ed.2d 251 (2001), **180**

Dupasseur v. Rochereau, 88 U.S. 130, 22 L.Ed. 588 (1874), 2, 3, 117

Edelman v. Jordan, 415 U.S. 651, 94 S.Ct. 1347, 39 L.Ed.2d 662 (1974), 231, 248

Edward J. DeBartolo Corp. v. Florida Gulf Coast Bldg. and Const. Trades Council, 485 U.S. 568, 108 S.Ct. 1392, 99 L.Ed.2d 645 (1988), 76

Edwards v. Carpenter, 529 U.S. 446, 120 S.Ct. 1587, 146 L.Ed.2d 518 (2000), 150, 177

Ellis v. Dyson, 421 U.S. 426, 95 S.Ct. 1691, 44 L.Ed.2d 274 (1975), 115

Employees of Dept. of Public Health and Welfare, Missouri v. Department of Public Health and Welfare, Missouri, 411 U.S. 279, 93 S.Ct. 1614, 36 L.Ed.2d 251 (1973), 247, 252

Engle v. Isaac, 456 U.S. 107, 102 S.Ct. 1558, 71 L.Ed.2d 783 (1982), 205
Erie, City of v. Pap's A.M., 529 U.S. 277, 120 S.Ct. 1382, 146 L.Ed.2d 265 (2000), 109
Erie R. Co. v. Tompkins, 304 U.S. 64, 58 S.Ct. 817, 82 L.Ed. 1188 (1938), 1, 12, 116, 117, 119, 120
Estelle v. McGuire, 502 U.S. 62, 112 S.Ct. 475, 116 L.Ed.2d 385 (1991), 191
Ex parte (see name of party)

Fairfax's Devisee v. Hunter's Lessee, 11 U.S. 603, 3 L.Ed. 453 (1812), 14, 25
Fay v. Noia, 372 U.S. 391, 83 S.Ct. 822, 9 L.Ed.2d 837 (1963), 177
Fay v. South Colonie Cent. School Dist., 802 F.2d 21 (2nd Cir.1986), 66
FCC v. Beach Communications, Inc., 508 U.S. 307, 113 S.Ct. 2096, 124 L.Ed.2d 211 (1993), 270, 279
FDIC v. Meyer, 510 U.S. 471, 114 S.Ct. 996, 127 L.Ed.2d 308 (1994), 67
Federal Election Com'n v. Akins, 524 U.S. 11, 118 S.Ct. 1777, 141 L.Ed.2d 10 (1998), **100**
Federal Maritime Com'n v. South Carolina State Ports Authority, ___ U.S. ___, 122 S.Ct. 1864 (2002), 283
Felker v. Turpin, 518 U.S. 651, 116 S.Ct. 2333, 135 L.Ed.2d 827 (1996), 76, 77, 88
Fiore v. White, 528 U.S. 23, 120 S.Ct. 469, 145 L.Ed.2d 353 (1999), 3, 25
Fitzpatrick v. Bitzer, 427 U.S. 445, 96 S.Ct. 2666, 49 L.Ed.2d 614 (1976), 230, 243, 244, 268, 282
Flast v. Cohen, 392 U.S. 83, 88 S.Ct. 1942, 20 L.Ed.2d 947 (1968), 103, 107
Florida Dept. of Health and Rehabilitative Services v. Florida Nursing Home Ass'n, 450 U.S. 147, 101 S.Ct. 1032, 67 L.Ed.2d 132 (1981), 246
Florida Prepaid Postsecondary Educ. Expense Bd. v. College Sav. Bank, 527 U.S. 627, 119 S.Ct. 2199, 144 L.Ed.2d 575 (1999), **255,** 264, 265, 281
Ford v. Wainwright, 477 U.S. 399, 106 S.Ct. 2595, 91 L.Ed.2d 335 (1986), 178, 179, 180
Franchise Tax Bd. of State of Cal. v. Construction Laborers Vacation Trust for Southern California, 463 U.S. 1, 103 S.Ct. 2841, 77 L.Ed.2d 420 (1983), 110, 111
Franklin v. Gwinnett County Public Schools, 503 U.S. 60, 112 S.Ct. 1028, 117 L.Ed.2d 208 (1992), 39, 40, 41, 44, 46, 54
Friends of the Earth, Inc. v. Laidlaw Environmental Services (TOC), Inc., 528 U.S. 167, 120 S.Ct. 693, 145 L.Ed.2d 610 (2000), 97, 99, 100

Garcia v. San Antonio Metropolitan Transit Authority, 469 U.S. 528, 105 S.Ct. 1005, 83 L.Ed.2d 1016 (1985), 239, 241
Gasperini v. Center for Humanities, Inc., 518 U.S. 415, 116 S.Ct. 2211, 135 L.Ed.2d 659 (1996), 116
Gebser v. Lago Vista Independent School Dist., 524 U.S. 274, 118 S.Ct. 1989, 141 L.Ed.2d 277 (1998), **38**
General Motors Corp. v. Romein, 503 U.S. 181, 112 S.Ct. 1105, 117 L.Ed.2d 328 (1992), 24
Gideon v. Wainwright, 372 U.S. 335, 83 S.Ct. 792, 9 L.Ed.2d 799 (1963), 151
Gonzaga University v. Doe, ___ U.S. ___, 122 S.Ct. 2268 (2002), 292, 293
Gore v. Harris, 772 So.2d 1243 (Fla.2000), 6, 8, 17, 21, 23, 24, 31
Graham v. Collins, 506 U.S. 461, 113 S.Ct. 892, 122 L.Ed.2d 260 (1993), 142, 195
Gray v. Sanders, 372 U.S. 368, 83 S.Ct. 801, 9 L.Ed.2d 821 (1963), 9
Green v. French, 143 F.3d 865 (4th Cir.1998), 139, 140, 141, 142
Green, In re, 134 U.S. 377, 10 S.Ct. 586, 33 L.Ed. 951 (1890), 12
Greenholtz v. Inmates of Nebraska Penal and Correctional Complex, 442 U.S. 1, 99 S.Ct. 2100, 60 L.Ed.2d 668 (1979), 93
Gregory v. Ashcroft, 501 U.S. 452, 111 S.Ct. 2395, 115 L.Ed.2d 410 (1991), 26, 76
Griggs v. Duke Power Co., 401 U.S. 424, 91 S.Ct. 849, 28 L.Ed.2d 158 (1971), 281
Grove City College v. Bell, 465 U.S. 555, 104 S.Ct. 1211, 79 L.Ed.2d 516 (1984), 54
Guardians Ass'n v. Civil Service Com'n of City of New York, 463 U.S. 582, 103 S.Ct. 3221, 77 L.Ed.2d 866 (1983), 49, 50, 54, 55, 57, 58, 60, 61

Hanna v. Plumer, 380 U.S. 460, 85 S.Ct. 1136, 14 L.Ed.2d 8 (1965), 117, 119, 120
Hans v. Louisiana, 134 U.S. 1, 10 S.Ct. 504, 33 L.Ed. 842 (1890), 213, 219, 220, 221, 230, 237, 249, 250
Harlow v. Fitzgerald, 457 U.S. 800, 102 S.Ct. 2727, 73 L.Ed.2d 396 (1982), 287
Harper v. Virginia State Bd. of Elections, 383 U.S. 663, 86 S.Ct. 1079, 16 L.Ed.2d 169 (1966), 7
Heckler v. Chaney, 470 U.S. 821, 105 S.Ct. 1649, 84 L.Ed.2d 714 (1985), 105
Heikkila v. Barber, 345 U.S. 229, 73 S.Ct. 603, 97 L.Ed. 972 (1953), 77, 78, 79, 81, 87, 91
Heller v. Doe, 509 U.S. 312, 113 S.Ct. 2637, 125 L.Ed.2d 257 (1993), 270, 276
Henderson v. Morgan, 426 U.S. 637, 96 S.Ct. 2253, 49 L.Ed.2d 108 (1976), 203, 207, 210, 211
Henry v. Rock Hill, 376 U.S. 776, 84 S.Ct. 1042, 12 L.Ed.2d 79 (1964), 195

Highland Farms Dairy v. Agnew, 300 U.S. 608, 57 S.Ct. 549, 81 L.Ed. 835 (1937), 26

Hilton v. South Carolina Public Railways Com'n, 502 U.S. 197, 112 S.Ct. 560, 116 L.Ed.2d 560 (1991), 222, 223, 240, 241

Holmes Group, Inc. v. Vornado Air Circulation Systems, Inc., ___ U.S. ___, 122 S.Ct. 1889 (2002), 110

Hooper v. California., 155 U.S. 648, 15 S.Ct. 207, 39 L.Ed. 297 (1895), 76

Horn v. Banks, ___ U.S. ___, 122 S.Ct. 2147 (2002), 148

Howlett v. Rose, 496 U.S. 356, 110 S.Ct. 2430, 110 L.Ed.2d 332 (1990), 225, 239

Hudson & Goodwin, United States v., 11 U.S. 32, 3 L.Ed. 259 (1812), 204

Hunter v. Fairfax's Devisee, 15 Va. 218 (Va. 1810), 14

Idaho v. Coeur d'Alene Tribe of Idaho, 521 U.S. 261, 117 S.Ct. 2028, 138 L.Ed.2d 438 (1997), 227, 231, 240, 285, 286

Indiana ex rel. Anderson v. Brand, 303 U.S. 95, 58 S.Ct. 443, 82 L.Ed. 685 (1938), 36

In re (see name of party)

INS v. St. Cyr, 533 U.S. 289, 121 S.Ct. 2271, 150 L.Ed.2d 347 (2001), 70, 71, **72**

INS v. Yueh–Shaio Yang, 519 U.S. 26, 117 S.Ct. 350, 136 L.Ed.2d 288 (1996), 93

James v. Kentucky, 466 U.S. 341, 104 S.Ct. 1830, 80 L.Ed.2d 346 (1984), 158, 162

Jay v. Boyd, 351 U.S. 345, 76 S.Ct. 919, 100 L.Ed. 1242 (1956), 79

Jefferson v. City of Tarrant, Ala., 522 U.S. 75, 118 S.Ct. 481, 139 L.Ed.2d 433 (1997), 120

J.I. Case Co. v. Borak, 377 U.S. 426, 84 S.Ct. 1555, 12 L.Ed.2d 423 (1964), 51, 52, 63

Johnson v. Transportation Agency, Santa Clara County, Cal., 480 U.S. 616, 107 S.Ct. 1442, 94 L.Ed.2d 615 (1987), 54

JPMorgan Chase Bank v. Traffic Stream (BVI) Infrastructure Ltd., ___ U.S. ___, 122 S.Ct. 2054 (2002), 115

Kaiser Aetna v. United States, 444 U.S. 164, 100 S.Ct. 383, 62 L.Ed.2d 332 (1979), 245

Katzenbach v. Morgan, 384 U.S. 641, 86 S.Ct. 1717, 16 L.Ed.2d 828 (1966), 278, 281, 282

Keaukaha–Panaewa Community Ass'n v. Hawaiian Homes Com'n, 739 F.2d 1467 (9th Cir.1984), 66

Keeney v. Tamayo–Reyes, 504 U.S. 1, 112 S.Ct. 1715, 118 L.Ed.2d 318 (1992), 172, 173, 175

Kennecott Copper Corp. v. State Tax Com'n, 327 U.S. 573, 66 S.Ct. 745, 90 L.Ed. 862 (1946), 246

Kimel v. Florida Bd. of Regents, 528 U.S. 62, 120 S.Ct. 631, 145 L.Ed.2d 522 (2000), 263, 264, 265, 268, 269, 272, 281

Klein, United States v., 80 U.S. 128, 20 L.Ed. 519 (1871), 68

Krivanek v. Take Back Tampa Political Committee, 625 So.2d 840 (Fla.1993), 17

Lackawanna County Dist. Attorney v. Coss, 532 U.S. 394, 121 S.Ct. 1567, 149 L.Ed.2d 608 (2001), 151

Lambrix v. Singletary, 520 U.S. 518, 117 S.Ct. 1517, 137 L.Ed.2d 771 (1997), 142

Lampf, Pleva, Lipkind, Prupis & Petigrow v. Gilbertson, 501 U.S. 350, 111 S.Ct. 2773, 115 L.Ed.2d 321 (1991), 51

Landgraf v. United StatesI Film Products, 511 U.S. 244, 114 S.Ct. 1483, 128 L.Ed.2d 229 (1994), 83

Lane County v. Oregon, 74 U.S. 71, 19 L.Ed. 101 (1868), 241

Lapides v. Board of Regents of University System of Georgia, ___ U.S. ___, 122 S.Ct. 1640, 152 L.Ed.2d 806 (2002), 214

Lau v. Nichols, 414 U.S. 563, 94 S.Ct. 786, 39 L.Ed.2d 1 (1974), 50, 51, 55, 56, 58, 59

Lawrence v. Chater, 516 U.S. 163, 116 S.Ct. 604, 133 L.Ed.2d 545 (1996), 195

Lee v. Kemna, 534 U.S. 362, 122 S.Ct. 877, 151 L.Ed.2d 820 (2002), **152,** 170, 171, 175, 176

Lehman Bros. v. Schein, 416 U.S. 386, 94 S.Ct. 1741, 40 L.Ed.2d 215 (1974), 25

Lincoln County v. Luning, 133 U.S. 529, 10 S.Ct. 363, 33 L.Ed. 766 (1890), 231, 271

Lindh v. Murphy, 96 F.3d 856 (7th Cir.1996), 129, 133, 150

Lochner v. New York, 198 U.S. 45, 25 S.Ct. 539, 49 L.Ed. 937 (1905), 243, 253

Lockhart v. Fretwell, 506 U.S. 364, 113 S.Ct. 838, 122 L.Ed.2d 180 (1993), 127, 134, 135, 137, 144, 145

Lonchar v. Thomas, 517 U.S. 314, 116 S.Ct. 1293, 134 L.Ed.2d 440 (1996), 189

Lopez, United States v., 514 U.S. 549, 115 S.Ct. 1624, 131 L.Ed.2d 626 (1995), 214

L. Singer & Sons v. Union Pac. R. Co., 311 U.S. 295, 61 S.Ct. 254, 85 L.Ed. 198 (1940), 104

Lucas v. South Carolina Coastal Council, 505 U.S. 1003, 112 S.Ct. 2886, 120 L.Ed.2d 798 (1992), 14

Lujan v. Defenders of Wildlife, 504 U.S. 555, 112 S.Ct. 2130, 119 L.Ed.2d 351 (1992), 97, 98, 99, 104, 107, 108

Luther v. Borden, 48 U.S. 1, 7 How. 1, 12 L.Ed. 581 (1849), 26

Mabry v. Johnson, 467 U.S. 504, 104 S.Ct. 2543, 81 L.Ed.2d 437 (1984), 204

Mackey v. United States, 401 U.S. 667, 91 S.Ct. 1160, 28 L.Ed.2d 404 (1971), 129
Maine v. Thiboutot, 448 U.S. 1, 100 S.Ct. 2502, 65 L.Ed.2d 555 (1980), 65, 222
Mallett v. Wisconsin Div. of Vocational Rehabilitation, 130 F.3d 1245 (7th Cir.1997), 66
Marbury v. Madison, 5 U.S. 137, 2 L.Ed. 60 (1803), 128, 242, 250, 299
Martin v. Hunter's Lessee, 14 U.S. 304, 4 L.Ed. 97 (1816), 25, 36, 224
Massachusetts Bd. of Retirement v. Murgia, 427 U.S. 307, 96 S.Ct. 2562, 49 L.Ed.2d 520 (1976), 270
Massachusetts Mut. Life Ins. Co. v. Russell, 473 U.S. 134, 105 S.Ct. 3085, 87 L.Ed.2d 96 (1985), 53
McCardle, Ex parte, 74 U.S. 506, 19 L.Ed. 264 (1868), 81
McCarthy v. United States, 394 U.S. 459, 89 S.Ct. 1166, 22 L.Ed.2d 418 (1969), 208
McCleskey v. Zant, 499 U.S. 467, 111 S.Ct. 1454, 113 L.Ed.2d 517 (1991), 169
McPherson v. Blacker, 146 U.S. 1, 13 S.Ct. 3, 36 L.Ed. 869 (1892), 7, 12, 30
McCulloch v. Maryland, 17 U.S. 316, 4 L.Ed. 579 (1819), 229, 239
Mendoza–Lopez, United States v., 481 U.S. 828, 107 S.Ct. 2148, 95 L.Ed.2d 772 (1987), 87
Merrill Lynch, Pierce, Fenner & Smith, Inc. v. Curran, 456 U.S. 353, 102 S.Ct. 1825, 72 L.Ed.2d 182 (1982), 52, 54, 63, 111
Middlesex County Sewerage Authority v. National Sea Clammers Ass'n, 453 U.S. 1, 101 S.Ct. 2615, 69 L.Ed.2d 435 (1981), 53
Miller v. French, 530 U.S. 327, 120 S.Ct. 2246, 147 L.Ed.2d 326 (2000), 94, 96
Mills v. Maryland, 486 U.S. 367, 108 S.Ct. 1860, 100 L.Ed.2d 384 (1988), 148, 149
Missouri v. Holland, 252 U.S. 416, 40 S.Ct. 382, 64 L.Ed. 641 (1920), 242
Moor v. Alameda County, 411 U.S. 693, 93 S.Ct. 1785, 36 L.Ed.2d 596 (1973), 115
Moore v. Ogilvie, 394 U.S. 814, 89 S.Ct. 1493, 23 L.Ed.2d 1 (1969), 9
Mt. Healthy City School Dist. Bd. of Educ. v. Doyle, 429 U.S. 274, 97 S.Ct. 568, 50 L.Ed.2d 471 (1977), 225
Mullaney v. Wilbur, 421 U.S. 684, 95 S.Ct. 1881, 44 L.Ed.2d 508 (1975), 13
Murray v. Carrier, 477 U.S. 478, 106 S.Ct. 2639, 91 L.Ed.2d 397 (1986), 169, 176, 205

NAACP v. Alabama ex rel. Patterson, 357 U.S. 449, 78 S.Ct. 1163, 2 L.Ed.2d 1488 (1958), 13, 14, 25
National Credit Union Admin. v. First Nat. Bank & Trust Co., 522 U.S. 479, 118 S.Ct. 927, 140 L.Ed.2d 1 (1998), 102

National League of Cities v. Usery, 426 U.S. 833, 96 S.Ct. 2465, 49 L.Ed.2d 245 (1976), 241
Nevada v. Hall, 440 U.S. 410, 99 S.Ct. 1182, 59 L.Ed.2d 416 (1979), 222, 223, 224, 228
New Orleans, City of v. Dukes, 427 U.S. 297, 96 S.Ct. 2513, 49 L.Ed.2d 511 (1976), 280
Newton v. Rumery, 480 U.S. 386, 107 S.Ct. 1187, 94 L.Ed.2d 405 (1987), 83
New York, ex parte, 256 U.S. 490, 41 S.Ct. 588, 65 L.Ed. 1057 (1921), 220, 230
New York v. United States, 505 U.S. 144, 112 S.Ct. 2408, 120 L.Ed.2d 120 (1992), 4, 223, 229
Nix v. Whiteside, 475 U.S. 157, 106 S.Ct. 988, 89 L.Ed.2d 123 (1986), 135
Northern Pipeline Const. Co. v. Marathon Pipe Line Co., 458 U.S. 50, 102 S.Ct. 2858, 73 L.Ed.2d 598 (1982), 93
Norton v. Mathews, 427 U.S. 524, 96 S.Ct. 2771, 49 L.Ed.2d 672 (1976), 113

O'Dell v. Netherland, 521 U.S. 151, 117 S.Ct. 1969, 138 L.Ed.2d 351 (1997), 24, 196, 200
Ohio Adult Parole Authority v. Woodard, 523 U.S. 272, 118 S.Ct. 1244, 140 L.Ed.2d 387 (1998), 93
Ohio ex rel. Davis v. Hildebrant, 241 U.S. 565, 36 S.Ct. 708, 60 L.Ed. 1172 (1916), 26
Oregon v. Mitchell, 400 U.S. 112, 91 S.Ct. 260, 27 L.Ed.2d 272 (1970), 279
Osborne v. Ohio, 495 U.S. 103, 110 S.Ct. 1691, 109 L.Ed.2d 98 (1990), 153, 158, 159, 162, 165
O'Sullivan v. Boerckel, 526 U.S. 838, 119 S.Ct. 1728, 144 L.Ed.2d 1 (1999), 177

Pacific States Box & Basket Co. v. White, 296 U.S. 176, 56 S.Ct. 159, 80 L.Ed. 138 (1935), 279
Palm Beach County Canvassing Bd. v. Harris, 772 So.2d 1273 (Fla.2000), 17, 19
Palm Beach County Canvassing Bd. v. Harris, 772 So.2d 1220 (Fla.2000), 15, 16
Parden v. Terminal Ry. of Alabama State Docks Dept., 377 U.S. 184, 84 S.Ct. 1207, 12 L.Ed.2d 233 (1964), 223, 226, 227, 246, 247, 248, 250, 251, 252, 253
Parratt v. Taylor, 451 U.S. 527, 101 S.Ct. 1908, 68 L.Ed.2d 420 (1981), 258
Patterson v. McLean Credit Union, 491 U.S. 164, 109 S.Ct. 2363, 105 L.Ed.2d 132 (1989), 54, 207
Paul v. Davis, 424 U.S. 693, 96 S.Ct. 1155, 47 L.Ed.2d 405 (1976), 245, 291
Pennhurst State School and Hospital v. Halderman, 451 U.S. 1, 101 S.Ct. 1531, 67 L.Ed.2d 694 (1981), 55, 293
Pennsylvania v. Ritchie, 480 U.S. 39, 107 S.Ct. 989, 94 L.Ed.2d 40 (1987), 120

TABLE OF CASES

Pennsylvania v. Union Gas Co., 491 U.S. 1, 109 S.Ct. 2273, 105 L.Ed.2d 1 (1989), 215, 223, 227, 262
Pennsylvania v. Wheeling & Belmont Bridge Co., 59 U.S. 421, 18 How. 421, 15 L.Ed. 435 (1855), 95
Plaut v. Spendthrift Farm, Inc., 514 U.S. 211, 115 S.Ct. 1447, 131 L.Ed.2d 328 (1995), 94, 95
Powell v. State of Ala., 287 U.S. 45, 53 S.Ct. 55, 77 L.Ed. 158 (1932), 165
Principality of Monaco v. Mississippi, 292 U.S. 313, 54 S.Ct. 745, 78 L.Ed. 1282 (1934), 220, 230
Printz v. United States, 521 U.S. 898, 117 S.Ct. 2365, 138 L.Ed.2d 914 (1997), 1, 4, 216, 223, 226, 229
Public Citizen v. United States Dept. of Justice, 491 U.S. 440, 109 S.Ct. 2558, 105 L.Ed.2d 377 (1989), 103, 104
Pulliam v. Allen, 466 U.S. 522, 104 S.Ct. 1970, 80 L.Ed.2d 565 (1984), 290

Randolph, Ex parte, 20 F.Cas. 242 (C.C.D.Va. 1833), 89
Reed v. Farley, 512 U.S. 339, 114 S.Ct. 2291, 129 L.Ed.2d 277 (1994), 204, 207, 208
Reed v. Ross, 468 U.S. 1, 104 S.Ct. 2901, 82 L.Ed.2d 1 (1984), 205
Reich v. Collins, 513 U.S. 106, 115 S.Ct. 547, 130 L.Ed.2d 454 (1994), 224, 225
Reno v. American–Arab Anti–Discrimination Committee, 525 U.S. 471, 119 S.Ct. 936, 142 L.Ed.2d 940 (1999), 82, 85
Reynolds v. Sims, 377 U.S. 533, 84 S.Ct. 1362, 12 L.Ed.2d 506 (1964), 7
Richardson, United States v., 418 U.S. 166, 94 S.Ct. 2940, 41 L.Ed.2d 678 (1974), 103, 104, 106, 107, 108
Rivers v. Roadway Exp., Inc., 511 U.S. 298, 114 S.Ct. 1510, 128 L.Ed.2d 274 (1994), 207, 210
Rivet v. Regions Bank of Louisiana, 522 U.S. 470, 118 S.Ct. 921, 139 L.Ed.2d 912 (1998), 122
Rome, City of v. United States, 446 U.S. 156, 100 S.Ct. 1548, 64 L.Ed.2d 119 (1980), 282
Rooker v. Fidelity Trust Co., 263 U.S. 413, 44 S.Ct. 149, 68 L.Ed. 362 (1923), 121
Rosa H. v. San Elizario Independent School Dist., 106 F.3d 648 (5th Cir.1997), 41
Rose v. Lundy, 455 U.S. 509, 102 S.Ct. 1198, 71 L.Ed.2d 379 (1982), 178, 184, 185, 189
Ruhrgas AG v. Marathon Oil Co., 526 U.S. 574, 119 S.Ct. 1563, 143 L.Ed.2d 760 (1999), 114

Sacramento, County of v. Lewis, 523 U.S. 833, 118 S.Ct. 1708, 140 L.Ed.2d 1043 (1998), 291

Saenz v. Roe, 526 U.S. 489, 119 S.Ct. 1518, 143 L.Ed.2d 689 (1999), 27
Saffle v. Parks, 494 U.S. 484, 110 S.Ct. 1257, 108 L.Ed.2d 415 (1990), 197
Sandoval v. Hagan, 197 F.3d 484 (11th Cir. 1999), 48
Sandoval v. Hagan, 7 F.Supp.2d 1234 (M.D.Ala.1998), 48
Sawyer v. Smith, 497 U.S. 227, 110 S.Ct. 2822, 111 L.Ed.2d 193 (1990), 195, 196, 200
Sawyer v. Whitley, 505 U.S. 333, 112 S.Ct. 2514, 120 L.Ed.2d 269 (1992), 206
Scheuer v. Rhodes, 416 U.S. 232, 94 S.Ct. 1683, 40 L.Ed.2d 90 (1974), 231
Schlup v. Delo, 513 U.S. 298, 115 S.Ct. 851, 130 L.Ed.2d 808 (1995), 163, 169, 170, 205, 209, 210, 211, 212
South Carolina v. Katzenbach, 383 U.S. 301, 86 S.Ct. 803, 15 L.Ed.2d 769 (1966), 274, 281
Seminole Tribe of Florida v. Florida, 517 U.S. 44, 116 S.Ct. 1114, 134 L.Ed.2d 252 (1996), 193, 200, 214, 215, 220, 221, 223, 231, 233, 234, 238, 239, 244, 248, 249, 252, 253, 254, 256, 257, 259, 262, 263, 284, 285, 286
Semtek Intern. Inc. v. Lockheed Martin Corp., 531 U.S. 497, 121 S.Ct. 1021, 149 L.Ed.2d 32 (2001), 2, 116, 117, 118, 120
Shafer v. South Carolina, 532 U.S. 36, 121 S.Ct. 1263, 149 L.Ed.2d 178 (2001), 93
Shaughnessy v. Pedreiro, 349 U.S. 48, 75 S.Ct. 591, 99 L.Ed. 868 (1955), 87
Shaughnessy, United States ex rel. Accardi v., 347 U.S. 260, 74 S.Ct. 499, 98 L.Ed. 681 (1954), 79, 91, 92
Shaw v. Reno, 509 U.S. 630, 113 S.Ct. 2816, 125 L.Ed.2d 511 (1993), 35
Siegert v. Gilley, 500 U.S. 226, 111 S.Ct. 1789, 114 L.Ed.2d 277 (1991), 288
Sierra Club v. Morton, 405 U.S. 727, 92 S.Ct. 1361, 31 L.Ed.2d 636 (1972), 98
Simmons v. South Carolina, 512 U.S. 154, 114 S.Ct. 2187, 129 L.Ed.2d 133 (1994), 196, 200
Slack v. McDaniel, 529 U.S. 473, 120 S.Ct. 1595, 146 L.Ed.2d 542 (2000), 177, 190
Smith v. Murray, 477 U.S. 527, 106 S.Ct. 2661, 91 L.Ed.2d 434 (1986), 205
Smith v. O'Grady, 312 U.S. 329, 61 S.Ct. 572, 85 L.Ed. 859 (1941), 203, 207
Smith v. Phillips, 455 U.S. 209, 102 S.Ct. 940, 71 L.Ed.2d 78 (1982), 175
Smith v. Reeves, 178 U.S. 436, 20 S.Ct. 919, 44 L.Ed. 1140 (1900), 220, 246
South Camden Citizens in Action v. New Jersey Dept. of Environmental Protection, 145 F.Supp.2d 446 (D.N.J.2001), 65, 66
South Dakota v. Dole, 483 U.S. 203, 107 S.Ct. 2793, 97 L.Ed.2d 171 (1987), 230
State of (see name of state)

TABLE OF CASES   **xix**

Staub v. City of Baxley, 355 U.S. 313, 78 S.Ct. 277, 2 L.Ed.2d 302 (1958), 162, 163, 166

Steel Co. v. Citizens for a Better Environment, 523 U.S. 83, 118 S.Ct. 1003, 140 L.Ed.2d 210 (1998), 98, 112, 114, 115

Stewart v. Martinez–Villareal, 523 U.S. 637, 118 S.Ct. 1618, 140 L.Ed.2d 849 (1998), 178, 180, 190

Strickland v. Washington, 466 U.S. 668, 104 S.Ct. 2052, 80 L.Ed.2d 674 (1984), 124, 126, 127, 134, 135, 137, 138, 140, 141, 144, 145, 146, 148

Sullivan v. Little Hunting Park, Inc., 396 U.S. 229, 90 S.Ct. 400, 24 L.Ed.2d 386 (1969), 160

Sullivan v. Louisiana, 508 U.S. 275, 113 S.Ct. 2078, 124 L.Ed.2d 182 (1993), 194, 195, 198, 199, 200, 201

Sumner v. Mata, 449 U.S. 539, 101 S.Ct. 764, 66 L.Ed.2d 722 (1981), 24

Suter v. Artist M., 503 U.S. 347, 112 S.Ct. 1360, 118 L.Ed.2d 1 (1992), 292

Swain v. Pressley, 430 U.S. 372, 97 S.Ct. 1224, 51 L.Ed.2d 411 (1977), 82

Swint v. Chambers County Com'n, 514 U.S. 35, 115 S.Ct. 1203, 131 L.Ed.2d 60 (1995), 120, 290

Teague v. Lane, 489 U.S. 288, 109 S.Ct. 1060, 103 L.Ed.2d 334 (1989), 128, 129, 130, 131, 142, 143, 148, 149, 195, 196, 197, 198, 199, 200, 201, 203, 204, 206

Testa v. Katt, 330 U.S. 386, 67 S.Ct. 810, 91 L.Ed. 967 (1947), 4, 229

Thompson v. Thompson, 484 U.S. 174, 108 S.Ct. 513, 98 L.Ed.2d 512 (1988), 52, 63

Timmreck, United States v., 441 U.S. 780, 99 S.Ct. 2085, 60 L.Ed.2d 634 (1979), 204, 208

Touche Ross & Co. v. Redington, 442 U.S. 560, 99 S.Ct. 2479, 61 L.Ed.2d 82 (1979), 51, 293

Town of (see name of town)

Townsend v. Sain, 372 U.S. 293, 83 S.Ct. 745, 9 L.Ed.2d 770 (1963), 170

Transamerica Mortg. Advisors, Inc. (TAMA) v. Lewis, 444 U.S. 11, 100 S.Ct. 242, 62 L.Ed.2d 146 (1979), 51

Trest v. Cain, 522 U.S. 87, 118 S.Ct. 478, 139 L.Ed.2d 444 (1997), 152

Tyler v. Cain, 533 U.S. 656, 121 S.Ct. 2478, 150 L.Ed.2d 632 (2001), **191**

United Mine Workers of America v. Gibbs, 383 U.S. 715, 86 S.Ct. 1130, 16 L.Ed.2d 218 (1966), 110, 111

United States v. _____ (see opposing party)

United States Dept. of Agriculture v. Moreno, 413 U.S. 528, 93 S.Ct. 2821, 37 L.Ed.2d 782 (1973), 278

United States ex rel. v. _____ (see opposing party and relator)

United States Term Limits, Inc. v. Thornton, 514 U.S. 779, 115 S.Ct. 1842, 131 L.Ed.2d 881 (1995), 27

Universities Research Ass'n, Inc. v. Coutu, 450 U.S. 754, 101 S.Ct. 1451, 67 L.Ed.2d 662 (1981), 52

Verizon Maryland, Inc. v. Public Service Com'n of Maryland, ___ U.S. ___, 122 S.Ct. 1753 (2002), 285

Victor v. Nebraska, 511 U.S. 1, 114 S.Ct. 1239, 127 L.Ed.2d 583 (1994), 191

Virginia, Ex parte, 100 U.S. 339, 10 Otto 339, 25 L.Ed. 676 (1879), 281

Wainwright v. Sykes, 433 U.S. 72, 97 S.Ct. 2497, 53 L.Ed.2d 594 (1977), 163, 169, 170, 172, 175, 176, 205

Waley v. Johnston, 316 U.S. 101, 62 S.Ct. 964, 86 L.Ed. 1302 (1942), 204

Warth v. Seldin, 422 U.S. 490, 95 S.Ct. 2197, 45 L.Ed.2d 343 (1975), 104

Washington v. Davis, 426 U.S. 229, 96 S.Ct. 2040, 48 L.Ed.2d 597 (1976), 60, 274, 275, 280

Welch v. Texas Dept. of Highways and Public Transp., 483 U.S. 468, 107 S.Ct. 2941, 97 L.Ed.2d 389 (1987), 247, 249

Wilder v. Virginia Hosp. Ass'n, 496 U.S. 498, 110 S.Ct. 2510, 110 L.Ed.2d 455 (1990), 293, 294, 295

Will v. Michigan Dept. of State Police, 491 U.S. 58, 109 S.Ct. 2304, 105 L.Ed.2d 45 (1989), 222, 241

Williams v. Taylor, 529 U.S. 362, 120 S.Ct. 1495, 146 L.Ed.2d 389 (2000), 194

Williams (Michael Wayne) v. Taylor, 529 U.S. 420, 120 S.Ct. 1479, 146 L.Ed.2d 435 (2000), 171, 175, 176, 177, 183

Williams (Terry) v. Taylor, 529 U.S. 362, 120 S.Ct. 1495, 146 L.Ed.2d 389 (2000), **124,** 146, 147, 148, 149

Williams v. Warden, 254 Va. 16, 487 S.E.2d 194 (Va.1997), 145

Wilson v. Layne, 526 U.S. 603, 119 S.Ct. 1692, 143 L.Ed.2d 818 (1999), 289

Wright v. Roanoke Redevelopment and Housing Authority, 479 U.S. 418, 107 S.Ct. 766, 93 L.Ed.2d 781 (1987), 294

Wright v. West, 505 U.S. 277, 112 S.Ct. 2482, 120 L.Ed.2d 225 (1992), 130, 147

Yerger, Ex parte, 75 U.S. 85, 19 L.Ed. 332 (1868), 76, 81, 88

Young, Ex parte, 209 U.S. 123, 28 S.Ct. 441, 52 L.Ed. 714 (1908), 213, 227, 231, 254, 274, 284, 285, 286

Younger v. Harris, 401 U.S. 37, 91 S.Ct. 746, 27 L.Ed.2d 669 (1971), 115, 121

Zinermon v. Burch, 494 U.S. 113, 110 S.Ct. 975, 108 L.Ed.2d 100 (1990), 258

TABLE OF SECONDARY AUTHORITIES

ABA Section of Individual Rights and Responsibilities, see Capital Punishment: Is There Any Habeas Left in This Corpus?, 27 Loyola U. Chi. L.J. 523 (1996)--p. 124

Achtenberg, A "Milder Measure of Villainy": The Unknown History of 42 U.S.C. § 1983 and the Meaning of "Under Color of" Law, 1999 Utah L.Rev. 1--p. 287

Adler, Stand or Deliver: Citizen Suits, Standing, and Environmental Protection, 12 Duke Env. L. & Pol. Forum 39 (2001)--p. 99

Anderson, Congressional Control Over the Jurisdiction of the Federal Courts: A New Threat to James Madison's Compromise, 39 Brandeis L. J. 417 (2000–01)--p. 96

Anderson, Responding to the Challenge of Actual Innocence Claims After *Herrera v. Collins*, 71 Temple L.Rev. 489 (1998)--p. 201

Araiza, *Alden v. Maine* and the Web of Environmental Law, 33 Loy. L. Rev. 1513 (2000)--p. 266

Armacost, Qualified Immunity: Ignorance Excused, 51 Vand.L.Rev. 583 (1998)--p. 288

Armacost, Race and Reputation: The Real Legacy of *Paul v. Davis*, 85 Va. L. Rev. 569 (1999)--p. 291

Baker, Seminole Speaks to Sovereign Immunity and Ex Parte Young, 71 St. John's L.Rev. 739 (1997)--p. 215

Bailey, An Universal Etymological English Dictionary (1789)--p. 90

Bandes, *Erie* and the History of the One True Federalism, 110 Yale L. J. 829 (2001)--p. 1

Bandes, Introduction: The Emperor's New Clothes, 48 DePaul L. Rev. 619 (1999)--p. 290

Bandes, The *Rooker–Feldman* Doctrine: Evaluating Its Jurisdictional Status, 74 Notre Dame L. Rev. 1175 (1999)--p. 121

Barkow, More Supreme Than Court? The Fall of the Political Question Doctrine and the Rise of Judicial Supremacy, 102 Colum. L. Rev. 237 (2002)--p. 109

Barnett and Terrell, Economic Observations on Citizen–Suit Provisions of Environmental Legislation, 12 Duke Env. L. & Pol. Forum 1 (2001)--p. 99

Bauer, The *Erie* Doctrine Revisited: How a Conflicts Perspective Can Aid the Analysis, 74 Notre Dame L. Rev. 1235 (1999)--p. 120

Bederman, Admiralty and the Eleventh Amendment, 72 Notre Dame L.Rev. 935 (1997)--p. 213

Beermann, Comments on *Rooker–Feldman* or Let State Law Be Our Guide, 74 Notre Dame L. Rev. 1209 (1999)--p. 121

Beermann, Municipal Responsibility for Constitutional Torts, 48 DePaul L. Rev. 627 (1999)--p. 290

Bellia, Federal Regulation of State Court Procedures, 110 Yale L. J. 947 (2001)--p. 4

Bohannon and Cotter, When the State Steals Ideas: Is the Abrogation of State Sovereign Immunity from Federal Infringement Claims Constitutional in Light of *Seminole Tribe*?, 67 Fordham L.Rev. 1435 (1999)--pp. 262, 264

Blum, Municipal Liability: Derivative or Direct? Statutory or Constitutional? Distinguishing the *Canton* Case from the *Collins* Case, 48 DePaul L. Rev. 687 (2000)--p. 290

Bone, From Property to Contract: The Eleventh Amendment and University–Private Sector Intellectual Property Relationships, 33 Loy. L. Rev. 1467 (2000)--p. 266

Bone, Revisiting the Policy Case for Supplemental Jurisdiction, 74 Ind.L.J. 139 (1998)--p. 115

Bradley and Goldsmith, Federal Courts and the Incorporation of International Law, 111 Harv.L.Rev. 2260 (1998)--p. 1

Braveman, Enforcement of Federal Rights Against States: *Alden* and Federalism Non–Sense, 49 Am. U. L. Rev. 611 (2000)--p. 265

Bright, Elected Judges and the Death Penalty in Texas: Why Full Habeas Corpus Review by Independent Federal Judges is Indispensable to Protecting Constitutional

Rights, 78 Tex. L. Rev. 1805 (2000)--p. 123

Bright, Is Fairness Irrelevant?: The Evisceration of Federal Habeas Corpus Review and Limits on the Ability of State Courts to Protect Fundamental Rights, 54 Wash. & Lee L. Rev. 1 (1997)--p. 124

Brown, Deterring Bully Government: A Sovereign Dilemma, 76 Tulane L. Rev. 149 (2001)--p. 290

Brown and Enrich, Nostalgic Federalism, 28 Hastings Const. L. Q. 1 (2002) (criticizing *Kimel*)--p. 264

Buzbee, Expanding the Zone, Tilting the Field: Zone of Interests and Article III Standing Analysis After *Bennett v. Spear*, 49 Admin.L.Rev. 763 (1997)--p. 97

Buzbee, Standing and the Statutory Universe, 11 Duke Env. L. & Pol. Forum 247 (2001)--p. 99

Caminker, Allocating the Judicial Power in a "Unified Judiciary," 78 Tex. L. Rev. 1513 (2000)--p. 69

Chase and Chase, *Monell:* The Story Behind the Landmark, 31 Urb. Law 491 (1999)--p. 291

Chemerinsky, Against Sovereign Immunity, 53 Stan. L. Rev. 1201 (2001)--p. 213

Chemerinsky, A Framework for Analyzing the Constitutionality of Restrictions on Federal Court Jurisdiction in Immigration Cases, 29 U. Memphis L. Rev. 295 (1999)--p. 68

Chemerinsky, The Hypocrisy of *Alden v. Maine:* Judicial Review, Sovereign Immunity, and the Rehnquist Court, 33 Loy. L. Rev. 1283 (2000)--p. 265

Chen, The Ultimate Standard: Qualified Immunity in the Age of Constitutional Balancing Tests, 81 Iowa L.Rev. 261 (1995)--p. 288

Clark, Ascertaining the Laws of the Several States: Positivism and Judicial Federalism After Erie, 145 U.Pa.L Rev. 1459 (1997)--p. 3

Clarke, Habeas Corpus: The Historical Debate, 13 N.Y. Law School J. Human Rights 375 (1998)--p. 123

Clermont & Eisenberg, Do Case Outcomes Really Reveal Anything About the Legal System? Win Rates and Removal Jurisdiction, 83 Cornell L.Rev. 581 (1998)--p. 69

Cole, Jurisdiction and Liberty: Habeas Corpus and Due Process as Limits on Congress's Control of Federal Jurisdiction, 86 Geo.L.J. 2481 (1998)--pp. 68, 150

Collings, Habeas Corpus for Convicts—Constitutional Right or Legislative Grace?, 40 Calif. L. Rev. 335 (1952)--p. 90

Coplan, Direct Environmental Standing for Chartered Conservation Corporations, 12 Duke Env. L. & Pol. Forum 183 (2001)--p. 100

Cooper, An Alternative and Discretionary § 1367, 74 Ind.L.J. 153 (1998)--p. 115

Coverdale, Remedies for Unconstitutional State Taxes, 32 Conn. L. Rev. 73 (1999)--p. 286

Cross, The *Erie* Doctrine in Equity, 60 La. L. Rev. 173 (1999)--p. 120

Currie, Response: Ex Parte Young After Seminole Tribe, 72 N.Y.U.L.Rev. 547 (1997)--p. 284

Dauenhauer and Wells, Corrective Justice and Constitutional Torts, 35 Ga. L. Rev. 903 (2001)--p. 290

Davies, Federal Civil Rights Practice in the 1990's: The Dichotomy Between Reality and Practice, 48 Hastings L.J. 197 (1997)--p. 295

Degnan and Burbank, see Howard M. Erichson, Interjurisdictional Preclusion, 96 Mich.L.Rev. 945 (1998)--p. 296

Devins and Fitts, The Triumph of Timing: Raines v. Byrd and the Modern Supreme Court's Attempt to Control Constitutional Confrontations, 86 Geo.L.J. 351 (1997)--p. 108

Duffy, Administrative Common Law in Judicial Review, 77 Texas L.Rev. 113 (1998)--p. 108

Durchslag, Accommodation by Declaration, 33 Loy. L. Rev. 1375 (2000)--p. 265

Echeverria, Critiquing *Laidlaw:* Congressional Power to Confer Standing and the Irrelevance of Mootness Doctrine to Civil Penalties, 11 Duke Env. L. & Pol. Forum 287 (2001)--p. 99

Engdahl, Intrinsic Limits of Congress' Power Regarding the Judicial Branch, 1999 B.Y.U.L.Rev. 75--p. 69

Epstein, "In Such Manner as the Legislature Thereof May Direct": The Outcome of *Bush v. Gore* Defended, 68 U. Chi. L. Rev. 613, 614 (2001)--pp. 34, 35, 36

Eskridge and Frickey, Quasi-Constitutional Law: Clear Statement Rules as Constitutional Lawmaking, 45 Vand. L. Rev. 593 (1992)--p. 76

Fallon, Applying the Suspension Clause to Immigration Cases, 98 Colum.L.Rev. 1068 (1998)--p. 123

Farber, Pledging a New Allegiance: An Essay on Sovereignty and the New Federalism, 75 Notre Dame L. Rev. 1133 (2000)--p. 264

Federal Evidentiary Hearings Under the New Habeas Corpus Statute, 6 B.U. Pub. Interest L.J. 135 (1996)--p. 170

Fink, Supplemental Jurisdiction–Take it to the Limit!, 74 Ind.L.J. 161 (1998)--p. 115

Fitzgerald, Beyond *Marbury*: Jurisdictional Self–Dealing in *Seminole Tribe*, 52 Vand. L. Rev. 407 (1999)--p. 284

Fletcher, "Common Nucleus of Operative Fact" and Defensive Set–Off: Beyond the *Gibbs* Test, 74 Ind.L.J. 171 (1998)--p. 115

Fletcher, The Eleventh Amendment: Unfinished Business, 75 Notre Dame L. Rev. 843 (2000)--p. 214

Floyd, *Erie* Awry: A Comment on *Gasperini v. Center for Humanities, Inc.*, Brigham Young L.Rev. 267 (1997)--p. 116

Force, An Essay on Federal Common Law and Admiralty, 43 St. Louis U. L.J. 1367 (1999)--p. 1

Fountaine, Article III and the Adequate and Independent State Grounds Doctrine, 48 American U. L. Rev. 1053 (1999)--p. 37

Freedman, Milestones in Habeas Corpus: Part II: Leo Frank Lives: Untangling the Historical Roots of Meaningful Federal Habeas Corpus Review of State Convictions, 51 Ala. L. Rev. 1467 (2000)--p. 123

Freedman, Milestones in Habeas Corpus: Part III: *Brown v. Allen*: The Habeas Corpus Revolution That Wasn't, 51 Ala. L. Rev. 1541 (2000)--p. 123

Freer, Some Thoughts on the State of *Erie* After *Gasperini*, 76 Texas L.Rev. 1637 (1998)--p. 116

Freer, Toward a Principled Statutory Approach to Supplemental Jurisdiction in Diversity of Citizenship Cases, 74 Ind.L.J. 5 (1998)--p. 116

Friedell, The Diverse Nature of Admiralty Jurisdiction, 43 St. Louis U. L.J. 1389 (1999)--p. 1

Friedman & Gaylord, *Rooker–Feldman*, from the Ground Up, 74 Notre Dame L. Rev. 1129 (1999)--p. 121

Gelfand, Introduction, Reconsidering *Monell*'s Limitation on Municipal Liability for Civil Rights Violations, 31 Urb. Law. 395 (1999)--p. 291

Gerhardt, Institutional Analysis of Municipal Liability Under Section 1983, 48 DePaul L. Rev. 669 (2000)--p. 290

Gilles, Breaking the Code of Silence: Rediscovering "Custom" in Section 1983 Municipal Liability, 80 B.U. L. Rev. 17 (2000)--p. 291

Gilles, In Defense of Making Government Pay: The Deterrent Effect of Constitutional Tort Remedies, 35 Ga. L. Rev. 845 (2001)--p. 290

Goldsmith and Walt, *Erie* and the Irrelevance of Legal Positivism, 84 Va.L.Rev. 673 (1998)--p. 1

Goldsmith, Federal Courts, Foreign Affairs, and Federalism, 83 Va.L.Rev. 1617 (1997)--p. 2

Goldstein, Federal Common Law in Admiralty: An Introduction to the Beginning of an Exchange, 43 St. Louis U. L.J. 1337 (1999)--p. 1

Greabe, *Mirabile Dictum!*: The Case for "Unnecessary" Constitutional Ruling in Civil Rights Damages Actions, 74 Notre Dame L.Rev. 403 (1999)--p. 289

Greve, *Friends of the Earth,* Foes of Federalism, 12 Duke Env. L. & Pol. Forum 167 (2001)--p. 100

Griffin, The Correction of Wrongful Convictions: A Comparative Perspective, 16 Am. U. Int'l L. Rev. 1241 (2001)--p. 201

Gutoff, Federal Common Law and Congressional Delegation: A Reconceptualization of Admiralty, 61 U. Pitt. L. Rev. 367 (2000)--p. 2

Hafetz, The Untold Story of Noncriminal Habeas Corpus and the 1996 Immigration Acts, 107 Yale L. J. 2509 (1998)--pp. 78, 92

Hamilton, The Importance and Overuse of Policy and Custom Claims: A View from One Trench, 48 DePaul L. Rev. 723 (2000)--p. 290

Harrison, Jurisdiction, Congressional Power, and Constitutional Remedies, 86 Geo.L.J. 2513 (1998)--pp. 68, 150

Harrison, The Constitutional Origins and Implications of Judicial Review, 84 Va. L. Rev. 333 (1998)--p. 299

Harrison, The Power of Congress Over the Rules of Precedent, 50 Duke L. J. 503 (2000)--p. 3

Hart, Conflating Scope of Right with Standard of Review: the Supreme Court's "Strict Scrutiny" of Congressional Efforts to Enforce the Fourteenth Amendment, 46 Vill. L. Rev. 1091 (2001)--p. 264

Hart, The Power of Congress to Limit the Jurisdiction of Federal Courts: An Exercise in Dialectic, 66 Harv. L. Rev. 1362 (1953)--p. 78

Hartnett, § 1367 Producamus, 51 Duke L.J. 687 (2001)--p. 116

Hartnett, The Standing of the United States: How Criminal Prosecutions Show That Standing Doctrine Is Looking for Answers in All the Wrong Places, 97 Mich. L. Rev. 2239 (1999)--p. 97

Hartnett, Would the *Kroger* Rule Survive the ALI's Proposed Revision of § 1367?, 51 Duke L.J. 647 (2001)--p. 116

Heald and Wells, Remedies for the Misappropriation of Intellectual Property by State and Municipal Governments Before and After *Seminole Tribe*: The Eleventh

Amendment and Other Immunity Doctrines, 55 W. & L.L.Rev. 849 (1998)--pp. 262, 265

Hill, In Defense of Our Law of Sovereign Immunity, 42 B.C.L. Rev. 485 (2001)--p. 213

Hills, The Eleventh Amendment as Curb on Bureaucratic Power, 53 Stan. L. Rev. 1225 (2001)--p. 266

Hoffman, Removal Jurisdiction and the All Writs Act, 148 U. Pa. L. Rev. 401 (1999)--p. 121

Hoffman, Substance and Procedure in Capital Cases: Why Federal Habeas Courts Should Review the Merits of Every Death Sentence, 78 Tex. L. Rev. 1771 (2000)--p. 123

Hoffman, Thinking Out Loud About the Myth of *Erie*: Plus a Good Word for Section 1652, 70 Miss. L.J. 163 (2000)--p. 120

Hoffstadt, How Congress Might Redesign a Leaner, Cleaner Writ of Habeas Corpus, 49 Duke L. J. 947 (2000)--p. 123

Hovenkamp, Judicial Restraint and Constitutional Federalism: The Supreme Court's *Lopez* and *Seminole Tribe* Decisions, 96 Colum. L. Rev. 2213 (1996)--p. 214

Huang, A New Options Theory for Risk Multipliers of Attorney's Fees in Federal Civil Rights Litigation, 73 N.Y.U.L.Rev. 1943 (1998)--p. 295

Idelman, The Demise of Hypothetical Jurisdiction in the Federal Courts, 52 Vand. L.Rev. 235 (1999)--p. 114

Issacharoff, Political Judgments, 68 U. Chi. L. Rev. 637 (2001)--p. 37

Jackson, Federalism and the Uses and Limits of Law: *Printz* and Principle, 111 Harv. L.Rev. 2181 (1998)--p. 1

Jackson, Holistic Interpretation: *Fitzpatrick v. Bitzer* and Our Bifurcated Constitution, 53 Stan. L. Rev. 1259 (2001)--p. 265

Jackson, Introduction: Congressional Control of Jurisdiction and the Future of the Federal Courts–Opposition, Agreement, and Hierarchy, 86 Geo.L.J. 2445 (1998)--pp. 68, 150

Jackson, Principle and Compromise in Constitutional Adjudication: The Eleventh Amendment and State Sovereign Immunity, 75 Notre Dame L. Rev. 953 (2000)--p. 263

Jackson, Seminole Tribe, the Eleventh Amendment, and the Potential Evisceration of Ex Parte Young, 72 N.Y.U.L.Rev. 495 (1997)--p. 284

Jackson, The Infrastructure of Federal Supremacy, 32 Ind.L.Rev. 111 (1998)--p. 4

Jeffries, Disaggregating Constitutional Torts, 110 Yale L.J. 259 (2000)--p. 288

Jeffries, In Praise of the Eleventh Amendment and Section 1983, 84 Va. L. Rev. 47, 49 (1998)--pp. 214, 284

Jeffries, The Right–Remedy Gap in Constitutional Law, 109 Yale L. J. 87 (1999)--p. 289

Johnson, A Dictionary of the English Language (1773)--p. 90

Kaczorowski, Reflections on *Monell*'s Analysis of the Legislative History of Section 1983, 31 Urb. Law. 407 (1999)--p. 291

Karlan, Nothing Personal: The Evolution of the Newest Equal Protection from *Shaw v. Reno* to *Bush v. Gore,* 79 U.N.C. L. Rev. 1345 (2001)--p. 35

Karlan, The Irony of Immunity: The Eleventh Amendment, Irreparable Injury, and Section 1983, 53 Stan. L. Rev. 1311 (2001)--p. 264

Karlan, The Newest Equal Protection: Regressive Doctrine on a Changeable Court, in Sunstein and Epstein, eds., The Vote: Bush, Gore, and the Supreme Court 79 (2001)--pp. 35, 36

Kelleher, Taking "Substantive Rights" (in the Rules Enabling Act) More Seriously, 74 Notre Dame L.Rev. 47 (1998)--p. 116

Kinports, Implied Waiver After Seminole Tribe, 82 Minn.L.Rev. 793 (1998)--p. 215

Koh, Is International Law Really State Law, 111 Harv.L.Rev. 1824 (1998)--p. 1

Krent, Judging Judging: The Problem of Second–Guessing State Judges' Interpretation of State Law in *Bush v. Gore*, 29 Fla. State U. L. Rev. 493 (2001)--p. 37

Krent, *Laidlaw:* Redressing the Law of Redressability, 12 Duke Env. L. & Pol. Forum 85--p. 99

Kritchevsky, Reexamining *Monell*: Basing Section 1983 Municipal Liability Doctrine on the Statutory Language, 31 Urb. Law. 437 (1999)--p. 291

Lee, On the Received Wisdom in Federal Courts, 147 U. Pa. L. Rev. 1111 (1999)--p. 69

Lee, Section 2254(d) of the New Habeas Statute: An (Opinionated) User's Manual, 51 Vand.L.Rev. 103 (1998)--p. 150

Lessig, Erie-Effects of Volume 110: An Essay on Context in Interpretive Theory, 110 Harv.L.Rev. 1785 (1997)--p. 2

Levinson, In Making Government Pay: Markets, Politics, and the Allocation of Constitutional Costs, 67 U. Chi. L. Rev. 345 (2000)--p. 289

Liebman and Ryan, "Some Effectual Power": The Quantity and Quality of Decisionmaking Required of Article III Courts, 98 Colum.L.Rev. 696 (1998)--pp. 69, 150

Lilly, Making Sense of Nonsense: Reforming Supplemental Jurisdiction, 74 Ind.L.J. 181 (1998)--p. 116

Logan, Federal Habeas in the Information Age, 85 Minn. L. Rev. 147 (2000)--p. 123

Lund, The Decline of Federal Common Law, 76 B.U.L. Rev. 895 (1996)--p. 1

Manley, Effective But Messy, *Monell* Should Endure, 31 Urb. Law. 481 (1999)--p. 291

Massey, Federalism and the Rehnquist Court, 53 Hastings L. J. 431 (2002)--p. 265

McConnell, Two-and-a-Half Cheers for *Bush v. Gore*, 68 U. Chi. L. Rev. 657 (2001)--p. 36

Meltzer, Congress, Courts, and Constitutional Remedies, 86 Geo.L.J. 2537 (1998)--pp. 68, 150

Meltzer, Overcoming Immunity: The Case of Federal Regulation of Intellectual Property, 53 Stan. L. Rev. 1331 (2001)--p. 265

Meltzer, State Sovereign Immunity: Five Authors in Search of a Theory, 75 Notre Dame L. Rev. 1011 (2000)--p. 264

Meltzer, The *Seminole* Decision and State Sovereign Immunity, 1996 Sup. Ct. Rev. 1--pp. 215, 284

Menell, Economic Implications of State Sovereign Immunity from Infringement of Federal Intellectual Property Rights, 33 Loy. L. Rev. 1399 (2000)--p. 266

Michelman, Suspicion, or the New Prince, 68 U. Chi. L. Rev. 679 (2001)--p. 37

Monaghan, The Sovereign Immunity "Exception," 110 Harv. L. Rev. 102 (1995)--p. 214

Nahmod, The Restructuring of Narrative and Empathy in Section 1983 Cases, 72 Chi.-Kent L.Rev. 819 (1997)--p. 288

Nelson, Resolving Native American Land Claims and the Eleventh Amendment: Changing the Balance of Power, 39 Villanova L. Rev. 525 (1994)--p. 215

Nelson, Sovereign Immunity as a Doctrine of Personal Jurisdiction, 115 Harv. L. Rev. 1561 (2002)--p. 214

Neuman, Habeas Corpus, Executive Detention, and the Removal of Aliens, 98 Colum.L.Rev. 961 (1998)--pp. 77, 123

Neuman, Jurisdiction and the Rule of Law After the 1996 Immigration Act, 113 Harv. L. Rev. 1963 (2000)--p. 79

Nichol, The Impossibility of *Lujan*'s Project, 11 Duke Env. L. & Pol. Forum 193 (2001)--p. 99

Nicolas, Fighting the Probate Mafia: A Dissection of the Probate Exception to Federal Court Jurisdiction, 74 So. Cal. L. Rev. 1479 (2001)--p. 115

Note, Developments in the Law—Federal Habeas Corpus, 83 Harv. L.Rev. 1038, 1238 (1970)--p. 77

Note, Developments in the Law—Federal Habeas Corpus, 83 Harv. L.Rev. 1038, 1113–14, and nn. 9–11 (1970)--p. 92

Note, Rewriting the Great Writ: Standards of Review for Habeas Corpus under the New 28 U.S.C. § 2254, 110 Harv.L.Rev. 1868 (1997)--p. 150

Nowak, The Gang of Five & the Second Coming of an Anti-Reconstruction Supreme Court, 75 Notre Dame L. Rev. 1091 (2000)--p. 264

Oakley, Federal Jurisdiction and the Problem of the Litigative Unit: When Does What "Arise Under" Federal Law, 76 Texas L.Rev. 1829 (1998)--p. 111

Oakley, Fiat Lux, 51 Duke L.J. 699 (2001)--p. 116

Oakley, Integrating Supplemental Jurisdiction and Diversity Jurisdiction: A Progress Report on the Work of the American Law Institute, 74 Ind.L.J. 25 (1998)--p. 116

Oakley, *Kroger* Redux, 51 Duke L.J. 663 (2001)--p. 116

Oaks, Legal History in the High Court—Habeas Corpus, 64 Mich. L. Rev. 451 (1966)--p. 92

Opinion on the Writ of Habeas Corpus, 97 Eng. Rep. 29, 43 (H.L.1758)--p. 92

Oren, If *Monell* Were Reconsidered: Sexual Abuse and the Scope-of-Employment Doctrine in the Common Law, 31 Urb. Law. 527 (1999)--p. 291

Orth, History and the Eleventh Amendment, 75 Notre Dame L. Rev. 1147 (2000)--p. 264

Percival and Goger, Escaping the Common Law's Shadow: Standing in the Light of *Laidlaw*, 12 Duke Env. L. & Pol. Forum 119 (2001)--p. 99

Peterson, Controlling the Federal Courts Through the Appropriations Process, [1998] Wisc.L.Rev. 993--p. 68

Pfander, History and State Suability: An "Explanatory" Account of the Eleventh Amendment, 83 Corn.L.Rev. 1269 (1998)--p. 213

Pfander, Jurisdiction-Stripping and the Supreme Court's Power to Supervise Inferior Tribunals, 78 Tex. L. Rev. 1433 (2000)--p. 69

Pfander, Once More Unto the Breach: Eleventh Amendment Scholarship and the

Court, 75 Notre Dame L. Rev. 817 (2000)--p. 263

Pfander, Supplemental Jurisdiction and Section 1367: The Case for a Sympathetic Textualism, 148 U. Pa. L. Rev. 109 (1999)--p. 116

Pierce, Issues Raised by *Friends of the Earth v. Laidlaw Environmental Services:* Access to the Court for Environmental Plaintiffs, 11 Duke Env. L. & Pol. Forum 207 (2001)--p. 99

Pillard, Taking Fiction Seriously: The Strange Results of Public Officials' Individual Liability Under *Bivens,* 88 Geo. L.J. 65 (1999)--p. 288

Posner, *Bush v. Gore:* Prolegomenon to an Assessment, 68 U. Chi. L. Rev. 719 (2001)--p. 36

Pushaw, Congressional Power Over Federal Court Jurisdiction: A Defense of the Neo–Federalist Interpretation of Article III, Brigham Young L.Rev. 847 (1997)--p. 69

Pushaw, Justiciability and Separation of Powers: A Neo–Federalist Approach, 81 Corn.L.Rev. 393 (1996)--p. 97

Pushaw, The Inherent Powers of Federal Courts and the Structural Constitution, 86 Iowa L. Rev. 735 (2001)--p. 3

Rannik, The Anti–Terrorism and Effective Death Penalty Act of 1996: A Death Sentence for the 212(c) Waiver, 29 Miami Inter–Am. L. Rev. 123 (1996)--p. 74

Raven–Hansen, The Forgotten Proviso of § 1376(b) (And Why We Forgot), 74 Ind. L.J. 197 (1998)--p. 116

Redish and Sklaver, Federal Power to Commandeer State Courts: Implications for the Theory of Judicial Federalism, 32 Ind. L.Rev. 71 (1998)--p. 4

Resnick, The Federal Courts and Congress: Additional Sources, Alternative Texts, and Altered Aspirations, 86 Geo.L.J. 2589 (1998)--pp. 68, 150

Rich, Privileges or Immunities: The Missing Link in Establishing Congressional Power to Abrogate State Eleventh Amendment Immunity, 28 Hastings C.L.Q. 235 (2001)--p. 265

Rowe, Not Bad for Government Work: Does Anyone Else Think the Supreme Court is Doing a Halfway Decent Job in its *Erie-Hanna* Jurisprudence?, 73 Notre Dame L.Rev. 963 (1998)--p. 116

Rowe, *Rooker–Feldman*: Worth Only the Powder to Blow It Up?, 74 Notre Dame L. Rev. 1081 (1999)--p. 121

Rowe, 1367 and All That: Recodifying Supplemental Jurisdiction, 74 Ind.L.J. 53 (1998)--p. 116

Rutherglen, Structural Uncertainty Over Habeas Corpus and the Jurisdiction of Military Tribunals, 5 Green Bag 2d 285 (2002)--p. 123

Sager, *Klein's* First Principle: A Proposed Solution, 86 Geo.L.J. 2525 (1998)--pp. 68, 150

Savage, The Vote Case Fallout, 87 A.B.A.J. 32 (2001)--p. 34

Schapiro, Conceptions and Misconceptions of State Constitutional Law in *Bush v. Gore,* 29 Fla. State U. L. Rev. 661 (2001)--p. 37

Scheidegger, Habeas Corpus, Relitigation, and the Legislative Power, 98 Colum.L.Rev. 888 (1998)--p. 150

Seamon, The Sovereign Immunity of States in Their Own Courts, 37 Brandeis L.Rev. 319 (1998–99)--pp. 4, 243

Serr, Turning Section 1983's Protection of Civil Rights Into an Attractive Nuisance: Extra–Textual Barriers in Municipal Liability Under *Monell,* 35 Ga. L. Rev. 881 (2001)--p. 290

Shapiro, Supplemental Jurisdiction: A Confession, an Avoidance, and a Proposal, 74 Ind.L.J. 211 (1998)--p. 116

Sherry, Judicial Federalism in the Trenches: The *Rooker-Feldman* Doctrine in Action, 74 Notre Dame L.Rev. 1085 (1999)--p. 121

Sherry, States Are People Too, 75 Notre Dame L. Rev. 1121 (2000)--p. 264

Siegel, Congress's Power to Authorize Suits Against States, 68 Geo. Wash. L. Rev. 44 (1999)--p. 264

Stagner, Avoiding Abstention: The Younger Exceptions, 29 Texas Tech L.Rev. 137 (1998)--p. 121

Stearns, From *Lujan* to *Laidlaw:* A Preliminary Model of Environmental Standing, 11 Duke Env. L. & Pol. Forum 321 (2001)--p. 99

Steiker, Habeas Exceptionalism, 78 Tex. L. Rev. 1703 (2000)--p. 69

Steinman, After *Steel Co.*: "Hypothetical Jurisdiction" in the Federal Appellate Courts, 58 Wash. & Lee L. Rev. 855 (2001)--p. 114

Steinman, Crosscurrents: Supplemental Jurisdiction, Removal, and the ALI Revision Project, 74 Ind.L.J. 75 (1998)--p. 116

Steinman, The Newest Frontier of Judicial Activism: Removal Under the All Writs Act, 80 Boston U. L. Rev. 773 (2000)--p. 121

Steinman, The Scope of Appellate Jurisdiction: Pendent Appellate Jurisdiction Before and After *Swint,* 49 Hastings L.J. 1337 (1998)--pp. 120, 290

Stephens, The Law of Our Land: Customary International Law as Federal Law After Erie, 66 Fordham L.Rev. 393 (1997)--p. 2

Stephens, The New Retroactivity Doctrine: Equality, Reliance and Stare Decisis, 48 Syracuse L.Rev. 1515 (1998)--p. 123

Strasser, *Chisholm,* the Eleventh Amendment, and Sovereign Immunity: On *Alden*'s Return to Confederation Principles, 28 Fla. St. L. Rev. 605 (2001)--p. 266

Strasser, *Hans, Ayers,* and Eleventh Amendment Jurisprudence: On Justification, Rationalization, and Sovereign Immunity, 10 Geo. Mason L. Rev. 251 (2001)--p. 213

Strasser, Taking Exception to Traditional Exceptions Clause Jurisprudence: On Congress's Power to Limit the Court's Jurisdiction, 2001 Utah L. Rev. 125--p. 69

Strauss, *Bush v. Gore*: What Were They Thinking?, 68 U. Chi. L. Rev. 737 (2001)--p. 37

Sunstein, Order Without Law, 68 U. Chi. L. Rev. 737 (2001)--p. 34

Sward, Legislative Courts, Article III, and the Seventh Amendment, 77 N.C.L.Rev. 1037 (1999)--p. 94

Taylor, A Litigator's View of Discovery and Proof in Police Misconduct Policy and Practice Cases, 48 DePaul L. Rev. 747 (2000)--p. 290

Tidmarsh, A Dialogic Defense of *Alden*, 75 Notre Dame L. Rev. 1161 (2000)--p. 264

Turner, Employer Liability for Supervisory Hostile Environment Sexual Harassment: Comparing Title VII's and Section 1983's Regulatory Regimes, 31 Urb. Law. 503 (1999)--p. 291

Tushnet & Yackle, Symbolic Statutes and Real Laws: The Pathologies of the Antiterrorism and Effective Death Penalty Act and the Prison Litigation Reform Act, 47 Duke L.J. 1 (1997)--p. 150

Vázquez, Eleventh Amendment Schizophrenia, 75 Notre Dame L. Rev. 859 (2000)--p. 263

Vázquez, Sovereign Immunity, Due Process, and the *Alden* Trilogy, 109 Yale L.J. 1927 (2000)--p. 64

Vázquez, What Is Eleventh Amendment Immunity?, 106 Yale L.J. 1683 (1997)--p. 215

Velasco, Congressional Control Over Federal Court Jurisdiction: A Defense of the Traditional View, 46 Catholic U.L.Rev. 671 (1997)--p. 68

Webster, American Dictionary of the English Language (1828)--p. 90

Weinberg, The Article III Box: The Power of "Congress" to Attack the "Jurisdiction" of "Federal Courts", 78 Tex. L. Rev. 1405 (2000)--p. 69

Weinberg, Of Sovereignty and Union: The Legends of *Alden,* 76 Notre Dame L. Rev. 1113 (2001)--p. 265

Weiser, Federal Common Law, Cooperative Federalism, and the Enforcement of the Telecom Act, 76 N.Y.U. L. Rev. 1692 (2001)--p. 3

Wells, Available State Remedies and the Fourteenth Amendment: Comments on *Florida Prepaid v. College Savings Bank,* 33 Loy. L. Rev. 1665 (2000)--p. 265

Wilson, The Eleventh Amendment Cases: Going "Too Far" with Judicial Neofederalism, 33 Loy. L. Rev. 1687 (2000)--p. 265

Winter, What If Justice Scalia Took History and the Rule of Law Seriously?, 12 Duke Env. L. & Pol. Forum 155 (2001)--p. 100

Wolf, Comment on the Supplemental-Jurisdiction Statute: 28 U.S.C. § 1367, 74 Ind. L.J. 223 (1998)--p. 116

Woolhandler and Collins, Judicial Federalism and the Administrative States, 87 Cal. L.Rev. 613 (1999)--p. 121

Woolhandler, Old Property, New Property, and Sovereign Immunity, 75 Notre Dame L. Rev. 919 (2000)--p. 263

Woolhandler, The Common Law Origins of Constitutionally Compelled Remedies, 107 Yale L.J. 77 (1997)--p. 213

Yackle, The American Bar Association and Federal Habeas Corpus, 61 Law & Contemp Probs. 171 (1998)--p. 152

Yackle, The Figure in the Carpet, 78 Tex. L. Rev. 1731 (2000)--p. 123

Yeazell, Teaching Supplemental Jurisdiction, 74 Ind.L.J. 241 (1998)--p. 116

Yonover, A Kinder, Gentler Erie: Reigning in the Use of Certification, 47 Ark.L.Rev. 305 (1994)--p. 3

Yoo, The Judicial Safeguards of Federalism, 70 Southern Cal. L. Rev. 1311 (1997)--p. 214

Young, Constitutional Avoidance, Resistance Norms, and the Preservation of Judicial Review, 78 Tex. L. Rev. 1549 (2000)--p. 69

Young, State Sovereign Immunity and the Future of Federalism, 1999 Sup.Ct. Rev. 1 (1999)--p. 266

Young, The Last Brooding Omnipresence: *Erie Railroad Co. v. Tompkins* and the Unconstitutionality of Preemptive Federal Maritime Law, 43 St. Louis U. L.J. 1349 (1999)--p. 1

Zeigler, Rights, Rights of Action, and Remedies: An Integrated Approach, 76 Wash. L. Rev. 67 (2001)--p. 38

2002 SUPPLEMENT

FEDERAL COURTS AND THE LAW OF FEDERAL–STATE RELATIONS

*

CHAPTER I

CHOICE OF LAW IN THE FEDERAL SYSTEM

Page 9, add at the beginning of footnote a:

For a thoughtful analysis of a recent book on *Erie*, see Susan Bandes, *Erie* and the History of the One True Federalism (Reviewing Edward A. Purcell, Jr., Brandeis and the Progressive Constitution: *Erie*, the Judicial Power, and the Politics of the Federal Courts in Twentieth–Century America), 110 Yale L.J. 829 (2001).

Page 12, add at the end of footnote d:

Compare Jack Goldsmith and Steven Walt, *Erie* and the Irrelevance of Legal Positivism, 84 Va. L. Rev. 673 (1998), which argues that the historical connection between *Erie* and legal positivism has not been shown and that "*Erie's* commitment to legal positivism is conceptually and normatively independent of its constitutional holding."

Page 13, Change Footnote 9 to footnote f; add at the end of the footnote:

For commentary on the implications of *Printz* and an argument in favor of appropriately limited judicial enforcement of federalism limits on Congressional power, see Vicki C. Jackson, Federalism and the Uses and Limits of Law: *Printz* and Principle, 111 Harv. L. Rev. 2181 (1998).

Page 14, add to the first sentence of footnote g:

Paul Lund, The Decline of Federal Common Law, 76 B.U. L. Rev. 895 (1996).

Page 15, add to the second sentence of footnote h:

; Joel K. Goldstein, Federal Common Law in Admiralty: An Introduction to the Beginning of an Exchange, 43 St. Louis U. L.J. 1337 (1999) (advocating "a fairly robust federal common law-making role for admiralty courts"); Ernest A. Young, The Last Brooding Omnipresence: *Erie Railroad Co. v. Tompkins* and the Unconstitutionality of Preemptive Federal Maritime Law, 43 St. Louis U. L.J. 1349 (1999) (arguing that the "broad role of maritime preemption is unconstitutional"); Robert Force, An Essay on Federal Common Law and Admiralty, 43 St. Louis U. L.J. 1367 (1999) (defending the "constitutional authority [of federal courts] to create substantive rules of maritime law"); Steven F. Friedell, The Diverse Nature of Admiralty Jurisdiction, 43 St. Louis U. L.J. 1389 (1999) (arguing that Congress has confirmed the law-making authority of the federal admiralty courts on numerous occasions).

Page 15, add at the end of footnote h:

For reactions, see Harold Hongju Koh, Is International Law Really State Law, 111 Harv. L. Rev. 1824 (1998); Curtis A. Bradley and Jack L. Goldsmith, Federal Courts and the Incorporation of International Law, 111

Harv. L. Rev. 2260 (1998). See also Jack L. Goldsmith, Federal Courts, Foreign Affairs, and Federalism, 83 Va. L. Rev. 1617 (1997); Beth Stephens, The Law of Our Land: Customary International Law as Federal Law After *Erie*, 66 Fordham L. Rev. 393 (1997). For an interesting extrapolation from the Bradley and Goldsmith article cited above, see Lawrence Lessig, *Erie*–Effects of Volume 110: An Essay on Context in Interpretive Theory, 110 Harv. L. Rev. 1785 (1997). See also Jonathan M. Gutoff, Federal Common Law and Congressional Delegation: A Reconceptualization of Admiralty, 61 U. Pitt. L. Rev. 367 (2000).

Page 17, add a new Note 7(iv) and renumber the present Note 7(iv) to Note 7(v):

(iv) ***Semtek International Inc. v. Lockheed Martin Corp.*** Semtek's suit against Lockheed, based on diversity jurisdiction, was dismissed by a California federal district court as barred by the California two-year statute of limitations. A suit alleging the same claims was then filed in a Maryland state court, based on the Maryland three-year limitations period. The Maryland courts held that the preclusive effect of the California federal court judgment was to be determined by federal law and that, under the applicable federal law, the suit was barred.

In Semtek International Inc. v. Lockheed Martin Corp., 531 U.S. 497 (2001), the Supreme Court unanimously reversed. Writing for the Court, Justice Scalia found no answer in the Federal Rules of Civil Procedure. There was one prior Supreme Court case on point, Dupasseur v. Rochereau, 88 U.S. (21 Wall.) 130 (1875), which held that state law controlled the res judicata effect of a federal trial court exercising diversity jurisdiction. But *Dupasseur* was "not dispositive because it was decided under the Conformity Act of 1872, which required federal courts to apply the procedural law of the forum State in nonequity cases." What, then, to do? Scalia answered:

> Having concluded that the claim-preclusive effect, in Maryland, of this California federal diversity judgment is dictated neither by *Dupasseur v. Rochereau,* as petitioner contends, nor by Rule 41(b), as respondent contends, we turn to consideration of what determines the issue. Neither the Full Faith and Credit Clause, U.S. Const., Art. IV, § 1, nor the full faith and credit statute, 28 U.S.C. § 1738, addresses the question. By their terms they govern the effects to be given only to state-court judgments (and, in the case of the statute, to judgments by courts of territories and possessions). And no other federal textual provision, neither of the Constitution nor of any statute, addresses the claim-preclusive effect of a judgment in a federal diversity action.
>
> It is also true, however, that no federal textual provision addresses the claim-preclusive effect of a federal-court judgment in a federal-question case, yet we have long held that States cannot give those judgments merely whatever effect they would give their own judgments, but must accord them the effect that this Court prescribes. The reasoning of that line of cases suggests, moreover, that even when States are allowed to give federal judgments

(notably, judgments in diversity cases) no more than the effect accorded to state judgments, that disposition is by direction of *this* Court, which has the last word on the claim-preclusive effect of *all* federal judgments....

In other words, in *Dupasseur* the State was allowed (indeed, required) to give a federal diversity judgment no more effect than it would accord one of its own judgments only because reference to state law was *the federal rule that this Court deemed appropriate.* In short, federal common law governs the claim-preclusive effect of a dismissal by a federal court sitting in diversity.... It is left to us, then, to determine the appropriate federal rule.

And the appropriate federal rule, Scalia said, was to follow state law: "[T]here is no conceivable federal interest in giving that time bar more effect in other courts than the California courts themselves would impose." The case was accordingly remanded so that the Maryland courts could determine the applicable California preclusion rules.

Did the Court have any other choice but "to determine the appropriate federal rule"? What else could it have done?[j]

j. Cf. Robert J. Pushaw, The Inherent Powers of Federal Courts and the Structural Constitution, 86 Iowa L. Rev. 735 (2001). See also John Harrison, The Power of Congress Over the Rules of Precedent, 50 Duke L.J. 503 (2000).

Page 18, add at the end of footnote j:

See also Phillip J. Weiser, Federal Common Law, Cooperative Federalism, and the Enforcement of the Telecom Act, 76 N.Y.U. L. Rev. 1692 (2001), which advances a vision of the law-making role of federal courts in the implementation of modern regulatory programs.

Page 22, revise the first sentence of Note 5(iii) and substitute a new footnote c:

Forty-three states, plus the District of Columbia and Puerto Rico, now permit some form of certification of uncertain state law to the highest local court for resolution.[c]

c. Bradford R. Clark, Ascertaining the Laws of the Several States: Positivism and Judicial Federalism After *Erie*, 145 U. Pa. L. Rev. 1459, 1548 (1997). Clark examines alternative approaches to uncertain state law and concludes that a presumption in favor of certification is the preferred approach. See also Geri J. Yonover, A Kinder, Gentler *Erie*: Reigning in the Use of Certification, 47 Ark. L. Rev. 305 (1994).

Page 22, add a footnote after the second sentence in Note 5(iii):

d. For an example of unanimous use of the certification procedure by the Supreme Court seeking the answer to a question of state law that would shape the federal constitutional question presented by a petition for federal habeas corpus, see Fiore v. White, 528 U.S. 23 (1999).

Page 50, add a new Note:

5. The Anti–Commandeering Principle. In Printz v. United States, 521 U.S. 898 (1997), the Supreme Court ruled that Congress could not constitutionally require local law enforcement to conduct background checks of firearms purchasers, as specified in the Brady Handgun Violence Prevention Act. The Court found the requirement violative of what has been called the anti-commandeering principle, namely, that "[t]he federal government may not compel the states to enact or administer a federal regulatory program." New York v. United States, 505 U.S. 144, 188 (1992).

Although the anti-commandeering principle in terms applies only to executive officers, there is perhaps some tension between that view of state sovereignty as a limit on federal legislative power and the requirement, often associated with *Testa v. Katt*, that state courts hear federal claims. The *Printz* Court distinguished congressional "commandeering" of state judges on the ground that they are bound by the supremacy clause to enforce state law. This reasoning, though not the conclusion to which it leads, is questioned and its implications explored in Martin H. Redish and Steven G. Sklaver, Federal Power to Commandeer State Courts: Implications for the Theory of Judicial Federalism, 32 Ind. L. Rev. 71 (1998), and Vicki C. Jackson, The Infrastructure of Federal Supremacy, 32 Ind. L. Rev. 111 (1998).

The problem became more acute after Alden v. Maine, 527 U.S. 706 (1999) (reprinted, infra, as a main case in this Supplement), where the Supreme Court invoked *Printz* and the anti-commandeering principle in support of its conclusion that Congress lacked power to override state sovereign immunity in state courts. For an anticipatory endorsement of that reasoning and careful examination of its relation to *Testa v. Katt*, see Richard H. Seamon, The Sovereign Immunity of States in Their Own Courts, 37 Brandeis L. Rev. 319 (1998–99).

Page 62, add at the beginning of footnote d:

For an analysis of Congressional power over state court procedures, see Anthony J., Bellia, Jr., Federal Regulation of State Court Procedures, 110 Yale L.J. 947 (2001).

Page 84, add the following main case:

Bush v. Gore

Supreme Court of the United States, 2000.
531 U.S. 98.

■ PER CURIAM.

I

On December 8, 2000, the Supreme Court of Florida ordered that the Circuit Court of Leon County tabulate by hand 9,000 ballots in Miami–

Dade County. It also ordered the inclusion in the certified vote totals of 215 votes identified in Palm Beach County and 168 votes identified in Miami–Dade County for Vice President Albert Gore, Jr., and Senator Joseph Lieberman, Democratic Candidates for President and Vice President. The Supreme Court noted that petitioner, Governor George W. Bush asserted that the net gain for Vice President Gore in Palm Beach County was 176 votes, and directed the Circuit Court to resolve that dispute on remand. The court further held that relief would require manual recounts in all Florida counties where so-called "undervotes" had not been subject to manual tabulation. The court ordered all manual recounts to begin at once. Governor Bush and Richard Cheney, Republican Candidates for the Presidency and Vice Presidency, filed an emergency application for a stay of this mandate. On December 9, we granted the application, treated the application as a petition for a writ of certiorari, and granted certiorari.

The proceedings leading to the present controversy are discussed in some detail in our opinion in Bush v. Palm Beach County Canvassing Bd., 531 U.S. 70 (2000) (*Bush I*). On November 8, 2000, the day following the Presidential election, the Florida Division of Elections reported that petitioner, Governor Bush, had received 2,909,135 votes, and respondent, Vice President Gore, had received 2,907,351 votes, a margin of 1,784 for Governor Bush. Because Governor Bush's margin of victory was less than "one-half of a percent . . . of the votes cast," an automatic machine recount was conducted under § 102.141(4) of the election code, the results of which showed Governor Bush still winning the race but by a diminished margin. Vice President Gore then sought manual recounts in Volusia, Palm Beach, Broward, and Miami–Dade Counties, pursuant to Florida's election protest provisions. Fla. Stat. § 102.166 (2000). A dispute arose concerning the deadline for local county canvassing boards to submit their returns to the Secretary of State (Secretary). The Secretary declined to waive the November 14 deadline imposed by statute. §§ 102.111, 102.112. The Florida Supreme Court, however, set the deadline at November 26. We granted certiorari and vacated the Florida Supreme Court's decision, finding considerable uncertainty as to the grounds on which it was based. On December 11, the Florida Supreme Court issued a decision on remand reinstating that date.

On November 26, the Florida Elections Canvassing Commission certified the results of the election and declared Governor Bush the winner of Florida's 25 electoral votes. On November 27, Vice President Gore, pursuant to Florida's contest provisions, filed a complaint in Leon County Circuit Court contesting the certification. He sought relief pursuant to § 102.168(3)(c), which provides that "receipt of a number of illegal votes or rejection of a number of legal votes sufficient to change or place in doubt the result of the election" shall be grounds for a contest. The Circuit Court denied relief, stating that Vice President Gore failed to meet his burden of proof. He appealed to the First District Court of Appeal, which certified the matter to the Florida Supreme Court.

Accepting jurisdiction, the Florida Supreme Court affirmed in part and reversed in part. Gore v. Harris, 772 So.2d 1243 (Fla.2000). The court held that the Circuit Court had been correct to reject Vice President Gore's challenge to the results certified in Nassau County and his challenge to the Palm Beach County Canvassing Board's determination that 3,300 ballots cast in that county were not, in the statutory phrase, "legal votes."

The Supreme Court held that Vice President Gore had satisfied his burden of proof under § 102.168(3)(c) with respect to his challenge to Miami–Dade County's failure to tabulate, by manual count, 9,000 ballots on which the machines had failed to detect a vote for President ("undervotes"). Noting the closeness of the election, the Court explained that "on this record, there can be no question that there are legal votes within the 9,000 uncounted votes sufficient to place the results of this election in doubt." A "legal vote," as determined by the Supreme Court, is "one in which there is a 'clear indication of the intent of the voter.'" The court therefore ordered a hand recount of the 9,000 ballots in Miami–Dade County. Observing that the contest provisions vest broad discretion in the circuit judge to "provide any relief appropriate under such circumstances," Fla. Stat. § 102.168(8) (2000), the Supreme Court further held that the Circuit Court could order "the Supervisor of Elections and the Canvassing Boards, as well as the necessary public officials, in all counties that have not conducted a manual recount or tabulation of the undervotes ... to do so forthwith, said tabulation to take place in the individual counties where the ballots are located."

The Supreme Court also determined that both Palm Beach County and Miami–Dade County, in their earlier manual recounts, had identified a net gain of 215 and 168 legal votes for Vice President Gore. Rejecting the Circuit Court's conclusion that Palm Beach County lacked the authority to include the 215 net votes submitted past the November 26 deadline, the Supreme Court explained that the deadline was not intended to exclude votes identified after that date through ongoing manual recounts. As to Miami–Dade County, the Court concluded that although the 168 votes identified were the result of a partial recount, they were "legal votes [that] could change the outcome of the election." The Supreme Court therefore directed the Circuit Court to include those totals in the certified results, subject to resolution of the actual vote total from the Miami–Dade partial recount.

The petition presents the following questions: whether the Florida Supreme Court established new standards for resolving Presidential election contests, thereby violating Art. II, § 1, cl. 2, of the United States Constitution and failing to comply with 3 U.S.C. § 5, and whether the use of standardless manual recounts violates the Equal Protection and Due Process Clauses. With respect to the equal protection question, we find a violation of the Equal Protection Clause.

II

A

The closeness of this election, and the multitude of legal challenges which have followed in its wake, have brought into sharp focus a common, if heretofore unnoticed, phenomenon. Nationwide statistics reveal that an estimated 2% of ballots cast do not register a vote for President for whatever reason, including deliberately choosing no candidate at all or some voter error, such as voting for two candidates or insufficiently marking a ballot. In certifying election results, the votes eligible for inclusion in the certification are the votes meeting the properly established legal requirements.

This case has shown that punch card balloting machines can produce an unfortunate number of ballots which are not punched in a clean, complete way by the voter. After the current counting, it is likely legislative bodies nationwide will examine ways to improve the mechanisms and machinery for voting.

B

The individual citizen has no federal constitutional right to vote for electors for the President of the United States unless and until the state legislature chooses a statewide election as the means to implement its power to appoint members of the Electoral College. U.S. Const., Art. II, § 1. This is the source for the statement in McPherson v. Blacker, 146 U.S. 1, 35 (1892), that the State legislature's power to select the manner for appointing electors is plenary; it may, if it so chooses, select the electors itself, which indeed was the manner used by State legislatures in several States for many years after the Framing of our Constitution. Id. at 28–33. History has now favored the voter, and in each of the several States the citizens themselves vote for Presidential electors. When the state legislature vests the right to vote for President in its people, the right to vote as the legislature has prescribed is fundamental; and one source of its fundamental nature lies in the equal weight accorded to each vote and the equal dignity owed to each voter. . . .

The right to vote is protected in more than the initial allocation of the franchise. Equal protection applies as well to the manner of its exercise. Having once granted the right to vote on equal terms, the State may not, by later arbitrary and disparate treatment, value one person's vote over that of another. See, e.g., Harper v. Virginia Bd. of Elections, 383 U.S. 663, 665 (1966) ("Once the franchise is granted to the electorate, lines may not be drawn which are inconsistent with the Equal Protection Clause of the Fourteenth Amendment"). It must be remembered that "the right of suffrage can be denied by a debasement or dilution of the weight of a citizen's vote just as effectively as by wholly prohibiting the free exercise of the franchise." Reynolds v. Sims, 377 U.S. 533, 555 (1964).

There is no difference between the two sides of the present controversy on these basic propositions.... The question before us, however, is whether the recount procedures the Florida Supreme Court has adopted are consistent with its obligation to avoid arbitrary and disparate treatment of the members of its electorate.

Much of the controversy seems to revolve around ballot cards designed to be perforated by a stylus but which, either through error or deliberate omission, have not been perforated with sufficient precision for a machine to count them. In some cases a piece of the card—a chad—is hanging, say by two corners. In other cases there is no separation at all, just an indentation.

The Florida Supreme Court has ordered that the intent of the voter be discerned from such ballots. For purposes of resolving the equal protection challenge, it is not necessary to decide whether the Florida Supreme Court had the authority under the legislative scheme for resolving election disputes to define what a legal vote is and to mandate a manual recount implementing that definition. The recount mechanisms implemented in response to the decisions of the Florida Supreme Court do not satisfy the minimum requirement for non-arbitrary treatment of voters necessary to secure the fundamental right. Florida's basic command for the count of legally cast votes is to consider the "intent of the voter." *Gore v. Harris*, 772 So.2d at 1262. This is unobjectionable as an abstract proposition and a starting principle. The problem inheres in the absence of specific standards to ensure its equal application. The formulation of uniform rules to determine intent based on these recurring circumstances is practicable and, we conclude, necessary.

The law does not refrain from searching for the intent of the actor in a multitude of circumstances; and in some cases the general command to ascertain intent is not susceptible to much further refinement. In this instance, however, the question is not whether to believe a witness but how to interpret the marks or holes or scratches on an inanimate object, a piece of cardboard or paper which, it is said, might not have registered as a vote during the machine count. The factfinder confronts a thing, not a person. The search for intent can be confined by specific rules designed to ensure uniform treatment.

The want of those rules here has led to unequal evaluation of ballots in various respects. As seems to have been acknowledged at oral argument, the standards for accepting or rejecting contested ballots might vary not only from county to county but indeed within a single county from one recount team to another.

The record provides some examples. A monitor in Miami–Dade County testified at trial that he observed that three members of the county canvassing board applied different standards in defining a legal vote. And testimony at trial also revealed that at least one county changed its evaluative standards during the counting process. Palm Beach County, for example, began the process with a 1990 guideline which precluded counting completely attached chads, switched to a rule that considered a vote to be legal if any light could be seen through a chad, changed back to the 1990 rule, and then abandoned any pretense of a per se rule, only to have a court order that the county consider dimpled chads legal. This is not a process with sufficient guarantees of equal treatment.

An early case in our one person, one vote jurisprudence arose when a State accorded arbitrary and disparate treatment to voters in its different counties. Gray v. Sanders, 372 U.S. 368 (1963). The Court found a constitutional violation. We relied on these principles in the context of the Presidential selection process in Moore v. Ogilvie, 394 U.S. 814 (1969), where we invalidated a county-based procedure that diluted the influence of citizens in larger counties in the nominating process. There we observed that "the idea that one group can be granted greater voting strength than another is hostile to the one man, one vote basis of our representative government."

The State Supreme Court ratified this uneven treatment. It mandated that the recount totals from two counties, Miami–Dade and Palm Beach, be included in the certified total. The court also appeared to hold sub silentio that the recount totals from Broward County, which were not completed until after the original November 14 certification by the Secretary of State, were to be considered part of the new certified vote totals even though the county certification was not contested by Vice President Gore. Yet each of the counties used varying standards to determine what was a legal vote. Broward County used a more forgiving standard than Palm Beach County, and uncovered almost three times as many new votes, a result markedly disproportionate to the difference in population between the counties.

In addition, the recounts in these three counties were not limited to so-called undervotes but extended to all of the ballots. The distinction has real consequences. A manual recount of all ballots identifies not only those ballots which show no vote but also those which contain more than one, the so-called overvotes. Neither category will be counted by the machine. This is not a trivial concern. At oral argument, respondents estimated there are as many as 110,000 overvotes statewide. As a result, the citizen whose ballot was not read by a machine because he failed to vote for a candidate in a way readable by a machine may still have his vote counted in a manual recount; on the other hand, the citizen who marks two candidates in a way discernible by the machine will not have the same opportunity to have his vote count, even if a manual examination of the ballot would reveal the requisite indicia of intent. Furthermore, the citizen who marks two candidates, only one of which is discernible by the machine, will have his vote counted even though it should have been read as an invalid ballot. The State Supreme Court's inclusion of vote counts based on these variant standards exemplifies concerns with the remedial processes that were under way.

That brings the analysis to yet a further equal protection problem. The votes certified by the court included a partial total from one county, Miami–Dade. The Florida Supreme Court's decision thus gives no assurance that the recounts included in a final certification must be complete. Indeed, it is respondent's submission that it would be consistent with the rules of the recount procedures to include whatever partial counts are done by the time of final certification, and we interpret the Florida Supreme Court's decision to permit this. See 772 So.2d at 1261–62 n.21 (noting "practical difficulties" may control outcome of election, but certifying partial Miami–Dade total nonetheless). This accommodation no doubt results from the truncated contest period established by the Florida Supreme Court in *Bush I*, at respondents' own urging. The press of time does not diminish the constitutional concern. A desire for speed is not a general excuse for ignoring equal protection guarantees.

In addition to these difficulties the actual process by which the votes were to be counted under the Florida Supreme Court's decision raises further concerns. That order did not specify who would recount the ballots. The county canvassing boards were forced to pull together ad hoc teams comprised of judges from various Circuits who had no previous training in handling and interpreting ballots. Furthermore, while others were permitted to observe, they were prohibited from objecting during the recount.

The recount process, in its features here described, is inconsistent with the minimum procedures necessary to protect the fundamental right of each voter in the special instance of a statewide recount under the authority of a single state judicial officer. Our consideration is limited to the present circumstances, for the problem of equal protection in election processes generally presents many complexities.

The question before the Court is not whether local entities, in the exercise of their expertise, may develop different systems for implementing elections. Instead, we are presented with a situation where a state court with the power to assure uniformity has ordered a statewide recount with minimal procedural safeguards. When a court orders a statewide remedy, there must be at least some assurance that the rudimentary requirements of equal treatment and fundamental fairness are satisfied.

Given the Court's assessment that the recount process underway was probably being conducted in an unconstitutional manner, the Court stayed the order directing the recount so it could hear this case and render an expedited decision. The contest provision, as it was mandated by the State Supreme Court, is not well calculated to sustain the confidence that all citizens must have in the outcome of elections. The State has not shown that its procedures include the necessary safeguards. The problem, for instance, of the estimated 110,000 overvotes has not been addressed....

Upon due consideration of the difficulties identified to this point, it is obvious that the recount cannot be conducted in compliance with the requirements of equal protection and due process without substantial additional work. It would require not only the adoption (after opportunity for argument) of adequate statewide standards for determining what is a legal vote, and practicable procedures to implement them, but also orderly judicial review of any disputed matters that might arise. In addition, the Secretary of State has advised that the recount of only a portion of the ballots requires that the vote tabulation equipment be used to screen out undervotes, a function for which the machines were not designed. If a recount of overvotes were also required, perhaps even a second screening would be necessary. Use of the equipment for this purpose, and any new software developed for it, would have to be evaluated for accuracy by the Secretary of State, as required by Fla. Stat. § 101.015 (2000).

The Supreme Court of Florida has said that the legislature intended the State's electors to "participate fully in the federal electoral process," as provided in 3 U.S.C. § 5. 772 So.2d at 1289. That statute, in turn, requires that any controversy or contest that is designed to lead to a conclusive selection of electors be completed by December 12. That date is upon us, and there is no recount procedure in place under the State Supreme Court's order that comports with minimal constitutional standards. Because it is evident that any recount seeking to meet the December 12 date will be unconstitutional for the reasons we have discussed, we reverse the judgment of the Supreme Court of Florida ordering a recount to proceed.

Seven Justices of the Court agree that there are constitutional problems with the recount ordered by the Florida Supreme Court that demand a remedy. See infra (Souter, J., dissenting); infra (Breyer, J., dissenting). The only disagreement is as to the remedy. Because the Florida Supreme Court has said that the Florida Legislature intended to obtain the safe-harbor benefits of 3 U.S.C. § 5, Justice Breyer's proposed remedy—remanding to the Florida Supreme Court for its ordering of a constitutionally proper contest until December 18—contemplates action in violation of the Florida election code, and hence could not be part of an "appropriate" order authorized by Fla. Stat. § 102.168(8) (2000).

None are more conscious of the vital limits on judicial authority than are the members of this Court, and none stand more in admiration of the Constitution's design to leave the selection of the President to the people, through their legislatures, and to the political sphere. When contending parties invoke the process of the courts, however, it becomes our unsought responsibility to resolve the federal and constitutional issues the judicial system has been forced to confront.

The judgment of the Supreme Court of Florida is reversed, and the case is remanded for further proceedings not inconsistent with this opinion.

Pursuant to this Court's Rule 45.2, the Clerk is directed to issue the mandate in this case forthwith.

It is so ordered.

■ CHIEF JUSTICE REHNQUIST, with whom JUSTICE SCALIA and JUSTICE THOMAS join, concurring.

We join the per curiam opinion. We write separately because we believe there are additional grounds that require us to reverse the Florida Supreme Court's decision.

I

We deal here not with an ordinary election, but with an election for the President of the United States. In Burroughs v. United States, 290 U.S. 534, 545 (1934), we said:

> While presidential electors are not officers or agents of the federal government (In re Green, 134 U.S. 377, 379), they exercise federal functions under, and discharge duties in virtue of authority conferred by, the Constitution of the United States. The President is vested with the executive power of the nation. The importance of his election and the vital character of its relationship to and effect upon the welfare and safety of the whole people cannot be too strongly stated.

Likewise, in Anderson v. Celebrezze, 460 U.S. 780, 794–95 (1983) (footnote omitted), we said: "In the context of a Presidential election, state-imposed restrictions implicate a uniquely important national interest. For the President and the Vice President of the United States are the only elected officials who represent all the voters in the Nation."

In most cases, comity and respect for federalism compel us to defer to the decisions of state courts on issues of state law. That practice reflects our understanding that the decisions of state courts are definitive pronouncements of the will of the States as sovereigns. Cf. Erie R. Co. v. Tompkins, 304 U.S. 64 (1938). Of course, in ordinary cases, the distribution of powers among the branches of a State's government raises no questions of federal constitutional law, subject to the requirement that the government be republican in character. See U.S. Const., Art. IV, § 4. But there are a few exceptional cases in which the Constitution imposes a duty or confers a power on a particular branch of a State's government. This is one of them. Article II, § 1, cl. 2, provides that "each State shall appoint, in such Manner as the *Legislature* thereof may direct," electors for President and Vice President. (Emphasis added.) Thus, the text of the election law itself, and not just its interpretation by the courts of the States, takes on independent significance.

In McPherson v. Blacker, 146 U.S. 1 (1892), we explained that Art. II, § 1, cl. 2, "conveys the broadest power of determination" and "leaves it to the legislature exclusively to define the method" of appointment. A significant departure from the legislative scheme for appointing Presidential electors presents a federal constitutional question.

3 U.S.C. § 5 informs our application of Art. II, § 1, cl. 2, to the Florida statutory scheme, which, as the Florida Supreme Court acknowledged, took that statute into account. Section 5 provides that the State's selection of electors "shall be conclusive, and shall govern in the counting of the electoral votes" if the electors are chosen under laws enacted prior to election day, and if the selection process is completed six days prior to the meeting of the electoral college. As we noted in Bush v. Palm Beach County Canvassing Bd., 531 U.S. 78, 121 (2000):

> Since § 5 contains a principle of federal law that would assure finality of the State's determination if made pursuant to a state law in effect before the election, a legislative wish to take advantage of the 'safe harbor' would counsel against any construction of the Election Code that Congress might deem to be a change in the law.

If we are to respect the legislature's Article II powers, therefore, we must ensure that postelection state-court actions do not frustrate the legislative desire to attain the "safe harbor" provided by § 5.

In Florida, the legislature has chosen to hold statewide elections to appoint the State's 25 electors. Importantly, the legislature has delegated the authority to run the elections and to oversee election disputes to the Secretary of State (Secretary), Fla. Stat. § 97.012(1) (2000), and to state circuit courts, §§ 102.168(1), 102.168(8). Isolated sections of the code may well admit of more than one interpretation, but the general coherence of the legislative scheme may not be altered by judicial interpretation so as to wholly change the statutorily provided apportionment of responsibility among these various bodies. In any election but a Presidential election, the Florida Supreme Court can give as little or as much deference to Florida's executives as it chooses, so far as Article II is concerned, and this Court will have no cause to question the court's actions. But, with respect to a Presidential election, the court must be both mindful of the legislature's role under Article II in choosing the manner of appointing electors and deferential to those bodies expressly empowered by the legislature to carry out its constitutional mandate.

In order to determine whether a state court has infringed upon the legislature's authority, we necessarily must examine the law of the State as it existed prior to the action of the court. Though we generally defer to state courts on the interpretation of state law—see, e.g., Mullaney v. Wilbur, 421 U.S. 684, 44 L. Ed. 2d 508, 95 S. Ct. 1881 (1975)—there are of course areas in which the Constitution requires this Court to undertake an independent, if still deferential, analysis of state law.

For example, in NAACP v. Alabama ex rel. Patterson, 357 U.S. 449 (1958), it was argued that we were without jurisdiction because the petitioner had not pursued the correct appellate remedy in Alabama's state courts. Petitioners had sought a state-law writ of certiorari in the Alabama Supreme Court when a writ of mandamus, according to that court, was proper. We found this state-law ground inadequate to defeat our jurisdiction because we were "unable to reconcile the procedural holding of the Alabama Supreme Court" with prior Alabama precedent. The purported state-law ground was so novel, in our independent estimation, that "petitioner could not fairly be deemed to have been apprised of its existence."

Six years later we decided Bouie v. City of Columbia, 378 U.S. 347 (1964), in which the state court had held, contrary to precedent, that the state trespass law applied to black sit-in demonstrators who had consent to enter private property but were then asked to leave. Relying upon *NAACP*, we concluded that the South Carolina Supreme Court's interpretation of a state penal statute had impermissibly broadened the scope of that statute beyond what a fair reading provided, in violation of due process. What we would do in the present case is precisely parallel: Hold that the Florida Supreme Court's interpretation of the Florida election laws impermissibly distorted them beyond what a fair reading required, in violation of Article II.[1]

This inquiry does not imply a disrespect for state *courts* but rather a respect for the constitutionally prescribed role of state *legislatures*. To attach definitive weight to the pronouncement of a state court, when the very question at issue is whether the court has actually departed from the statutory meaning, would be to abdicate our responsibility to enforce the explicit requirements of Article II.

II

Acting pursuant to its constitutional grant of authority, the Florida Legislature has created a detailed, if not perfectly crafted, statutory scheme that provides for appointment of Presidential electors by direct election. Fla. Stat. § 103.011 (2000). Under the statute, "votes cast for the actual candidates for President and Vice President shall be counted as votes cast for the presidential electors supporting such candidates." Ibid. The legislature has designated the Secretary of State as the "chief election officer," with the responsibility to "obtain and maintain uniformity in the application, operation, and interpretation of the election laws." § 97.012. The state legislature has delegated to county canvassing boards the duties of

---

1. Similarly, our jurisprudence requires us to analyze the "background principles" of state property law to determine whether there has been a taking of property in violation of the Takings Clause. That constitutional guarantee would, of course, afford no protection against state power if our inquiry could be concluded by a state supreme court holding that state property law accorded the plaintiff no rights. See Lucas v. South Carolina Coastal Council, 505 U.S. 1003 (1992). In one of our oldest cases, we similarly made an independent evaluation of state law in order to protect federal treaty guarantees. In Fairfax's Devisee v. Hunter's Lessee, 11 U.S. (7 Cranch) 603 (1813), we disagreed with the Supreme Court of Appeals of Virginia that a 1782 state law had extinguished the property interests of one Denny Fairfax, so that a 1789 ejectment order against Fairfax supported by a 1785 state law did not constitute a future confiscation under the 1783 peace treaty with Great Britain. See 11 U.S. at 623; Hunter v. Fairfax's Devisee, 15 Va. 218, 1 Munf. 218 (Va.1809).

administering elections. § 102.141. Those boards are responsible for providing results to the state Elections Canvassing Commission, comprising the Governor, the Secretary of State, and the Director of the Division of Elections. § 102.111. Cf. Boardman v. Esteva, 323 So.2d 259, 268 n. 5 (1975) ("The election process ... is committed to the executive branch of government through duly designated officials all charged with specific duties.... [The] judgments [of these officials] are entitled to be regarded by the courts as presumptively correct ...").

After the election has taken place, the canvassing boards receive returns from precincts, count the votes, and in the event that a candidate was defeated by .5% or less, conduct a mandatory recount. Fla. Stat. § 102.141(4) (2000). The county canvassing boards must file certified election returns with the Department of State by 5 p.m. on the seventh day following the election. § 102.112(1). The Elections Canvassing Commission must then certify the results of the election. § 102.111(1).

The state legislature has also provided mechanisms both for protesting election returns and for contesting certified election results. Section 102.166 governs protests. Any protest must be filed prior to the certification of election results by the county canvassing board. § 102.166(4)(b). Once a protest has been filed, "the county canvassing board may authorize a manual recount." § 102.166(4)(c). If a sample recount conducted pursuant to § 102.166(5) "indicates an error in the vote tabulation which could affect the outcome of the election," the county canvassing board is instructed to: "(a) Correct the error and recount the remaining precincts with the vote tabulation system; (b) Request the Department of State to verify the tabulation software; or (c) Manually recount all ballots," § 102.166(5). In the event a canvassing board chooses to conduct a manual recount of all ballots, § 102.166(7) prescribes procedures for such a recount.

Contests to the certification of an election, on the other hand, are controlled by § 102.168. The grounds for contesting an election include "receipt of a number of illegal votes or rejection of a number of legal votes sufficient to change or place in doubt the result of the election." § 102.168(3)(c). Any contest must be filed in the appropriate Florida circuit court, Fla. Stat. § 102.168(1), and the canvassing board or election board is the proper party defendant, § 102.168(4). Section 102.168(8) provides that "the circuit judge to whom the contest is presented may fashion such orders as he or she deems necessary to ensure that each allegation in the complaint is investigated, examined, or checked, to prevent or correct any alleged wrong, and to provide any relief appropriate under such circumstances." In Presidential elections, the contest period necessarily terminates on the date set by 3 U.S.C. § 5 for concluding the State's "final determination" of election controversies.

In its first decision, Palm Beach County Canvassing Bd. v. Harris, 772 So.2d 1220 (Fla.2000) (*Harris I*), the Florida Supreme Court extended the

7–day statutory certification deadline established by the legislature.[2] This modification of the code, by lengthening the protest period, necessarily shortened the contest period for Presidential elections. Underlying the extension of the certification deadline and the shortchanging of the contest period was, presumably, the clear implication that certification was a matter of significance: The certified winner would enjoy presumptive validity, making a contest proceeding by the losing candidate an uphill battle. In its latest opinion, however, the court empties certification of virtually all legal consequence during the contest, and in doing so departs from the provisions enacted by the Florida Legislature.

The court determined that canvassing boards' decisions regarding whether to recount ballots past the certification deadline (even the certification deadline established by *Harris I*) are to be reviewed de novo, although the election code clearly vests discretion whether to recount in the boards, and sets strict deadlines subject to the Secretary's rejection of late tallies and monetary fines for tardiness. See Fla. Stat. § 102.112 (2000). Moreover, the Florida court held that all late vote tallies arriving during the contest period should be automatically included in the certification regardless of the certification deadline (even the certification deadline established by *Harris I*), thus virtually eliminating both the deadline and the Secretary's discretion to disregard recounts that violate it.

Moreover, the court's interpretation of "legal vote," and hence its decision to order a contest-period recount, plainly departed from the legislative scheme. Florida statutory law cannot reasonably be thought to *require* the counting of improperly marked ballots. Each Florida precinct before election day provides instructions on how properly to cast a vote, § 101.46; each polling place on election day contains a working model of the voting machine it uses, § 101.5611; and each voting booth contains a sample ballot, § 101.46. In precincts using punch-card ballots, voters are instructed to punch out the ballot cleanly:

> AFTER VOTING, CHECK YOUR BALLOT CARD TO BE SURE YOUR VOTING SELECTIONS ARE CLEARLY AND CLEANLY PUNCHED AND THERE ARE NO CHIPS LEFT HANGING ON THE BACK OF THE CARD.

No reasonable person would call it "an error in the vote tabulation," Fla. Stat. § 102.166(5), or a "rejection of legal votes," Fla. Stat. § 102.168(3)(c),[4] when electronic or electromechanical equipment performs precisely in the manner designed, and fails to count those ballots that are

---

2. We vacated that decision and remanded that case; the Florida Supreme Court reissued the same judgment with a new opinion on December 11, 2000, 772 So.2d 1273.

4. It is inconceivable that what constitutes a vote that must be counted under the "error in the vote tabulation" language of the protest phase is different from what constitutes a vote that must be counted under the "legal votes" language of the contest phase.

not marked in the manner that these voting instructions explicitly and prominently specify. The scheme that the Florida Supreme Court's opinion attributes to the legislature is one in which machines are required to be "capable of correctly counting votes," § 101.5606(4), but which nonetheless regularly produces elections in which legal votes are predictably not tabulated, so that in close elections manual recounts are regularly required. This is of course absurd. The Secretary of State, who is authorized by law to issue binding interpretations of the election code, §§ 97.012, 106.23, rejected this peculiar reading of the statutes. See DE 00–13 (opinion of the Division of Elections). The Florida Supreme Court, although it must defer to the Secretary's interpretations, see Krivanek v. Take Back Tampa Political Committee, 625 So.2d 840, 844 (Fla.1993), rejected her reasonable interpretation and embraced the peculiar one. See Palm Beach County Canvassing Board v. Harris, 772 So.2d 1273 (Fla.2000) (*Harris III*).

But as we indicated in our remand of the earlier case, in a Presidential election the clearly expressed intent of the legislature must prevail. And there is no basis for reading the Florida statutes as requiring the counting of improperly marked ballots, as an examination of the Florida Supreme Court's textual analysis shows. We will not parse that analysis here, except to note that the principal provision of the election code on which it relied, § 101.5614(5), was, as the Chief Justice pointed out in his dissent from *Harris II*, entirely irrelevant. See Gore v. Harris, 772 So.2d 1243, 1267 (Fla.2000). The State's Attorney General (who was supporting the Gore challenge) confirmed in oral argument here that never before the present election had a manual recount been conducted on the basis of the contention that "undervotes" should have been examined to determine voter intent. Cf. Broward County Canvassing Board v. Hogan, 607 So.2d 508, 509 (Fla.Ct.App.1992) (denial of recount for failure to count ballots with "hanging paper chads"). For the court to step away from this established practice, prescribed by the Secretary of State, the state official charged by the legislature with "responsibility to ... obtain and maintain uniformity in the application, operation, and interpretation of the election laws," § 97.012(1), was to depart from the legislative scheme.

III

The scope and nature of the remedy ordered by the Florida Supreme Court jeopardizes the "legislative wish" to take advantage of the safe harbor provided by 3 U.S.C. § 5. *Bush v. Palm Beach County Canvassing Bd.*, supra, at 78. December 12, 2000, is the last date for a final determination of the Florida electors that will satisfy § 5. Yet in the late afternoon of December 8th—four days before this deadline—the Supreme Court of Florida ordered recounts of tens of thousands of so-called "undervotes" spread through 64 of the State's 67 counties. This was done in a search for elusive—perhaps delusive—certainty as to the exact count of 6 million votes. But no one claims that these ballots have not previously been tabulated; they were initially read by voting machines at the time of the election, and thereafter reread by virtue of Florida's automatic recount provision. No one claims there was any fraud in the election. The Supreme Court of Florida ordered this additional recount under the provision of the election code giving the circuit judge the authority to provide relief that is "appropriate under such circumstances." Fla. Stat. § 102.168(8) (2000).

Surely when the Florida Legislature empowered the courts of the State to grant "appropriate" relief, it must have meant relief that would have become final by the cut-off date of 3 U.S.C. § 5. In light of the inevitable legal challenges and ensuing appeals to the Supreme Court of Florida and petitions for certiorari to this Court, the entire recounting process could not possibly be completed by that date. Whereas the majority in the Supreme Court of Florida stated its confidence that "the remaining undervotes in these counties can be [counted] within the required time frame," 772 So.2d at 1262 n.22, it made no assertion that the seemingly inevitable appeals could be disposed of in that time. Although the Florida Supreme Court . . . has heard and decided the appeals in the present case with great promptness . . ., the federal deadlines for the Presidential election simply do not permit even such a shortened process.

As the dissent noted:

> In [the four days remaining], all questionable ballots must be reviewed by the judicial officer appointed to discern the intent of the voter in a process open to the public. Fairness dictates that a provision be made for either party to object to how a particular ballot is counted. Additionally, this short time period must allow for judicial review. I respectfully submit this cannot be completed without taking Florida's presidential electors outside the safe harbor provision, creating the very real possibility of disenfranchising those nearly 6 million voters who are able to correctly cast their ballots on election day.

772 So.2d at 1269 (Wells, C. J., dissenting). . . .

Given all these factors, and in light of the legislative intent identified by the Florida Supreme Court to bring Florida within the "safe harbor" provision of 3 U.S.C. § 5, the remedy prescribed by the Supreme Court of Florida cannot be deemed an "appropriate" one as of December 8. It significantly departed from the statutory framework in place on November 7, and authorized open-ended further proceedings which could not be completed by December 12, thereby preventing a final determination by that date.

For these reasons, in addition to those given in the per curiam, we would reverse.

■ JUSTICE STEVENS, with whom JUSTICE GINSBURG and JUSTICE BREYER join, dissenting.

The Constitution assigns to the States the primary responsibility for determining the manner of selecting the Presidential electors. See Art. II,

§ 1, cl. 2. When questions arise about the meaning of state laws, including election laws, it is our settled practice to accept the opinions of the highest courts of the States as providing the final answers.... On rare occasions, however, either federal statutes or the Federal Constitution may require federal judicial intervention in state elections. This is not such an occasion.

The federal questions that ultimately emerged in this case are not substantial. Article II provides that "each *State* shall appoint, in such Manner as the Legislature *thereof* may direct, a Number of Electors." Ibid. (emphasis added). It does not create state legislatures out of whole cloth, but rather takes them as they come—as creatures born of, and constrained by, their state constitutions.... The legislative power in Florida is subject to judicial review pursuant to Article V of the Florida Constitution, and nothing in Article II of the Federal Constitution frees the state legislature from the constraints in the state constitution that created it. Moreover, the Florida Legislature's own decision to employ a unitary code for all elections indicates that it intended the Florida Supreme Court to play the same role in Presidential elections that it has historically played in resolving electoral disputes. The Florida Supreme Court's exercise of appellate jurisdiction therefore was wholly consistent with, and indeed contemplated by, the grant of authority in Article II....

[N]either in this case, nor in its earlier opinion in Palm Beach County Canvassing Bd. v. Harris, 772 So.2d 1273 (Fla.2000), did the Florida Supreme Court make any substantive change in Florida electoral law. Its decisions were rooted in long-established precedent and were consistent with the relevant statutory provisions, taken as a whole. It did what courts do—it decided the case before it in light of the legislature's intent to leave no legally cast vote uncounted. In so doing, it relied on the sufficiency of the general "intent of the voter" standard articulated by the state legislature, coupled with a procedure for ultimate review by an impartial judge, to resolve the concern about disparate evaluations of contested ballots. If we assume—as I do—that the members of that court and the judges who would have carried out its mandate are impartial, its decision does not even raise a colorable federal question.

What must underlie petitioners' entire federal assault on the Florida election procedures is an unstated lack of confidence in the impartiality and capacity of the state judges who would make the critical decisions if the vote count were to proceed. Otherwise, their position is wholly without merit. The endorsement of that position by the majority of this Court can only lend credence to the most cynical appraisal of the work of judges throughout the land. It is confidence in the men and women who administer the judicial system that is the true backbone of the rule of law. Time will one day heal the wound to that confidence that will be inflicted by today's decision. One thing, however, is certain. Although we may never know with complete certainty the identity of the winner of this year's

Presidential election, the identity of the loser is perfectly clear. It is the Nation's confidence in the judge as an impartial guardian of the rule of law.

I respectfully dissent.

■ JUSTICE SOUTER, with whom JUSTICE BREYER joins and with whom JUSTICE STEVENS and JUSTICE GINSBURG join with regard to all but Part C, dissenting.

The Court should not have reviewed either Bush v. Palm Beach County Canvassing Bd., 531 U.S. 70 (2000), or this case, and should not have stopped Florida's attempt to recount all undervote ballots by issuing a stay of the Florida Supreme Court's orders during the period of this review. If this Court had allowed the State to follow the course indicated by the opinions of its own Supreme Court, it is entirely possible that there would ultimately have been no issue requiring our review, and political tension could have worked itself out in the Congress following the procedure provided in 3 U.S.C. § 15. The case being before us, however, its resolution by the majority is another erroneous decision.

As will be clear, I am in substantial agreement with the dissenting opinions of Justice Stevens, Justice Ginsburg, and Justice Breyer. I write separately only to say how straightforward the issues before us really are.

There are three issues: whether the State Supreme Court's interpretation of the statute providing for a contest of the state election results somehow violates 3 U.S.C. § 5; whether that court's construction of the state statutory provisions governing contests impermissibly changes a state law from what the State's legislature has provided, in violation of Article II, § 1, cl. 2, of the national Constitution; and whether the manner of interpreting markings on disputed ballots failing to cause machines to register votes for President (the undervote ballots) violates the equal protection or due process guaranteed by the Fourteenth Amendment. None of these issues is difficult to describe or to resolve.

A

The 3 U.S.C. § 5 issue is not serious. That provision sets certain conditions for treating a State's certification of Presidential electors as conclusive in the event that a dispute over recognizing those electors must be resolved in the Congress under 3 U.S.C. § 15. Conclusiveness requires selection under a legal scheme in place before the election, with results determined at least six days before the date set for casting electoral votes. But no State is required to conform to § 5 if it cannot do that (for whatever reason); the sanction for failing to satisfy the conditions of § 5 is simply loss of what has been called its "safe harbor." And even that determination is to be made, if made anywhere, in the Congress.

B

The second matter here goes to the State Supreme Court's interpretation of certain terms in the state statute governing election "contests," Fla.

Stat. § 102.168 (2000); there is no question here about the state court's interpretation of the related provisions dealing with the antecedent process of "protesting" particular vote counts, § 102.166, which was involved in the previous case, *Bush v. Palm Beach County Canvassing Board*, supra. The issue is whether the judgment of the state supreme court has displaced the state legislature's provisions for election contests: is the law as declared by the court different from the provisions made by the legislature, to which the national Constitution commits responsibility for determining how each State's Presidential electors are chosen? See U.S. Const., Art. II, § 1, cl. 2. Bush does not, of course, claim that any judicial act interpreting a statute of uncertain meaning is enough to displace the legislative provision and violate Article II; statutes require interpretation, which does not without more affect the legislative character of a statute within the meaning of the Constitution. What Bush does argue, as I understand the contention, is that the interpretation of § 102.168 was so unreasonable as to transcend the accepted bounds of statutory interpretation, to the point of being a nonjudicial act and producing new law untethered to the legislative act in question.

The starting point for evaluating the claim that the Florida Supreme Court's interpretation effectively re-wrote § 102.168 must be the language of the provision on which Gore relies to show his right to raise this contest: that the previously certified result in Bush's favor was produced by "rejection of a number of legal votes sufficient to change or place in doubt the result of the election." Fla. Stat. § 102.168(3)(c) (2000). None of the state court's interpretations is unreasonable to the point of displacing the legislative enactment quoted. . . .

1. The statute does not define a "legal vote," the rejection of which may affect the election. The State Supreme Court was therefore required to define it, and in doing that the court looked to another election statute, § 101.5614(5), dealing with damaged or defective ballots, which contains a provision that no vote shall be disregarded "if there is a clear indication of the intent of the voter as determined by a canvassing board." The court read that objective of looking to the voter's intent as indicating that the legislature probably meant "legal vote" to mean a vote recorded on a ballot indicating what the voter intended. Gore v. Harris, 772 So.2d 1243, 1256–57 (Fla.2000). It is perfectly true that the majority might have chosen a different reading. See, e.g., Brief for Respondent Harris et al. 10 (defining "legal votes" as "votes properly executed in accordance with the instructions provided to all registered voters in advance of the election and in the polling places"). But even so, there is no constitutional violation in following the majority view; Article II is unconcerned with mere disagreements about interpretive merits.

2. The Florida court next interpreted "rejection" to determine what act in the counting process may be attacked in a contest. Again, the statute does not define the term. The court majority read the word to mean simply

a failure to count. 772 So.2d at 1257. That reading is certainly within the bounds of common sense, given the objective to give effect to a voter's intent if that can be determined. A different reading, of course, is possible. The majority might have concluded that "rejection" should refer to machine malfunction, or that a ballot should not be treated as "rejected" in the absence of wrongdoing by election officials, lest contests be so easy to claim that every election will end up in one. There is, however, nothing nonjudicial in the Florida majority's more hospitable reading.

3. The same is true about the court majority's understanding of the phrase "votes sufficient to change or place in doubt" the result of the election in Florida. The court held that if the uncounted ballots were so numerous that it was reasonably possible that they contained enough "legal" votes to swing the election, this contest would be authorized by the statute. While the majority might have thought (as the trial judge did) that a probability, not a possibility, should be necessary to justify a contest, that reading is not required by the statute's text, which says nothing about probability. Whatever people of good will and good sense may argue about the merits of the Florida court's reading, there is no warrant for saying that it transcends the limits of reasonable statutory interpretation to the point of supplanting the statute enacted by the "legislature" within the meaning of Article II.

In sum, the interpretations by the Florida court raise no substantial question under Article II. That court engaged in permissible construction in determining that Gore had instituted a contest authorized by the state statute, and it proceeded to direct the trial judge to deal with that contest in the exercise of the discretionary powers generously conferred by Fla. Stat. § 102.168(8) (2000), to "fashion such orders as he or she deems necessary to ensure that each allegation in the complaint is investigated, examined, or checked, to prevent or correct any alleged wrong, and to provide any relief appropriate under such circumstances." As Justice Ginsburg has persuasively explained in her own dissenting opinion, our customary respect for state interpretations of state law counsels against rejection of the Florida court's determinations in this case.

C

It is only on the third issue before us that there is a meritorious argument for relief, as this Court's Per Curiam opinion recognizes. It is an issue that might well have been dealt with adequately by the Florida courts if the state proceedings had not been interrupted, and if not disposed of at the state level it could have been considered by the Congress in any electoral vote dispute. But because the course of state proceedings has been interrupted, time is short, and the issue is before us, I think it sensible for the Court to address it.

Petitioners have raised an equal protection claim (or, alternatively, a due process claim) in the charge that unjustifiably disparate standards are applied in different electoral jurisdictions to otherwise identical facts. It is true that the Equal Protection Clause does not forbid the use of a variety of voting mechanisms within a jurisdiction, even though different mechanisms will have different levels of effectiveness in recording voters' intentions; local variety can be justified by concerns about cost, the potential value of innovation, and so on. But evidence in the record here suggests that a different order of disparity obtains under rules for determining a voter's intent that have been applied (and could continue to be applied) to identical types of ballots used in identical brands of machines and exhibiting identical physical characteristics (such as "hanging" or "dimpled" chads). I can conceive of no legitimate state interest served by these differing treatments of the expressions of voters' fundamental rights. The differences appear wholly arbitrary.

In deciding what to do about this, we should take account of the fact that electoral votes are due to be cast in six days. I would therefore remand the case to the courts of Florida with instructions to establish uniform standards for evaluating the several types of ballots that have prompted differing treatments, to be applied within and among counties when passing on such identical ballots in any further recounting (or successive recounting) that the courts might order.

Unlike the majority, I see no warrant for this Court to assume that Florida could not possibly comply with this requirement before the date set for the meeting of electors, December 18. Although one of the dissenting justices of the State Supreme Court estimated that disparate standards potentially affected 170,000 votes, *Gore v. Harris,* supra, at 1272–73, the number at issue is significantly smaller. The 170,000 figure apparently represents all uncounted votes, both undervotes (those for which no Presidential choice was recorded by a machine) and overvotes (those rejected because of votes for more than one candidate). Tr. of Oral Arg. 61–62. But as Justice Breyer has pointed out, no showing has been made of legal overvotes uncounted, and counsel for Gore made an uncontradicted representation to the Court that the statewide total of undervotes is about 60,000. Id. at 62. To recount these manually would be a tall order, but before this Court stayed the effort to do that the courts of Florida were ready to do their best to get that job done. There is no justification for denying the State the opportunity to try to count all disputed ballots now.

I respectfully dissent.

■ JUSTICE GINSBURG, with whom JUSTICE STEVENS joins, and with whom JUSTICE SOUTER and JUSTICE BREYER join as to Part I, dissenting.

I

The Chief Justice acknowledges that provisions of Florida's Election Code "may well admit of more than one interpretation." But instead of respecting the state high court's province to say what the State's Election Code means, the Chief Justice maintains that Florida's Supreme Court has veered so far from the ordinary practice of judicial review that what it did cannot properly be called judging. My colleagues have offered a reasonable construction of Florida's law. Their construction coincides with the view of one of Florida's seven Supreme Court justices. Gore v. Harris, 772 So.2d 1243, 1264 (Fla.2000) (Wells, C. J., dissenting). I might join the Chief Justice were it my commission to interpret Florida law. But disagreement with the Florida court's interpretation of its own State's law does not warrant the conclusion that the justices of that court have legislated. There is no cause here to believe that the members of Florida's high court have done less than "their mortal best to discharge their oath of office," Sumner v. Mata, 449 U.S. 539, 549 (1981), and no cause to upset their reasoned interpretation of Florida law.

This Court more than occasionally affirms statutory, and even constitutional, interpretations with which it disagrees. For example, when reviewing challenges to administrative agencies' interpretations of laws they implement, we defer to the agencies unless their interpretation violates "the unambiguously expressed intent of Congress." Chevron U.S.A. Inc. v. Natural Resources Defense Council, Inc., 467 U.S. 837, 843 (1984). We do so in the face of the declaration in Article I of the United States Constitution that "All legislative Powers herein granted shall be vested in a Congress of the United States." Surely the Constitution does not call upon us to pay more respect to a federal administrative agency's construction of federal law than to a state high court's interpretation of its own state's law. And not uncommonly, we let stand state-court interpretations of *federal* law with which we might disagree. Notably, in the habeas context, the Court ... "validates reasonable, good-faith interpretations of existing precedents made by state courts even though they are shown to be contrary to later decisions," [quoting O'Dell v. Netherland, 521 U.S. 151, 156 (1997)].

No doubt there are cases in which the proper application of federal law may hinge on interpretations of state law. Unavoidably, this Court must sometimes examine state law in order to protect federal rights. But we have dealt with such cases ever mindful of the full measure of respect we owe to interpretations of state law by a State's highest court. In the Contract Clause case, General Motors Corp. v. Romein, 503 U.S. 181 (1992), for example, we said that although "ultimately we are bound to decide for ourselves whether a contract was made," the Court "accords respectful consideration and great weight to the views of the State's highest court." Id., at 187 (citation omitted). And in Central Union Telephone Co. v. Edwardsville, 269 U.S. 190 (1925), we upheld the Illinois Supreme Court's interpretation of a state waiver rule, even though that interpretation resulted in the forfeiture of federal constitutional rights. Refusing to supplant Illinois law with a federal definition of waiver, we explained that the state court's declaration "should bind us unless so unfair or unreasonable in its application to those asserting a federal right as to obstruct it." Id., at 195.

In deferring to state courts on matters of state law, we appropriately recognize that this Court acts as an " 'outsider' lacking the common exposure to local law which comes from sitting in the jurisdiction." Lehman Brothers v. Schein, 416 U.S. 386, 391 (1974). That recognition has sometimes prompted us to resolve doubts about the meaning of state law by certifying issues to a State's highest court, even when federal rights are at stake.... Just last Term, in Fiore v. White, 528 U.S. 23 (1999), we took advantage of Pennsylvania's certification procedure. In that case, a state prisoner brought a federal habeas action claiming that the State had failed to prove an essential element of his charged offense in violation of the Due Process Clause. Instead of resolving the state-law question on which the federal claim depended, we certified the question to the Pennsylvania Supreme Court for that court to "help determine the proper state-law predicate for our determination of the federal constitutional questions raised." Id., at 29; id. at 28 (asking the Pennsylvania Supreme Court whether its recent interpretation of the statute under which Fiore was convicted "was always the statute's meaning, even at the time of Fiore's trial"). The Chief Justice's willingness to *reverse* the Florida Supreme Court's interpretation of Florida law in this case is at least in tension with our reluctance in *Fiore* even to interpret Pennsylvania law before seeking instruction from the Pennsylvania Supreme Court. I would have thought the "cautious approach" we counsel when federal courts address matters of state law ... demanded greater restraint.

Rarely has this Court rejected outright an interpretation of state law by a state high court. Fairfax's Devisee v. Hunter's Lessee, 11 U.S. (7 Cranch) 603 (1813), NAACP v. Alabama ex rel. Patterson, 357 U.S. 449 (1958), and Bouie v. City of Columbia, 378 U.S. 347 (1964), cited by the Chief Justice are three such rare instances. But those cases are embedded in historical contexts hardly comparable to the situation here. *Fairfax's Devisee*, which held that the Virginia Court of Appeals had misconstrued its own forfeiture laws to deprive a British subject of lands secured to him by federal treaties, occurred amidst vociferous States' rights attacks on the Marshall Court. Gerald Gunther & Kathleen Sullivan, Constitutional Law 61–62 (13th ed. 1997). The Virginia court refused to obey this Court's *Fairfax's Devisee* mandate to enter judgment for the British subject's successor in interest. That refusal led to the Court's pathmarking decision in Martin v. Hunter's Lessee, 14 U.S. (1 Wheat.) 304 (1816). *Patterson*, a case decided three months after Cooper v. Aaron, 358 U.S. 1 (1958), in the face of Southern resistance to the civil rights movement, held that the Alabama Supreme Court had irregularly applied its own procedural rules to deny review of a contempt order against the NAACP arising from its refusal to disclose membership lists. We said that "our jurisdiction is not defeated if the nonfederal ground relied on by the state court is without any fair or substantial support." 357 U.S. at 455. *Bouie*, stemming from a lunch counter "sit-in" at the height of the civil rights movement, held that the South Carolina Supreme Court's construction of its trespass laws—

criminalizing conduct not covered by the text of an otherwise clear statute—was "unforeseeable" and thus violated due process when applied retroactively to the petitioners. 378 U.S. at 350, 354.

The Chief Justice's casual citation of these cases might lead one to believe they are part of a larger collection of cases in which we said that the Constitution impelled us to train a skeptical eye on a state court's portrayal of state law. But one would be hard pressed, I think, to find additional cases that fit the mold. As Justice Breyer convincingly explains, this case involves nothing close to the kind of recalcitrance by a state high court that warrants extraordinary action by this Court. The Florida Supreme Court concluded that counting every legal vote was the overriding concern of the Florida Legislature when it enacted the State's Election Code. The court surely should not be bracketed with state high courts of the Jim Crow South.

The Chief Justice says that Article II, by providing that state legislatures shall direct the manner of appointing electors, authorizes federal superintendence over the relationship between state courts and state legislatures, and licenses a departure from the usual deference we give to state court interpretations of state law. The Framers of our Constitution, however, understood that in a republican government, the judiciary would construe the legislature's enactments. See U.S. Const., Art. III; The Federalist No. 78 (A. Hamilton). In light of the constitutional guarantee to States of a "Republican Form of Government," U.S. Const., Art. IV, § 4, Article II can hardly be read to invite this Court to disrupt a State's republican regime. Yet the Chief Justice today would reach out to do just that. By holding that Article II requires our revision of a state court's construction of state laws in order to protect one organ of the State from another, the Chief Justice contradicts the basic principle that a State may organize itself as it sees fit. See, e.g., Gregory v. Ashcroft, 501 U.S. 452, 460 (1991) ("Through the structure of its government, and the character of those who exercise government authority, a State defines itself as a sovereign."); Highland Farms Dairy, Inc. v. Agnew, 300 U.S. 608, 612 (1937) ("How power shall be distributed by a state among its governmental organs is commonly, if not always, a question for the state itself.").[2] Article II does not call for the scrutiny undertaken by this Court.

The extraordinary setting of this case has obscured the ordinary principle that dictates its proper resolution: Federal courts defer to state high courts' interpretations of their state's own law. This principle reflects

---

2. Even in the rare case in which a State's "manner" of making and construing laws might implicate a structural constraint, Congress, not this Court, is likely the proper governmental entity to enforce that constraint. See U.S. Const. amend. XII; 3 U.S.C. §§ 1–15; cf. Ohio ex rel. Davis v. Hildebrant, 241 U.S. 565, 569 (1916) (treating as a nonjusticiable political question whether use of a referendum to override a congressional districting plan enacted by the state legislature violates Art. I, § 4); Luther v. Borden, 48 U.S. (7 How.) 1, 42 (1849).

the core of federalism, on which all agree. "The Framers split the atom of sovereignty. It was the genius of their idea that our citizens would have two political capacities, one state and one federal, each protected from incursion by the other." Saenz v. Roe, 526 U.S. 489, 504 n. 17 (1999) (citing U.S. Term Limits, Inc. v. Thornton, 514 U.S. 779, 838 (1995) (Kennedy, J., concurring)). The Chief Justice's solicitude for the Florida Legislature comes at the expense of the more fundamental solicitude we owe to the legislature's sovereign. U.S. Const., Art. II, § 1, cl. 2 ("Each *State* shall appoint, in such Manner as the Legislature *thereof* may direct," the electors for President and Vice President) (emphasis added). Were the other members of this Court as mindful as they generally are of our system of dual sovereignty, they would affirm the judgment of the Florida Supreme Court.

II

[P]etitioners have not presented a substantial equal protection claim. Ideally, perfection would be the appropriate standard for judging the recount. But we live in an imperfect world, one in which thousands of votes have not been counted. I cannot agree that the recount adopted by the Florida court, flawed as it may be, would yield a result any less fair or precise than the certification that preceded that recount.

Even if there were an equal protection violation, I would agree with Justice Stevens, Justice Souter, and Justice Breyer that the Court's concern about "the December 12 deadline" is misplaced. Time is short in part because of the Court's entry of a stay on December 9, several hours after an able circuit judge in Leon County had begun to superintend the recount process. More fundamentally, the Court's reluctance to let the recount go forward—despite its suggestion that "the search for intent can be confined by specific rules designed to ensure uniform treatment"—ultimately turns on its own judgment about the practical realities of implementing a recount, not the judgment of those much closer to the process....

The Court assumes that time will not permit "orderly judicial review of any disputed matters that might arise." But no one has doubted the good faith and diligence with which Florida election officials, attorneys for all sides of this controversy, and the courts of law have performed their duties. Notably, the Florida Supreme Court has produced two substantial opinions within 29 hours of oral argument. In sum, the Court's conclusion that a constitutionally adequate recount is impractical is a prophecy the Court's own judgment will not allow to be tested. Such an untested prophecy should not decide the Presidency of the United States.

I dissent.

■ JUSTICE BREYER with whom JUSTICE STEVENS and JUSTICE GINSBURG join except as to Part I–A–1, and with whom JUSTICE SOUTER joins as to Part I, dissenting.

The Court was wrong to take this case. It was wrong to grant a stay. It should now vacate that stay and permit the Florida Supreme Court to decide whether the recount should resume.

I

The political implications of this case for the country are momentous. But the federal legal questions presented, with one exception, are insubstantial.

A

1. The majority raises three Equal Protection problems with the Florida Supreme Court's recount order: first, the failure to include overvotes in the manual recount; second, the fact that *all* ballots, rather than simply the undervotes, were recounted in some, but not all, counties; and third, the absence of a uniform, specific standard to guide the recounts. As far as the first issue is concerned, petitioners presented no evidence, to this Court or to any Florida court, that a manual recount of overvotes would identify additional legal votes. The same is true of the second, and, in addition, the majority's reasoning would seem to invalidate any state provision for a manual recount of individual counties in a statewide election.

The majority's third concern does implicate principles of fundamental fairness. The majority concludes that the Equal Protection Clause requires that a manual recount be governed not only by the uniform general standard of the "clear intent of the voter," but also by uniform subsidiary standards (for example, a uniform determination whether indented, but not perforated, "undervotes" should count). The opinion points out that the Florida Supreme Court ordered the inclusion of Broward County's undercounted "legal votes" even though those votes included ballots that were not perforated but simply "dimpled," while newly recounted ballots from other counties will likely include only votes determined to be "legal" on the basis of a stricter standard. In light of our previous remand, the Florida Supreme Court may have been reluctant to adopt a more specific standard than that provided for by the legislature for fear of exceeding its authority under Article II. However, since the use of different standards could favor one or the other of the candidates, since time was, and is, too short to permit the lower courts to iron out significant differences through ordinary judicial review, and since the relevant distinction was embodied in the order of the State's highest court, I agree that, in these very special circumstances, basic principles of fairness may well have counseled the adoption of a uniform standard to address the problem. In light of the majority's disposition, I need not decide whether, or the extent to which, as a remedial matter, the Constitution would place limits upon the content of the uniform standard.

2. Nonetheless, there is no justification for the majority's remedy, which is simply to reverse the lower court and halt the recount entirely. An appropriate remedy would be, instead, to remand this case with instructions that, even at this late date, would permit the Florida Supreme Court to require recounting *all* undercounted votes in Florida, including those from Broward, Volusia, Palm Beach, and Miami–Dade Counties, whether or not previously recounted prior to the end of the protest period, and to do so in accordance with a [uniform standard].

The majority justifies stopping the recount entirely on the ground that there is no more time. In particular, the majority relies on the lack of time for the Secretary to review and approve equipment needed to separate undervotes. But the majority reaches this conclusion in the absence of *any* record evidence that the recount could not have been completed in the time allowed by the Florida Supreme Court. The majority finds facts outside of the record on matters that state courts are in a far better position to address. Of course, it is too late for any such recount to take place by December 12, the date by which election disputes must be decided if a State is to take advantage of the safe harbor provisions of 3 U.S.C. § 5. Whether there is time to conduct a recount prior to December 18, when the electors are scheduled to meet, is a matter for the state courts to determine. And whether, under Florida law, Florida could or could not take further action is obviously a matter for Florida courts, not this Court, to decide.

By halting the manual recount, and thus ensuring that the uncounted legal votes will not be counted under any standard, this Court crafts a remedy out of proportion to the asserted harm. And that remedy harms the very fairness interests the Court is attempting to protect. The manual recount would itself redress a problem of unequal treatment of ballots. [T]he ballots of voters in counties that use punch-card systems are more likely to be disqualified than those in counties using optical-scanning systems. . . . Thus, in a system that allows counties to use different types of voting systems, voters already arrive at the polls with an unequal chance that their votes will be counted. I do not see how the fact that this results from counties' selection of different voting machines rather than a court order makes the outcome any more fair. Nor do I understand why the Florida Supreme Court's recount order, which helps to redress this inequity, must be entirely prohibited based on a deficiency that could easily be remedied.

B

The remainder of petitioners' claims, which are the focus of the Chief Justice's concurrence, raise no significant federal questions. I cannot agree that the Chief Justice's unusual review of state law in this case is justified by reference either to Art. II, § 1, or to 3 U.S.C. § 5. Moreover, even were such review proper, the conclusion that the Florida Supreme Court's decision contravenes federal law is untenable.

While conceding that, in most cases, "comity and respect for federalism compel us to defer to the decisions of state courts on issues of state law," the concurrence relies on some combination of Art. II, § 1, and 3 U.S.C. § 5 to justify the majority's conclusion that this case is one of the few in which we may lay that fundamental principle aside. The concurrence's primary foundation for this conclusion rests on an appeal to plain text: Art. II, § 1's grant of the power to appoint Presidential electors to the State "Legislature." But neither the text of Article II itself nor the only case the concurrence cites that interprets Article II, McPherson v. Blacker, 146 U.S. 1, 3 (1892), leads to the conclusion that Article II grants unlimited power to the legislature, devoid of any state constitutional limitations, to select the manner of appointing electors....

The concurrence's treatment of § 5 as "informing" its interpretation of Article II, § 1, cl. 2, is no more convincing. The Chief Justice contends that our opinion in Bush v. Palm Beach County Canvassing Bd., 531 U.S. 70 (2000) *(Bush I)*, in which we stated that "a legislative wish to take advantage of [§ 5] would counsel against" a construction of Florida law that Congress might deem to be a change in law, now means that *this Court* "must ensure that post-election state court actions do not frustrate the legislative desire to attain the 'safe harbor' provided by § 5." However, § 5 is part of the rules that govern Congress' recognition of slates of electors. Nowhere in *Bush I* did we establish that *this Court* had the authority to enforce § 5. Nor did we suggest that the permissive "counsel against" could be transformed into the mandatory "must ensure." And nowhere did we intimate, as the concurrence does here, that a state court decision that threatens the safe harbor provision of § 5 does so in violation of Article II. The concurrence's logic turns the presumption that legislatures would wish to take advantage of § 5's "safe harbor" provision into a mandate that trumps other statutory provisions and overrides the intent that the legislature *did* express.

But, in any event, the concurrence, having conducted its review, now reaches the wrong conclusion. It says that "the Florida Supreme Court's interpretation of the Florida election laws impermissibly distorted them beyond what a fair reading required, in violation of Article II." But what precisely is the distortion? Apparently, it has three elements. First, the Florida court, in its earlier opinion, changed the election certification date from November 14 to November 26. Second, the Florida court ordered a manual recount of "undercounted" ballots that could not have been fully completed by the December 12 "safe harbor" deadline. Third, the Florida court, in the opinion now under review, failed to give adequate deference to the determinations of canvassing boards and the Secretary.

To characterize the first element as a "distortion," however, requires the concurrence to second-guess the way in which the state court resolved a plain conflict in the language of different statutes....

To characterize the second element as a "distortion" requires the concurrence to overlook the fact that the inability of the Florida courts to conduct the recount on time is, in significant part, a problem of the Court's own making. The Florida Supreme Court thought that the recount could be completed on time, and, within hours, the Florida Circuit Court was moving in an orderly fashion to meet the deadline. This Court improvidently entered a stay. As a result, we will never know whether the recount could have been completed.

Nor can one characterize the third element as "impermissible distorting" once one understands that there are two sides to the opinion's argument that the Florida Supreme Court "virtually eliminated the Secretary's discretion." The Florida statute in question was amended in 1999 to provide that the "grounds for contesting an election" include the "rejection of a number of legal votes sufficient to . . . place in doubt the result of the election." Fla. Stat. §§ 102.168(3), (3)(c) (2000). And the parties have argued about the proper meaning of the statute's term "legal vote." The Secretary has claimed that a "legal vote" is a vote "properly executed in accordance with the instructions provided to all registered voters." On that interpretation, punchcard ballots for which the machines cannot register a vote are not "legal" votes. The Florida Supreme Court did not accept her definition. But it had a reason. Its reason was that a different provision of Florida election laws (a provision that addresses damaged or defective ballots) says that no vote shall be disregarded "if there is a clear indication of the intent of the voter as determined by the canvassing board" (adding that ballots should not be counted "if it is impossible to determine the elector's choice"). Fla. Stat. § 101.5614(5) (2000). Given this statutory language, . . . the Florida Supreme Court concluded that the term "legal vote" means a vote recorded on a ballot that clearly reflects what the voter intended. Gore v. Harris, 772 So.2d 1243, 1254 (Fla.2000). That conclusion differs from the conclusion of the Secretary. But nothing in Florida law requires the Florida Supreme Court to accept as determinative the Secretary's view on such a matter. Nor can one say that the Court's ultimate determination is so unreasonable as to amount to a constitutionally "impermissible distortion" of Florida law.

The Florida Supreme Court, applying this definition, decided, on the basis of the record, that respondents had shown that the ballots undercounted by the voting machines contained enough "legal votes" to place "the results" of the election "in doubt." Since only a few hundred votes separated the candidates, and since the "undercounted" ballots numbered tens of thousands, it is difficult to see how anyone could find this conclusion unreasonable—however strict the standard used to measure the voter' "clear intent." . . .

The statute goes on to provide the Florida circuit judge with authority to "fashion such orders as he or she deems necessary to ensure that each allegation . . . is *investigated, examined, or checked,* . . . and to provide any relief appropriate." Fla. Stat. § 102.168(8) (2000) (emphasis added). The Florida Supreme Court did just that. One might reasonably disagree with the Florida Supreme Court's interpretation of these, or other, words in the statute. But I do not see how one could call its plain language interpretation of a 1999 statutory change so misguided as no longer to qualify as judicial interpretation or as a usurpation of the authority of the State legislature. Indeed, other state courts have interpreted roughly similar state statutes in similar ways....

I repeat, where is the "impermissible" distortion?

II

Despite the reminder that this case involves "an election for the President of the United States," no preeminent legal concern, or practical concern related to legal questions, required this Court to hear this case, let alone to issue a stay that stopped Florida's recount process in its tracks. With one exception, petitioners' claims do not ask us to vindicate a constitutional provision designed to protect a basic human right. Petitioners invoke fundamental fairness, namely, the need for procedural fairness, including finality. But with the one "equal protection" exception, they rely upon law that focuses, not upon that basic need, but upon the constitutional allocation of power. Respondents invoke a competing fundamental consideration—the need to determine the voter's true intent. But they look to state law, not to federal constitutional law, to protect that interest. Neither side claims electoral fraud, dishonesty, or the like. And the more fundamental equal protection claim might have been left to the state court to resolve if and when it was discovered to have mattered. It could still be resolved through a remand conditioned upon issuance of a uniform standard; it does not require reversing the Florida Supreme Court.

Of course, the selection of the President is of fundamental national importance. But that importance is political, not legal. And this Court should resist the temptation unnecessarily to resolve tangential legal disputes, where doing so threatens to determine the outcome of the election.

The Constitution and federal statutes themselves make clear that restraint is appropriate. They set forth a road map of how to resolve disputes about electors, even after an election as close as this one. That road map foresees resolution of electoral disputes by *state* courts. See 3 U.S.C. § 5 (providing that, where a "State shall have provided, by laws enacted prior to [election day], for its final determination of any controversy or contest concerning the appointment of ... electors ... by *judicial* or other methods," the subsequently chosen electors enter a safe harbor free from congressional challenge). But it nowhere provides for involvement by the United States Supreme Court.

To the contrary, the Twelfth Amendment commits to Congress the authority and responsibility to count electoral votes. A federal statute, the Electoral Count Act, enacted after the close 1876 Hayes–Tilden Presidential election, specifies that, after States have tried to resolve disputes (through "judicial" or other means), Congress is the body primarily authorized to resolve remaining disputes. See Electoral Count Act of 1887, 3 U.S.C. §§ 5, 6, and 15.

The legislative history of the Act makes clear its intent to commit the power to resolve such disputes to Congress, rather than the courts:

> The two Houses are, by the Constitution, authorized to make the count of electoral votes. They can only count legal votes, and in doing so must determine, from the best evidence to be had, what are legal votes.... The power to determine rests with the two Houses, and there is no other constitutional tribunal.

H. Rep. No. 1638, 49th Cong., 1st Sess., 2 (1886) (report submitted by Rep. Caldwell, Select Committee on the Election of President and Vice-President).

... The Act goes on to set out rules for the congressional determination of disputes about those votes. If, for example, a state submits a single slate of electors, Congress must count those votes unless both Houses agree that the votes "have not been ... regularly given." 3 U.S.C. § 15. If, as occurred in 1876, one or more states submits two sets of electors, then Congress must determine whether a slate has entered the safe harbor of § 5, in which case its votes will have "conclusive" effect. Ibid. If, as also occurred in 1876, there is controversy about "which of two or more of such State authorities ... is the lawful tribunal" authorized to appoint electors, then each House shall determine separately which votes are "supported by the decision of such State so authorized by its law." Ibid. If the two Houses of Congress agree, the votes they have approved will be counted. If they disagree, then "the votes of the electors whose appointment shall have been certified by the executive of the State, under the seal thereof, shall be counted." Ibid.

Given this detailed, comprehensive scheme for counting electoral votes, there is no reason to believe that federal law either foresees or requires resolution of such a political issue by this Court. Nor, for that matter, is there any reason to that think the Constitution's Framers would have reached a different conclusion. Madison, at least, believed that allowing the judiciary to choose the presidential electors "was out of the question." Madison, July 25, 1787 (reprinted in 5 Elliot's Debates on the Federal Constitution 363 (2d ed. 1876)).

The decision by both the Constitution's Framers and the 1886 Congress to minimize this Court's role in resolving close federal presidential elections is as wise as it is clear. However awkward or difficult it may be for Congress to resolve difficult electoral disputes, Congress, being a political body, expresses the people's will far more accurately than does an unelected Court. And the people's will is what elections are about....

[T]he Court is not acting to vindicate a fundamental constitutional principle, such as the need to protect a basic human liberty. No other strong reason to act is present. Congressional statutes tend to obviate the need. And, above all, in this highly politicized matter, the appearance of a split decision runs the risk of undermining the public's confidence in the Court itself. That confidence is a public treasure. It has been built slowly over many years, some of which were marked by a Civil War and the tragedy of segregation. It is a vitally necessary ingredient of any successful effort to protect basic liberty and, indeed, the rule of law itself. We run no risk of returning to the days when a President (responding to this Court's efforts to protect the Cherokee Indians) might have said, "John Marshall has made his decision; now let him enforce it!" Loth, Chief Justice John Marshall and The Growth of the American Republic 365 (1948). But we do risk a self-inflicted wound—a wound that may harm not just the Court, but the Nation.

I fear that in order to bring this agonizingly long election process to a definitive conclusion, we have not adequately attended to that necessary "check upon our own exercise of power," "our own sense of self-restraint." United States v. Butler, 297 U.S. 1, 79 (1936) (Stone, J., dissenting). Justice Brandeis once said of the Court, "The most important thing we do is not doing." Bickel, supra, at 71. What it does today, the Court should have left undone. I would repair the damage done as best we now can, by permitting the Florida recount to continue under uniform standards.

I respectfully dissent.

NOTES ON *BUSH v. GORE*

1. Equal Protection. Of the two grounds advanced for the decision in *Bush v. Gore*, the equal protection argument is the more difficult to understand, despite the fact that it commanded the votes of five Justices and elicited the sympathy of two more. Even defenders of the result have been reluctant to embrace the equal protection rationale. See, e.g., Richard A. Epstein, "In such Manner as the Legislature Thereof May Direct": The Outcome of *Bush v. Gore* Defended, 68 U. Chi. L. Rev. 613, 614 (2001) (dismissing the equal protection ground as "a confused nonstarter ... which deserves much of the scorn that has been heaped upon it").

The first problem with the equal protection rationale is the lack of precedent. The notion that variable standards for manual recounts violates equal protection has no foundation in prior decisions. In the words of Cass Sunstein, it came as a "bolt from the blue." Cass Sunstein, Order Without Law, 68 U. Chi. L. Rev. 737, 766 (2001). See also; David G. Savage, The Vote Case Fallout, 87 A.B.A.J. 32 (2001) (quoting A.E. Dick Howard as saying, "This is a remarkable use of the equal protection clause. It is not consistent with anything they have done in the past 25 years.").

Bush v. Gore's closest equal protection antecedents may be the racial gerrymandering decisions, beginning with Shaw v. Reno, 509 U.S. 630 (1993). As Pam Karlan has explained, "Prior to *Shaw*, there were basically two types of voting rights injuries: disenfranchisement and dilution. Disenfranchisement involved outright denial of the ability to cast a ballot. Dilution, by contrast, occurred when the votes of some identifiable group counted for less than the votes of other voters." Pamela S. Karlan, The Newest Equal Protection: Regressive Doctrine on a Changeable Court, in Cass R. Sunstein and Richard A. Epstein, eds., The Vote: Bush, Gore, and the Supreme Court 79 (2001). Karlan sees *Shaw* as a launching a new kind of claim, which she calls "structural equal protection" and describes not as the protection of individual voters but as an effort "to regulate the institutional arrangements within which politics is conducted." She sees the same kind of agenda in *Bush v. Gore*: "[W]hatever interest the Supreme Court's decision vindicated, it was *not* the interest of an identifiable individual voter. Rather it was a perceived systemic interest in having recounts conducted according to a uniform standard or not at all." In any event, the equality interest at stake in *Bush v. Gore* bore scant relation to those vindicated in the poll tax and reapportionment cases relied on by the Court. See Epstein, supra, at 615–16.

A second problem is that the Court's equal protection rationale focuses on a very narrow slice of the potential inequalities in voting. The different technologies used for recording and counting votes produce disparities far greater than differences in standards for recounts. Even if conducted under less than perfect standards, manual recounts might reduce, rather than exacerbate, the kinds of inequalities that offended the Justices. In striking down the recount, the Court seemed uncommonly selective in its sensitivity to inequality. In the words of Pam Karlan, "A Court that believes that the real problem in Florida was the disparities in the manual recount standards, rather than the disparities in a voter's overall chance of casting a ballot that is actually counted for the candidate for whom he intended to vote, has strained at a gnat only to swallow an elephant." See Karlan, The Newest Equal Protection, supra, at 91. See also Pamela S. Karlan, Nothing Personal: The Evolution of the Newest Equal Protection from *Shaw v. Reno* to *Bush v. Gore*, 79 N.C. L. Rev. 1345 (2001).

A third problem is the remedy. Even if one assumes that differing recount standards and practices violate equal protection, why should the remedy be ending the recount? As the dissenters argued, a more appropriate remedy might have been to remand for better recount, rather than precluding one altogether. See Epstein, The Outcome in *Bush v. Gore* Defended, supra, at 616–18.

A final problem is standing. If the equal protection violation consists of a systemic inadequacy in the mechanisms for recounts, it is not entirely clear why Governor Bush had standing. Injury, of course, is quite clear, given the prospect of losing a presidential election, but the rights Bush raised were arguably not his own. Apparently, the Court assumed—but did not say—that Bush had third-party standing to raise the rights of Florida voters, but the effort to identify the precise third-party rights for which Bush would be an appropriate champion has been found difficult. See Karlan, The Newest Equal Protection, supra, at 81–90.

2. Article II. The quite different ground advanced in the Chief Justice's concurrence has met with a mixed reception. In principle, nearly everyone agrees that manipulation of state law to defeat federal rights states a violation of federal law, a la Martin v. Hunter's Lessee, 14 U.S. (1 Wheat.) 304 (1816); Indiana ex rel. Anderson v. Brand, 303 U.S. 95 (1938). Whether the Florida Supreme Court's actions fairly can be so characterized, however, is a matter of intense dispute. For what he calls "a qualified rear-guard defense" of *Bush v. Gore* on this ground, see Epstein, supra, at 619–35. Epstein describes in detail "the manifest errors in the Florida Supreme Court's decisions" and concludes that

> It is, to say the least, a regrettable truth that the outcome of a presidential election necessarily turns on a question of degree, by asking just how wrong is wrong enough to topple the decision of the Florida Supreme Court. But the peculiar determination to override at various times the decisions of Florida's canvassing boards, Secretary of State, and circuit court judges crosses that line.

For a similar review of the performance of the Florida Supreme Court, see Richard A. Posner, *Bush v. Gore*: Prolegomenon to an Assessment, 68 U. Chi. L. Rev. 719 (2001). Judge Posner examines in detail "what the Florida Supreme Court did to Florida's election statute," finds that the Florida Supreme Court "erred grievously" in interpreting Florida law, and concludes:

> Had Gore been declared the winner on the basis of the recount ordered by the Florida court on December 8, he would have owed his victory to a legal error, whether or not it was a legal error that the U. S. Supreme Court should have corrected. The result of the Supreme Court's interpretation was, therefore, at the least, rough justice....

In much the same vein are the views of Michael W. McConnell, Two-and-a-Half Cheers for *Bush v. Gore*, 68 U. Chi. L. Rev. 657 (2001). McConnell examined the questions of state law and concluded:

> On grounds that seemed dubious at best and disingenuous at worst, the Florida court ruled each time in favor of Gore. That put the U.S. Supreme Court in an awkward position. It could either allow a state court to decide the national presidential election through what appeared to be one-sided interpretations of the law, or render a decision that would call its own position, above politics, into question.

As the title indicates, McConnell thought the Court deserved "two-and-a-half cheers" for its resolution.

On the other side, many academics have joined the dissenters in expressing considerable skepticism about the Article II rationale. For one example, see Samuel Issacharoff, Political Judgments, 68 U. Chi. L. Rev. 637 (2001). Issacharoff examines the Article II argument in some detail and concludes that it "provides little basis for a robust approach to the problem of elections gone bad." For a similar reaction, see Frank I. Michelman, Suspicion, or the New Prince, 68 U. Chi. L. Rev. 679, 683 (2001) (describing the Article II argument in terms that can fairly be called dismissive). And David Strauss has concluded that "several members of the Court—perhaps a majority—were determined to overturn any ruling of the Florida Supreme Court that was favorable to Vice President Gore" and that the actions of the Supreme Court majority "show a relentless search for some reason that could be put forward to justify a decision reversing the Florida Supreme Court." David Strauss, *Bush v. Gore*: What Were They Thinking?, 68 U. Chi. L. Rev. 737, 738 (2001). Strauss also characterized the majority's action on the question of remedy as "simply indefensible."

For further analysis of the Court's treatment of state law, see also Harold J. Krent, Judging Judging: The Problem of Second-Guessing State Judges' Interpretation of State Law in *Bush v. Gore*, 29 Fla. State U. L. Rev. 493 (2001), and Robert A. Schapiro, Conceptions and Misconceptions of State Constitutional Law in *Bush v. Gore*, 29 Fla. State U. L. Rev. 661 (2001), which are part of a wide-ranging symposium on the decision.

Page 92, add at the end of footnote a:

For an argument that "the Constitution dictates the boundaries" of the adequate and independent state ground doctrine, see Cynthia L. Fountaine, Article III and the Adequate and Independent State Grounds Doctrine, 48 American U. L. Rev. 1053 (1999).

CHAPTER II

THE POWER OF THE FEDERAL COURTS TO CREATE FEDERAL LAW

Page 175, add at the end of Note 8:

See also Donald H. Zeigler, Rights, Rights of Action, and Remedies: An Integrated Approach, 76 Wash. L. Rev. 67 (2001) (arguing that rights, private rights of action, and remedies are inextricably related and that courts should integrate these questions into a single inquiry: "Does the applicable statutory provision entitle the plaintiff to the remedy he or she seeks?").

Page 175, add a new main case immediately before Section 3:

Gebser v. Lago Vista Independent School District
Supreme Court of the United States, 1998.
524 U.S. 274.

■ JUSTICE O'CONNOR delivered the opinion of the Court.

The question in this case is when a school district may be held liable in damages in an implied right of action under title IX of the Education Amendments of 1972 as amended, 20 U.S.C. § 1681 et seq., for the sexual harassment of a student by one of the district's teachers. We conclude that damages may not be recovered in those circumstances unless an official of the school district who at a minimum has authority to institute corrective measures on the district's behalf has actual notice of, and is deliberately indifferent to, the teacher's misconduct.

I

In the spring of 1991, when petitioner Alida Star Gebser was an eighth-grade student at a middle school in respondent Lago Vista Independent School District (Lago Vista), she joined a high school book discussion group led by Frank Waldrop, a teacher at Lago Vista's high school. Lago Vista received federal funds at all pertinent times. During the book discussion sessions, Waldrop often made sexually suggestive comments to the students. Gebser entered high school in the fall and was assigned to classes taught by Waldrop in both semesters. Waldrop continued to make inappropriate remarks to the students, and he began to direct more of his suggestive comments toward Gebser, including the substantial amount of time that the two were alone in his classroom. He initiated sexual contact with Gebser in the spring, when, while visiting her home ostensibly to give her a book, he kissed and fondled her. The two had sexual intercourse on a number of occasions during the remainder of the school year. . . .

Gebser did not report the relationship to school officials, testifying that while she realized Waldrop's conduct was improper, she was uncertain how to react and she wanted to continue having him as a teacher. In October 1992, the parents of two other students complained to the high school principal about Waldrop's comments in class. The principal arranged a meeting, at which, according to the principal, Waldrop indicated that he did not believe he had made offensive remarks but apologized to the parents and said it would not happen again. The principal also advised Waldrop to be careful about his classroom comments and told the school guidance counselor about the meeting, but he did not report the parents' complaint to Lago Vista's superintendent, who was the district's title IX coordinator. A couple of months later, in January 1993, a police officer discovered Waldrop and Gebser engaging in sexual intercourse and arrested Waldrop. Lago Vista terminated his employment. . . .

Gebser and her mother filed suit against Lago Vista and Waldrop in state court in November 1993, raising claims against the school district under title IX, 42 U.S.C. § 1983, and state negligence law, and claims against Waldrop primarily under state law. . . . After the case was removed, the United States District Court for the Western District of Texas granted summary judgment in favor of Lago Vista on all claims, and remanded the allegations against Waldrop to state court. In rejecting the title IX claim against the school district, the court reasoned that the statute "was enacted to counter *policies* of discrimination . . . in federally funded education programs," and that "[o]nly if school administrators have some type of notice of the gender discrimination and fail to respond in good faith can the discrimination be interpreted as a *policy* of the school district." . . . The Court of Appeals for the Fifth Circuit affirmed . . . and we now affirm.

II

Title IX provides in pertinent part that, "[n]o person . . . shall, on the basis of sex, be excluded from participation in, be denied the benefits of, or be subjected to discrimination under any education program or activity receiving federal financial assistance." 20 U.S.C. § 1681(a). The express statutory means of enforcement is administrative: The statute directs federal agencies who distribute education funding to establish requirements to effectuate the nondiscrimination mandate, and permit the agencies to enforce those requirements through "any means authorized by law," including ultimately the termination of federal funding. § 1682. The Court held in Cannon v. University of Chicago, 441 U.S. 677 (1979), that title IX is also enforceable through an implied private right of action, a conclusion we do not revisit here. We subsequently established in Franklin v. Gwinnett County Public Schools, 503 U.S. 60 (1992), that monetary damages are available in the implied action. ...

Franklin ... establishes that a school district can be held liable in damages in cases involving a teachers' sexual harassment of a student; the decision, however, does not purport to define the contours of that liability.

We face that issue squarely in this case. Petitioners, joined by the United States as amicus curiae, would invoke standards used by the courts of appeals in title VII cases involving a supervisor's sexual harassment of an employee in the workplace. [One approach, based on common-law agency theory, would impose respondeat superior liability "whenever a teacher's authority over a student facilities the harassment," "irrespective of whether school district officials had any knowledge of the harassment and irrespective of their response upon becoming aware." Alternatively, petitioners argued that liability should be imposed on a theory of constructive notice when the district knew or should have known of the harassment "but failed to uncover and eliminate it."]

In this case ..., petitioners seek not just to establish a title IX violation but to recover *damages* based on theories of respondeat superior and constructive notice. It is that aspect of their action, in our view, which is most critical to resolving the case. Unlike title IX, title VII contains an express cause of action and specifically provides for relief in the form of money damages. Congress ... has directly addressed the subject of damages relief under title VII and has set out the particular situations in which damages are available as well as the maximum amounts recoverable. With respect to title IX, however, the private right of action is judicially implied, and there is thus no legislative expression of the scope of available remedies, including when it is appropriate to award monetary damages. ...

III

Because the private right of action under title IX is judicially implied, we have a measure of latitude to shape a sensible remedial scheme that best comports with the statute. That endeavor inherently entails a degree of speculation, since it addresses an issue on which Congress has not specifically spoken. To guide the analysis, we generally examine the relevant statute to ensure that we do not fashion the parameters of an implied right in an manner at odds with the statutory structure and purpose.

Those considerations, we think, are pertinent not only to the scope of the implied right, but also the scope of the available remedies. ... Applying those principles here, we conclude that it would "frustrate the purposes" of title IX to permit a damages recovery against a school district for a teacher's sexual harassment of a student based on principles of respondeat superior or constructive notice, i.e., without actual notice to a school district official. ...

As a general matter, it does not appear that Congress contemplated unlimited recovery in damages against a funding recipient where the recipient is unaware of discrimination in its programs. When title IX was enacted in 1972, the principal civil rights statutes containing an express right of action did not provide for recovery of monetary damages at all, instead allowing only injunctive and equitable relief. It was not until 1991 that Congress made damages available under title VII, and even then, Congress carefully limited the amount recoverable in any individual case, calibrating the maximum recovery to the size of the employer. Adopting petitioners' position would amount, then, to allowing unlimited recovery of damages under title IX where Congress has not spoken on the subject of either the right or the remedy, and in the face of evidence that when Congress expressly considered both in title VII it restricted the amount of damages available.

Congress enacted title IX in 1972 with two principal objectives in mind: "to avoid the use of federal resources to support discriminatory practices" and "to provide individual citizens effective protection against those practices." *Cannon*, supra, at 704. The statute was modeled after title VI of the Civil Rights Act of 1964, which is parallel to title IX except that it prohibits race discrimination, not sex discrimination, and applies in all programs receiving federal funds, not only in education programs. See 42 U.S.C. § 2000d et seq. The two statutes operate in the same manner, conditioning an offer of federal funding on a promise by the recipient not to discriminate, in what amounts essentially to a contract between the government and the recipient of funds.

That contractual framework distinguishes title IX from title VII, which is framed in terms not of a condition but of an outright prohibition . . . [W]hereas title VII aims centrally to compensate victims of discrimination, title IX focuses more on "protecting" individuals from discriminatory practices carried out by recipients of federal funds. That might explain why, when the Court first recognized the implied right under title IX in *Cannon*, the opinion referred to injunctive or equitable relief in a private action, but not to a damages remedy.

Title IX's contractual nature has implications for our construction of the scope of available remedies. When Congress attaches conditions to the award of federal funds under its spending power, . . . we examine closely the propriety of private actions holding the recipient liable in monetary damages for noncompliance with the condition. Our central concern . . . is with ensuring "that the receiving entity of federal funds [has] notice that it will be liable for a monetary award." *Franklin*, supra, at 74. . . . If a school district's liability for a teacher's sexual harassment rests on principles of constructive notice or respondeat superior, it will . . . be the case that the recipient of funds was unaware of the discrimination. It is sensible to assume that Congress did not envision a recipient's liability in damages in that situation. See Rosa H. v. San Elizario Independent School Dist., 106

F.3d 648, 654 (5th Cir.1997) ("When the school board accepted federal funds, it agreed not to discriminate on the basis of sex. We think it unlikely that it further agreed to suffer liability whenever its employees discriminate on the basis of sex.").

Most significantly, title IX contains important clues that Congress did not intend to allow recovery in damages where liability rests solely on principles of vicarious liability or constructive notice. Title IX's express means of enforcement—by administrative agencies—operates on an assumption of actual notice to officials of the funding recipient. [A]n agency may not initiate enforcement proceedings until it "has advised the appropriate person or persons of the failure to comply with the requirement and has determined that compliance cannot be secured by voluntary means." 20 U.S.C. § 1682. ...

Presumably, a central purpose of requiring notice of the violation "to the appropriate person" and an opportunity for voluntary compliance before administrative enforcement proceedings can commence is to avoid diverting education funding from beneficial uses where a recipient was unaware of discrimination in its programs and is willing to institute prompt corrective measures. The scope of private damages relief proposed by petitioners is at odds with that basic objective. ...

It would be unsound, we think for a statute's *express* system of enforcement to require notice to the recipient and an opportunity to come into voluntary compliance while a judicially *implied* system of enforcement permits substantial liability without regard to the recipient's knowledge or its corrective actions upon receiving notice. Moreover, an award of damages in a particular case might well exceed a recipient's level of federal funding. See Tr. of Oral Arg. 35 (Lago Vista's federal funding for 1992–1993 was roughly $120,000). Where a statute's express enforcement scheme hinges its most severe sanction on notice and unsuccessful efforts to obtain compliance, we cannot attribute to Congress the intention to have implied an enforcement scheme that allows imposition of greater liability without comparable conditions.

IV

Because the express remedial scheme under title IX is predicated upon notice to an "appropriate person" and an opportunity to rectify any violation, we conclude, in the absence of further direction from Congress, that an implied damages remedy should be fashioned along the same lines. An "appropriate person" under § 1682 is, at a minimum, an official of the recipient entity with authority to take corrective action to end the discrimination. Consequently, in cases like this one that do not involve official policy of the recipient entity, we hold that a damages remedy will not lie under title IX unless an official who at a minimum has authority to address the alleged discrimination and to institute correction measures on the recipient's behalf has actual knowledge of discrimination in the recipient's programs and fails adequately to respond.

We think, moreover, that the response must amount to deliberate indifference to discrimination. The administrative enforcement scheme presupposes that an official who is advised of a title IX violation refuses to take action to bring the recipient into compliance. The premise, in other words, is an official decision by the recipient not to remedy the violation. That framework finds rough parallel in the standard of deliberate indifference. . . .

Applying the framework to this case is fairly straightforward, as petitioners do not contend they can prevail under an actual notice standard. . . . Petitioners focus primarily on Lago Vista's asserted failure to promulgate and publicize an effective policy and grievance procedure for sexual harassment claims. They point to Department of Education regulations requiring [such procedures]. Lago Vista's alleged failure to comply with the regulations, however, does not establish the requisite actual notice and deliberate indifference. And in any event, the failure to promulgate a grievance procedure does not itself constitute "discrimination" under title IX. . . .

V

The number of reported cases involving sexual harassment of students in schools confirms that harassment unfortunately is an all too common aspect of the educational experience. No one questions that a student suffers extraordinary harm when subjected to sexual harassment and abuse by a teacher, and that the teacher's conduct is reprehensible and undermines the basic purposes of the educational system. The issue in this case, however, is whether the independent misconduct of a teacher is attributable to the school district that employs him under a specific federal statute designed primarily to prevent recipients of federal financial assistance from using the funds in a discriminatory manner. Our decision does not affect any right of recovery that an individual may have against a school district as a matter of state law or against the teacher in his individual capacity under state law or under 42 U.S.C. § 1983. Until Congress speaks directly on the subject, however, we will not hold a school district liable in damages under title IX for a teacher's sexual harassment of a student absent actual notice and deliberate indifference. We therefore affirm the judgment of the court of appeals.

■ JUSTICE STEVENS, with whom JUSTICE SOUTER, JUSTICE GINSBURG, and JUSTICE BREYER join, dissenting.

. . . As a basis for its decision, the majority relies heavily on the notion that because the private cause of action under title IX is "judicially implied," the Court has "a measure of latitude" to use its own judgment in shaping a remedial scheme. This assertion of lawmaking authority is not faithful either to our precedents or to our duty to interpret, rather than to revise, congressional commands. Moreover, the majority's policy judgment about the appropriate remedy in this case thwarts the purposes of title IX.

I

It is important to emphasize that in Cannon v. University of Chicago, 441 U.S. 677 (1979), the court confronted a question of statutory construction. The decision represented our considered judgment about the intent of the Congress that enacted title IX in 1972. After noting that title IX had been patterned after title VI of the Civil Rights Act of 1964, which had been interpreted to include a private right of action, we concluded that Congress intended to authorize the same private enforcement of title IX. As long as the intent of Congress is clear, an implicit command has the same legal force as one that is explicit. . . .

In Franklin v. Gwinnett County Public Schools, 503 U.S. 60 (1992), we unanimously concluded that title IX authorized a high school student who had been sexually harassed by a sports coach/teacher to recover damages from the school district. That conclusion was supported by two considerations. In his opinion for the Court, Justice White first relied on the presumption that Congress intends to authorize "all appropriate remedies" unless it expressly indicates otherwise. He then noted that two amendments to title IX enacted after the decision in *Cannon* had validated *Cannon*'s holding and supported the conclusion that "Congress did not intend to limit the remedies available in a suit brought under title IX." Justice Scalia, concurring in the judgment, agreed that Congress' amendment of title IX to eliminate the states' 11th amendment immunity, see 42 U.S.C. § 2000d–7(a)(1), must be read "not only 'as a validation of *Cannon*'s holding,' but also as an implicit acknowledgment that damages are available."

Because these constructions of the statute have been accepted by Congress and are unchallenged here, they have the same legal effect as if the private cause of action seeking damages had been explicitly, rather than implicitly, authorized by Congress. We should therefore seek guidance from the text of the statute and settled legal principles rather than from our views about sound policy.

II

. . . *Franklin* . . . stands for the proposition that sexual harassment of a student by her teacher violates the duty—assumed by the school district in exchange for federal funds—not to discriminate on the basis of sex, and that a student may recover damages from a school district for such a violation.

Although the opinion the Court announces today is not entirely clear, it does not purport to overrule *Franklin*. Moreover, I do not understand the Court to question the conclusion that an intentional violation of title IX, of the type we recognized in *Franklin*, has been alleged in this case. During her freshman and sophomore years of high school, petitioner Alida Star Gebser was repeatedly subjected to sexual abuse by her teacher, Frank Waldrop, whom she had met in the eighth grade when she joined his high school book discussion group. Waldrop's conduct was surely intentional and it occurred during, and as a part of, a curriculum activity in which he wielded authority over Gebser that had been delegated to him by respondent. . . .

The Court nevertheless holds that the law does not provide a damages remedy for the title IX violation alleged in this case because no official of the school district with "authority to institute corrective measures on the district's behalf" had actual notice of Waldrop's misconduct. That holding is at odds with settled principles of agency law, under which the district is responsible for Waldrop's misconduct because "he was aided in accomplishing the tort by the existence of the agency relation." Restatement (Second) of Agency, § 219(2)(d) (1957). This case presents a paradigmatic example of a tort that was made possible, that was effected, and that was repeated over a prolonged period because of the powerful influence that Waldrop had over Gebser by reason of the authority that his employer, the school district, had delegated to him. As a secondary school teacher, Waldrop exercised even greater authority over his students than employers and supervisors exercise over their employees. His gross misuse of that authority allowed him to abuse this young student's trust.

Reliance on the principle set out in § 219(2)(d) of the Restatement comports with the relevant agency's interpretation of title IX. The United States Department of Education, through its Office for Civil Rights, recently issued a policy "guidance" stating that a school district is liable under title IX if one of its teachers "was aided in carrying out the sexual harassment of students by his or her position of authority with the institution." Dept. of Ed., Office for Civil Rights, Sexual Harassment Guidance: Harassment of Students by School Employees, Other Students, or Third Parties, 62 Fed. Reg. 12034, 12039 (1997). . . .

The reason why the common law imposes liability on the principal in such circumstances is the same as the reason why Congress included the prohibition against discrimination on the basis of sex in title IX: to induce school boards to adopt and enforce practices that will minimize the danger that vulnerable students will be exposed to such odious behavior. The rule that the court has crafted creates the opposite incentive. As long as school boards can insulate themselves from knowledge about this sort of conduct, they can claim immunity from damages liability. . . .

III

The Court advances several reasons why it would "frustrate the purposes" of title IX to allow recovery against a school district that does not have actual notice of a teacher's sexual harassment of a student. As the Court acknowledges, however, the two principal purposes that motivated the enactment of title IX were: (1) " 'to avoid the use of federal resources to support discriminatory practices' "; and (2) " 'to provide individual citizens effective protection against those practices,' " (quoting *Cannon*, supra, at 704). It seems quite obvious that both of these purposes would be served—not frustrated—by providing a damages remedy in a case of this kind. To the extent that the Court's reasons for its policy choice have any merit, they suggest that no damages should ever be awarded in a title IX case—in other words, that our unanimous holding in *Franklin* should be repudiated.

First, the Court observes that at the time title IX was enacted, "the principal civil rights statutes containing an express right of action did not provide for recovery of monetary damages at all." *Franklin*, however, forecloses this reevaluation of legislative intent; in that case, we "evaluate[d] the state of the law when the legislature passed title IX," 503 U.S., at 71, and concluded that "the same contextual approach used to justify an implied right of action more than amply demonstrates the lack of any legislative intent to abandon the traditional presumption in favor of all available remedies," id., at 72. . . .

Second, the Court suggests that the school district did not have fair notice when it accepted federal funding that it might be held liable " 'for a monetary award' " under title IX (quoting *Franklin*, supra, at 74). The Court cannot mean, however, that respondent was not on notice that sexual harassment of a student by a teacher constitutes an "intentional" violation of title IX for which damages are available, because we so held shortly before Waldrop began abusing Gebser. See *Franklin*, supra, at 74–75. . . .

The majority nevertheless takes the position that a school district that accepts federal funds under title IX should not be held liable in damages for an intentional violation of that statute if the district itself "was unaware of the discrimination." The Court reasons that because administrative proceedings to terminate funding cannot be commenced until after the grant recipient has received notice of its noncompliance and the agency determines that voluntary compliance is not possible, there should be no damages liability unless the grant recipient has actual notice of the violation (and thus an opportunity to end the harassment).

The fact that Congress has specified a particular administrative procedure to be followed when a subsidy is to be terminated, however, does not illuminate the question of what the victim of discrimination on the basis of sex must prove in order to recover damages in an implied right of action. Indeed, in *Franklin*, we noted that the Department of Education's Office of Civil Rights had declined to terminate federal funding of the school district at issue—despite its finding that a title IX violation had occurred—because "the district had come into compliance with title IX" after the harassment at issue. That fact did not affect the Court's analysis, much less persuade the Court that a damages remedy was unavailable. Cf. *Cannon*, supra, at 711 ("The fact that other provisions of a complex statutory scheme create express remedies has not been accepted as a sufficient reason for refusing to imply an otherwise appropriate remedy under a separate section"). . . .

IV

. . . It is possible, of course, that in some cases the recoverable damages, in either a title IX action or a state-law tort action, would exceed the amount of a federal grant. That is surely not relevant to the question whether the school district or the injured student should bear the risk of harm—a risk against which the district, but not the student, can insure. It is not clear to me why the well-settled rules of law that impose responsibility on the principal for the misconduct of its agents should not apply in this case. As a matter of policy, the Court ranks protection of the school district's purse above the protection of immature high school students that those rules would provide. Because those students are members of the class for whose special benefit Congress enacted title IX, that policy choice is not faithful to the intent of the policymaking branch of our government.

I respectfully dissent.

■ JUSTICE GINSBURG, with whom JUSTICE SOUTER and JUSTICE BREYER join, dissenting. . . .

I join [Justice Stevens'] opinion [and add that] I would recognize as an affirmative defense to a title IX charge of sexual harassment, an effective policy for reporting and redressing such misconduct. School districts subject to title IX's governance have been instructed by the Secretary of Education to install procedures for "prompt and equitable resolution" of complaints, 34 CFR § 106.8(b) (1977), and the Department of Education's Office of Civil Rights has detailed elements of an effective grievance process, with specific reference to sexual harassment. 62 Fed. Reg. 12034, 12044–45 (1997).

The burden would be on the school district to show that its internal remedies were adequate publicized and likely would have provided redress without exposing the complainant to undue risk, effort, or expense. Under such a regime, to the extent that a plaintiff unreasonably failed to avail herself of the school district's preventive and remedial measures, and consequently suffered avoidable harm, she would not qualify for title IX relief.

NOTE ON *GEBSER v. LAGO VISTA*

What question should the Court be asking in this case? Is the issue the standard of liability that the Court thinks most consistent with sound policy (as informed by explicit legislative choices), or is the question one of legislative intent? If the latter, how is that intent to be discerned? Does the (wholly unsurprising) fact that Congress did not impose explicit limits on a liability it did not explicitly create preclude the Court from crafting restrictive standards? Or affirmative defenses? How much of the dispute in this case turns on competing methodologies, and how much springs from differing conceptions of what the law should be?

Alexander v. Sandoval

Supreme Court of the United States, 2001.
532 U.S. 275.

■ JUSTICE SCALIA delivered the opinion of the Court.

This case presents the question whether private individuals may sue to enforce disparate-impact regulations promulgated under Title VI of the Civil Rights Act of 1964.

I

The Alabama Department of Public Safety (Department), of which petitioner James Alexander is the Director, accepted grants of financial assistance from the United States Department of Justice (DOJ) and Department of Transportation (DOT) and so subjected itself to the restrictions of Title VI of the Civil Rights Act of 1964, 42 U.S.C. § 2000d et seq. Section 601 of that Title provides that no person shall, "on the ground of race, color, or national origin, be excluded from participation in, be denied the benefits of, or be subjected to discrimination under any program or activity" covered by Title VI. 42 U.S.C. § 2000d. Section 602 authorizes federal agencies "to effectuate the provisions of [§ 601] ... by issuing rules, regulations, or orders of general applicability," 42 U.S.C. § 2000d–1, and the DOJ in an exercise of this authority promulgated a regulation forbidding funding recipients to "utilize criteria or methods of administration which have the effect of subjecting individuals to discrimination because of their race, color, or national origin...." 28 CFR § 42.104(b)(2) (1999). See also 49 CFR § 21.5(b)(2) (2000) (similar DOT regulation).

The State of Alabama amended its Constitution in 1990 to declare English "the official language of the state of Alabama." Amdt. 509. Pursuant to this provision and, petitioners have argued, to advance public safety, the Department decided to administer state driver's license examinations only in English. Respondent Sandoval, as representative of a class, brought suit in the United States District Court for the Middle District of Alabama to enjoin the English-only policy, arguing that it violated the DOJ regulation because it had the effect of subjecting non-English speakers to discrimination based on their national origin. The District Court agreed. It enjoined the policy and ordered the Department to accommodate non-English speakers. Sandoval v. Hagan, 7 F.Supp.2d 1234 (M.D.Ala.1998). Petitioners appealed to the Court of Appeals for the Eleventh Circuit, which affirmed. Sandoval v. Hagan, 197 F.3d 484 (11th Cir.1999). Both courts rejected petitioners' argument that Title VI did not provide respondents a cause of action to enforce the regulation.

We do not inquire here whether the DOJ regulation was authorized by § 602, or whether the courts below were correct to hold that the English-only policy had the effect of discriminating on the basis of national origin. The petition for writ of certiorari raised, and we agreed to review, only the question posed in the first paragraph of this opinion: whether there is a private cause of action to enforce the regulation.

II

[T]hree aspects of Title VI must be taken as given. First, private individuals may sue to enforce § 601 of Title VI and obtain both injunctive relief and damages. In Cannon v. University of Chicago, 441 U.S. 677 (1979), the Court held that a private right of action existed to enforce Title IX of the Education Amendments of 1972, as amended, 20 U.S.C. §§ 1681 et seq. The reasoning of that decision embraced the existence of a private right to enforce Title VI as well. "Title IX," the Court noted, "was patterned after Title VI of the Civil Rights Act of 1964." 441 U.S. at 694. And, "in 1972 when Title IX was enacted, the [parallel] language in Title VI had already been construed as creating a private remedy." Id., at 696. That meant, the Court reasoned, that Congress had intended Title IX, like Title VI, to provide a private cause of action. Id., at 699, 703, 710–711. Congress has since ratified *Cannon*'s holding. Section 1003 of the Rehabilitation Act Amendments of 1986, 42 U.S.C. § 2000d–7, expressly abrogated States' sovereign immunity against suits brought in federal court to enforce Title VI and provided that in a suit against a State "remedies (including remedies both at law and in equity) are available ... to the same extent as such remedies are available ... in the suit against any public or private entity other than a State," § 2000d–7(a)(2).... It is thus beyond dispute that private individuals may sue to enforce § 601.

Second, it is similarly beyond dispute—and no party disagrees—that § 601 prohibits only intentional discrimination.... What we said in Alexander v. Choate, 469 U.S. 287, 293 (1985), is true today: "Title VI itself directly reaches only instances of intentional discrimination."

Third, we must assume for purposes of deciding this case that regulations promulgated under § 602 of Title VI may validly proscribe activities that have a disparate impact on racial groups, even though such activities are permissible under § 601. Though no opinion of this Court has held that, five Justices in Guardians Assn. v. Civil Service Comm'n of New York City, 463 U.S. 582 (1983), voiced that view of the law at least as alternative grounds for their decisions, see id., at 591–592 (opinion of White, J.); id., at 623, n. 15 (Marshall, J., dissenting); id., at 643–45 (Stevens, J., joined by Brennan and Blackmun, JJ., dissenting), and dictum in *Alexander* v. *Choate* is to the same effect, see 469 U.S. at 293, 295 n. 11. These statements are in considerable tension with the rule ... that § 601 forbids only intentional discrimination, but petitioners have not challenged the regulations here. We therefore assume for the purposes of deciding this case that the DOJ and DOT regulations proscribing activities that have a disparate impact on the basis of race are valid.

Respondents assert that the issue in this case, like the first two described above, has been resolved by our cases. To reject a private cause of action to enforce the disparate-impact regulations, they say, we would "[have] to ignore the actual language of *Guardians* and *Cannon*." The language in *Cannon* to which respondents refer does not in fact support their position, [but] in any event, this Court is bound by holdings, not language. *Cannon* was decided on the assumption that the University of Chicago had intentionally discriminated against petitioner. See 441 U.S. at 680 (noting that respondents "admitted arguendo" that petitioner's "application for admission to medical school was denied by the respondents because she is a woman"). It therefore *held* that Title IX created a private right of action to enforce its ban on intentional discrimination, but had no occasion to consider whether the right reached regulations barring disparate-impact discrimination. In *Guardians*, the Court *held* that private individuals could not recover compensatory damages under Title VI except for intentional discrimination. Five Justices in addition voted to uphold the disparate-impact regulations (four would have declared them invalid), but of those five, three expressly reserved the question of a direct private right of action to enforce the regulations, saying that "whether a cause of action against private parties exists directly under the regulations ... [is a] question that [is] not presented by this case." 463 U.S. at 645 n. 18 (Stevens, J., dissenting). Thus, only two Justices had cause to reach the issue that respondents say the "actual language" of *Guardians* resolves. Neither that case, nor any other in this Court, has held that the private right of action exists.

Nor does it follow straightaway from the three points we have taken as given that Congress must have intended a private right of action to enforce disparate-impact regulations. We do not doubt that regulations applying § 601's ban on intentional discrimination are covered by the cause of action to enforce that section. Such regulations, if valid and reasonable, authoritatively construe the statute itself, and it is therefore meaningless to talk about a separate cause of action to enforce the regulations apart from the statute. A Congress that intends the statute to be enforced through a private cause of action intends the authoritative interpretation of the statute to be so enforced as well. The many cases that respondents say have "assumed" that a cause of action to enforce a statute includes one to enforce its regulations illustrate (to the extent that cases in which an issue was not presented can illustrate anything) only this point; each involved regulations of the type we have just described, as respondents conceded at oral argument, [citing cases]. Our decision in Lau v. Nichols, 414 U.S. 563 (1974), falls within the same category. The Title VI regulations at issue in *Lau*, similar to the ones at issue here, forbade funding recipients to take actions which had the effect of discriminating on the basis of race, color, or national origin. Unlike our later cases, however, the Court in *Lau* interpreted § 601 itself to proscribe disparate-impact discrimination, saying that ... the disparate-impact regulations simply "[made] sure that recipients of federal aid ... conducted any federally financed projects consistently with § 601."[5]

We must face now the question avoided by *Lau*, because we have since rejected *Lau*'s interpretation of § 601 as reaching beyond intentional discrimination. It is clear now that the disparate-impact regulations do not simply apply § 601—since they indeed forbid conduct that § 601 permits—and therefore clear that the private right of action to enforce § 601 does not include a private right to enforce these regulations. That right must come, if at all, from the independent force of § 602. As stated earlier, we assume for purposes of this decision that § 602 confers the authority to promulgate disparate-impact regulations; the question remains whether it confers a private right of action to enforce them. If not, we must conclude that a failure to comply with regulations promulgated under § 602 that is not also a failure to comply with § 601 is not actionable.

Implicit in our discussion thus far has been a particular understanding of the genesis of private causes of action. Like substantive federal law itself, private rights of action to enforce federal law must be created by Congress. Touche Ross & Co. v. Redington, 442 U.S. 560, 578 (1979) (remedies available are those "that Congress enacted into law"). The judicial task is to interpret the statute Congress has passed to determine whether it displays an intent to create not just a private right but also a private remedy. Transamerica Mortgage Advisors, Inc. v. Lewis, 444 U.S. 11, 15 (1979). Statutory intent on this latter point is determinative. Without it, a cause of action does not exist and courts may not create one, no matter how desirable that might be as a policy matter, or how compatible with the statute. "Raising up causes of action where a statute has not created them may be a proper function for common-law courts, but not for federal tribunals." Lampf, Pleva, Lipkind, Prupis & Petigrow v. Gilbertson, 501 U.S. 350, 365 (1991) (Scalia, J., concurring in part and concurring in judgment).

Respondents would have us revert in this case to the understanding of private causes of action that held sway 40 years ago when Title VI was enacted. That understanding is captured by the Court's statement in J. I. Case Co. v. Borak, 377 U.S. 426, 433 (1964), that "it is the duty of the courts to be alert to provide such remedies as are necessary to make effective the congressional purpose" expressed by a statute. We abandoned that understanding in Cort v. Ash, 422 U.S. 66, 78 (1975)—which itself interpreted a statute enacted under the ancien regime—and have not returned to it since. Not even when interpreting the same Securities

---

5. It is true, as the dissent points out, that three Justices who concurred in the result in *Lau* relied on regulations promulgated under § 602 to support their position, see Lau v. Nichols, 414 U.S. 563, 570–71 (1974) (Stewart, J., concurring in result). But the five Justices who made up the majority did not....

Exchange Act of 1934 that was at issue in *Borak* have we applied *Borak*'s method for discerning and defining causes of action [citing cases]. Having sworn off the habit of venturing beyond Congress's intent, we will not accept respondents' invitation to have one last drink.

Nor do we agree with the Government that our cases interpreting statutes enacted prior to *Cort v. Ash* have given "dispositive weight" to the "expectations" that the enacting Congress had formed "in light of the 'contemporary legal context.'" Only three of our legion implied-right-of-action cases have found this sort of "contemporary legal context" relevant, and two of those involved Congress's enactment (or reenactment) of the verbatim statutory text that courts had previously interpreted to create a private right of action. See Merrill Lynch, Pierce, Fenner & Smith, Inc. v. Curran, 456 U.S. 353, 378–79 (1982); *Cannon*, 441 U.S. at 698–99. In the third case, this sort of "contemporary legal context" simply buttressed a conclusion independently supported by the text of the statute. See Thompson v. Thompson, 484 U.S. 174 (1988). We have never accorded dispositive weight to context shorn of text. In determining whether statutes create private rights of action, as in interpreting statutes generally, legal context matters only to the extent it clarifies text.

We therefore begin (and find that we can end) our search for Congress's intent with the text and structure of Title VI. Section 602 authorizes federal agencies "to effectuate the provisions of [§ 601] . . . by issuing rules, regulations, or orders of general applicability." 42 U.S.C. § 2000d–1. It is immediately clear that the "rights-creating" language so critical to the Court's analysis in *Cannon* of § 601, see 441 U.S. at 690 n.13, is completely absent from § 602. Whereas § 601 decrees that "no person . . . shall . . . be subjected to discrimination," 42 U.S.C. § 2000d, the text of § 602 provides that "each Federal department and agency . . . is authorized and directed to effectuate the provisions of [§ 601]," 42 U.S.C. § 2000d–1. Far from displaying congressional intent to create new rights, § 602 limits agencies to "effectuating" rights already created by § 601. And the focus of § 602 is twice removed from the individuals who will ultimately benefit from Title VI's protection. Statutes that focus on the person regulated rather than the individuals protected create "no implication of an intent to confer rights on a particular class of persons." California v. Sierra Club, 451 U.S. 287, 294 (1981). Section 602 is yet a step further removed: it focuses neither on the individuals protected nor even on the funding recipients being regulated, but on the agencies that will do the regulating. Like the statute found not to create a right of action in Universities Research Assn., Inc. v. Coutu, 450 U.S. 754 (1981), § 602 is "phrased as a directive to federal agencies engaged in the distribution of public funds," id., at 772. When this is true, "there [is] far less reason to infer a private remedy in favor of individual persons," *Cannon*, supra, at 690–91. So far as we can tell, this authorizing portion of § 602 reveals no congressional intent to create a private right of action.

Nor do the methods that § 602 goes on to provide for enforcing its authorized regulations manifest an intent to create a private remedy; if anything, they suggest the opposite. Section 602 empowers agencies to enforce their regulations either by terminating funding to the "particular program, or part thereof," that has violated the regulation or "by any other means authorized by law," 42 U.S.C. § 2000d–1. No enforcement action may be taken, however, "until the department or agency concerned has advised the appropriate person or persons of the failure to comply with the requirement and has determined that compliance cannot be secured by voluntary means." Ibid. And every agency enforcement action is subject to judicial review. § 2000d–2. If an agency attempts to terminate program funding, still more restrictions apply. The agency head must "file with the committees of the House and Senate having legislative jurisdiction over the program or activity involved a full written report of the circumstances and the grounds for such action." § 2000d–1. And the termination of funding does not "become effective until thirty days have elapsed after the filing of such report." Ibid. Whatever these elaborate restrictions on agency enforcement may imply for the private enforcement of rights created *outside* of § 602, they tend to contradict a congressional intent to create privately enforceable rights through § 602 itself. The express provision of one method of enforcing a substantive rule suggests that Congress intended to preclude others. Sometimes the suggestion is so strong that it precludes a finding of congressional intent to create a private right of action, even though other aspects of the statute (such as language making the would-be plaintiff "a member of the class for whose benefit the statute was enacted") suggest the contrary. Massachusetts Mut. Life Ins. Co. v. Russell, 473 U.S. 134, 145 (1985). And as our 42 U.S.C. § 1983 cases show, some remedial schemes foreclose a private cause of action to enforce even those statutes that admittedly create substantive private rights. See, e.g., Middlesex County Sewerage Authority v. National Sea Clammers Assn., 453 U.S. 1, 19–20 (1981). In the present case, the claim of exclusivity for the express remedial scheme does not even have to overcome such obstacles. The question whether § 602's remedial scheme can overbear other evidence of congressional intent is simply not presented, since we have found no evidence anywhere in the text to suggest that Congress intended to create a private right to enforce regulations promulgated under § 602.

Both the Government and respondents argue that the *regulations* contain rights-creating language and so must be privately enforceable, but that argument skips an analytical step. Language in a regulation may invoke a private right of action that Congress through statutory text created, but it may not create a right that Congress has not. Thus, when a statute has provided a general authorization for private enforcement of regulations, it may perhaps be correct that the intent displayed in each regulation can determine whether or not it is privately enforceable. But it is most certainly incorrect to say that language in a regulation can conjure up a private cause of action that has not been authorized by Congress. Agencies may play the sorcerer's apprentice but not the sorcerer himself.

The last string to respondents' and the Government's bow is their argument that two amendments to Title VI "ratified" this Court's decisions finding an implied private right of action to enforce the disparate-impact regulations. See Rehabilitation Act Amendments of 1986, § 1003, 42 U.S.C. § 2000d–7; Civil Rights Restoration Act of 1987, § 6, 42 U.S.C. § 2000d–4a. One problem with this argument is that, as explained above, none of our decisions establishes (or even assumes) the private right of action at issue here, which is why in *Guardians* three Justices were able expressly to reserve the question. Incorporating our cases in the amendments would thus not help respondents. Another problem is that the incorporation claim itself is flawed. Section 1003 of the Rehabilitation Act Amendments of 1986, on which only respondents rely, by its terms applies only to suits "for a violation of a *statute*," 42 U.S.C. § 2000d–7(a)(2) (emphasis added). It therefore does not speak to suits for violations of regulations that go beyond the statutory proscription of § 601. Section 6 of the Civil Rights Restoration Act of 1987 is even less on point. That provision amends Title VI to make the term "program or activity" cover larger portions of the institutions receiving federal financial aid than it had previously covered, see Grove City College v. Bell, 465 U.S. 555 (1984). It is impossible to understand what this has to do with implied causes of action—which is why we declared in *Franklin v. Gwinnett County Public Schools*, 503 U.S. at 73, that § 6 did not "in any way alter the existing rights of action and the corresponding remedies permissible under ... Title VI." Respondents point to *Merrill Lynch, Pierce, Fenner & Smith, Inc. v. Curran*, 456 U.S. at 381–382, which inferred congressional intent to ratify lower court decisions regarding a particular statutory provision when Congress comprehensively revised the statutory scheme but did not amend that provision. But we recently criticized *Curran*'s reliance on congressional inaction, saying that "as a general matter ... [the] argument deserves little weight in the interpretive process." Central Bank of Denver, N. A. v. First Interstate Bank of Denver, N. A., 511 U.S. 164, 187 (1994). And when, as here, Congress has not comprehensively revised a statutory scheme but has made only isolated amendments, we have spoken more bluntly: "It is 'impossible to assert with any degree of assurance that congressional failure to act represents' affirmative congressional approval of the Court's statutory interpretation." Patterson v. McLean Credit Union, 491 U.S. 164, 175 n. 1 (1989) (quoting Johnson v. Transportation Agency, Santa Clara Cty., 480 U.S. 616, 671–72 (1987) (Scalia, J., dissenting)).

Neither as originally enacted nor as later amended does Title VI display an intent to create a freestanding private right of action to enforce regulations promulgated under § 602. We therefore hold that no such right of action exists. Since we reach this conclusion applying our standard test for discerning private causes of action, we do not address petitioners' additional argument that implied causes of action against States (and perhaps nonfederal state actors generally) are inconsistent with the clear statement rule of Pennhurst State School and Hospital v. Halderman, 451 U.S. 1 (1981). See Davis v. Monroe County Bd. of Ed., 526 U.S. 629, 656–57 (1999) (Kennedy, J., dissenting).

The judgment of the Court of Appeals is reversed.

It is so ordered.

■ JUSTICE STEVENS, with whom JUSTICE SOUTER, JUSTICE GINSBURG, and JUSTICE BREYER join, dissenting.

In 1964, as part of a groundbreaking and comprehensive civil rights Act, Congress prohibited recipients of federal funds from discriminating on the basis of race, ethnicity, or national origin. Title VI of the Civil Rights Act of 1964, 42 U.S.C. §§ 2000d to 2000d–7. Pursuant to powers expressly delegated by that Act, the federal agencies and departments responsible for awarding and administering federal contracts immediately adopted regulations prohibiting federal contractees from adopting policies that have the "effect" of discriminating on those bases. At the time of the promulgation of these regulations, prevailing principles of statutory construction assumed that Congress intended a private right of action whenever such a cause of action was necessary to protect individual rights granted by valid federal law. Relying both on this presumption and on independent analysis of Title VI, this Court has repeatedly and consistently affirmed the right of private individuals to bring civil suits to enforce rights guaranteed by Title VI. A fair reading of those cases, and coherent implementation of the statutory scheme, requires the same result under Title VI's implementing regulations.

In separate lawsuits spanning several decades, we have endorsed an action identical in substance to the one brought in this case, see Lau v. Nichols, 414 U.S. 563 (1974); demonstrated that Congress intended a private right of action to protect the rights guaranteed by Title VI, see Cannon v. University of Chicago, 441 U.S. 677 (1979); and concluded that private individuals may seek declaratory and injunctive relief against state officials for violations of regulations promulgated pursuant to Title VI, see Guardians Assn. v. Civil Serv. Comm'n of New York City, 463 U.S. 582 (1983). Giving fair import to our language and our holdings, every Court of Appeals to address the question has concluded that a private right of action exists to enforce the rights guaranteed both by the text of Title VI and by any regulations validly promulgated pursuant to that Title, and Congress has adopted several statutes that appear to ratify the status quo.

Today, in a decision unfounded in our precedent and hostile to decades of settled expectations, a majority of this Court carves out an important exception to the right of private action long recognized under Title VI. In so doing, the Court makes three distinct, albeit interrelated, errors. First, the Court provides a muddled account of both the reasoning and the breadth of our prior decisions endorsing a private right of action under Title VI, thereby obscuring the conflict between those opinions and today's decision. Second, the Court offers a flawed and unconvincing analysis of the relationship between §§ 601 and 602 of the Civil Rights Act of 1964, ignoring more plausible and persuasive explanations detailed in our prior opinions. Finally, the Court badly misconstrues the theoretical linchpin of our decision in *Cannon v. University of Chicago,* supra, mistaking that decision's careful contextual analysis for judicial fiat.

I

The majority is undoubtedly correct that this Court has never said in so many words that a private right of action exists to enforce the disparate-impact regulations promulgated under § 602. However, the failure of our cases to state this conclusion explicitly does not absolve the Court of the responsibility to canvass our prior opinions for guidance. Reviewing these opinions with the care they deserve, I reach the same conclusion as the Courts of Appeals: This Court has already considered the question presented today and concluded that a private right of action exists.

When this Court faced an identical case 27 years ago, all the Justices believed that private parties could bring lawsuits under Title VI and its implementing regulations to enjoin the provision of governmental services in a manner that discriminated against non-English speakers. See *Lau v. Nichols,* supra. While five Justices saw no need to go beyond the command of § 601, Chief Justice Burger, Justice Stewart, and Justice Blackmun relied specifically and exclusively on the regulations to support the private action, see id., at 569 (Stewart, J., concurring in result). There is nothing in the majority's opinion in *Lau,* or in earlier opinions of the Court, that is not fully consistent with the analysis of the concurring Justices or that would have differentiated between private actions to enforce the text of § 601 and private actions to enforce the regulations promulgated pursuant to § 602.

Five years later, we more explicitly considered whether a private right of action exists to enforce the guarantees of Title VI and its gender-based twin, Title IX. See *Cannon v. University of Chicago,* supra. In that case, we examined the text of the statutes, analyzed the purpose of the laws, and canvassed the relevant legislative history. Our conclusion was unequivocal: "We have no doubt that Congress intended to create Title IX remedies comparable to those available under Title VI and that it understood Title VI as authorizing an implied private cause of action for victims of the prohibited discrimination." 441 U.S. at 703.

The majority acknowledges that *Cannon* is binding precedent with regard to both Title VI and Title IX, but seeks to limit the scope of its holding to cases involving allegations of intentional discrimination. The distinction the majority attempts to impose is wholly foreign to *Cannon's* text and reasoning. The opinion in *Cannon* consistently treats the question presented in that case as whether a private right of action exists to enforce "Title IX" (and by extension "Title VI"), and does not draw any distinctions between the various types of discrimination outlawed by the operation of those statutes. Though the opinion did not reach out to affirmatively preclude the drawing of every conceivable distinction, it could hardly have been more clear as to the scope of its holding: A private right of action exists for "victims of *the* prohibited discrimination." 441 U.S. at 703 (emphasis added). Not some of the prohibited discrimination, but all of it.

Moreover, *Cannon* was itself a disparate-impact case. In that case, the plaintiff brought suit against two private universities challenging medical school admissions policies that set age limits for applicants. Plaintiff, a 39-year-old woman, alleged that these rules had the effect of discriminating against women because the incidence of interrupted higher education is higher among women than among men. In providing a shorthand description of her claim in the text of the opinion, we ambiguously stated that she had alleged that she was denied admission "because she is a woman," but we appended a lengthy footnote setting forth the details of her disparate-impact claim. Other than the shorthand description of her claim, there is not a word in the text of the opinion even suggesting that she had made the improbable allegation that the University of Chicago and Northwestern University had intentionally discriminated against women. In the context of the entire opinion (including both its analysis and its uncontested description of the facts of the case), that single ambiguous phrase provides no basis for limiting the case's holding to incidents of intentional discrimination. If anything, the fact that the phrase "because she is a woman" encompasses both intentional and disparate-impact claims should have made it clear that the reasoning in the opinion was equally applicable to both types of claims. In any event, the *holding* of the case certainly applied to the disparate-impact claim that was described in detail in footnote 1 of the opinion, 413 U.S., at 680.

Our fractured decision in Guardians Assn. v. Civil Serv. Comm'n of New York City, 463 U.S. 582 (1983), reinforces the conclusion that this issue is effectively settled. While the various opinions in that case took different views as to the spectrum of relief available to plaintiffs in Title VI cases, a clear majority of the Court expressly stated that private parties may seek injunctive relief against governmental practices that have the effect of discriminating against racial and ethnic minorities. Id., at 594–95, 607 (White, J.); id., at 634 (Marshall, J., dissenting); id., at 638 (Stevens, J., joined by Brennan and Blackmun, JJ., dissenting). As this case involves just such an action, its result ought to follow naturally from *Guardians*.

As I read today's opinion, the majority declines to accord precedential value to *Guardians* because the five Justices in the majority were arguably divided over the mechanism through which private parties might seek such injunctive relief.[5] This argument inspires two responses. First, to the extent that the majority denies relief to the respondents merely because they neglected to mention 42 U.S.C. § 1983 in framing their Title VI claim, this case is something of a sport. Litigants who in the future wish to enforce the Title VI regulations against state actors in all likelihood must only reference § 1983 to obtain relief; indeed, the plaintiffs in this case (or other similarly situated individuals) presumably retain the option of re-challenging Alabama's English-only policy in a complaint that invokes § 1983 even after today's decision.

More important, the majority's reading of *Guardians* is strained even in reference to the broader question whether injunctive relief is available to remedy violations of the Title VI regulations by nongovernmental grantees. As *Guardians* involved an action against a governmental entity, making § 1983 relief available, the Court might have discussed the availability of judicial relief without addressing the scope of the implied private right of action available directly under Title VI. However, the analysis in each of the relevant opinions did not do so. Rather than focusing on considerations specific to § 1983, each of these opinions looked instead to our opinion in *Cannon*, to the intent of the Congress that adopted Title VI and the contemporaneous executive decisionmakers who crafted the disparate-impact regulations, and to general principles of remediation.

In summary, there is clear precedent of this Court for the proposition that the plaintiffs in this case can seek injunctive relief either through an implied right of action or through § 1983. Though the holding in *Guardians* does not compel the conclusion that a private right of action exists to enforce the Title VI regulations against private parties, the rationales of the relevant opinions strongly imply that result. When that fact is coupled with our holding in *Cannon* and our unanimous decision in *Lau*, the answer to the question presented in this case is overdetermined. Even absent my continued belief that Congress intended a private right of action to enforce both Title VI and its implementing regulations, I would answer the question presented in the affirmative and affirm the decision of the Court of Appeals as a matter of stare decisis.

II

Underlying the majority's dismissive treatment of our prior cases is a flawed understanding of the structure of Title VI and, more particularly, of the relationship between §§ 601 and 602. To some extent, confusion as to the relationship between the provisions is understandable, as Title VI is a deceptively simple statute. Section 601 of the Act lays out its straightforward commitment: "No person in the United States shall, on the ground of race, color, or national origin, be excluded from participation in, be denied the benefits of, or be subjected to discrimination under any program or

---

5. None of the relevant opinions was absolutely clear as to whether it envisioned such suits as being brought directly under the statute or under 42 U.S.C. § 1983....

activity receiving Federal financial assistance." 42 U.S.C. § 2000d. Section 602 "authorizes and directs" all federal departments and agencies empowered to extend federal financial assistance to issue "rules, regulations, or orders of general applicability" in order to "effectuate" § 601's antidiscrimination mandate. 42 U.S.C. § 2000d–1.

On the surface, the relationship between §§ 601 and 602 is unproblematic—§ 601 states a basic principle, § 602 authorizes agencies to develop detailed plans for defining the contours of the principle and ensuring its enforcement. In the context of federal civil rights law, however, nothing is ever so simple. As actions to enforce § 601's antidiscrimination principle have worked their way through the courts, we have developed a body of law giving content to § 601's broadly worded commitment. As the majority emphasizes today, the Judiciary's understanding of what conduct may be remedied in actions brought directly under § 601 is, in certain ways, more circumscribed than the conduct prohibited by the regulations.

Given that seeming peculiarity, it is necessary to examine closely the relationship between §§ 601 and 602, in order to understand the purpose and import of the regulations at issue in this case. For the most part, however, the majority ignores this task, assuming that the judicial decisions interpreting § 601 provide an authoritative interpretation of its true meaning and treating the regulations promulgated by the agencies charged with administering the statute as poor step-cousins—either parroting the text of § 601 (in the case of regulations that prohibit intentional discrimination) or forwarding an agenda untethered to § 601's mandate (in the case of disparate-impact regulations).

The majority's statutory analysis does violence to both the text and the structure of Title VI. Section 601 does not stand in isolation, but rather as part of an integrated remedial scheme. Section 602 exists for the sole purpose of forwarding the antidiscrimination ideals laid out in § 601. The majority's persistent belief that the two sections somehow forward different agendas finds no support in the statute. Nor does Title VI anywhere suggest, let alone state, that for the purpose of determining their legal effect, the "rules, regulations, [and] orders of general applicability" adopted by the agencies are to be bifurcated by the judiciary into two categories based on how closely the courts believe the regulations track the text of § 601.

What makes the Court's analysis even more troubling is that our cases have already adopted a simpler and more sensible model for understanding the relationship between the two sections. For three decades, we have treated § 602 as granting the responsible agencies the power to issue broad prophylactic rules aimed at realizing the vision laid out in § 601, even if the conduct captured by these rules is at times broader than that which would otherwise be prohibited.

In *Lau*, our first Title VI case, the only three Justices whose understanding of § 601 required them to reach the question explicitly endorsed the power of the agencies to adopt broad prophylactic rules to enforce the aims of the statute. As Justice Stewart explained, regulations promulgated pursuant to § 602 may "go beyond ... § 601" as long as they are "reasonably related" to its antidiscrimination mandate. 414 U.S. at 571 (Stewart, J., joined by Burger, C. J., and Blackmun, J., concurring in result). In *Guardians*, at least three Members of the Court adopted a similar understanding of the statute. See 463 U.S. at 643 (Stevens, J., joined by Brennan and Blackmun, JJ., dissenting). Finally, just 16 years ago, our unanimous opinion in Alexander v. Choate, 469 U.S. 287 (1985), treated this understanding of Title VI's structure as settled law. Writing for the Court, Justice Marshall aptly explained the interpretation of § 602's grant of regulatory power that necessarily underlies our prior caselaw: "In essence, then, we [have] held that Title VI [has] delegated to the agencies in the first instance the complex determination of what sorts of disparate impacts upon minorities constituted sufficiently significant social problems, and [are] readily enough remediable, to warrant altering the practices of the federal grantees that have produced those impacts." Id., at 293–94.

This understanding is firmly rooted in the text of Title VI. As § 602 explicitly states, the agencies are authorized to adopt regulations to "effectuate" § 601's antidiscrimination mandate. 42 U.S.C. § 2000d–1. The plain meaning of the text reveals Congress' intent to provide the relevant agencies with sufficient authority to transform the statute's broad aspiration into social reality. So too does a lengthy, consistent, and impassioned legislative history.

This legislative design reflects a reasonable—indeed inspired—model for attacking the often-intractable problem of racial and ethnic discrimination. On its own terms, the statute supports an action challenging policies of federal grantees that explicitly or unambiguously violate antidiscrimination norms (such as policies that on their face limit benefits or services to certain races). With regard to more subtle forms of discrimination (such as schemes that limit benefits or services on ostensibly race-neutral grounds but have the predictable and perhaps intended consequence of materially benefiting some races at the expense of others), the statute does not establish a static approach but instead empowers the relevant agencies to evaluate social circumstances to determine whether there is a need for stronger measures.[13] Such an approach builds into the law flexibility, an

---

13. It is important, in this context, to note that regulations prohibiting policies that have a disparate impact are not necessarily aimed only—or even primarily—at unintentional discrimination. Many policies whose very intent is to discriminate are framed in a race-neutral manner. It is often difficult to obtain direct evidence of this motivating animus. Therefore, an agency decision to adopt disparate-impact regulations may very well reflect a determination by that agency that substantial intentional discrimination pervades the industry it is charged with regulating but that such discrimination is difficult to prove directly. As I have stated before: "Frequently the most probative evidence of intent will be objective evidence of what actually happened rather than evidence describing the subjective state of mind of the actor." Washington v. Davis, 426 U.S. 229, 253 (1976)

ability to make nuanced assessments of complex social realities, and an admirable willingness to credit the possibility of progress.

The "effects" regulations at issue in this case represent the considered judgment of the relevant agencies that discrimination on the basis of race, ethnicity, and national origin by federal contractees are significant social problems that might be remedied, or at least ameliorated, by the application of a broad prophylactic rule. Given the judgment underlying them, the regulations are inspired by, at the service of, and inseparably intertwined with § 601's antidiscrimination mandate. Contrary to the majority's suggestion, they "apply" § 601's prohibition on discrimination just as surely as the intentional discrimination regulations the majority concedes are privately enforceable.

To the extent that our prior cases mischaracterize the relationship between §§ 601 and 602, they err on the side of underestimating, not overestimating, the connection between the two provisions. While our cases have explicitly adopted an understanding of § 601's scope that is somewhat narrower than the reach of the regulations, they have done so in an unorthodox and somewhat haphazard fashion. . . .

In addition, these Title VI cases seemingly ignore the well-established principle of administrative law that is now most often described as the "*Chevron* doctrine." See Chevron U.S.A. Inc. v. Natural Resources Defense Council, Inc., 467 U.S. 837 (1984). In most other contexts, when the agencies charged with administering a broadly-worded statute offer regulations interpreting that statute or giving concrete guidance as to its implementation, we treat their interpretation of the statute's breadth as controlling unless it presents an unreasonable construction of the statutory text. While there may be some dispute as to the boundaries of *Chevron* deference, it is paradigmatically appropriate when Congress has clearly delegated agencies the power to issue regulations with the force of law and established formal procedures for the promulgation of such regulations.

If we were writing on a blank slate, we might very well conclude that *Chevron* and similar cases decided both before and after *Guardians* provide the proper framework for understanding the structure of Title VI. Under such a reading there would be no incongruity between §§ 601 and 602. Instead, we would read § 602 as granting the federal agencies responsible for distributing federal funds the authority to issue regulations interpreting § 601 on the assumption that their construction will—if reasonable—be incorporated into our understanding of § 601's meaning. To resolve this case, however, it is unnecessary to answer the question whether our cases interpreting the reach of § 601 should be reinterpreted in light of *Chevron*. If one understands the relationship between §§ 601 and 602 through the

(concurring opinion). On this reading, Title VI simply accords the agencies the power to decide whether or not to credit such evidence.

prism of *either Chevron* or our prior Title VI cases, the question presented all but answers itself. If the regulations promulgated pursuant to § 602 are either an authoritative construction of § 601's meaning or prophylactic rules necessary to actualize the goals enunciated in § 601, then it makes no sense to differentiate between private actions to enforce § 601 and private actions to enforce § 602. There is but one private action to enforce Title VI, and we already know that such an action exists. See *Cannon*, 441 U.S. at 703.

III

The majority couples its flawed analysis of the structure of Title VI with an uncharitable understanding of the substance of the divide between those on this Court who are reluctant to interpret statutes to allow for private rights of action and those who are willing to do so if the claim of right survives a rigorous application of the criteria set forth in Cort v. Ash, 422 U.S. 66 (1975). As the majority narrates our implied right of action jurisprudence, the Court's shift to a more skeptical approach represents the rejection of a common-law judicial activism in favor of a principled recognition of the limited role of a contemporary "federal tribunal." According to its analysis, the recognition of an implied right of action when the text and structure of the statute do not absolutely compel such a conclusion is an act of judicial self-indulgence. As much as we would like to help those disadvantaged by discrimination, we must resist the temptation to pour ourselves "one last drink." To do otherwise would be to "venture beyond Congress's intent."

Overwrought imagery aside, it is the majority's approach that blinds itself to congressional intent. While it remains true that, if Congress intends a private right of action to support statutory rights, "the far better course is for it to specify as much when it creates those rights," *Cannon*, 441 U.S. at 717, its failure to do so does not absolve us of the responsibility to endeavor to discern its intent. In a series of cases since *Cort* v. *Ash*, we have laid out rules and developed strategies for this task.

The very existence of these rules and strategies assumes that we will sometimes find manifestations of an implicit intent to create such a right. Our decision in *Cannon* represents one such occasion. As the *Cannon* opinion iterated and reiterated, the question whether the plaintiff had a right of action that could be asserted in federal court was a "question of statutory construction," 441 U.S. at 688, see also id., at 717 (Rehnquist, J., concurring), not a question of policy for the Court to decide. Applying the *Cort* v. *Ash* factors, we examined the nature of the rights at issue, the text and structure of the statute, and the relevant legislative history. Our conclusion was that Congress unmistakably intended a private right of action to enforce both Title IX and Title VI. Our reasoning—and, as I have demonstrated, our holding—was equally applicable to intentional discrimination and disparate impact claims. . . .

In order to impose its own preferences as to the availability of judicial remedies, the Court today adopts a methodology that blinds itself to important evidence of congressional intent. It is one thing for the Court to ignore the import of our holding in *Cannon*, as the breadth of that precedent is a matter upon which reasonable jurists may differ. It is entirely another thing for the majority to ignore the reasoning of that opinion and the evidence contained therein, as those arguments and that evidence speak directly to the question at issue today. As I stated above, *Cannon* carefully explained that both Title VI and Title IX were intended to benefit a particular class of individuals, that the purposes of the statutes would be furthered rather than frustrated by the implication of a private right of action, and that the legislative histories of the statutes support the conclusion that Congress intended such a right. Those conclusions and the evidence supporting them continue to have force today.

Similarly, if the majority is genuinely committed to deciphering congressional intent, its unwillingness to even consider evidence as to the context in which Congress legislated is perplexing. Congress does not legislate in a vacuum. As the respondent and the Government suggest, and as we have held several times, the objective manifestations of congressional intent to create a private right of action must be measured in light of the enacting Congress' expectations as to how the judiciary might evaluate the question. See Thompson v. Thompson, 484 U.S. 174 (1988); Merrill Lynch, Pierce, Fenner & Smith, Inc. v. Curran, 456 U.S. 353, 378–79 (1982); *Cannon*, 441 U.S. at 698–99.

At the time Congress was considering Title VI, it was normal practice for the courts to infer that Congress intended a private right of action whenever it passed a statute designed to protect a particular class that did not contain enforcement mechanisms which would be thwarted by a private remedy. See *Merrill Lynch*, 456 U.S. at 374–75 (discussing this history). Indeed, the very year Congress adopted Title VI, this Court specifically stated that "it is the duty of the courts to be alert to provide such remedies as are necessary to make effective the congressional purpose." J. I. Case Co. v. Borak, 377 U.S. 426, 433 (1964). Assuming, as we must, that Congress was fully informed as to the state of the law, the contemporary context presents important evidence as to Congress' intent—evidence the majority declines to consider.

Ultimately, respect for Congress' prerogatives is measured in deeds, not words. Today, the Court coins a new rule, holding that a private cause of action to enforce a statute does not encompass a substantive regulation issued to effectuate that statute unless the regulation does nothing more than "authoritatively construe the statute itself." This rule might be proper if we were the kind of "common-law court" the majority decries, inventing private rights of action never intended by Congress. For if we are not construing a statute, we certainly may refuse to create a remedy for violations of federal regulations. But if we are faithful to the commitment to discerning congressional intent that all Members of this Court profess, the distinction is untenable. There is simply no reason to assume that Congress contemplated, desired, or adopted a distinction between regulations that merely parrot statutory text and broader regulations that are authorized by statutory text.

IV

Beyond its flawed structural analysis of Title VI and an evident antipathy toward implied rights of action, the majority offers little affirmative support for its conclusion that Congress did not intend to create a private remedy for violations of the Title VI regulations. The Court offers essentially two reasons for its position. First, it attaches significance to the fact that the "rights-creating" language in § 601 that defines the classes protected by the statute is not repeated in § 602. But, of course, there was no reason to put that language in § 602 because it is perfectly obvious that the regulations authorized by § 602 must be designed to protect precisely the same people protected by § 601. Moreover, it is self-evident that, linguistic niceties notwithstanding, any statutory provision whose stated purpose is to "effectuate" the eradication of racial and ethnic discrimination has as its "focus" those individuals who, absent such legislation, would be subject to discrimination.

Second, the Court repeats the argument advanced and rejected in *Cannon* that the express provision of a fund cut-off remedy "suggests that Congress intended to preclude others." In *Cannon*, 441 U.S. at 704–08, we carefully explained why the presence of an explicit mechanism to achieve one of the statute's objectives (ensuring that federal funds are not used "to support discriminatory practices") does not preclude a conclusion that a private right of action was intended to achieve the statute's other principal objective ("to provide individual citizens effective protection against those practices"). In support of our analysis, we offered policy arguments, cited evidence from the legislative history, and noted the active support of the relevant agencies. In today's decision, the Court does not grapple with—indeed, barely acknowledges—our rejection of this argument in *Cannon*.

Like much else in its opinion, the present majority's unwillingness to explain its refusal to find the reasoning in *Cannon* persuasive suggests that today's decision is the unconscious product of the majority's profound distaste for implied causes of action rather than an attempt to discern the intent of the Congress that enacted Title VI of the Civil Rights Act of 1964. Its colorful disclaimer of any interest in "venturing beyond Congress's intent" has a hollow ring.

V

The question the Court answers today was only an open question in the most technical sense. Given the prevailing consensus in the Courts of Appeals, the Court should have declined to take this case. Having granted certiorari, the Court should have answered the question differently by simply according respect to our prior decisions. But most importantly, even if it were to ignore all of our post–1964 writing, the Court should have answered the question differently on the merits.

I respectfully dissent.

NOTE ON *ALEXANDER v. SANDOVAL*

An interesting question concerns the intersection of *Alexander v. Sandoval* and the Supreme Court's interpretation of 42 U.S.C. § 1983 to authorize a private right of action against anyone who violates a federal statute while acting "under color of" state law. Maine v. Thiboutot, 448 U.S. 1 (1980) (see casebook, page 173, Note 7). Obviously, the defendants in *Sandoval* were state officers and so could have been sued under § 1983 without resort to an "implied" cause of action under Title VI. It was this possibility that led Justice Stevens to remark, in dissent:

> [T]o the extent that the majority denies relief to the respondents merely because they neglected to mention 42 U.S.C. § 1983 in framing their Title VI claim, this case is something of a sport. Litigants who in the future wish to enforce the Title VI regulations against state actors in all likelihood must only reference § 1983 to obtain relief; indeed, the plaintiffs in this case (or other similarly situated individuals) presumably retain the option of re-challenging Alabama's English-only policy in a complaint that invokes § 1983 even after today's decision.

Picking up on Justice Stevens's suggestion, the District Court in South Camden Citizens in Action v. New Jersey Department of Environmental Protection, 145 F.Supp.2d 446 (D.N.J.2001), held that *Sandoval* does not preclude § 1983 actions to enforce § 602 regulations:

> As the Supreme Court has observed, the inquiry whether an action may be brought under § 1983 is separate and distinct from the inquiry courts must perform to determine whether Congress intended that a statute create an implied private right of action, which is the inquiry the Supreme Court undertook in *Sandoval*. To discern whether an implied right of action exists under a particular statute, courts employ the four-factor test articulated by the Supreme Court in Cort v. Ash, 422 U.S. 66 (1975).... The *Cort* test "reflects a concern, grounded in separation of powers, that Congress rather than the courts control the availability of remedies for violations of statutes." While the *Cort* test ... considers whether the provision was enacted for the benefit of the putative plaintiff, the central inquiry of the *Cort* test is the second prong of that test, specifically, "whether Congress intended to create, either expressly or by implication, a private cause of action." ... In contrast, the [inquiry under § 1983] is concerned

with whether the statute creates a federal right in favor of the plaintiff. Whether the statute provides a remedy is of less concern because § 1983 itself provides the remedy.... Section 1983 explicitly authorizes a private right of action, thereby obviating the need, in cases brought under § 1983, for courts to scrutinize the underlying statute giving rise to the claim to determine whether plaintiffs have a private right of action under that statute itself....[a]

Is it conceivable that *Sandoval* actually involved only a pleading error in the plaintiffs' failure to invoke § 1983? If the Justices in the *Sandoval* majority intend to say more than that, they will eventually have to specify what they mean to say. One possibility is that regulations prohibiting disparate impact are not valid under either § 601 or § 602, in which case no question of private enforcement arises. Alternatively, if they are unwilling to strike down disparate-impact regulations altogether, they will have to find not only that Title VI does not itself create a private right of action to enforce those regulations but also, and more controversially, that the statutory remedies provided by Title VI somehow preclude and limit the express cause of action under § 1983. For more detailed discussion of the latter question, see the materials in Chapter IX, Section 4C, on the enforceability of non-constitutional rights under 42 U.S.C. § 1983.

Page 212, add a new Note 3 and renumber the remaining notes:

3. *Correctional Services Corp. v. Malesko.* In Correctional Services Corp. v. Malesko, 534 U.S. 61 (2001), a divided Supreme Court refused to extend *Bivens* to actions against a private corporation operating a halfway house under contract with the Federal Bureau of Prisons. An inmate assigned to that facility developed a heart condition and was given special permission to use the elevator to reach his room on the fifth floor. On one occasion, however, an employee of the corporation refused to let him use the elevator. The inmate climbed the stairs and suffered a heart attack. Malesko then sued CSC and its employees under the authority of *Bivens*. The *Bivens* claims against various individual defendants were

---

a. For similar cases, relied on in *South Camden Citizens in Action*, see Fay v. South Colonie Cent. School District, 802 F.2d 21, 33 (2d Cir.1986) (holding that, although the Family Educational Rights and Privacy Act, 20 U.S.C. § 1232g, does not support inference of a private cause of action, plaintiffs can nonetheless bring suit under § 1983 to enforce rights created by that statute); Chan v. City of New York, 1 F.3d 96 (2d Cir.1993) (holding that, although the Housing and Community Development Act did not create a private right of action, it did create substantive rights that could be enforced against state officers under § 1983); Mallett v. Wisconsin Div. of Vocational Rehab., 130 F.3d 1245, 1248–57 (7th Cir.1997) (finding no private right of action under the Rehabilitation Act but determining that its provisions could be enforced via § 1983); Keaukaha–Panaewa Comm. Ass'n v. Hawaiian Homes Comm'n, 739 F.2d 1467, 1470–71 (9th Cir.1984) (again finding no private right of action under a statute but concluding that its terms could be enforced under § 1983).

dismissed on statute-of-limitations grounds, but the action against the corporation triggered a different statute and was allowed to proceed.

In FDIC v. Meyer, 510 U.S. 471 (1994), the Court held that *Bivens* actions would not lie against federal agencies, as distinct from the individual officers employed by them. In *Malesko*, the Court extended that reasoning to private corporations operating under color of federal law. Speaking for the Court, the Chief Justice said that the "purpose of *Bivens* is to deter *individual* federal officers from committing constitutional violations" (emphasis added). The Court also noted that the plaintiff in *Malesko* did not lack for alternative remedies, as the corporation could have been sued for negligence under state law. Justices Stevens, Souter, Ginsburg, and Breyer, dissented.

CHAPTER III

CONGRESSIONAL CONTROL OF THE FEDERAL COURTS

Page 215, add a footnote after the words "constitutional rights" in the second sentence of the first full paragraph:

e. Erwin Chemerinsky, A Framework for Analyzing the Constitutionality of Restrictions on Federal Court Jurisdiction in Immigration Cases, 29 U. Memphis L. Rev. 295 (1999), suggests that the Court will need to address this issue because of the exclusions of immigration cases from federal court jurisdiction in the 1996 Antiterrorism and Effective Death Penalty Act, Pub. L. No. 104-132, 110 Stat. 1214 (1996), and the Illegal Immigration Reform and Immigrant Responsibility Act of 1996, Pub. L. No. 104-208, div. C, 110 Stat. 3009 (1996).

Page 218, add to the second sentence of footnote f:

Julian Velasco, Congressional Control Over Federal Court Jurisdiction: A Defense of the Traditional View, 46 Catholic U. L. Rev. 671 (1997).

Page 218, add at the end of footnote f:

Of course, control over jurisdiction is not the only mechanism through which Congress can influence the actions of the federal courts. See Todd D. Peterson, Controlling the Federal Courts Through the Appropriations Process, [1998] Wisc. L. Rev. 993.

Page 224, add to the end of footnote c:

For treatments of *Klein* provoked by 1996 legislation in which Congress restricted federal court authority to impose remedial decrees on state prison systems, to grant writs of habeas corpus, and to review deportation orders, see Lawrence G. Sager, *Klein*'s First Principle: A Proposed Solution, 86 Geo. L.J. 2525 (1998), and the response in Daniel J. Meltzer, Congress, Courts, and Constitutional Remedies, 86 Geo. L.J. 2537 (1998). For additional articles in the same symposium addressing the issues covered in these and the following series of Notes, see Vicki C. Jackson, Introduction: Congressional Control of Jurisdiction and the Future of the Federal Courts—Opposition, Agreement, and Hierarchy, 86 Geo. L.J. 2445 (1998); David Cole, Jurisdiction and Liberty: Habeas Corpus and Due Process as Limits on Congress's Control of Federal Jurisdiction, 86 Geo. L.J. 2481 (1998); John Harrison, Jurisdiction, Congressional Power, and Constitutional Remedies, 86 Geo. L.J. 2513 (1998); Judith Resnick, The Federal Courts and Congress: Additional Sources, Alternative Texts, and Altered Aspirations, 86 Geo. L.J. 2589 (1998).

Page 232, add to the second sentence of footnote e:

Julian Velasco, Congressional Control Over Federal Court Jurisdiction: A Defense of the Traditional View, 46 Catholic U. L. Rev. 671 (1997).

Page 232, add to the end of the first paragraph of footnote e:

For a friendly elaboration of the Amar position, see Robert J. Pushaw, Jr., Congressional Power Over Federal Court Jurisdiction: A Defense of the Neo–Federalist Interpretation of Article III, [1997] Brigham Young L. Rev. 847.

Page 232, add to the end of the second paragraph of footnote e:

See also David E. Engdahl, Intrinsic Limits of Congress' Power Regarding the Judicial Branch, 1999 B.Y.U. L. Rev. 75. Engdahl criticizes Amar's analysis, suggests that one key to the scope of Congressional power over federal court jurisdiction lies in properly understanding the necessary and proper clause, and concludes that "[w]hile Congress may create or abolish inferior tribunals and may shuffle assignments among such federal courts as exist, no category of subject matter jurisdiction, once vested, may be divested from the judiciary as a whole, except by constitutional amendment."

Page 232, add to the end of the third paragraph of footnote e:

See also Evan Tsen Lee, On the Received Wisdom in Federal Courts, 147 U. Pa. L. Rev. 1111 (1999), which criticizes the received wisdom that constitutional claims should be channeled to state courts and "attempts to make an affirmative case for the normative attractiveness of a system that generally guarantees federal constitutional claimants at least one full hearing in federal court."

Page 235, add to footnote o:

For additional entries in the ongoing debate, see Evan Caminker, Allocating the Judicial Power in a "Unified Judiciary", 78 Tex. L. Rev. 1513 (2000); James S. Liebman and William F. Ryan, "Some Effectual Power": The Quantity and Quality of Decisionmaking Required of Article III Courts, 98 Colum. L. Rev. 696 (1998); James E. Pfander, Jurisdiction-Stripping and the Supreme Court's Power to Supervise Inferior Tribunals, 78 Tex. L. Rev. 1433 (2000); Jordan Steiker, Habeas Exceptionalism, 78 Tex. L. Rev. 1703 (2000); Mark Strasser, Taking Exception to Traditional Exceptions Clause Jurisprudence: On Congress's Power to Limit the Court's Jurisdiction, 2001 Utah L. Rev. 125; Ernest A. Young, Constitutional Avoidance, Resistance Norms, and the Preservation of Judicial Review, 78 Tex. L. Rev. 1549 (2000).

Page 236, add at the end of footnote t:

For further discussion of this issue, see Louise Weinberg, The Article III Box: The Power of "Congress" to Attack the "Jurisdiction" of "Federal Courts", 78 Tex. L. Rev. 1405 (2000).

Page 238, add at the end of footnote y:

See also Kevin M. Clermont & Theodore Eisenberg, Do Case Outcomes Really Reveal Anything About the Legal System? Win Rates and Removal Jurisdiction, 83 Cornell L. Rev. 581 (1998), which examines statistics leading them to the conclusions that forum effects outcome and removal takes defendants "to a forum much more favorable."

Page 239, add before Section 2:

Calcano–Martinez v. Immigration and Naturalization Service

Supreme Court of the United States, 2001.
533 U.S. 348.

■ JUSTICE STEVENS delivered the opinion of the Court.

Deboris Calcano–Martinez, Sergio Madrid, and Fazila Khan are all lawful permanent residents of the United States subject to administratively final orders of removal. They conceded that they are deportable based upon their past criminal convictions, but each filed both a petition for review in the Second Circuit pursuant to 8 U.S.C. § 1252(a)(1) (1994 ed., Supp. V) and a habeas corpus petition in the District Court pursuant to 28 U.S.C. § 2241 in order to challenge the Board of Immigration Appeals' determination that, as a matter of law, petitioners were ineligible to apply for a discretionary waiver of deportation under former § 212(c) of the Immigration and Nationality Act, 66 Stat. 182, 8 U.S.C. § 1182(c) (1994 ed.). Their petitions for review were consolidated in the Court of Appeals, which subsequently dismissed the petitions for lack of jurisdiction, holding that petitioners could nevertheless pursue their constitutional and statutory claims in a district court habeas action brought pursuant to 28 U.S.C. § 2241. We granted certiorari in this case and in INS v. St. Cyr, 533 U.S. 289 (2001) [the next main case], in order to comprehensively consider whether aliens in the petitioners' position may seek relief in the Court of Appeals (pursuant to 8 U.S.C. § 1252(a)(1)); in the district court (pursuant to 28 U.S.C. § 2241); or not at all. For the reasons stated below and in our opinion in *INS v. St. Cyr*, we agree with the Court of Appeals that it lacks jurisdiction to hear the petitions for direct review at issue in this case and that petitioners must, therefore, proceed with their petitions for habeas corpus if they wish to obtain relief.

As part of the Illegal Immigration Reform and Immigrant Responsibility Act of 1996 (IIRIRA), 110 Stat. 3009–546, Congress adopted new provisions governing the judicial review of immigration orders. See 8 U.S.C. § 1252 (1994 ed., Supp. V) (codifying these procedures). Like the prior statute, the new provision vests the courts of appeals with the authority to consider petitions challenging "final orders" commanding the "removal" of aliens from the United States. § 1252(a)(1).[1] However, unlike the previous provisions, the new statute expressly precludes the courts of appeals from

---

[1] An additional difference between the old and the new statute with regard to petitions for review is one of nomenclature. In keeping with a statute-wide change in terminology, the new provision refers to orders of "removal" rather than orders of "deportation" or "exclusion." Compare 8 U.S.C. § 1252(a)(1) (1994 ed., Supp. V), with § 1105a (1994 ed.).

exercising "jurisdiction to review any final order of removal against any alien who is removable by reason of" a conviction for certain criminal offenses, including any aggravated felony. § 1252(a)(2)(C).[2]

As petitioners in this case were convicted of "aggravated felonies" within the meaning of the relevant statutes, the plain language of § 1252(a)(2)(C) fairly explicitly strips the courts of appeals of jurisdiction to hear their claims on petitions for direct review. Without much discussion, the Court of Appeals so held.

Before this Court, petitioners primarily argue that constitutional considerations and background principles of statutory interpretation require that they be afforded some forum for the adjudication of the merits of their claims. They devote the bulk of their briefs to arguing that the Court of Appeals—motivated by these concerns—properly interpreted IIRIRA's jurisdiction-stripping provision not to preclude aliens such as petitioners from pursuing habeas relief pursuant to 28 U.S.C. § 2241. In the alternative, they argue that we might construe the same provisions as stripping jurisdiction from the courts of appeals over only some matters, leaving in place their jurisdiction to directly review petitions raising claims previously cognizable under § 2241.

We agree with petitioners that leaving aliens without a forum for adjudicating claims such as those raised in this case would raise serious constitutional questions. We also agree with petitioners—and the Court of Appeals—that these concerns can best be alleviated by construing the jurisdiction-stripping provisions of that statute not to preclude aliens such as petitioners from pursuing habeas relief pursuant to § 2241. See *INS v. St. Cyr.*

Finding no support in the text or history of § 1252 for concluding that the courts of appeals retain jurisdiction to hear petitions such as those brought in this case, but concluding that Congress has not spoken with sufficient clarity to strip the district courts of jurisdiction to hear habeas petitions raising identical claims, we affirm the judgment of the Court of Appeals in all particulars.

It is so ordered.

---

2. The scope of this preclusion is not entirely clear. Though the text of the provision is quite broad, it is not without its ambiguities. Throughout this litigation, the government has conceded that the courts of appeals have the power to hear petitions challenging the factual determinations thought to trigger the jurisdiction-stripping provision (such as whether an individual is an alien and whether he or she has been convicted of an "aggravated felony" within the meaning of the statute). In addition, the government has also conceded that the courts of appeals retain jurisdiction to review "substantial constitutional challenges" raised by aliens who come within the strictures of § 1252(a)(2)(C). As the petitions in this case do not raise any of these types of issues, we need not address this point further. Nonetheless, it remains instructive that the government acknowledges that background principles of statutory construction and constitutional concerns must be considered in determining the scope of IIRIRA's jurisdiction-stripping provisions.

■ JUSTICE O'CONNOR, dissenting.

For the reasons stated in my dissenting opinion in the companion case of INS v. St. Cyr, 533 U.S. 289 (2001), I agree with Justice Scalia's proposed disposition of the instant case.

■ JUSTICE SCALIA, with whom THE CHIEF JUSTICE and JUSTICE THOMAS join, dissenting.

For the reasons stated in my dissenting opinion in the companion case of INS v. St. Cyr, 533 U.S. 289 (2001), I would vacate the judgment of the court below and remand with instructions to dismiss for want of jurisdiction, with prejudice to petitioners Calcano–Martinez's and Madrid's refiling in the District Court.

Immigration and Naturalization Service v. St. Cyr
Supreme Court of the United States, 2001.
533 U.S. 289.

■ JUSTICE STEVENS delivered the opinion of the Court.

Both the Antiterrorism and Effective Death Penalty Act of 1996 (AEDPA), enacted on April 24, 1996, 110 Stat. 1214, and the Illegal Immigration Reform and Immigrant Responsibility Act of 1996 (IIRIRA), enacted on September 30, 1996, 110 Stat. 3009–546, contain comprehensive amendments to the Immigration and Nationality Act (INA), 66 Stat. 163, as amended, 8 U.S.C. § 1101 et seq. This case raises two important questions about the impact of those amendments. The first question is a procedural one, concerning the effect of those amendments on the availability of habeas corpus jurisdiction under 28 U.S.C. § 2241. The second question is a substantive one, concerning the impact of the amendments on conduct that occurred before their enactment and on the availability of discretionary relief from deportation.

Respondent, Enrico St. Cyr, is a citizen of Haiti who was admitted to the United States as a lawful permanent resident in 1986. Ten years later, on March 8, 1996, he pled guilty in a state court to a charge of selling a controlled substance in violation of Connecticut law. That conviction made him deportable. Under pre-AEDPA law applicable at the time of his conviction, St. Cyr would have been eligible for a waiver of deportation at the discretion of the Attorney General. However, removal proceedings against him were not commenced until April 10, 1997, after both AEDPA and IIRIRA became effective, and, as the Attorney General interprets those statutes, he no longer has discretion to grant such a waiver.

In his habeas corpus petition, respondent has alleged that the restrictions on discretionary relief from deportation contained in the 1996 statutes do not apply to removal proceedings brought against an alien who pled guilty to a deportable crime before their enactment. The District Court accepted jurisdiction of his application and agreed with his submission. In accord with the decisions of four other Circuits, the Court of Appeals for the Second Circuit affirmed. The importance of both questions warranted our grant of certiorari.

I

The character of the pre-AEDPA and pre-IIRIRA law that gave the Attorney General discretion to waive deportation in certain cases is relevant to our appraisal of both the substantive and the procedural questions raised by the petition of the Immigration and Naturalization Service (INS). We shall therefore preface our discussion of those questions with an overview of the sources, history, and scope of that law.

Subject to certain exceptions, § 3 of the Immigration Act of 1917 excluded from admission to the United States several classes of aliens, including, for example, those who had committed crimes "involving moral turpitude." 39 Stat. 875. The seventh exception provided "[t]hat aliens returning after a temporary absence to an unrelinquished United States domicile of seven consecutive years may be admitted in the discretion of the Secretary of Labor, and under such conditions as he may prescribe." Id., at 878.[2] Although that provision applied literally only to exclusion proceedings, and although the deportation provisions of the statute did not contain a similar provision, the Immigration and Naturalization Service (INS) relied on § 3 to grant relief in deportation proceedings involving aliens who had departed and returned to this country after the ground for deportation arose.[3]

Section 212 of the Immigration and Nationality Act of 1952, which replaced and roughly paralleled § 3 of the 1917 Act, excluded from the United States several classes of aliens, including those convicted of offenses involving moral turpitude or the illicit traffic in narcotics. See 66 Stat. 182–87. As with the prior law, this section was subject to a proviso granting the Attorney General broad discretion to admit excludable aliens. See id., at 187. That proviso, codified at 8 U.S.C. § 1182(c), stated:

> Aliens lawfully admitted for permanent residence who temporarily proceeded abroad voluntarily and not under an order of deportation, and who are returning to a lawful unrelinquished domicile of seven consecutive years, may be admitted in the discretion of the Attorney General....

Like § 3 of the 1917 Act, § 212(c) was literally applicable only to exclusion proceedings, but it too has been interpreted by the Board of Immigration

---

2. The INS was subsequently transferred to the Department of Justice. As a result, the powers previously delegated to the Secretary of Labor were transferred to the Attorney General.

3. The exercise of discretion was deemed a nunc pro tunc correction of the record of reentry. In approving of this construction, the Attorney General concluded that strictly limiting the seventh exception to exclusion proceedings would be "capricious and whimsical."

Appeals (BIA) to authorize any permanent resident alien with "a lawful unrelinquished domicile of seven consecutive years" to apply for a discretionary waiver from deportation. If relief is granted, the deportation proceeding is terminated and the alien remains a permanent resident.

The extension of § 212(c) relief to the deportation context has had great practical importance, because deportable offenses have historically been defined broadly. For example, under the Immigration and Nationality Act, aliens are deportable upon conviction for two crimes of "moral turpitude" (or for one such crime if it occurred within five years of entry into the country and resulted in a jail term of at least one year). See 8 U.S.C. §§ 1227(a)(2)(A)(i)-(ii) (1994 ed., Supp. V). In 1988, Congress further specified that an alien is deportable upon conviction for any "aggravated felony," Anti–Drug Abuse Act of 1988, 102 Stat. 4469–70, § 1227(a)(2)(A)(iii), which was defined to include numerous offenses without regard to how long ago they were committed.[4] Thus, the class of aliens whose continued residence in this country has depended on their eligibility for § 212(c) relief is extremely large, and not surprisingly, a substantial percentage of their applications for § 212(c) relief have been granted.[5] Consequently, in the period between 1989 and 1995 alone, § 212(c) relief was granted to over 10,000 aliens.[6]

---

4. While the term has always been defined expansively, it was broadened substantially by IIRIRA. For example, as amended by that statute, the term includes all convictions for theft or burglary for which a term of imprisonment of at least one year is imposed and all convictions involving fraud or deceit in which the loss to the victim exceeds $10,000. In addition, the term includes any "crime of violence" resulting in a prison sentence of at least one year and that phrase is itself broadly defined. See 18 U.S.C. § 16 ("[A]n offense that has as an element the use, attempted use, or threatened use of physical force against the person or property of another," or "any other offense that is a felony and that, by its nature, involves a substantial risk that physical force against the person or property of another may be used in the course of committing the offense").

5. See, e.g., Julie K. Rannik, The Anti–Terrorism and Effective Death Penalty Act of 1996: A Death Sentence for the 212(c) Waiver, 28 Miami Inter–Am. L.Rev. 123, 150, n. 80 (1996) (providing statistics indicating that 51.5% of the applications for which a final decision was reached between 1989 and 1995 were granted).

In developing these changes, the Board developed criteria, comparable to common-law rules, for deciding when deportation is appropriate. Those criteria, which have been set forth in several Board opinions, include the seriousness of the offense, evidence of either rehabilitation or recidivism, the duration of the alien's residence, the impact of deportation on the family, the number of citizens in the family, and the character of any service in the Armed Forces.

6. See Rannik, at 150, n. 80. However, based on these statistics, one cannot form a reliable estimate of the number of individuals who will be affected by today's decision. Since the 1996 statutes expanded the definition of "aggravated felony" substantially—and retroactively—the number of individuals now subject to deportation absent § 212(c) relief is significantly higher than these figures would suggest. In addition, the nature of the changes (bringing under the definition more minor crimes which may have been committed many years ago) suggests that an increased percentage of applicants will meet the stated criteria for § 212(c) relief.

Three statutes enacted in recent years have reduced the size of the class of aliens eligible for such discretionary relief. In 1990, Congress amended § 212(c) to preclude from discretionary relief anyone convicted of an aggravated felony who had served a term of imprisonment of at least five years. § 511, 104 Stat. 5052 (amending 8 U.S.C. § 1182(c)). In 1996, in § 440(d) of AEDPA, Congress identified a broad set of offenses for which convictions would preclude such relief. See 110 Stat. 1277 (amending 8 U.S.C. § 1182(c)).[7] And finally, that same year, Congress passed IIRIRA. That statute, inter alia, repealed § 212(c), and replaced it with a new section that gives the Attorney General the authority to cancel removal for a narrow class of inadmissible or deportable aliens, see id., at 3009–594 (creating 8 U.S.C. § 1229b). So narrowed, that class does not include anyone previously "convicted of any aggravated felony." § 1229b(a)(3) (1994 ed., Supp. V).

In the Attorney General's opinion, these amendments have entirely withdrawn his § 212(c) authority to waive deportation for aliens previously convicted of aggravated felonies. Moreover, as a result of other amendments adopted in AEDPA and IIRIRA, the Attorney General also maintains that there is no judicial forum available to decide whether these statutes did, in fact, deprive him of the power to grant such relief. As we shall explain below, we disagree on both points. In our view, a federal court does have jurisdiction to decide the merits of the legal question, and the District Court and the Court of Appeals decided that question correctly in this case.

II

The first question we must consider is whether the District Court retains jurisdiction under the general habeas corpus statute, 28 U.S.C. § 2241, to entertain St. Cyr's challenge. His application for a writ raises a pure question of law. He does not dispute any of the facts that establish his deportability or the conclusion that he is deportable. Nor does he contend that he would have any right to have an unfavorable exercise of the Attorney General's discretion reviewed in a judicial forum. Rather, he contests the Attorney General's conclusion that, as a matter of statutory interpretation, he is not eligible for discretionary relief.

The District Court held, and the Court of Appeals agreed, that it had jurisdiction to answer that question in a habeas corpus proceeding. The INS argues, however, that four sections of the 1996 statutes—specifically, § 401(e) of AEDPA and three sections of IIRIRA (8 U.S.C. §§ 1252(a)(1); 1252(a)(2)(C), and 1252(b)(9) (1994 ed., Supp. V))—stripped the courts of jurisdiction to decide the question of law presented by respondent's habeas corpus application.

---

7. The new provision barred review for individuals ordered deported because of a conviction for an aggravated felony, for a drug conviction, for certain weapons or national security violations, and for multiple convictions involving crimes of moral turpitude. See 110 Stat. 1277.

For the INS to prevail it must overcome both the strong presumption in favor of judicial review of administrative action and the longstanding rule requiring a clear statement of congressional intent to repeal habeas jurisdiction. See Ex parte Yerger, 75 U.S. (8 Wall.) 85, 102 (1869) ("We are not at liberty to except from [habeas corpus jurisdiction] any cases not plainly excepted by law"); Felker v. Turpin, 518 U.S. 651, 660–61 (1996) (noting that "[n]o provision of Title I mentions our authority to entertain original habeas petitions," and the statute "makes no mention of our authority to hear habeas petitions filed as original matters in this Court").[10] Implications from statutory text or legislative history are not sufficient to repeal habeas jurisdiction; instead, Congress must articulate specific and unambiguous statutory directives to effect a repeal. *Ex parte Yerger*, 8 Wall., at 105 ("Repeals by implication are not favored. They are seldom admitted except on the ground of repugnancy; and never, we think, when the former act can stand together with the new act").

In this case, the plain statement rule draws additional reinforcement from other canons of statutory construction. First, as a general matter, when a particular interpretation of a statute invokes the outer limits of Congress' power, we expect a clear indication that Congress intended that result. Second, if an otherwise acceptable construction of a statute would raise serious constitutional problems, and where an alternative interpretation of the statute is "fairly possible," see Crowell v. Benson, 285 U.S. 22, 62 (1932), we are obligated to construe the statute to avoid such problems. See Ashwander v. TVA, 297 U.S. 288, 341, 345–48 (1936) (Brandeis, J., concurring).[12]

A construction of the amendments at issue that would entirely preclude review of a pure question of law by any court would give rise to substantial constitutional questions. Article I, § 9, cl. 2, of the Constitution provides: "The Privilege of the Writ of Habeas Corpus shall not be suspended, unless when in Cases of Rebellion or Invasion the public Safety may require it." Because of that Clause, some "judicial intervention in

---

10. "In traditionally sensitive areas, ... the requirement of [a] clear statement assures that the legislature has in fact faced, and intended to bring into issue, the critical matters involved in the judicial decision." Gregory v. Ashcroft, 501 U.S. 452, 461 (1991); see also William N. Eskridge, Jr. & Philip P. Frickey, Quasi-Constitutional Law: Clear Statement Rules as Constitutional Lawmaking, 45 Vand. L.Rev. 593, 597 (1992) ("[T]he Court ... has tended to create the strongest clear statement rules to confine Congress's power in areas in which Congress has the constitutional power to do virtually anything").

12. "As was stated in Hooper v. California, 155 U.S. 648, 657 (1895), '[t]he elementary rule is that every reasonable construction must be resorted to, in order to save a statute from unconstitutionality.' This approach ... also recognizes that Congress, like this Court, is bound by and swears an oath to uphold the Constitution. The courts will therefore not lightly assume that Congress intended to infringe constitutionally protected liberties or usurp power constitutionally forbidden it." Edward J. DeBartolo Corp. v. Florida Gulf Coast Building & Constr. Trades Council, 485 U.S. 568, 575 (1988).

deportation cases" is unquestionably "required by the Constitution." Heikkila v. Barber, 345 U.S. 229, 235 (1953).

Unlike the provisions of AEDPA that we construed in Felker v. Turpin, 518 U.S. 651 (1996), this case involves an alien subject to a federal removal order rather than a person confined pursuant to a state-court conviction. Accordingly, regardless of whether the protection of the Suspension Clause encompasses all cases covered by the 1867 Amendment extending the protection of the writ to state prisoners or by subsequent legal developments, at the absolute minimum, the Suspension Clause protects the writ "as it existed in 1789."[13]

At its historical core, the writ of habeas corpus has served as a means of reviewing the legality of executive detention, and it is in that context that its protections have been strongest.[14] See, e.g., Brown v. Allen, 344 U.S. 443, 533 (1953) (Jackson, J., concurring in result) ("The historic purpose of the writ has been to relieve detention by executive authorities without judicial trial"). In England prior to 1789, in the Colonies, and in this Nation during the formative years of our Government, the writ of habeas corpus was available to nonenemy aliens as well as to citizens. It enabled them to challenge executive and private detention in civil cases as well as criminal. Moreover, the issuance of the writ was not limited to challenges to the jurisdiction of the custodian, but encompassed detentions based on errors of law, including the erroneous application or interpretation of statutes. It was used to command the discharge of seamen who had a statutory exemption from impressment into the British Navy, to emancipate slaves, and to obtain the freedom of apprentices and asylum inmates. Most important, for our purposes, those early cases contain no suggestion that habeas relief in cases involving executive detention was only available for constitutional error.

Notwithstanding the historical use of habeas corpus to remedy unlawful executive action, the INS argues that this case falls outside the traditional scope of the writ at common law. It acknowledges that the writ protected an individual who was held without legal authority, but argues that the writ would not issue where "an official had statutory authorization to detain the individual but ... the official was not properly exercising his discretionary power to determine whether the individual should be re-

---

13. The fact that this Court would be required to answer the difficult question of what the Suspension Clause protects is in and of itself a reason to avoid answering the constitutional questions that would be raised by concluding that review was barred entirely. Cf. Gerald L. Neuman, Habeas Corpus, Executive Detention, and the Removal of Aliens, 98 Colum. L.Rev. 961, 980 (1998) (noting that "reconstructing habeas corpus law [for purposes of a Suspension Clause analysis] would be a difficult enterprise, given fragmentary documentation, state-by-state disuniformity, and uncertainty about how state practices should be transferred to new national institutions").

14. At common law, "[w]hile habeas review of a court judgment was limited to the issue of the sentencing court's jurisdictional competency, an attack on an executive order could raise all issues relating to the legality of the detention." Note, Developments in the Law—Federal Habeas Corpus, 83 Harv. L.Rev. 1038, 1238 (1970).

leased." In this case, the INS points out, there is no dispute that the INS had authority in law to hold St. Cyr, as he is eligible for removal. St. Cyr counters that there is historical evidence of the writ issuing to redress the improper exercise of official discretion. See Jonathan L. Hafetz, The Untold Story of Noncriminal Habeas Corpus and the 1996 Immigration Acts, 107 Yale L.J. 2509 (1998).

St. Cyr's constitutional position also finds some support in our prior immigration cases. In *Heikkila v. Barber*, the Court observed that the then-existing statutory immigration scheme "had the effect of precluding judicial intervention in deportation cases *except insofar as it was required by the Constitution*," 345 U.S., at 234–35 (emphasis added)—and that scheme, as discussed below, did allow for review on habeas of questions of law concerning an alien's eligibility for discretionary relief. Therefore, while the INS' historical arguments are not insubstantial, the ambiguities in the scope of the exercise of the writ at common law identified by St. Cyr, and the suggestions in this Court's prior decisions as to the extent to which habeas review could be limited consistent with the Constitution, convince us that the Suspension Clause questions that would be presented by the INS' reading of the immigration statutes before us are difficult and significant.

In sum, even assuming that the Suspension Clause protects only the writ as it existed in 1789, there is substantial evidence to support the proposition that pure questions of law like the one raised by the respondent in this case could have been answered in 1789 by a common law judge with power to issue the writ of habeas corpus. It necessarily follows that a serious Suspension Clause issue would be presented if we were to accept the INS's submission that the 1996 statutes have withdrawn that power from federal judges and provided no adequate substitute for its exercise. See H. M. Hart, The Power of Congress to Limit the Jurisdiction of Federal Courts: An Exercise in Dialectic, 66 Harv. L.Rev. 1362, 1395–97 (1953). The necessity of resolving such a serious and difficult constitutional issue—and the desirability of avoiding that necessity—simply reinforce the reasons for requiring a clear and unambiguous statement of constitutional intent.

Moreover, to conclude that the writ is no longer available in this context would represent a departure from historical practice in immigration law. The writ of habeas corpus has always been available to review the legality of executive detention. Federal courts have been authorized to issue writs of habeas corpus since the enactment of the Judiciary Act of 1789, and § 2241 of the Judicial Code provides that federal judges may grant the writ of habeas corpus on the application of a prisoner held "in custody in violation of the Constitution or laws or treaties of the United States." 28 U.S.C. § 2241. Before and after the enactment in 1875 of the first statute regulating immigration, 18 Stat. 477, that jurisdiction was regularly invoked on behalf of noncitizens, particularly in the immigration context.

Until the enactment of the 1952 Immigration and Nationality Act, the sole means by which an alien could test the legality of his or her deportation order was by bringing a habeas corpus action in district court.[26] In such cases, other than the question whether there was some evidence to support the order, the courts generally did not review factual determinations made by the Executive. However, they did review the Executive's legal determinations. See ... Gerald L. Neuman, Jurisdiction and the Rule of Law after the 1996 Immigration Act, 113 Harv. L.Rev.1963, 1965–1969 (2000). In case after case, courts answered questions of law in habeas corpus proceedings brought by aliens challenging Executive interpretations of the immigration laws.

Habeas courts also regularly answered questions of law that arose in the context of discretionary relief.[30] Traditionally, courts recognized a distinction between eligibility for discretionary relief, on the one hand, and the favorable exercise of discretion, on the other hand. See Neuman, 113 Harv. L.Rev., at 1991 (noting the "strong tradition in habeas corpus law ... that subjects the legally erroneous failure to exercise discretion, unlike a substantively unwise exercise of discretion, to inquiry on the writ"). Eligibility that was "governed by specific statutory standards" provided "a right to a ruling on an applicant's eligibility," even though the actual granting of relief was "not a matter of right under any circumstances, but rather is in all cases a matter of grace." Jay v. Boyd, 351 U.S. 345, 353–54 (1956). Thus, even though the actual suspension of deportation authorized by § 19(c) of the Immigration Act of 1917 was a matter of grace, in United States ex rel. Accardi v. Shaughnessy, 347 U.S. 260 (1954), we held that a deportable alien had a right to challenge the Executive's failure to exercise the discretion authorized by the law. The exercise of the District Court's habeas corpus jurisdiction to answer a pure question of law in this case is entirely consistent with the exercise of such jurisdiction in *Accardi*.

Thus, under the pre–1996 statutory scheme—and consistent with its common-law antecedents—it is clear that St. Cyr could have brought his challenge to the Board of Immigration Appeals' legal determination in a habeas corpus petition under 28 U.S.C. § 2241. The INS argues, however, that AEDPA and IIRIRA contain four provisions that express a clear and unambiguous statement of Congress' intent to bar petitions brought under § 2241, despite the fact that none of them mention that section. The first of those provisions is AEDPA's § 401(e).

While the title of § 401(e)—"Elimination of Custody Review by Habeas Corpus"—would seem to support the INS' submission, the actual text of

---

26. After 1952, judicial review of deportation orders could also be obtained by declaratory judgment actions brought in federal district court. However, in 1961, Congress acted to consolidate review in the courts of appeals.

30. Indeed, under the pre–1952 regime which provided only what *Heikkila* termed the constitutional minimum of review, on habeas lower federal courts routinely reviewed decisions under the Seventh Proviso, the statutory predecessor to § 212(c), to ensure the lawful exercise of discretion. During the same period, habeas was also used to review legal questions that arose in the context of the Government's exercise of other forms of discretionary relief under the 1917 Act.

that provision does not.[31] As we have previously noted, a title alone is not controlling. The actual text of § 401(e), unlike its title, merely repeals a subsection of the 1961 statute amending the judicial review provisions of the 1952 Immigration and Nationality Act. Neither the title nor the text makes any mention of 28 U.S.C. § 2241.

Under the 1952 Act, district courts had broad authority to grant declaratory and injunctive relief in immigration cases, including orders adjudicating deportability and those denying suspensions of deportability. The 1961 Act withdrew that jurisdiction from the district courts and provided that the procedures set forth in the Hobbs Act would be the "sole and exclusive procedure" for judicial review of final orders of deportation, subject to a series of exceptions. See 75 Stat. 651. The last of those exceptions stated that "any alien held in custody pursuant to an order of deportation may obtain review thereof by habeas corpus proceedings." See id., at 652, codified at 8 U.S.C. § 1105a(10) (repealed Sept. 30, 1996).

The INS argues that the inclusion of that exception in the 1961 Act indicates that Congress must have believed that it would otherwise have withdrawn the pre-existing habeas corpus jurisdiction in deportation cases, and that, as a result, the repeal of that exception in AEDPA in 1996 implicitly achieved that result. It seems to us, however, that the 1961 exception is best explained as merely confirming the limited scope of the new review procedures. In fact, the 1961 House Report provides that this section "in no way disturbs the Habeas Corpus Act."[32] H.R.Rep. No. 1086, 87th Cong., 1st Sess., 29 (1961). Moreover, a number of the courts that considered the interplay between the general habeas provision and INA § 106(a)(10) after the 1961 Act and before the enactment of AEDPA did not read the 1961 Act's specific habeas provision as supplanting jurisdiction under § 2241.

In any case, whether § 106(a)(10) served as an independent grant of habeas jurisdiction or simply as an acknowledgment of continued jurisdiction pursuant to § 2241, its repeal cannot be sufficient to eliminate what it

---

31. The section reads as follows:

(e) ELIMINATION OF CUSTODY REVIEW BY HABEAS CORPUS.—Section 106(a) of the Immigration and Nationality Act (8 U.S.C. 1105a(a)) is amended—

(1) in paragraph (8), by adding 'and' at the end;

(2) in paragraph (9), by striking; 'and' at the end and inserting a period; and

(3) by striking paragraph (10).
110 Stat. 1268.

32. Moreover, the focus of the 1961 amendments appears to have been the elimination of Administrative Procedure Act (APA) suits that were brought in the district court and that sought declaratory relief. See, e.g., H.R. No. 2478, 85th Cong., 2d Sess., 9 (1958) ("[H]abeas corpus is a far more expeditious judicial remedy than that of declaratory judgment"); 104 Cong. Rec. 17173 (1958) (statement of Rep. Walter) (stating that courts would be "relieved of a great burden" once declaratory actions were eliminated and noting that habeas corpus was an "expeditious" means of review).

did not originally grant—namely, habeas jurisdiction pursuant to 28 U.S.C. § 2241.[33] See *Ex parte Yerger*, 75 U.S. (8 Wall.), at 105–06 (concluding that the repeal of "an additional grant of jurisdiction" does not "operate as a repeal of jurisdiction theretofore allowed"); Ex parte McCardle, 74 U.S. (7 Wall.) 506, 515 (1869) (concluding that the repeal of portions of the 1867 statute conferring appellate jurisdiction on the Supreme Court in habeas proceedings did "not affect the jurisdiction which was previously exercised").

The INS also relies on three provisions of IIRIRA, now codified at 8 U.S.C. §§ 1252(a)(1), 1252(a)(2)(C), and 1252(b)(9). As amended by § 306 of IIRIRA, 8 U.S.C. § 1252(a)(1) (1994 ed., Supp. V) now provides that, with certain exceptions, including those set out in subsection (b) of the same statutory provision, "[j]udicial review of a final order of removal . . . is governed only by" the Hobbs Act's procedures for review of agency orders in the courts of appeals. Similarly, § 1252(b)(9), which addresses the "[c]onsolidation of questions for judicial review," provides that "[j]udicial review of all questions of law and fact, including interpretation and application of constitutional and statutory provisions, arising from any action taken or proceeding brought to remove an alien from the United States under this subchapter shall be available only in judicial review of a final order under this section." Finally, § 1252(a)(2)(C), which concerns "[m]atters not subject to judicial review," states: "Notwithstanding any other provision of law, no court shall have jurisdiction to review any final order of removal against an alien who is removable by reason of having committed" certain enumerated criminal offenses.

The term "judicial review" or "jurisdiction to review" is the focus of each of these three provisions. In the immigration context, "judicial review" and "habeas corpus" have historically distinct meanings. See Heikkila v. Barber, 345 U.S. 229 (1953). In *Heikkila*, the Court concluded that the finality provisions at issue "preclud[ed] judicial review" to the maximum extent possible under the Constitution, and thus concluded that the APA was inapplicable. Nevertheless, the Court reaffirmed the right to habeas corpus. Noting that the limited role played by the courts in habeas corpus proceedings was far narrower than the judicial review authorized by the APA, the Court concluded that "it is the scope of inquiry on habeas corpus that differentiates" habeas review from "judicial review." Both §§ 1252(a)(1) and (a)(2)(C) speak of "judicial review"—that is, full, nonhabeas review. Neither explicitly mentions habeas,[35] or 28 U.S.C. § 2241.[36] Accordingly, neither provision speaks with sufficient clarity to bar jurisdiction pursuant to the general habeas statute.

33. As the INS acknowledges, the overwhelming majority of Circuit Courts concluded that district courts retained habeas jurisdiction under § 2241 after AEDPA.

35. Contrary to the dissent, we do not think, given the longstanding distinction between "judicial review" and "habeas," that § 1252(e)(2)'s mention of habeas in the subsection governing "[j]udicial review of orders under section 1225(b)(1)" is sufficient to establish that Congress intended to abrogate the historical distinction between two terms

The INS also makes a separate argument based on 8 U.S.C. § 1252(b)(9) (1994 ed., Supp. V). We have previously described § 1252(b)(9) as a "zipper clause." Reno v. American–Arab Anti–Discrimination Committee, 525 U.S. 471, 483 (1999). Its purpose is to consolidate "judicial review" of immigration proceedings into one action in the court of appeals, but it applies only "[w]ith respect to review of an order of removal under subsection (a)(1)." 8 U.S.C. § 1252(b) (1994 ed., Supp. V). Accordingly, this provision, by its own terms, does not bar habeas jurisdiction over removal orders *not* subject to judicial review under § 1252(a)(1)—including orders against aliens who are removable by reason of having committed one or more criminal offenses. Subsection (b)(9) simply provides for the consolidation of issues to be brought in petitions for "[j]udicial review," which, as we note above, is a term historically distinct from habeas. It follows that § 1252(b)(9) does not clearly apply to actions brought pursuant to the general habeas statute, and thus cannot repeal that statute either in part or in whole.

If it were clear that the question of law could be answered in another judicial forum, it might be permissible to accept the INS' reading of § 1252. But the absence of such a forum, coupled with the lack of a clear, unambiguous, and express statement of congressional intent to preclude judicial consideration on habeas of such an important question of law, strongly counsels against adopting a construction that would raise serious constitutional questions.[38] Accordingly, we conclude that habeas jurisdiction under § 2241 was not repealed by AEDPA and IIRIRA.

III

The absence of a clearly expressed statement of congressional intent also pervades our review of the merits of St. Cyr's claim. Two important

---

of art in the immigration context when enacting IIRIRA.... At most, § 1252(e)(2) introduces additional statutory ambiguity, but ambiguity does not help the INS in this case. As we noted above, only the clearest statement of congressional intent will support the INS' position.

36. It is worth noting that in enacting the provisions of AEDPA and IIRIRA that restricted or altered judicial review, Congress did refer specifically to several different sources of jurisdiction.... At no point, however, does IIRIRA make express reference to § 2241. Given the historic use of § 2241 jurisdiction as a means of reviewing deportation and exclusion orders, Congress' failure to refer specifically to § 2241 is particularly significant.

38. The dissent argues that our decision will afford more rights to criminal aliens than to noncriminal aliens. However, as we have noted, the scope of review on habeas is considerably more limited than on APA-style review. Moreover, this case raises only a pure question of law as to respondent's statutory eligibility for discretionary relief, not, as the dissent suggests, an objection to the manner in which discretion was exercised. As to the question of timing and congruent means of review, we note that Congress could, without raising any constitutional questions, provide an adequate substitute through the courts of appeals. See, e.g., Swain v. Pressley, 430 U.S. 372, 381 (1977) ("[T]he substitution of a collateral remedy which is neither inadequate nor ineffective to test the legality of a person's detention" does not violate the Suspension Clause).

legal consequences ensued from respondent's entry of a guilty plea in March 1996: (1) He became subject to deportation, and (2) he became eligible for a discretionary waiver of that deportation under the prevailing interpretation of § 212(c). When IIRIRA went into effect in April 1997, the first consequence was unchanged except for the fact that the term "removal" was substituted for "deportation." The issue that remains to be resolved is whether IIRIRA § 304(b) changed the second consequence by eliminating respondent's eligibility for a waiver.

The INS submits that the statute resolves the issue because it unambiguously communicates Congress' intent to apply the provisions of IIRIRA's Title III–A to all removals initiated after the effective date of the statute, and, in any event, its provisions only operate prospectively and not retrospectively. The Court of Appeals held, contrary to the INS' arguments, that Congress' intentions concerning the application of the "Cancellation of Removal" procedure are ambiguous and that the statute imposes an impermissible retroactive effect on aliens who, in reliance on the possibility of § 212(c) relief, pled guilty to aggravated felonies. We agree. . . .

Plea agreements involve a quid pro quo between a criminal defendant and the government. In exchange for some perceived benefit, defendants waive several of their constitutional rights (including the right to a trial) and grant the government numerous "tangible benefits, such as promptly imposed punishment without the expenditure of prosecutorial resources." Newton v. Rumery, 480 U.S. 386, 393 n. 3 (1987). There can be little doubt that, as a general matter, alien defendants considering whether to enter into a plea agreement are acutely aware of the immigration consequences of their convictions. Given the frequency with which § 212(c) relief was granted in the years leading up to AEDPA and IIRIRA, preserving the possibility of such relief would have been one of the principal benefits sought by defendants deciding whether to accept a plea offer or instead to proceed to trial.

. . . The potential for unfairness in the retroactive application of IIRIRA § 304(b) to people like . . . St. Cyr is significant and manifest. Relying upon settled practice, the advice of counsel, and perhaps even assurances in open court that the entry of the plea would not foreclose § 212(c) relief, a great number of defendants in . . . St. Cyr's position agreed to plead guilty. Now that prosecutors have received the benefit of these plea agreements, agreements that were likely facilitated by the aliens' belief in their continued eligibility for § 212(c) relief, it would surely be contrary to "familiar considerations of fair notice, reasonable reliance, and settled expectations," Landgraf v. USI Film Products, 511 U.S. 244, 270 (1994), to hold that IIRIRA's subsequent restrictions deprive them of any possibility of such relief.

[T]he fact that § 212(c) relief is discretionary does not affect the propriety of our conclusion. There is a clear difference, for the purposes of retroactivity analysis, between facing possible deportation and facing certain deportation. Prior to AEDPA and IIRIRA, aliens like St. Cyr had a significant likelihood of receiving § 212(c) relief. Because respondent, and other aliens like him, almost certainly relied upon that likelihood in deciding whether to forgo their right to a trial, the elimination of any possibility of § 212(c) relief by IIRIRA has an obvious and severe retroactive effect.

We find nothing in IIRIRA unmistakably indicating that Congress considered the question whether to apply its repeal of § 212(c) retroactively to such aliens. We therefore hold that § 212(c) relief remains available for aliens, like respondent, whose convictions were obtained through plea agreements and who, notwithstanding those convictions, would have been eligible for § 212(c) relief at the time of their plea under the law then in effect.

The judgment is affirmed.

It is so ordered.

■ JUSTICE O'CONNOR, dissenting.

I join Parts I and III of Justice Scalia's dissenting opinion in this case. I do not join Part II because I believe that, assuming, arguendo, that the Suspension Clause guarantees some minimum extent of habeas review, the right asserted by the alien in this case falls outside the scope of that review for the reasons explained by Justice Scalia in Part II–B of his dissenting opinion. The question whether the Suspension Clause assures habeas jurisdiction in this particular case properly is resolved on this ground alone, and there is no need to say more.

■ JUSTICE SCALIA, with whom THE CHIEF JUSTICE and JUSTICE THOMAS join, and with whom JUSTICE O'CONNOR joins as to Parts I and III, dissenting.

The Court today finds ambiguity in the utterly clear language of a statute that forbids the district court (and all other courts) to entertain the claims of aliens such as respondent St. Cyr, who have been found deportable by reason of their criminal acts. It fabricates a superclear statement, "magic words" requirement for the congressional expression of such an intent, unjustified in law and unparalleled in any other area of our jurisprudence. And as the fruit of its labors, it brings forth a version of the statute that affords *criminal* aliens *more* opportunities for delay-inducing judicial review than are afforded to non-criminal aliens, or even than were afforded to criminal aliens prior to this legislation concededly designed to *expedite* their removal. Because it is clear that the law deprives us of jurisdiction to entertain this suit, I respectfully dissent.

I

In categorical terms that admit of no exception, the Illegal Immigration Reform and Immigrant Responsibility Act of 1996 (IIRIRA), 110 Stat. 3009–546, unambiguously repeals the application of 28 U.S.C. § 2241 (the general habeas corpus provision), and of all other provisions for judicial review, to deportation challenges brought by certain kinds of criminal aliens. This would have been readily apparent to the reader, had the Court at the outset of its opinion set forth the relevant provisions of IIRIRA and of its statutory predecessor, the Antiterrorism and Effective Death Penalty Act of 1996 (AEDPA), 110 Stat. 1214. I will begin by supplying that deficiency, and explaining IIRIRA's jurisdictional scheme. It begins with what we have called a channeling or " 'zipper' clause," Reno v. American–Arab Anti–Discrimination Comm., 525 U.S. 471, 483 (1999)—namely, 8 U.S.C. § 1252(b)(9) (1994 ed., Supp. V). This provision, entitled "Consolidation of questions for judicial review," provides as follows:

> Judicial review of all questions of law and fact, including interpretation and application of constitutional and statutory provisions, arising from *any action taken or proceeding brought to remove an alien* from the United States under this subchapter shall be available *only* in judicial review of a final order under this section. (Emphases added.)

In other words, *if* any review is available of any "questio[n] of law ... arising from any action taken or proceeding brought to remove an alien from the United States under this subchapter," it is available "only in judicial review of a final order under this section [§ 1252]." What kind of review does that section provide? That is set forth in § 1252(a)(1), which states:

> Judicial review of a final order of removal (other than an order of removal without a hearing pursuant to [the expedited-removal provisions for undocumented aliens arriving at the border found in] section 1225(b)(1) of this title) is governed *only* by chapter 158 of title 28 [the Hobbs Act], except as provided in subsection (b) of this section [which modifies some of the Hobbs Act provisions] and except that the court may not order the taking of additional evidence under section 2347(c) of [Title 28]. (Emphasis added.)

In other words, *if* judicial review is available, it consists *only* of the modified Hobbs Act review specified in § 1252(a)(1).

In some cases (including, as it happens, the one before us), there can be no review at all, because IIRIRA categorically and unequivocally rules out judicial review of challenges to deportation brought by certain kinds of criminal aliens. Section 1252(a)(2)(C) provides:

> Notwithstanding *any* other provision of law, *no court* shall have jurisdiction to review any final order of removal against an alien who is removable by reason of having committed [one or more enumerated] criminal offense[s] [including drug-trafficking offenses of the sort of which respondent had been convicted]. (Emphases added).

Finally, the pre-IIRIRA antecedent to the foregoing provisions—AEDPA § 401(e)—and the statutory background against which that was enacted, confirm that § 2241 habeas review, in the district court or elsewhere, has been unequivocally repealed. In 1961, Congress amended the Immigration and Nationality Act of 1952 (INA), 66 Stat. 163, by directing that the procedure for Hobbs Act review in the courts of appeals "shall apply to, and shall be the *sole and exclusive procedure for*, the judicial review of all final orders of deportation" under the INA. 8 U.S.C. § 1105a(a) (repealed Sept. 30, 1996) (emphasis added). Like 8 U.S.C. § 1252(a)(2)(C) (1994 ed., Supp. V), this provision squarely prohibited § 2241 district-court habeas review. At the same time that it enacted this provision, however, the 1961 Congress enacted a specific exception: "any alien held in custody pursuant to an order of deportation may obtain judicial review thereof by habeas corpus proceedings," 8 U.S.C. § 1105a(a)(10) (1994 ed.). (This would of course have been surplusage had § 2241 habeas review not been covered by the "sole and exclusive procedure" provision.) Section 401(e) of AEDPA repealed this narrow exception, and there is no doubt what the repeal was thought to accomplish: the provision was entitled "ELIMINATION OF CUSTODY REVIEW BY HABEAS CORPUS." It gave universal preclusive effect to the "sole and exclusive procedure" language of § 1105a(a). And it is this regime that IIRIRA has carried forward.

The Court's efforts to derive ambiguity from this utmost clarity are unconvincing. First, the Court argues that §§ 1252(a)(2)(C) and 1252(b)(9) are not as clear as one might think—that, even though they are sufficient to repeal the jurisdiction of the courts of appeals, see Calcano-Martinez v. INS, 533 U.S. 348 (2001),[1] they do not cover habeas jurisdiction in the district court, since, "[i]n the immigration context, 'judicial review' and 'habeas corpus' have historically distinct meanings." Of course § 1252(a)(2)(C) does not even use the term "judicial review" (it says "jurisdiction to review")—but let us make believe it does. The Court's contention that in this statute it does not include habeas corpus is decisively refuted by the language of § 1252(e)(2), enacted along with §§ 1252(a)(2)(C) and 1252(b)(9): "*Judicial review* of any determination made under section 1225(b)(1) of this title [governing review of expedited removal orders against undocumented aliens arriving at the border] is available in *habeas corpus* proceedings...." (Emphases added.) It is hard to imagine how Congress could have made it any clearer that, when it used the term "judicial review" in IIRIRA, it included judicial review through habeas corpus. Research into the "historical" usage of the term "judicial review" is thus quite beside the point.

But the Court is demonstrably wrong about that as well. Before IIRIRA was enacted, from 1961 to 1996, the governing immigration statutes unquestionably treated "judicial review" as encompassing review by habeas corpus. As discussed earlier, 8 U.S.C. § 1105a (1994 ed.) made Hobbs Act review "the sole and exclusive procedure for, the *judicial review*

---

1. In the course of this opinion I shall refer to some of the Court's analysis in this companion case; the two opinions are intertwined.

of all final orders of deportation" (emphasis added), but created (in subsection (a)(10)) a limited exception for habeas corpus review. Section 1105a was entitled *"Judicial review* of orders of deportation and exclusion" (emphasis added), and the exception for habeas corpus stated that "any alien held in custody pursuant to an order of deportation may obtain *judicial review* thereof by *habeas corpus* proceedings," ibid. (emphases added). Apart from this prior statutory usage, many of our own immigration cases belie the Court's suggestion that the term "judicial review," when used in the immigration context, does not include review by habeas corpus. See, e.g., United States v. Mendoza–Lopez, 481 U.S. 828, 836–37 (1987) ("[A]ny alien held in custody pursuant to an order of deportation may obtain *judicial review* of that order in a *habeas corpus* proceeding" (emphases added)); Shaughnessy v. Pedreiro, 349 U.S. 48 (1955) ("Our holding is that there is a right of *judicial review* of deportation orders *other than by habeas corpus* . . ." (emphases added)).

The only support the Court offers in support of the asserted "longstanding distinction between 'judicial review' and 'habeas,'" is language from a single opinion of this Court, Heikkila v. Barber, 345 U.S. 229 (1953). There, we "differentiate [d]" "habeas corpus" from "judicial review *as that term is used in the Administrative Procedure Act*." (Emphasis added.) But that simply asserts that habeas corpus review is different from ordinary APA review, which no one doubts. It does *not* assert that habeas corpus review is not judicial review *at all*. Nowhere does *Heikkila* make such an implausible contention.

The Court next contends that the zipper clause, § 1252(b)(9), "by its own terms, does not bar" § 2241 district-court habeas review of removal orders because the opening sentence of subsection (b) states that "[w]ith respect to review of an order of removal *under subsection (a)(1) of this section*, the following requirements apply...." (Emphasis added.) But in the broad sense, § 1252(b)(9) does "apply" "to review of an order of removal under subsection (a)(1)," because it mandates that "review of all questions of law and fact ... arising from any action taken or proceeding brought to remove an alien from the United States under this subchapter" must take place *in connection with* such review. This is "application" enough—and to insist that subsection (b)(9) be given effect only *within* the review of removal orders that takes place under subsection (a)(1), is to render it meaningless. Moreover, other of the numbered subparagraphs of subsection (b) make clear that the introductory sentence does not at all operate as a limitation upon what follows. Subsection (b)(7) specifies the procedure by which "a defendant in a criminal proceeding" charged with failing to depart after being ordered to do so may contest "the validity of [a removal] order" before trial; and subsection (b)(8) prescribes some of the prerogatives and responsibilities of the Attorney General and the alien after entry of a final removal order. These provisions have no effect if they must apply (even in the broad sense that subsection (b)(9) can be said to apply) "to review of an order of removal under subsection (a)(1)."

Unquestionably, unambiguously, and unmistakably, IIRIRA expressly supersedes § 2241's general provision for habeas jurisdiction. The Court asserts that Felker v. Turpin, 518 U.S. 651 (1996), and Ex parte Yerger, 75 U.S. (8 Wall.) 85 (1869), reflect a "longstanding rule requiring a clear statement of congressional intent to repeal habeas jurisdiction." They do no such thing. Those cases simply applied the general principle—not unique to habeas—that "[r]epeals by implication are not favored." *Felker*, supra, at 660. *Felker* held that a statute which by its terms prohibited only further review by this Court (or by an en banc court of appeals) of a court-of-appeals panel's " 'grant or denial of . . . authorization . . . to file a second or successive [habeas] application' " should not be read to imply the repeal of this Court's separate and distinct "authority to hear habeas petitions filed as original matters in this Court." *Yerger* held that an 1868 Act that by its terms "repeal[ed] only so much of the act of 1867 as authorized appeals, or the exercise of appellate jurisdiction by this court," should be read to "reach no [further than] the act of 1867," and did not repeal by implication the appellate jurisdiction conferred by the Judiciary Act of 1789 and other pre–1867 enactments. In the present case, unlike in *Felker* and *Yerger*, none of the statutory provisions relied upon requires us to imply from one statutory provision the repeal of another. All *by their terms* prohibit the judicial review at issue in this case.

The Court insists, however, that since "[n]either [§ 1252(a)(1) nor § 1252(a)(2)(C)] explicitly mentions habeas, or 28 U.S.C. § 2241," "neither provision speaks with sufficient clarity to bar jurisdiction pursuant to the general habeas statute." Even in those areas of our jurisprudence where we *have* adopted a "clear statement" rule (notably, the sovereign immunity cases to which the Court adverts), clear statement has never meant the kind of magic words demanded by the Court today—explicit reference to habeas or to § 2241—rather than reference to "judicial review" in a statute that explicitly calls habeas corpus a form of judicial review.... For the reasons discussed above, the intent to eliminate habeas jurisdiction in the present case is entirely clear, and that is all that is required.

It has happened before—too frequently, alas—that courts have distorted plain statutory text in order to produce a "more sensible" result. The unique accomplishment of today's opinion is that the result it produces is as far removed from what is sensible as its statutory construction is from the language of the text. One would have to study our statute books for a long time to come up with a more unlikely disposition. By authorizing § 2241 habeas review in the district court but foreclosing review in the court of appeals, see *Calcano-Martinez*, 533 U.S., at ___, the Court's interpretation routes all legal challenges to removal orders brought by criminal aliens to the district court, to be adjudicated under that court's § 2241 habeas authority, which specifies no time limits. After review by that court, criminal aliens will presumably have an appeal as of right to the court of appeals, and can then petition this Court for a writ of certiorari. In contrast, noncriminal aliens seeking to challenge their removal orders—for example, those charged with having been inadmissible at the time of entry, with having failed to maintain their nonimmigrant status, with having procured a visa through a marriage that was not bona fide, or with having become, within five years after the date of entry, a public charge—will still presumably be required to proceed directly to the court of appeals by way of petition for review, under the restrictive modified Hobbs Act review provisions set forth in § 1252(a)(1), including the 30-day filing deadline, see § 1252(b)(1). In fact, prior to the enactment of IIRIRA, criminal aliens also had to follow this procedure for immediate modified Hobbs Act review in the court of appeals. See 8 U.S.C. § 1105a(a) (1994 ed.). The Court has therefore succeeded in perverting a statutory scheme designed to *expedite* the removal of criminal aliens into one that now affords them *more* opportunities for (and layers of) judicial review (and hence more opportunities for delay) than are afforded *non*-criminal aliens—and more than were afforded criminal aliens prior to the enactment of IIRIRA.[4] This outcome speaks for itself; no Congress ever imagined it.

To excuse the violence it does to the statutory text, the Court invokes the doctrine of constitutional doubt, which it asserts is raised by the Suspension Clause, U.S. Const., Art. I, § 9, cl. 2. This uses one distortion to justify another, transmogrifying a doctrine designed to maintain "a just respect for the legislature," Ex parte Randolph, 20 F.Cas. 242, 254 (No. 11,558) (C.C.D.Va.1833) (Marshall, on circuit), into a means of thwarting the clearly expressed intent of the legislature. The doctrine of constitutional doubt is meant to effectuate, not to subvert, congressional intent, by giving *ambiguous* provisions a meaning that will avoid constitutional peril, and that will conform with Congress's presumed intent not to enact measures of dubious validity. The condition precedent for application of the doctrine is that the statute can *reasonably be construed* to avoid the constitutional difficulty. It is a device for interpreting what the statute says—not for *ignoring* what the statute says in order to avoid the trouble of determining whether what it says is unconstitutional. For the reasons I have set forth above, it is crystal clear that the statute before us here bars criminal aliens from obtaining judicial review, including § 2241 district-court review, of their removal orders. It is therefore also crystal clear that the doctrine of constitutional doubt has no application.

In the remainder of this opinion I address the question the Court *should* have addressed: Whether these provisions of IIRIRA are unconstitutional.

---

4. The Court disputes this conclusion by observing that "the scope of review on habeas is considerably more limited than on APA-style review" (a statement, by the way, that confirms our contention that habeas is, along with the APA, one form of judicial review). It is more limited, to be sure—but not "considerably more limited" in any respect that would disprove the fact that criminal aliens are much better off than others. In all the many cases that (like the present one) involve "question[s] of law," the Court's statutory misconstruction gives criminal aliens a preferred position.

II

A

The Suspension Clause of the Constitution, Art. I, § 9, cl. 2, provides as follows:

> The Privilege of the Writ of Habeas Corpus shall not be suspended, unless when in Cases of Rebellion or Invasion the public Safety may require it.

A straightforward reading of this text discloses that it does not guarantee any content to (or even the existence of) the writ of habeas corpus, but merely provides that the writ shall not (except in case of rebellion or invasion) be suspended. Indeed, that was precisely the objection expressed by four of the state ratifying conventions—that the Constitution failed affirmatively to guarantee a right to habeas corpus. See Rex A. Collings, Jr., Habeas Corpus for Convicts–Constitutional Right or Legislative Grace?, 40 Calif. L.Rev. 335, 340, and nn. 39–41 (1952).

To "suspend" the writ was not to fail to enact it, much less to refuse to accord it particular content. Noah Webster, in his American Dictionary of the English Language, defined it—with patriotic allusion to the constitutional text—as "[t]o cause to cease for a time from operation or effect; as, to *suspend* the habeas corpus act." Vol. 2, p. 86 (1828 ed.). See also N. Bailey, An Universal Etymological English Dictionary (1789) ("To Suspend [in *Law*] signifies a temporal stop of a man's right"); 2 S. Johnson, A Dictionary of the English Language 1958 (1773) ("to make to stop for a time"). This was a distinct abuse of majority power, and one that had manifested itself often in the Framers' experience: temporarily but entirely eliminating the "Privilege of the Writ" for a certain geographic area or areas, or for a certain class or classes of individuals....

In the present case, of course, Congress has not temporarily withheld operation of the writ, but has permanently altered its content. That is, to be sure, an act subject to majoritarian abuse, as is Congress's framing (or its determination not to frame) a habeas statute in the first place. But that is not the majoritarian abuse against which the Suspension Clause was directed. It is no more irrational to guard against the common and well known "suspension" abuse, without guaranteeing any particular habeas right that enjoys immunity from suspension, than it is, in the Equal Protection Clause, to guard against unequal application of the laws, without guaranteeing any particular law which enjoys *that* protection. And it is no more acceptable for this Court to write a habeas law, in order that the Suspension Clause might have some effect, than it would be for this Court to write other laws, in order that the Equal Protection Clause might have some effect.

The Court cites many cases which it says establish that it is a "serious and difficult constitutional issue" whether the Suspension Clause prohibits the elimination of habeas jurisdiction effected by IIRIRA. Every one of those cases, however, pertains not to the meaning of the Suspension Clause, but to the content of the habeas corpus provision of the United States Code, which is quite a different matter. The closest the Court can come is a statement in one of those cases to the effect that the Immigration Act of 1917 "had the effect of precluding judicial intervention in deportation cases except insofar as it was required by the Constitution," *Heikkila*, 345 U.S., at 234–35. That statement (1) was pure dictum, since the Court went on to hold that the judicial review of petitioner's deportation order was unavailable; (2) does not specify to *what* extent judicial review *was* "required by the Constitution," which could (as far as the Court's holding was concerned) be zero; and, most important of all, (3) does not refer to the Suspension Clause, so could well have had in mind the due process limitations upon the procedures for determining deportability that our later cases establish. . . .

B

Even if one were to assume that the Suspension Clause, despite its text . . ., guarantees some constitutional minimum of habeas relief, that minimum would assuredly not embrace the rarified right asserted here: the right to judicial compulsion of the exercise of Executive *discretion* (which may be exercised favorably or unfavorably) regarding a prisoner's release. If one reads the Suspension Clause as a guarantee of habeas relief, the obvious question presented is: *What* habeas relief? There are only two alternatives, the first of which is too absurd to be seriously entertained. It could be contended that Congress "suspends" the writ whenever it eliminates *any* prior ground for the writ that it adopted. Thus, if Congress should ever (in the view of this Court) have authorized immediate habeas corpus—without the need to exhaust administrative remedies—for a person arrested as an illegal alien, Congress would *never* be able (in the light of sad experience) to revise that disposition. The Suspension Clause, in other words, would be a one-way ratchet that enshrines in the Constitution every grant of habeas jurisdiction. This is, as I say, too absurd to be contemplated, and I shall contemplate it no further.

The other alternative is that the Suspension Clause guarantees the common-law right of habeas corpus, as it was understood when the Constitution was ratified. There is no doubt whatever that this did not include the right to obtain discretionary release. The Court notes with apparent credulity respondent's contention "that there is historical evidence of the writ issuing to redress the improper exercise of official discretion." The only Framing-era or earlier cases it alludes to in support of that contention establish no such thing. . . .

[The] cases cited in the Court's opinion—indeed, *all the later Supreme Court cases until United States ex rel. Accardi v. Shaughnessy, 347 U.S. 260, in 1954*—provide habeas relief from executive detention only when the custodian had no legal authority to detain. See 3 J. Story, Commentaries on the Constitution of the United States § 1333, p. 206 (1833) (the writ lies to ascertain whether a "sufficient ground of detention appears"). The fact is that, far from forming a traditional basis for issuance of the writ of habeas corpus, the whole "concept of 'discretion' was not well developed at common law," Jonathan L. Hafetz, The Untold Story of Noncriminal Habeas Corpus and the 1996 Immigration Acts, 107 Yale L.J. 2509, 2534 (1998). An exhaustive search of cases antedating the Suspension Clause discloses few instances in which courts even discussed the concept of executive discretion; and on the rare occasions when they did, they simply confirmed what seems obvious from the paucity of such discussions—namely, that courts understood executive discretion as lying entirely beyond the judicial ken. That is precisely what one would expect, since even the executive's evaluation of the *facts*—a duty that was a good deal *more* than discretionary—was not subject to review on habeas. Both in this country, until passage of the Habeas Corpus Act of 1867, and in England, the longstanding rule had been that the truth of the custodian's return *could not be controverted*. See, e.g., Opinion on the Writ of Habeas Corpus, 97 Eng. Rep. 29, 43 (H.L.1758); Note, Developments in the Law–Federal Habeas Corpus, 83 Harv. L.Rev. 1038, 1113–14, and nn. 9–11 (1970); Dallin H. Oaks, Legal History in the High Court–Habeas Corpus, 64 Mich. L.Rev. 451, 453 (1966). And, of course, going beyond inquiry into the legal authority of the executive to detain would have been utterly incompatible with the well-established limitation upon habeas relief for a convicted prisoner: "[O]nce a person had been convicted by a superior court of general jurisdiction, a court disposing of a habeas corpus petition could not go behind the conviction for any purpose other than to verify the formal jurisdiction of the committing court." Id., at 468.

In sum, there is no authority whatever for the proposition that, at the time the Suspension Clause was ratified—or, for that matter, even for a century and a half thereafter—habeas corpus relief was available to compel the Executive's allegedly wrongful refusal to exercise discretion. The striking proof of that proposition is that when, in 1954, the Warren Court held that the Attorney General's alleged refusal to exercise his discretion under the Immigration Act of 1917 could be reviewed on habeas, see *United States ex rel. Accardi v. Shaughnessy*, supra, it did so without citation of any supporting authority, and over the dissent of Justice Jackson, joined by three other Justices, who wrote:

> Of course, it may be thought that it would be better government if even executive acts of grace were subject to judicial review. But the process of the Court seems adapted only to the determination of legal rights, and here the decision is thrusting upon the courts the task of reviewing a discretionary and purely executive function. Habeas corpus, like the currency, can be debased by over-issue quite as certainly as by too niggardly use. We would ... leave the responsibility for suspension or execution of this deportation squarely on the Attorney General, where Congress has put it.

III

Given the insubstantiality of the due process and Article III arguments against barring judicial review of respondent's claim (the Court does not even bother to mention them ...), I will address them only briefly.

The Due Process Clause does not [require judicial determination of] respondent's claim. Respondent has no legal entitlement to suspension of deportation, no matter how appealing his case. "[T]he Attorney General's suspension of deportation [is] 'an act of grace' which is accorded pursuant to her 'unfettered discretion,' ... and [can be likened, as Judge Learned Hand observed,] to 'a judge's power to suspend the execution of a sentence, or the President's to pardon a convict,'" INS v. Yueh–Shaio Yang, 519 U.S. 26, 30, (1996). The furthest our cases have gone in imposing due process requirements upon analogous exercises of executive discretion is the following. (1) We have required *"minimal* procedural safeguards" for death-penalty clemency proceedings, to prevent them from becoming so capricious as to involve "a state official flipp[ing] a coin to determine whether to grant clemency," Ohio Adult Parole Authority v. Woodard, 523 U.S. 272, 289 (1998) (O'Connor, J., concurring in part and concurring in judgment). Even assuming that this holding is not part of our "death-is-different" jurisprudence, Shafer v. South Carolina, 532 U.S. 36, 55 (2001) (Scalia, J., dissenting), respondent here is not complaining about the absence of procedural safeguards; he disagrees with the Attorney General's judgment on a point of law. (2) We have recognized the existence of a due process liberty interest when a State's statutory parole procedures prescribe that a prisoner "shall" be paroled if certain conditions are satisfied, see Board of Pardons v. Allen, 482 U.S. 369, 370–71 (1987); Greenholtz v. Inmates of Neb. Penal and Correctional Complex, 442 U.S. 1, 12 (1979). There is no such statutory entitlement to suspension of deportation, no matter what the facts. Moreover, in neither *Woodard,* nor *Allen,* nor *Greenholtz* did we intimate that the Due Process Clause conferred jurisdiction of its own force, without benefit of statutory authorization. All three cases were brought under 42 U.S.C. § 1983.

Article III, § 1's investment of the "judicial Power of the United States" in the federal courts does not prevent Congress from committing the adjudication of respondent's legal claim wholly to [non-Article III federal adjudicative bodies]. The notion that Article III requires every Executive determination, on a question of law or of fact, to be subject to judicial review has no support in our jurisprudence. Were it correct, the doctrine of sovereign immunity would not exist, and the APA's general permission of suits challenging administrative action, see 5 U.S.C. § 702, would have been superfluous. Of its own force, Article III does no more than commit to the courts matters that are "the stuff of the traditional actions at common law tried by the courts at Westminster in 1789," Northern Pipeline Constr. Co. v. Marathon Pipe Line Co., 458 U.S. 50, 90

(1982) (Rehnquist, J., concurring in judgment)—which (as I have discussed earlier) did not include supervision of discretionary executive action.

* * *

The Court has created a version of IIRIRA that is not only unrecognizable to its framers (or to anyone who can read) but gives the statutory scheme precisely the *opposite* of its intended effect, affording criminal aliens *more* opportunities for delay-inducing judicial review than others have, or even than criminal aliens had prior to the enactment of this legislation. Because § 2241's exclusion of judicial review is unmistakably clear, and unquestionably constitutional, both this Court and the courts below were without power to entertain respondent's claims. I would set aside the judgment of the court below and remand with instructions to have the District Court dismiss for want of jurisdiction. I respectfully dissent from the judgment of the Court.

Page 298, add at the end of Note 3:

For analysis of the intersection of non-article III courts and the seventh amendment, see Ellen E. Sward, Legislative Courts, Article III, and the Seventh Amendment, 77 N.C.L. Rev. 1037 (1999). Sward argues that the right to jury trial in civil cases should not necessarily be limited to article III courts but should extend as well to much non-article III adjudication.

Page 330, at the end of *Plaut*, add a note as follows:

NOTE ON *MILLER v. FRENCH*

A variation on the problem in *Plaut* arose in Miller v. French, 530 U.S. 327 (2000), which concerned the "automatic stay" provision of the Prison Litigation Reform Act of 1995. That statute curtails structural reform injunctions against prisons. Basically, § 3626(b) of the statute requires that courts issue or continue such injunctions only if the relief is narrowly drawn and extends no further than is necessary to correct the violation of a federal right. The automatic stay provision, § 3626(e)(2), provides that a motion to terminate prospective relief automatically operates as a stay of that relief after 30 days, or 90 days if extended for "good cause." Under this provision, when a prison subject to a court order regarding conditions of confinement moves to terminate the injunction, the injunction is automatically lifted after a maximum of 90 days, unless the district court denies the motion.

In *Miller*, four inmates challenged this provision as an indirect legislative "suspension" of a final judgment, as condemned in *Plaut*. Speaking for the Court, Justice O'Connor rejected that argument:

> *Plaut* ... was careful to distinguish the situation before the Court in that case—legislation that attempted to reopen the dismissal of a suit seeking money damages—from legislation that

"altered the prospective effect of injunctions entered by Article III courts." . . . Prospective relief under a continuing, executory decree remains subject to alteration due to changes in the underlying law. . . .

By establishing new standards for the enforcement of prospective relief in § 3626(b), Congress has altered the relevant underlying law. The PLRA has restricted courts' authority to issue and enforce prospective relief concerning prison conditions, requiring that such relief be supported by findings and precisely tailored to what is needed to remedy the violation of a federal right. [W]hen Congress changes the law underlying a judgment awarding prospective relief, that relief is no longer enforceable to the extent it is inconsistent with the new law. . . . Although the remedial injunction here is a "final judgment" for purposes of appeal, it is not the "last word of the judicial department." *Plaut*, 514 U.S., at 227. The provision of prospective relief is subject to the continuing supervisory jurisdiction of the court, and therefore may be altered according to subsequent changes in the law.

In reaching this conclusion, the Court relied particularly on Pennsylvania v. Wheeling & Belmont Bridge Co., 59 U.S. (18 How.) 421 (1856) (*Wheeling Bridge II*). In an earlier decision under the same name, the Court had ruled that a bridge across the Ohio River obstructed navigation (because it was too low) and therefore had to be removed. Congress thereafter enacted legislation declaring the bridge a "lawful structure." When the bridge was destroyed in a storm, the state of Pennsylvania sued to enjoin its reconstruction, claiming that the statute was an unconstitutional attempt to annul the Court's judgment requiring removal. In *Wheeling Bridge II*, the Court rejected that contention, saying that the intervening statute had altered the underlying law and rendered the bridge no longer unlawful. The Court noted that an award of damages would have been beyond Congress's power to undo, but concluded that a continuing injunction against maintaining the bridge could be rendered invalid by a change in the underlying law. Parallel reasoning suggested that Congress could also change the underlying law governing prison reform injunctions.

Having found no separation-of-powers problem, the Court found that there might be a due process violation if the time limit imposed by the automatic stay provision proved so short that it deprived litigants of a meaningful opportunity to be heard. That issue, not being before the Court, was left to another day.

Justice Breyer, joined by Justice Stevens, dissented. Breyer thought that there was a separation-of-powers problem and that the automatic stay provision could be construed to avoid it by allowing courts to suspend the automatic stay on appropriate facts. Justice Souter, joined by Justice Ginsburg, dissented in part. They agreed with the majority that the statute precluded judicial discretion but believed that there would be a separation-of-powers violation if the time authorized proved insufficient. As there had been no consideration of whether the 90 days allowed by the statute were sufficient in this case, Souter suggested that the case be remanded for consideration of that issue.[a]

[a] For criticism of the result in *Miller*, see Lloyd C. Anderson, Congressional Control Over the Jurisdiction of the Federal Courts: A New Threat to James Madison's Compromise, 39 Brandeis L. J. 417 (2000–01).

CHAPTER IV

JUSTICIABILITY

Page 357, add at the end of Note 6:

In a more recent article, Pushaw argues that "separation of powers in our democracy is frustrated by justiciability doctrines that permit courts to abdicate their role of enforcing federal law." See Robert J. Pushaw, Jr., Justiciability and Separation of Powers: A Neo–Federalist Approach, 81 Corn. L. Rev. 393 (1996). Pushaw includes extensive historical investigation of the origins and development of modern justiciability doctrines.

For another interesting perspective on the constitutional foundation of modern standing law, see Edward A. Hartnett, The Standing of the United States: How Criminal Prosecutions Show That Standing Doctrine Is Looking for Answers in All the Wrong Places, 97 Mich. L. Rev. 2239 (1999). Hartnett suggests that criminal prosecutions demonstrate that "injury in fact," in the sense of "concrete and particularized" harm, need not exist for the United States as plaintiff and consequently that injury is not part of the "irreducible constitutional minimum" of article III.

Page 382, add a footnote at the end of the first sentence of Note 4:

    d. For criticism of a subsequent decision holding that ranchers and other competing users of waters that the U.S. Fish and Wildlife Service had restricted in order to preserve endangered species had standing to challenge such restrictions, see William W. Buzbee, Expanding the Zone, Tilting the Field: Zone of Interests and Article III Standing Analysis After *Bennett v. Spear*, 49 Admin. L. Rev. 763 (1997).

Page 382, add a new Note 5:

    5. *Friends of the Earth v. Laidlaw.* The reasoning of *Lujan* was qualified, at least, in Friends of the Earth, Inc. v. Laidlaw Environmental Services, Inc., 528 U.S. 167 (2000). Friends of the Earth and other environmental organizations filed suit against Laidlaw under the citizen-suit provision of the Clean Water Act, 33 U.S.C. §§ 1251 et seq., after giving the requisite 60–days' notice. They complained of mercury discharges into South Carolina's North Tyger River in amounts exceeding the stringent limitations imposed in a discharge permit held by the company. The District Court found numerous discharge violations, but found that they had caused "no demonstrated proof of harm to the environment." The court accordingly denied injunctive relief (noting that the company had been in substantial compliance for some time), but imposed a civil penalty of $405,800, payable to the United States Treasury for discharge violations.

As the case came to the Supreme Court, a key issue was whether the plaintiffs had standing to maintain a citizen-suit for this remedy.

Under the Clean Water Act, a citizen suit is authorized by "a person or persons having an interest which is or may be adversely affected." 33 U.S.C. §§ 1365(a), (g). To establish the "injury in fact" required by Article III, plaintiff environmental organizations submitted affidavits recounting the environmental concerns of local members:

> For example, FOE member Kenneth Lee Curtis averred in an affidavits that he lived a half-mile from Laidlaw's facility; that he occasionally drove over the North Tyger River, and that it looked and smelled polluted; and that he would like to fish, camp, swim, and picnic in and near the river between three and 15 miles downstream from the facility, as he did when he was a teenager, but would not do so because he was concerned that the water was polluted by Laidlaw's discharges.

Speaking for the Court, Justice Ginsburg found these and similar allegations sufficient to satisfy Article III: "We have held that environmental plaintiffs adequately allege injury in fact when they aver that they use the affected area and are persons 'for whom the aesthetic and recreational values of the area will be lessened' by the challenged activity" (quoting Sierra Club v. Morton, 405 U.S. 727, 735 (1972). *Lujan* was found not to the contrary, because the allegations of harm there were more "general" and "conclusory."

Only Justices Scalia and Thomas dissented. Justice Scalia emphasized the trial court's finding of no harm to the environment and argued that plaintiffs' "concerns" were not enough:

> By accepting plaintiffs' vague, contradictory, and unsubstantiated allegations of "concern" about the environment as adequate to prove injury in fact, and accepting them even in the fact of a finding that the environment was not demonstrably harmed, the Court makes the injury-in-fact requirement a sham. If there are permit violations, and a member of a plaintiff environmental organization lives near the offending plant, it would be difficult not to satisfy today's lenient standard.

A related issue was redressability. The relief plaintiffs' obtained was a civil penalty payable not to them, but to the United States. In Steel Co. v. Citizens for Better Environment, 523 U.S. 83 (1998), the Court had said that civil penalties paid to the government do not redress environmental plaintiffs for past injuries suffered by them. *Steel Co.* was distinguished on the ground that FOE alleged continuing violations by Laidlaw, which would be deterred by the monetary penalty. Justice Ginsburg explained:

> It can scarcely be doubted that, for a plaintiff who is injured or faces the threat of future injury due to illegal conduct ongoing at the time of suit, a sanction that effectively abates that conduct and prevents its recurrence provides a form of redress. Civil penalties can fit that description.

In dissent, Justice Scalia asserted that the Court's holding that "a penalty payable to the public 'remedies' a threatened private harm, and suffices to sustain a private suit" was a holding that "has no precedent in our jurisprudence and takes this Court beyond the 'cases and controversies' that Article III of the Constitution has entrusted to its resolution."

Plainly, *Lujan* and *Laidlaw* are in tension. *Lujan* seemed to say that Article III restricted standing, even in the face of explicit congressional authorization to sue. *Laidlaw*, in contrast, seems to accommodate congressional objectives by finding standing on terms that make citizen suits possible. Can the two decisions be reconciled, or has *Lujan* effectively been overruled?

For commentary on these questions, see the symposium on Citizen Suits and the Future of Standing in the 21st Century: From *Lujan* to *Laidlaw* and Beyond in a double-issue of the Duke Environmental Law & Policy Forum. Contributors included Gene R. Nichol, The Impossibility of *Lujan*'s Project, 11 Duke Env. L. & Pol. Forum 193 (2001) (arguing that when Congress creates legal interests, the courts are "immensely hard-pressed" to deny injury in fact when those interests are transgressed); Richard J. Pierce, Jr., Issues Raised by *Friends of the Earth v. Laidlaw Environmental Services*: Access to the Court for Environmental Plaintiffs, 11 Duke Env. L. & Pol. Forum 207 (2001) (characterizing *Laidlaw* as a "major victory for environmentalist," but noting that the Court could "retract, recharacterize, or amend significantly" its analysis in *Laidlaw*, as *Laidlaw* did to *Lujan*); William W. Buzbee, Standing and the Statutory Universe, 11 Duke Env. L. & Pol. Forum 247 (2001) (concluding that "courts should heed explicit or implicit legislative judgments about interests created or protected and about the importance of legislatively chosen procedures for furthering those interests"); John D. Echeverria, Critiquing *Laidlaw*: Congressional Power to Confer Standing and the Irrelevance of Mootness Doctrine to Civil Penalties, 11 Duke Env. L. & Pol. Forum 287 (2001) (endorsing the rule that compliance does not moot a claim for civil penalty for past violations); Maxwell L. Stearns, From *Lujan* to *Laidlaw*: A Preliminary Model of Environmental Standing, 11 Duke Env. L. & Pol. Forum 321 (2001) (applying a model of standing based on social choice theory to statutory standing); A. H. Barnett and Timothy D. Terrell, Economic Observations on Citizen–Suit Provisions of Environmental Legislation, 12 Duke Env. L. & Pol. Forum 1 (2001) (analyzing the economic implications of citizen-suit standing); Jonathan D. Adler, Stand or Deliver: Citizen Suits, Standing, and Environmental Protection, 12 Duke Env. L. & Pol. Forum 39 (2001) (arguing that liberalized standing rules for citizen-suits will not necessarily enhance environmental quality); Harold J. Krent, *Laidlaw*: Redressing the Law of Redressability, 12 Duke Env. L. & Pol. Forum 85 (examining Congress's role in determining redressability); Robert V. Percival and Joanna B. Goger, Escaping the Common Law's Shadow: Standing in the Light of *Laidlaw*, 12 Duke Env. L. & Pol. Forum 119 (2001) (analyzing *Laidlaw* as a warranted rejection of a private-law model of standing); Steven L. Winter, What If Justice Scalia Took History and the Rule of Law Seriously?, 12 Duke Env. L. & Pol. Forum 155 (2001) (as the title suggests, criticizing Justice Scalia's dissent in *Laidlaw*); Michael S. Greve, *Friends of the Earth*, Foes of Federalism, 12 Duke Env. L. & Pol. Forum 167 (2001) (criticizing *Laidlaw* from the perspective of a desire to enhance political responsibility and federalism); Karl S. Coplan, Direct Environmental Standing for Chartered Conservation Corporations, 12 Duke Env. L. & Pol. Forum 183 (2001) (arguing that state-chartered organizations should have standing to assert their own interests, without reference to the individual interests of their members).

Page 383, add a new main case before *Raines v. Byrd*:

Federal Election Commission v. Akins

Supreme Court of the United States, 1998.
524 U.S. 11.

■ JUSTICE BREYER delivered the opinion of the Court.

The Federal Election Commission (FEC) has determined that the American Israel Public Affairs Committee (AIPAC) is not a "political committee" as defined by the Federal Election Campaign Act of 1971 as amended, 2 U.S.C. § 431(4) (FECA), and, for that reason, the Commission has refused to require AIPAC to make disclosures regarding its membership, contributions, and expenditures that FECA would otherwise require. We hold that respondents, a group of voters, have standing to challenge the Commission's determination in court, and we remand this case for further proceedings.

I

[T]he act imposes extensive recordkeeping and disclosure requirements upon groups that fall within the act's definition of a "political committee." Those groups must register with the FEC, appoint a treasurer, keep names and addresses of contributors, track the amount and purpose of disbursements, and file complex FEC reports that include lists of donors giving in excess of $200 per year (often, these donors may be the group's members), contributions, expenditures, and any other disbursements irrespective of their purposes.

The act's use of the word "political committee" calls to mind the term "political action committee" ..., [but the term] has a much broader scope. The act states that a "political committee" includes "*any* committee, club, association or other group of persons which receives" more than $1,000 in "contributions" or "which makes" more than $1,000 in "expenditures" in any given year. § 431(4)(A) (emphasis added).

This broad definition, however, is less universally encompassing than at first it may seem, for later definitional subsections limit its scope. The act defines the key terms "contribution" and "expenditure" as covering only those contributions and expenditures that are made "for the purpose of influencing any election for Federal office." §§ 431(8)(A)(i), (9)(A)(i). Moreover, the act sets forth detailed categories of disbursements, loans, and assistance-in-kind that do not count as a "contribution" or "expenditure," even when made for election-related purposes. §§ 431(8)(B), (9)(B). In particular, assistance given to help a particular candidate will not count toward the $1,000 "expenditure" ceiling that qualifies an organization as a "political committee" if it takes the form of a "communication" by an organization "to its members"—as long as the organization at issue is a "membership organization or corporation" and it is not "organized primarily for the purpose of influencing the nomination ... or election, of any individual." § 431(9)(B)(iii).

This case arises out of an effort by respondents, a group of voters with views often opposed to those of AIPAC, to persuade the FEC to treat AIPAC as a "political committee." Respondents filed a complaint with the FEC, stating that AIPAC had made more than $1,000 in qualifying "expenditures" last year, and thereby became a "political committee." ...

AIPAC asked the FEC to dismiss the complaint. AIPAC described itself as an issue-oriented organization that seeks to maintain friendship and promote goodwill between the United States and Israel. AIPAC conceded that it lobbies elected officials and disseminates information about candidates for public office. But ... AIPAC denied that it had made the kinds of "expenditures" that matter for FECA purposes....

To put the matter more specifically: AIPAC focused on certain "expenditures" that respondents had claimed were election-related, such as the costs of meetings with candidates, the introduction of AIPAC members to candidates, and the distribution of candidate position papers. AIPAC said that its spending on such activities, even if election-related, fell within a relevant exception. They amounted, said AIPAC, to communications by a membership organization with its members, which the act exempts from its definition of "expenditures." ...

The FEC's General Counsel concluded that, between 1983 and 1988, AIPAC had indeed funded communications of the sort described. The General Counsel said that those expenditures were campaign related, in that they amounted to advocating the election or defeat of particular candidates. He added that these expenditures were "likely to have crossed the $1,000 threshold." At the same time, the FEC said that, although it was a "close question," these expenditures were not membership communications, because that exception applies to a membership organization's communications with its members, and most of the persons who belonged to AIPAC did not qualify as "members" for purposes of the act. ...

The FEC's determination that many of the persons who belonged to AIPAC were not "members" effectively foreclosed any claim that AIPAC's communications did not count as "expenditures" for purposes of determining whether it was a "political committee." . . .

The FEC nonetheless held that AIPAC was not subject to the disclosure requirements, but for a different reason. In the FEC's view, the act's definition of "political committee" includes only those organizations that have as a "major purpose" the nomination or election of candidates. AIPAC, it added, was fundamentally an issue-oriented lobbying organization, not a campaign-related organization, and hence AIPAC fell outside the definition of a "political committee" regardless. The FEC consequently dismissed respondents' complaint.

Respondents filed a petition in federal district court seeking review of the FEC's determination dismissing their complaint. The district court granted summary judgment for the FEC, and a divided panel of the court of appeals affirmed. The en banc court of appeals reversed, however, on the ground that the FEC's "major purpose" test improperly interpreted the act's definition of a "political committee." We granted the government's petition for certiorari. . . .

II

The Solicitor General argues that respondents lack standing to challenge the FEC's decision not to proceed against AIPAC. . . .

We [disagree]. Congress has specifically provided in FECA that "[a]ny person who believes a violation of this act . . . has occurred, may file a complaint with the Commission." § 437g(a)(1). It has added that "[a]ny party aggrieved by an order of the Commission dismissing a complaint filed by such party . . . may file a petition" in district court seeking review of that dismissal. § 437g(a)(8)(A). History associates the word "aggrieved" with a congressional intent to cast the standing net broadly—beyond the common-law interests and substantive statutory rights upon which "prudential" standing traditionally rested.

Moreover, prudential standing is satisfied when the injury asserted by a plaintiff " 'arguably [falls] within the zone of interests to be protected or regulated by the statute . . . in question.' " National Credit Union Admin. v. First National Bank & Trust Co., 522 U.S. 479, 488 (1998) (quoting Association of Data Processing Service Organizations, Inc. v. Camp, 397 U.S. 150, 153 (1970)). The kind of injury of which respondents complain—their failure to obtain relevant information—is injury of a kind that FECA seeks to address. We have found nothing in the act that suggests Congress intended to exclude voters from the benefits of these provisions, or otherwise to restrict standing, say, to political parties, candidates, or their committees.

Given the language of the statute and the nature of the injury, we conclude that Congress, intending to protect voters such as respondents from suffering the kind of injury here at issue, intended to authorize this kind of suit. Consequently, respondents satisfy "prudential" standing requirements.

Nor do we agree ... that Congress lacks the constitutional power to authorize federal courts to adjudicate this lawsuit. Article III, of course, limits Congress' grant of judicial power to "cases" or "controversies." That limitation means that respondents must show, among other things, an "injury in fact"....

The "injury in fact" that respondents have suffered consists of their inability to obtain information—lists of AIPAC donors (who are, according to AIPAC, its members), and campaign-related contributions and expenditures—that, on respondents' view of the law, the statute requires that AIPAC make public. There is no reason to doubt their claim that the information would help them (and others to whom they would communicate it) to evaluate candidates for public office, especially candidates who received assistance from AIPAC, and to evaluate the role that AIPAC's financial assistance might play in a specific election. Respondents' injury consequently seems concrete and particular. Indeed, this Court has previously held that a plaintiff suffers an "injury in fact" when the plaintiff fails to obtain information which must be publicly disclosed pursuant to a statute. Public Citizen v. Department of Justice, 491 U.S. 440, 449 (1989) (failure to obtain information subject to disclosure under Federal Advisory Committee Act "constitutes a sufficiently distinct injury to provide standing to sue").

The dissent refers to United States v. Richardson, 418 U.S. 166 (1974), a case in which a plaintiff sought information (details of Central Intelligence Agency expenditures) to which, he said, the Constitution's accounts clause, art. I, § 9, cl. 7, entitled him. The Court held that the plaintiff there lacked article III standing. The dissent says that *Richardson* and this case are "indistinguishable." But as the parties' briefs suggest—for they do not mention *Richardson*—that case does not control the outcome here.

Richardson's plaintiff claimed that a statute permitting the CIA to keep its expenditures nonpublic violated the accounts clause, which requires that "a regular Statement and Account of the Receipts and Expenditures of all public Money shall be published from time to time." The Court held that the plaintiff lacked standing because there was "no 'logical nexus' between the [plaintiff's] asserted status of taxpayer and the claimed failure of the Congress to require the Executive to supply a more detailed report of the [CIA's] expenditures." 418 U.S., at 175 (quoting Flast v. Cohen, 392 U.S. 83, 102 (1968), for the proposition that in "taxpayer standing" cases, there must be "a logical nexus between the status asserted and the claim sought to be adjudicated").

In this case, however, the "logical nexus" inquiry is not relevant. Here, there is no constitutional provision requiring the demonstration of the "nexus" the Court believed must be shown in *Richardson* and *Flast*. Rather, there is a statute which, as we previously pointed out, does seek to protect individuals such as respondents from the kind of harm they say they have suffered, i.e., failing to receive particular information about campaign-related activities. . . .

The fact that the Court in *Richardson* focused upon taxpayer standing, not voter standing, places that case at still a greater distance from the case before us. . . .

The FEC's strongest argument is its contention that this lawsuit involves only a "generalized grievance." The Solicitor General points out that respondents' asserted harm (their failure to obtain information) is one which is " 'shared in substantially equal measure by all or a large class of citizens,' " quoting Warth v. Seldin, 422 U.S. 490, 499 (1975). This Court, he adds, has often said that "generalized grievance[s]" are not the kinds of harms that confer standing. See also Lujan v. Defenders of Wildlife, 504 U.S. 555, 573–74 (1992); Allen v. Wright, 468 U.S. 737, 755–56 (1984); [and others]. . . .

The kind of judicial language to which the FEC points, however, invariably appears in cases where the harm at issue is not only widely shared, but is also of an abstract and indefinite nature—for example, harm to the "common concern for obedience to law." L. Singer & Sons v. Union Pacific R. Co., 311 U.S. 295, 303 (1940); see also *Allen*, supra, 468 U.S., at 754. Cf. *Lujan*, supra, 504 U.S., at 572–78 (injury to interest in seeing that certain procedures are followed not normally sufficient by itself to confer standing). The abstract nature of the harm—for example, injury to the interest in seeing that the law is obeyed—deprives the case of the concrete specificity that characterized those controversies which were "the traditional concern of the courts at Westminster," and which today prevents a plaintiff from obtaining what would, in effect, amount to an advisory opinion.

Often the fact that an interest is abstract and the fact that it is widely shared go hand in hand. But their association is not invariable, and where a harm is concrete, though widely shared, the Court has found "injury in fact." See *Public Citizen*, supra, 491 U.S. at 449–50. Thus the fact that a political forum may be more readily available where an injury is widely shared (while counseling against, say, interpreting a statute as conferring standing) does not, by itself, automatically disqualify an interest for article III purposes. Such an interest, where sufficiently concrete, may count as an "injury in fact." This conclusion seems particularly obvious where (to use a hypothetical example) large numbers of individuals suffer the same common-law injury (say, a widespread mass tort), or where large numbers of voters suffer interference with voting rights conferred by law. We conclude that similarly, the informational injury at issue here, directly related to voting, the most basic of political rights, is sufficiently concrete and specific such that the fact that it is widely shared does not deprive Congress of constitutional power to authorize its vindication in the federal courts.

Respondents have also satisfied the remaining two constitutional standing requirements. The harm asserted is "fairly traceable" to the FEC's decision about which respondents complain. Of course, ... it is possible that even had the FEC agreed with respondents' view of the law, it would still have decided in the exercise of its discretion not to require the AIPAC to produce the information. Yet that fact does not destroy article III "causation," for we cannot know that the FEC would have exercised its prosecutorial discretion in this way. Agencies often have discretion about whether or not to take a particular action. Yet those adversely affected by a discretionary agency decision generally have standing to complain that the agency based its decision upon an improper legal ground. If a reviewing court agrees that the agency misinterpreted the law, it will set aside the agency's action and remand the case—even though the agency (like a new jury after a mistrial) might later, in the exercise of its lawful discretion, reach the same result for a different reason. Thus respondents' "injury in fact" is "fairly traceable" to the FEC's decision not to issue its complaint, even though the FEC might reach the same result exercising its discretionary powers lawfully. For similar reasons, the courts in this case can "redress" respondents' "injury in fact."

Finally, the FEC argues that we should deny respondents standing because this case involves an agency's decision not to undertake an enforcement action—an area generally not subject to judicial review. In Heckler v. Chaney, 470 U.S. 821, 832 (1985), this Court noted that agency enforcement decisions "ha[ve] traditionally been 'committed to agency discretion,'" and concluded that Congress did not intend to alter that tradition in enacting the APA. We deal here with a statute that explicitly indicates to the contrary.

In sum, respondents, as voters, have satisfied both prudential and constitutional standing requirements. They may bring this petition for a declaration that the FEC's dismissal of their complaint was unlawful. ...

■ JUSTICE SCALIA, with whom JUSTICE O'CONNOR and JUSTICE THOMAS join, dissenting.

The provision of law at issue in this case is an extraordinary one, conferring upon a private person the ability to bring an executive agency into court to compel its enforcement of the law against a third party. ... If provisions such as the present one were commonplace, the role of the executive branch in our system of separated and equilibrated powers would be greatly reduced, and that of the judiciary greatly expanded.

Because this provision is so extraordinary, we should be particularly careful not to expand it beyond its fair meaning. In my view, the Court's opinion does that. Indeed, it expands the meaning beyond what the Constitution permits.

I

It is clear that the Federal Election Campaign Act does not intend that *all* persons filing complaints with the Commission have the right to seek judicial review of the rejection of their complaints. This is evident from the fact that the act permits a complaint to be filed by "[a]ny *person* who believes a violation of this act ... has occurred," 2 U.S.C. § 437g(a)(1) (emphasis added), but accords a right to judicial relief only to "[a]ny *party aggrieved* by an order of the Commission dismissing a complaint filed by such party," 2 U.S.C. § 437g(a)(8)(A) (emphasis added). The interpretation that the Court gives the latter provision deprives it of almost all its limiting force. *Any voter* can sue to compel the agency to require registration of an entity as a political committee, even though the "aggrievement" consists of nothing more than the deprivation of access to information whose public availability would have been one of the consequences of registration.

This seems to me too much of a stretch. It should be borne in mind that the agency action complained of here is not the refusal to make available information in its possession that the act requires to be disclosed. A person demanding provision of information that the law requires the agency to furnish ... can reasonably be described as being "aggrieved" by the agency's refusal to provide it. What the respondents complain of in this suit, however, is not the refusal to provide information, but the refusal (for an allegedly improper reason) to commence an agency enforcement action against a third person. That refusal *itself* plainly does not render respondents "aggrieved" within the meaning of the act, for in that case there would have been no reason for the act to differentiate between "person" in subsection (a)(1) and "party aggrieved" in subsection (a)(8). ...

And finally, a narrower reading of "party aggrieved" is supported by the doctrine of constitutional doubt, which counsels us to interpret statutes, if possible, in such fashion as to avoid grave constitutional questions. ...

II

In United States v. Richardson, 418 U.S. 166 (1974), we dismissed for lack of standing a suit whose "aggrievement" was precisely the "aggrievement" respondents assert here: the government's unlawful refusal to place information within the public domain. The only difference, in fact, is that the aggrievement there was more direct, since the government already had the information within its possession, whereas here the respondents seek enforcement action that will bring information within the government's possession and *then* require the information to be made public. The plaintiff in *Richardson* challenged the government's failure to disclose the expenditures of the Central Intelligence Agency (CIA), in alleged violation of the constitutional requirement, art. I, § 9, cl. 7, that "a regular Statement and Account of the Receipts and Expenditures of all public Money shall be published from time to time." We held that such a claim was a nonjusticiable "generalized grievance" because "the impact on [plaintiff] is plainly undifferentiated and common to all members of the public."

It was alleged in *Richardson* that the government had denied a right conferred by the Constitution, whereas respondents here assert a right conferred by statute—but of course "there is absolutely no basis for making the article III inquiry turn on the source of the asserted right." Lujan v. Defenders of Wildlife, 504 U.S. 555, 576 (1992). The Court today distinguishes *Richardson* on a different basis—a basis that reduces it from a landmark constitutional holding to a curio. According to the Court, "*Richardson* focused upon taxpayer standing, . . . not voter standing." In addition to being a silly distinction, . . . this is also a distinction that the Court in *Richardson* went out of its way explicitly to eliminate. It is true enough that the narrow question presented in *Richardson* was " '[w]hether a federal taxpayer has standing.' " 418 U.S., at 167. But the *Richardson* Court did not hold only, as the Court today suggests, that the plaintiff failed to qualify for the exception to the rule of no taxpayer standing established by the "logical nexus" test of Flast v. Cohen, 392 U.S. 83 (1968). The plaintiff's complaint in *Richardson* had also alleged that he was " 'a member of the electorate,' " 418 U.S., at 167 n.1, and he asserted injury in that capacity as well. The *Richardson* opinion treated that as fairly included within the taxpayer-standing question, or at least as plainly indistinguishable from it. . . . Fairly read, and applying a fair understanding of its important purposes, *Richardson* is indistinguishable from the present case.

The Court's opinion asserts that our language disapproving generalized grievances "invariably appears in cases where the harm at issue is not only widely shared, but is also of an abstract and indefinite nature." . . . But . . . the Court is wrong to think that generalized grievances have only concerned us when they are abstract. One need go no further than *Richardson* to prove that—unless the Court believes that deprivation of information is an abstract injury, in which event this case could be disposed of on that much broader ground.

What is noticeably lacking in the Court's discussion of our generalized-grievance jurisprudence is all reference to two words that have figured in it prominently: "particularized" and "undifferentiated." "Particularized" means that "the injury must affect the plaintiff in a personal and individual way." *Lujan*, supra, 504 U.S., at 560 n.1. If the effect is "undifferentiated and common to all members of the public," *Richardson*, supra, 418 U.S., at 177, the plaintiff has a "generalized grievance" that must be pursued by political rather than judicial means. These terms explain why it is a gross oversimplification to reduce the concept of a generalized grievance to nothing more than "the fact that [the grievance] is widely shared, thereby enable the concept to be dismissed as a standing principle by such examples as 'large numbers of individuals suffer[ing] the same common-law injury (say, a widespread mass tort), or . . . large numbers of voters suffer[ing] interference with voting rights conferred by law.' " The exemplified injuries are widely shared, to be sure, but each individual suffers a particularized and differentiated harm. One tort victim suffers a burnt leg, another a burnt arm—or even if both suffer burnt arms they are *different* arms. One voter suffers the deprivation of *his* franchise, another the deprivation of *hers*. With the generalized grievance, on the other hand, the injury or deprivation is not only widely shared but is *undifferentiated*. The harm caused to Mr. Richardson by the alleged disregard of the statement-of-accounts clause was precisely the same as the harm caused to everyone else: unavailability of a description of CIA expenditures. Just as the (more indirect) harm caused to Mr. Akins by the allegedly unlawful failure to enforce FECA is precisely the same as the harm caused to everyone else: unavailability of a description of AIPAC's activities.

The Constitution's line of demarcation between the executive power and the judicial power presupposes a common understanding of the type of interest needed to sustain a "case or controversy" against the executive in the courts. A system in which the citizenry at large could sue to compel executive compliance with the law would be a system in which the courts, rather than the president, are given the primary responsibility to "take Care that the Laws be faithfully executed," art. II, § 3. We do not have such a system because the common understanding of the interest necessary to sustain suit has included the requirement, affirmed in *Richardson*, that the complained-of injury be particularized and differentiated, rather than common to all the electorate. When the executive can be directed by the courts, at the instance of any voter, to remedy a deprivation which affects the entire electorate in precisely the same way—and particularly when that deprivation (here, the unavailability of information) is one inseverable part of a larger enforcement scheme—there has occurred a shift of political responsibility to a branch designed not to protect the public at large but to protect individual rights. "To permit Congress to convert the undifferentiated public interest in executive officers' compliance with the law into an 'individual right' vindicable in the courts is to permit Congress to transfer from the president to the courts the chief executive's most important constitutional duty...." *Lujan*, supra, 504 U.S. at 577. If today's decision is correct, it is within the power of Congress to authorize any interested person to manage (through the courts) the executive's enforcement of any law that includes a requirement for the filing and public availability of a piece of paper. This is not the system we have had, and is not the system we should desire.

Page 388, add a footnote at the end of *Raines v. Byrd*:

a. For commentary on *Raines*, see Neal Devins and Michael A. Fitts, The Triumph of Timing: *Raines v. Byrd* and the Modern Supreme Court's Attempt to Control Constitutional Confrontations, 86 Geo. L. J. 351 (1997). [Footnote by eds.]

Page 414, add at end of Note 9 prior to Subsection C:

See also John F. Duffy, Administrative Common Law in Judicial Review, 77 Texas L. Rev. 113 (1998).

Page 418, add a new Note, as follows:

4A. *City of Erie v. Pap's "Kandyland."* The Supreme Court appeared to follow, but not acknowledge, Chief Justice Rehnquist's approach in City of Erie v. Pap's A.M., tdba "Kandyland," 529 U.S. 277 (2000). When the City of Erie passed an ordinance aimed at nude dancing, Pap's, operator of an establishment known as "Kandyland," raised a first amendment challenge. Eventually, the Pennsylvania Supreme Court ruled in the plaintiff's favor and enjoined enforcement of the ordinance. Thereafter, Pap's closed Kandyland and sold the building to a developer. Pap's sole shareholder, who was of an age to retire, submitted an affidavit recounting those facts and confirming that neither he nor the corporation had any current interest in nude dancing nor any intention to own or operate such an establishment in the future. Based on these facts, the case looked moot. The problem, however, was that if mootness deprived the Court of jurisdiction to reach the merits, it also lacked jurisdiction to direct a vacatur by the state court. See ASARCO, Inc. v. Kadish, 490 U.S. 605, 621 n. 1 (1989). That would mean that the judgment against Erie would remain in effect. Additionally, the Justices were irritated that the facts suggesting mootness had not been mentioned in Pap's response to the city's petition for certiorari but had first been raised in a motion to dismiss filed after certiorari was granted.

Speaking for the Court, Justice O'Connor found that the case was not moot. The Court refused to credit the owner's affidavit, noting that "Pap's is still incorporated under Pennsylvania law, and it could again decide to operate a nude dancing establishment in Erie." O'Connor noted that the city had an "ongoing injury because it is barred from enforcing the public nudity provisions of its ordinance," and concluded, somewhat obliquely, that "to the extent Pap's has an interest in resuming operations, it has an interest in preserving the judgment of the Pennsylvania Supreme Court." On the merits, the Court concluded that the ordinance was not unconstitutional.

Justice Scalia, joined by Justice Thomas, dissented on the mootness issue, arguing that the unfortunate situation of leaving in place an erroneous decision of the Pennsylvania Supreme Court did not justify "entertain[ing] a suit that the Constitution places beyond our power."

Page 448, add at the end of Note 4:

For a major recent article, see Rachel E. Barkow, More Supreme Than Court? The Fall of the Political Question Doctrine and the Rise of Judicial Supremacy, 102 Colum. L. Rev. 237 (2002). Barkow documents and criticizes the demise of the political question doctrine and relates that development to a "disconcerting" rise in "judicial immodesty" that has left the Supreme Court "blind to its own aggrandizement at the expense of the other branches."

CHAPTER V

SUBJECT MATTER JURISDICTION

Page 451, add at the end of footnote b:

For a reaffirmation and application of the face-of-the-complaint rule, see The Holmes Group, Inc. v. Vornado Air Circulation Systems, Inc., ___ U.S. ___ (2002).

Page 459, add a new Note:

    7a. *City of Chicago v. International College of Surgeons.* The interrelationship between federal question jurisdiction, removal, review of state administrative action, and supplemental jurisdiction was elaborated by a divided Court in City of Chicago v. International College of Surgeons, 522 U.S. 156 (1997). The College of Surgeons (ICS) owned two properties on North Lake Shore Drive in Chicago. The Chicago Landmarks Commission had determined that two mansions on ICS property were historical landmarks, but ICS wished to sell the property to a developer for construction of a high-rise condominium. ICS's application for permission to demolish the mansions was denied by the Landmarks Commission. ICS then sought administrative review of the Commission's decision in the Circuit Court of Cook County pursuant to the Illinois Administrative Review Law. It also challenged the decision on a number of federal and state constitutional grounds.

    The City removed the case to federal court. The District Court exercised jurisdiction over both the federal and state claims, ultimately ruling for the City on all counts. The Court of Appeals reversed, holding that the case had been improperly removed. The Supreme Court disagreed. It held the case properly removable, and upheld the District Court's jurisdiction over both federal and state claims.

    For the Court, Justice O'Connor began by observing that it "is true ... that the federal constitutional claims were raised by way of a cause of action created by state law, namely, the Illinois Administrative Review Law." But, quoting Franchise Tax Board of California v. Construction Laborers Vacation Trust for Southern California, 463 U.S. 1 (1983), " '[even though state law creates [a party's] cause of action, its case might 'arise under' the laws of the United States if a well-pleaded complaint established that its right to relief under state law requires resolution of a substantial question of federal law.]' " Given this, and given that the state claims for relief derived "from a common nucleus of operative fact" (quoting *United Mine Workers v. Gibbs*), the supplemental jurisdiction statute authorized the district court to hear all of the claims.

Joined by Justice Stevens, Justice Ginsburg had a different take. She saw the case as "a watershed decision" because it authorized, in her view, a "cross system appeal":

> "This now-federal case originated as an appeal in state court from a municipal agency's denials of demolition permits. The review that state law provides is classically appellate in character—on the agency's record, not de novo. Nevertheless, the court decides today that this standard brand of appellate review can be shifted from the appropriate state tribunal to a federal court of first instance at the option of either party—plaintiff originally or defendant by removal. . . . After today, litigants asserting federal-question . . . jurisdiction may routinely lodge in federal courts direct appeals from the actions of all manner of local (county and municipal) agencies, boards, and commissions. Exercising this cross-system appellate authority, federal courts may now directly superintend local agencies by affirming, reversing, or modifying their administrative rulings."

The Court's response was that "[o]f course, to say that the terms of § 1367(a) authorize the district courts to exercise supplemental jurisdiction over state law claims for on-the-record review of administrative decisions does not mean that the jurisdiction *must* be exercised in all cases." Accordingly, it remanded for consideration whether the district court should have refused to hear the state claims based on abstention principles or the discretion to deny supplemental jurisdiction contained in *Gibbs* and 28 U.S.C. § 1367(c).

For a general discussion of how to determine the existence of federal question jurisdiction using as the point of departure *City of Chicago*, *Merrill Dow*, *Franchise Tax Board* (the next main case), and the less well known case of Christianson v. Colt Industries Operating Corp., 486 U.S. 800 (1988), see John B. Oakley, Federal Jurisdiction and the Problem of the Litigative Unit: When Does What "Arise Under" Federal Law, 76 Texas L. Rev. 1829 (1998).

7b. The Primacy of Subject Matter Jurisdiction. Rule 12(h)(3) of the Federal Rules of Civil Procedure provides that "[w]henever it appears by suggestion of the parties or otherwise that the court lacks jurisdiction of the subject matter, the court shall dismiss the action." It is standard lore that this requirement operates at all levels of adjudication. If an appellate court notices at any stage of the proceedings that the district court lacked subject matter jurisdiction, it is obliged to order dismissal of the case for lack of jurisdiction and is foreclosed from reaching the merits of the case.[j]

---

j. "[I]f the record discloses that the lower court was without jurisdiction this Court will notice the defect, although the parties make no contention concerning it. [This Court will then have] jurisdiction on appeal, not of the merits but merely for the purpose of correcting the error of the lower court in entertaining the suit." United States v. Corrick, 298 U.S. 435, 440 (1936).

(i) Hypothetical Jurisdiction: *Steel Co. v. Citizens for a Better Environment*. In Steel Co. v. Citizens for a Better Environment, 523 U.S. 83 (1998), six Justices concluded that the plaintiff lacked article III standing to bring suit under a federal statute. The other three thought that the federal statute should not be interpreted to authorize the suit. In the course of his opinion for the Court on the standing question, Justice Scalia described a jurisdictional practice that had grown up in the Courts of Appeals:

> "[S]everal Courts of Appeals ... find it proper to proceed immediately to the merits ... despite jurisdictional objections, at least where (1) the merits question is more readily resolved, and (2) the prevailing party on the merits would be the same as the prevailing party were jurisdiction denied. The Ninth Circuit has denominated this practice—which it characterizes as 'assuming' jurisdiction for the purpose of deciding the merits—the 'doctrine of hypothetical jurisdiction.'"

Justice Scalia made it clear that such a doctrine was unacceptable:

> "We decline to endorse such an approach because it carries the courts beyond the bounds of authorized judicial action and thus offends fundamental principles of separation of powers. This conclusion should come as no surprise, since it is reflected in a long and venerable line of our cases. [Citations omitted.] This Court's insistence that proper jurisdiction appear begins at least as early as 1804, when we set aside a judgment for the defendant at the instance of the losing plaintiff *who had himself* failed to allege the basis for federal jurisdiction. Capron v. Van Noorden, 6 U.S. (2 Cranch) 126 (1804)."

Justice Scalia examined a line of Supreme Court cases that had been cited by the Courts of Appeals in support of its asserted authority. He distinguished them all and continued:

> "While some of the above cases must be acknowledged to have diluted the absolute purity of the rule that article III jurisdiction is always an antecedent question, none of them even approaches approval of a doctrine of 'hypothetical jurisdiction' that enables a court to resolve contested questions of law when its jurisdiction is in doubt. Hypothetical jurisdiction produces nothing more than a hypothetical judgment—which comes to the same thing as an advisory opinion, disapproved by this Court from the beginning. Much more than legal niceties are at stake here. The statutory and (especially) constitutional elements of jurisdiction are an essential ingredient of separation and equilibration of powers, restraining the courts from acting at certain times, and even restraining them from acting permanently regarding certain subjects. For a court to

pronounce upon the meaning or the constitutionality of a state or federal law when it has no jurisdiction to do so is, by very definition, for a court to act ultra vires."

Two Justices in the majority reserved judgment about whether the opinion should be read as an absolute prohibition. Joined by Justice Kennedy, Justice O'Connor wrote separately to say that, while she agreed "that federal courts should be certain of their jurisdiction before reaching the merits of a case," she nonetheless thought that "the Court's opinion should not be read as cataloguing an exhaustive list of circumstances under which federal courts may exercise judgment in 'reserv[ing] difficult questions of . . . jurisdiction when the case alternatively could be resolved on the merits in favor of the same party.' Norton v. Mathews, 427 U.S. 524, 532 (1976)."

Justice Breyer went further. He said:

"I agree with the Court that the respondent in this case lacks article III standing. I further agree that federal courts often and typically should decide standing questions at the outset of a case. That order of decision (first jurisdiction then the merits) helps better to restrict the use of the federal courts to those adversarial disputes that article III defines as the federal judiciary's business. But my qualifying words 'often' and 'typically' are important. The Constitution, in my view, does not require us to replace those words with the word 'always.' The Constitution does not impose a rigid judicial 'order of operations,' when doing so would cause serious practical problems.

"This Court has previously made clear that courts may 'reserve [ ] difficult questions of . . . jurisdiction when the case alternatively could be resolved on the merits in favor of the same party.' Norton v. Mathews, 427 U.S. 524, 532 (1976). That rule makes theoretical sense, for the difficulty of the jurisdictional question makes reasonable the court's jurisdictional assumption. And that rule makes enormous practical sense. Whom does it help to have appellate judges spend their time and energy puzzling over the correct answer to an intractable jurisdictional matter, when (assuming an easy answer on the substantive merits) the same party would win or lose regardless? More importantly, to insist upon a rigid 'order of operations' in today's world of federal court caseloads that have grown enormously over a generation means unnecessary delay and consequent added cost. It means a more cumbersome system. It thereby increases, to at least a small degree, the risk of the 'justice delayed' that means 'justice denied.' "

"For this reason, I would not make the ordinary sequence an absolute requirement. Nor, even though the case before us is ordinary, not exceptional, would I simply reserve judgment about the matter."[k]

(ii) In Personam v. Subject Matter Jurisdiction: *Ruhrgas AG v. Marathon Oil Co.* Ruhrgas AG v. Marathon Oil Co., 526 U.S. 574 (1999), involved an easy question of in personam jurisdiction and a hard question of subject matter jurisdiction (in this case, whether diversity or federal question jurisdiction could be established). Writing for a unanimous Court, Justice Ginsburg adhered to *Steel*, but held it appropriate to address the issue of in personam jurisdiction without resolving the question of subject matter jurisdiction:

> "This case concerns the authority of the federal courts to adjudicate controversies. Jurisdiction to resolve cases on the merits requires both authority over the category of claim in suit (subject-matter jurisdiction) and authority over the parties (personal jurisdiction), so that the court's decision will bind them. In Steel Co. v. Citizens for a Better Environment, 523 U.S. 83 (1998), this Court adhered to the rule that a federal court may not hypothesize subject-matter jurisdiction for the purpose of deciding the merits. *Steel Co.* is the backdrop for the issue now before us: If, as *Steel Co.* held, jurisdiction generally must precede merits in dispositional order, must subject-matter jurisdiction precede personal jurisdiction on the decisional line? Or, do federal district courts have discretion to avoid a difficult question of subject-matter jurisdiction when the absence of personal jurisdiction is the surer ground? . . .
>
> "We hold that in cases removed from state court to federal court, as in cases originating in federal court, there is no unyielding jurisdictional hierarchy. Customarily, a federal court first resolves doubts about its jurisdiction over the subject matter, but there are circumstances in which a district court appropriately accords priority to a personal jurisdiction inquiry. The proceeding before us is such a case. . . .
>
> "The Court of Appeals accorded priority to the requirement of subject-matter jurisdiction because it is nonwaivable and delimits federal-court power, while restrictions on a court's jurisdiction over the person are waivable and protect individual rights. The

---

k. For an extensive consideration of *Steel*, its Court of Appeals antecedents, and its likely effect on future decisions in the Courts of Appeals, see Scott C. Idelman, The Demise of Hypothetical Jurisdiction in the Federal Courts, 52 Vand. L. Rev. 235 (1999). Idelman concludes that "[w]hile the outward form and even the doctrinal core of hypothetical jurisdiction may have been eliminated by the Court's formalist decree, its value and thus its essence will long persist in the deliberations, and quite possibly the decisions, of the lower federal bench." See also Joan Steinman, After *Steel Co.*: "Hypothetical Jurisdiction" in the Federal Appellate Courts, 58 Wash. & Lee L. Rev. 855 (2001), which focuses "on matters left unclear by *Steel Co.* and, in particular, on the effects of the Court's denunciation of the work of the federal appellate courts."

character of the two jurisdictional bedrocks unquestionably differs. Subject-matter limitations on federal jurisdiction serve institutional interests. They keep the federal courts within the bounds the Constitution and Congress have prescribed. Accordingly, subject-matter delineations must be policed by the courts on their own initiative even at the highest level. . . .

"These distinctions do not mean that subject-matter jurisdiction is ever and always the more 'fundamental.' . . . While *Steel Co.* reasoned that subject-matter jurisdiction necessarily precedes a ruling on the merits, the same principle does not dictate a sequencing of jurisdictional issues. . . . It is hardly novel for a federal court to choose among threshold grounds for denying audience to a case on the merits. Thus, as the Court observed in *Steel Co.*, district courts do not overstep article III limits when they decline jurisdiction of state-law claims on discretionary grounds without determining whether those claims fall within their pendent jurisdiction, see Moor v. County of Alameda, 411 U.S. 693, 715–16 (1973), or abstain under Younger v. Harris, 401 U.S. 37 (1971), without deciding whether the parties present a case or controversy, see Ellis v. Dyson, 421 U.S. 426, 433–34 (1975). . . .

"Where, as here, . . . a district court has before it a straightforward personal jurisdiction issue presenting no complex question of state law, and the alleged defect in subject-matter jurisdiction raises a difficult and novel question, the court does not abuse its discretion by turning directly to personal jurisdiction."

Page 485, add at the end of the first paragraph of footnote m:

For an argument that the courts should construe the probate exception narrowly and that Congress should consider overruling it, see Peter Nicolas, Fighting the Probate Mafia: A Dissection of the Probate Exception to Federal Court Jurisdiction, 74 So. Cal. L. Rev. 1479 (2001).

Page 486, add at the end of footnote p:

A similar problem arises in the interpretation of § 1332(a)(2), which establishes federal court jurisdiction for suits between "citizens of a State and citizens or subjects of a foreign state." In JPMorgan Chase Bank v. Traffic Stream (BVI) Infrastructure Ltd., ___ U.S. ___ (2002), the court held unanimously that a corporation organized under the laws of the British Virgin Islands was a "citizen . . . of a foreign state" even though the British Virgin Islands is a British Overseas Territory rather than a separately recognized sovereign state.

Page 500, add to the last paragraph of Note 2:

Robert G. Bone, Revisiting the Policy Case for Supplement Jurisdiction, 74 Ind. L.J. 139 (1998); Edward H. Cooper, An Alternative and Discretionary § 1367, 74 Ind. L.J. 153 (1998); Howard P. Fink, Supplemental Jurisdiction—Take it to the Limit!, 74 Ind. L.J. 161 (1998); William A. Fletcher, "Common Nucleus of Operative Fact" and Defensive Set–Off: Beyond the

Gibbs Test, 74 Ind. L.J. 171 (1998); Richard D. Freer, Toward a Principled Statutory Approach to Supplemental Jurisdiction in Diversity of Citizenship Cases, 74 Ind. L.J. 5 (1998); Edward A. Hartnett, Would the *Kroger* Rule Survive the ALI's Proposed Revision of § 1367?, 51 Duke L.J. 647 (2001); Edward A. Hartnett, § 1367 Producamus, 51 Duke L.J. 687 (2001); Graham C. Lilly, Making Sense of Nonsense: Reforming Supplemental Jurisdiction, 74 Ind. L.J. 181 (1998); John B. Oakley, Integrating Supplemental Jurisdiction and Diversity Jurisdiction: A Progress Report on the Work of the American Law Institute, 74 Ind. L.J. 25 (1998); John B. Oakley, *Kroger* Redux, 51 Duke L.J. 663 (2001); John B. Oakley, Fiat Lux, 51 Duke L.J. 699 (2001); James E. Pfander, Supplemental Jurisdiction and Section 1367: The Case for a Sympathetic Textualism, 148 U. Pa. L. Rev. 109 (1999); Peter Raven–Hansen, The Forgotten Proviso of § 1376(b) (And Why We Forgot), 74 Ind. L.J. 197 (1998); Thomas D. Rowe, Jr., 1367 and All That: Recodifying Supplemental Jurisdiction, 74 Ind. L.J. 53 (1998); David L. Shapiro, Supplemental Jurisdiction: A Confession, An Avoidance, and a Proposal, 74 Ind. L.J. 211 (1998); Joan Steinman, Crosscurrents: Supplemental Jurisdiction, Removal, and the ALI Revision Project, 74 Ind. L.J. 75 (1998); Arthur D. Wolf, Comment on the Supplemental–Jurisdiction Statute: 28 U.S.C. § 1367, 74 Ind. L.J. 223 (1998); Stephen C. Yeazell, Teaching Supplemental Jurisdiction, 74 Ind. L.J. 241 (1998).

Page 518, add at the end of footnote c:

Gasperini has engendered a new round of debate in the *Erie* literature. See, e.g., C. Douglas Floyd, *Erie* Awry: A Comment on *Gasperini v. Center for Humanities, Inc.*, [1997] Brigham Young L. Rev. 267; Richard D. Freer, Some Thoughts on the State of *Erie* After *Gasperini*, 76 Texas L. Rev. 1637 (1998); Thomas D. Rowe, Jr., Not Bad for Government Work: Does Anyone Else Think the Supreme Court is Doing a Halfway Decent Job in its *Erie-Hanna* Jurisprudence?, 73 Notre Dame L. Rev. 963 (1998).

Page 529, add to footnote a:

For a more general discussion of how the Supreme Court should interpret the limitations of the Rules Enabling Act, see Leslie M. Kelleher, Taking "Substantive Rights" (in the Rules Enabling Act) More Seriously, 74 Notre Dame L. Rev. 47 (1998).

Page 538, add a new Note:

   6. ***Semtek International Inc. v. Lockheed Martin Corp.*** Semtek's suit against Lockheed, based on diversity jurisdiction, was dismissed by a California federal district court as barred by the California two-year statute of limitations. A suit alleging the same claims was then filed in a Maryland state court, based on the Maryland three-year limitations period. The Maryland courts held that the preclusive effect of the California federal court judgment was to be determined by federal law and that, under the applicable federal law, the suit was barred.

   In Semtek International Inc. v. Lockheed Martin Corp., 531 U.S. 497 (2001), the Supreme Court unanimously reversed. Writing for the Court, Justice Scalia found no answer in the Federal Rules of Civil Procedure.

There was one prior Supreme Court case on point, Dupasseur v. Rochereau, 88 U.S. (21 Wall.) 130 (1875), which held that state law controlled the res judicata effect of a federal trial court exercising diversity jurisdiction. But *Dupasseur* was "not dispositive because it was decided under the Conformity Act of 1872, which required federal courts to apply the procedural law of the forum State in nonequity cases." What, then, to do? Scalia's answer was that "federal common law governs the claim-preclusive effect of a dismissal by a federal court sitting in diversity.... It is left to us, then, to determine the appropriate federal rule."

And what should "the appropriate federal rule" be? Scalia answered:

> [D]espite the sea change that has occurred in the background law since *Dupasseur* was decided—not only repeal of the Conformity Act but also the watershed decision of this Court in *Erie*—we think the result decreed by *Dupasseur* continues to be correct for diversity cases. Since state, rather than federal, substantive law is at issue there is no need for a uniform federal rule. And indeed, nationwide uniformity in the substance of the matter is better served by having the same claim-preclusive rule (the state rule) apply whether the dismissal has been ordered by a state or a federal court. This is, it seems to us, a classic case for adopting, as the federally prescribed rule of decision, the law that would be applied by state courts in the State in which the federal diversity court sits. [A]ny other rule would produce the sort of "forum-shopping ... and ... inequitable administration of the laws" that *Erie* seeks to avoid, Hanna v. Plumer, 380 U.S. 460, 468 (1965), since filing in, or removing to, federal court would be encouraged by the divergent effects that the litigants would anticipate from likely grounds of dismissal.
>
> This federal reference to state law will not obtain, of course, in situations in which the state law is incompatible with federal interests. If, for example, state law did not accord claim-preclusive effect to dismissals for willful violation of discovery orders, federal courts' interest in the integrity of their own processes might justify a contrary federal rule. No such conflict with potential federal interests exists in the present case. Dismissal of this state cause of action was decreed by the California federal court only because the California statute of limitations so required; and there is no conceivable federal interest in giving that time bar more effect in other courts than the California courts themselves would impose.

The case was accordingly remanded so that the Maryland courts could determine the applicable California preclusion rules.

Is *Semtek* the beginning of a move towards a simpler analysis? Is Scalia's rationale essentially: if there is no applicable federal law or policy, follow state law? Why need any other questions be asked? Compare the three-part analysis suggested near the end of Note 1.

Semtek also involved a narrow interpretation of Rule 41(b). The order of dismissal by the California federal court said that the claims were dismissed "in [their] entirety on the merits and with prejudice." Rule 41(b) itself provided:

> Involuntary Dismissal: Effect Thereof. For failure of the plaintiff to prosecute or to comply with these rules or any order of court, a defendant may move for dismissal of an action or of any claim against the defendant. Unless the court in its order for dismissal otherwise specifies, a dismissal under this subdivision and any dismissal not provided for in this rule, other than a dismissal for lack of jurisdiction, for improper venue, or for failure to join a party under Rule 19, operates as an adjudication upon the merits.

Scalia said for the Court that the effect of a dismissal "without prejudice" was to allow the plaintiff to return to the rendering court with the same underlying claim. As to the effect of a dismissal "on the merits and with prejudice," Scalia said:

> We think, then, that the effect of the "adjudication upon the merits" default provision of Rule 41(b)—and, presumably, of the explicit order in the present case that used the language of that default provision—is simply that, unlike a dismissal "without prejudice," the dismissal in the present case barred refiling of the same claim in the United States District Court for the Central District of California. That is undoubtedly a necessary condition, but it is not a sufficient one, for claim-preclusive effect in other courts.

Why this narrow reading of Rule 41(b)? Scalia had a number of reasons:

> The original connotation of an "on the merits" adjudication is one that actually "pass[es] directly on the substance of [a particular] claim" before the court. Restatement § 19, Comment *a*, at 161. That connotation remains common to every jurisdiction of which we are aware. And it is, we think, the meaning intended in those many statements to the effect that a judgment "on the merits" triggers the doctrine of res judicata or claim preclusion.
>
> But over the years the meaning of the term "judgment on the merits" "has gradually undergone change," R. Marcus, M. Redish, & E. Sherman, Civil Procedure: A Modern Approach 1140–1141 (3d ed.2000), and it has come to be applied to some judgments (such as the one involved here) that do *not* pass upon the substantive merits of a claim and hence do *not* (in many jurisdictions) entail claim-preclusive effect. That is why the Restatement of

Judgments has abandoned the use of the term—"because of its possibly misleading connotations," Restatement § 19, Comment *a*, at 161.

In short, it is no longer true that a judgment "on the merits" is necessarily a judgment entitled to claim-preclusive effect; and there are a number of reasons for believing that the phrase "adjudication upon the merits" does not bear that meaning in Rule 41(b). To begin with, Rule 41(b) sets forth nothing more than a default rule for determining the import of a dismissal (a dismissal is "upon the merits," with the three stated exceptions, unless the court "otherwise specifies"). This would be a highly peculiar context in which to announce a federally prescribed rule on the complex question of claim preclusion, saying in effect, "All federal dismissals (with three specified exceptions) preclude suit elsewhere, unless the court otherwise specifies."

And even apart from the purely default character of Rule 41(b), it would be peculiar to find a rule governing the effect that must be accorded federal judgments by other courts ensconced in rules governing the internal procedures of the rendering court itself. Indeed, such a rule would arguably violate the jurisdictional limitation of the Rules Enabling Act: that the Rules "shall not abridge, enlarge or modify any substantive right," 28 U.S.C. § 2072(b). In the present case, for example, if California law left petitioner free to sue on this claim in Maryland even after the California statute of limitations had expired, the federal court's extinguishment of that right (through Rule 41(b)'s mandated claim-preclusive effect of its judgment) would seem to violate this limitation.

Moreover, as so interpreted, the Rule would in many cases violate the federalism principle of Erie R. Co. v. Tompkins, 304 U.S. 64, 78–80 (1938), by engendering " 'substantial' variations [in outcomes] between state and federal litigation" which would "[l]ikely ... influence the choice of a forum," Hanna v. Plumer, 380 U.S. 460, 467–68 (1965). With regard to the claim-preclusion issue involved in the present case, for example, the traditional rule is that expiration of the applicable statute of limitations merely bars the remedy and does not extinguish the substantive right, so that dismissal on that ground does not have claim-preclusive effect in other jurisdictions with longer, unexpired limitation periods. See Restatement (Second) of Conflict of Laws §§ 142(2), 143 (1969); Restatement of Judgments § 49, Comment *a* (1942). Out-of-state defendants sued on stale claims in California and in other States adhering to this traditional rule would systematically remove state-law suits brought against them to federal court—

where, unless otherwise specified, a statute-of-limitations dismissal would bar suit everywhere.

Finally, if Rule 41(b) did mean what respondent suggests, we would surely have relied upon it in our cases recognizing the claim-preclusive effect of federal judgments in federal-question cases. Yet for over half a century since the promulgation of Rule 41(b), we have not once done so.

Are the twin aims of *Erie* now principles that govern the interpretation of the Federal Rules and that call for narrow interpretations of those Rules in situations that might infringe on the "substantive" interests of the States? Indeed, has the entire rubric of *Hanna* been adjusted to call for (a) use of state rules—whether of substance or procedure—whenever no countervailing federal policy can be found and (b) narrow interpretation of the Federal Rules of Civil Procedure whenever inconsistencies with state practice can be found that might lead plaintiffs to select a federal diversity court over a state court? Is it surprising that *Semtek* was unanimous?

Page 538, add to last paragraph of Note 6:

Joseph P. Bauer, The *Erie* Doctrine Revisited: How a Conflicts Perspective Can Aid the Analysis, 74 Notre Dame L. Rev. 1235 (1999); John T. Cross, The *Erie* Doctrine in Equity, 60 La. L. Rev. 173 (1999); Jerome A. Hoffman, Thinking Out Loud About the Myth of *Erie*: Plus a Good Word for Section 1652, 70 Miss. L.J. 163 (2000).

Page 552, add to footnote f:

For an elaborate criticism of *Swint* and an argument in favor of a properly circumscribed doctrine of pendent appellate jurisdiction applicable to all categories of interlocutory review, see Joan Steinman, The Scope of Appellate Jurisdiction: Pendent Appellate Jurisdiction Before and After *Swint*, 49 Hastings L.J. 1337 (1998).

Page 568, add at the end of footnote d:

Jefferson v. City of Tarrant, 522 U.S. 75 (1997) (confining *Ritchie* to its precise circumstances).

CHAPTER VI

ABSTENTION

Page 590, add a footnote at the end of Note 1:

a. Yet another abstention rationale is known as the "*Rooker-Feldman* doctrine," under which lower federal courts are said to have no jurisdiction to hear functional appeals from state court decisions or to decide questions that are "inextricably intertwined" with prior state court judgments. The doctrine derives from Rooker v. Fidelity Trust Co., 263 U.S. 413 (1923), and District of Columbia Court of Appeals v. Feldman, 460 U.S. 462 (1983).

There are no recent Supreme Court explications of the doctrine, but as applied by the lower federal courts it appears to have broader preclusive effect than the normal application of res judicata principles. For a defense of the doctrine and an exploration of situations where it can legitimately be applied, see Suzanna Sherry, Judicial Federalism in the Trenches: The *Rooker–Feldman* Doctrine in Action, 74 Notre Dame L. Rev. 1085 (1999). The doctrine is also the subject of a Symposium in the Notre Dame Law Review. See Thomas D. Rowe, Jr., *Rooker–Feldman*: Worth Only the Powder to Blow It Up?, 74 Notre Dame L. Rev. 1081 (1999); Suzanna Sherry, Judicial Federalism in the Trenches: The *Rooker–Feldman* Doctrine in Action, 74 Notre Dame L. Rev. 1085 (1999); Barry Friedman & James E. Gaylord, *Rooker–Feldman*, from the Ground Up, 74 Notre Dame L. Rev. 1129 (1999); Susan Bandes, The *Rooker–Feldman* Doctrine: Evaluating Its Jurisdictional Status, 74 Notre Dame L. Rev. 1175 (1999); Jack M. Beermann, Comments on *Rooker–Feldman* or Let State Law Be Our Guide, 74 Notre Dame L. Rev. 1209 (1999).

Page 596, add at the end of paragraph of Note 6:

For an argument endorsing, on both historical and contemporary grounds, greater federal judicial review of state agency, see Ann Woolhandler and Michael G. Collins, Judicial Federalism and the Administrative States, 87 Cal. L. Rev. 613 (1999).

Page 629, add at the end of footnote k:

Brian Stagner, Avoiding Abstention: The *Younger* Exceptions, 29 Texas Tech L. Rev. 137 (1998). Based on cases litigated in the lower courts, Stagner adds two other exceptions to the *Younger* list: a colorable claim of double jeopardy; and waiver by the state of a *Younger* argument.

Page 680, add at the end of footnote f:

See also Lonny Sheinkopf Hoffman, Removal Jurisdiction and the All Writs Act, 148 U. Pa. L. Rev. 401 (1999), and Joan Steinman, The Newest Frontier of Judicial Activism: Removal Under the All Writs Act, 80 Boston U. L. Rev. 773 (2000), which consider federal court use of the All Writs Act (28 U.S.C. § 1651(a)) as the basis for removal of state claims that threaten a prior federal court order.

Page 683, add a footnote at the end of Note 4:

h. Can a defendant in state court remove to federal court on the ground that the plaintiff's claim is precluded by a prior federal court judgment? The Court said "no" in Rivet v. Regions Bank of Louisiana, 522 U.S. 470 (1998): "Under the well-pleaded complaint rule, [claim] preclusion [is] a defensive plea involving no recasting of the plaintiff's complaint, and is therefore not a proper basis for removal."

CHAPTER VII

HABEAS CORPUS

Page 686, add after the Duker citation in footnote a:

For debate about application of the suspension clause in the context of executive detention, see Gerald L. Neuman, Habeas Corpus, Executive Detention, and the Removal of Aliens, 98 Colum. L. Rev. 961 (1998), and the response in Richard H. Fallon, Jr., Applying the Suspension Clause to Immigration Cases, 98 Colum. L. Rev. 1068 (1998). See also George Rutherglen, Structural Uncertainty Over Habeas Corpus and the Jurisdiction of Military Tribunals, 5 Green Bag 2d 285 (2002).

Page 686, add at end of footnote b:

For an argument that the custody requirement should be broadened to encompass situations where convicted sex offenders are subject to registration and community notification laws, see Wayne A. Logan, Federal Habeas in the Information Age, 85 Minn. L. Rev. 147 (2000).

Page 709, add to footnote b:

Alan Clarke, Habeas Corpus: The Historical Debate, 13 N.Y. Law School J. Human Rights 375 (1998); Eric M. Freedman, Milestones in Habeas Corpus: Part II: Leo Frank Lives: Untangling the Historical Roots of Meaningful Federal Habeas Corpus Review of State Convictions, 51 Ala. L. Rev. 1467 (2000); Eric M. Freedman, Milestones in Habeas Corpus: Part III: *Brown v. Allen*: The Habeas Corpus Revolution that Wasn't, 51 Ala. L. Rev. 1541 (2000).

Page 711, add to paragraph of citations at bottom of page:

Stephen B. Bright, Elected Judges and the Death Penalty in Texas: Why Full Habeas Corpus Review by Independent Federal Judges is Indispensable to Protecting Constitutional Rights, 78 Tex. L. Rev. 1805 (2000); Joseph L. Hoffmann, Substance and Procedure in Capital Cases: Why Federal Habeas Courts Should Review the Merits of Every Death Sentence, 78 Tex. L. Rev. 1771 (2000); Brian M. Hoffstadt, How Congress Might Redesign a Leaner, Cleaner Writ of Habeas Corpus, 49 Duke L.J. 947 (2000); Larry W. Yackle, The Figure in the Carpet, 78 Tex. L. Rev. 1731 (2000).

Page 718, add to footnote c:

For comparison of the Court's criminal cases dealing with the retroactivity of constitutional decisions to their civil counterparts, see Pamela J. Stephens, The New Retroactivity Doctrine: Equality, Reliance and Stare Decisis, 48 Syracuse L. Rev. 1515 (1998).

Page 722, add a footnote after the citation in Note 6:

f. For a panel discussion criticizing the statute before it was enacted convened by the ABA Section of Individual Rights and Responsibilities, see Capital Punishment: Is There Any Habeas Left in This Corpus?, 27 Loyola U. Chi. L.J. 523 (1996). See also Stephen B. Bright, Is Fairness Irrelevant?: The Evisceration of Federal Habeas Corpus Review and Limits on the Ability of State Courts to Protect Fundamental Rights, 54 Wash. & Lee L. Rev. 1 (1997).

Page 722, omit *Lindh v. Murphy* and the Notes on the 1966 Legislation, pages 722–743, and substitute the following:

Terry Williams v. Taylor

Supreme Court of the United States, 2000.
529 U.S. 362.

■ JUSTICE STEVENS announced the judgment of the Court and delivered the opinion of the Court with respect to Parts, I, III, and IV, and an opinion with respect to Parts II and V.*

The questions presented are whether Terry Williams' constitutional right to the effective assistance of counsel as defined in Strickland v. Washington, 466 U.S. 668 (1984), was violated, and whether the judgment of the Virginia Supreme Court refusing to set aside his death sentence "was contrary to, or involved an unreasonable application of, clearly established Federal law, as determined by the Supreme Court of the United States," within the meaning of 28 U.S.C. § 2254(d)(1) (1994 ed., Supp. III). We answer both questions affirmatively.

I

On November 3, 1985, Harris Stone was found dead in his residence on Henry Street in Danville, Virginia. Finding no indication of a struggle, local officials determined that the cause of death was blood alcohol poisoning, and the case was considered closed. Six months after Stone's death, Terry Williams, who was then incarcerated in the "I" unit of the city jail for an unrelated offense, wrote a letter to the police stating that he had killed " 'that man down on Henry Street' " and also stating that he " 'did it' " to that " 'lady down on West Green Street' " and was " 'very sorry.' " The letter was unsigned, but it closed with a reference to "I cell." The police readily identified Williams as its author, and, on April 25, 1986, they obtained several statements from him. In one Williams admitted that, after Stone refused to lend him " 'a couple of dollars,' " he had killed Stone with a mattock and took the money from his wallet. In September 1986, Williams was convicted of robbery and capital murder.

---

* Justice Souter, Justice Ginsburg, and Justice Breyer join this opinion in its entirety. Justice O'Connor and Justice Kennedy join Parts I, III, and IV of this opinion.

At Williams' sentencing hearing, the prosecution proved that Williams had been convicted of armed robbery in 1976 and burglary and grand larceny in 1982. The prosecution also introduced the written confessions that Williams had made in April. The prosecution described two auto thefts and two separate violent assaults on elderly victims perpetrated after the Stone murder. On December 4, 1985, Williams had started a fire outside one victim's residence before attacking and robbing him. On March 5, 1986, Williams had brutally assaulted an elderly woman on West Green Street— an incident he had mentioned in his letter to the police. That confession was particularly damaging because other evidence established that the woman was in a "vegetative state" and not expected to recover. Williams had also been convicted of arson for setting a fire in the jail while awaiting trial in this case. Two expert witnesses employed by the State testified that there was a "high probability" that Williams would pose a serious continuing threat to society.

The evidence offered by Williams' trial counsel at the sentencing hearing consisted of the testimony of Williams' mother, two neighbors, and a taped excerpt from a statement by a psychiatrist. One of the neighbors had not been previously interviewed by defense counsel, but was noticed by counsel in the audience during the proceedings and asked to testify on the spot. The three witnesses briefly described Williams as a "nice boy" and not a violent person. The recorded psychiatrist's testimony did little more than relate Williams' statement during an examination that in the course of one of his earlier robberies, he had removed the bullets from a gun so as not to injure anyone.

In his cross-examination of the prosecution witnesses, Williams' counsel repeatedly emphasized the fact that Williams had initiated the contact with the police that enabled them to solve the murder and to identify him as the perpetrator of the recent assaults, as well as the car thefts. In closing argument, Williams' counsel characterized Williams' confessional statements as "dumb," but asked the jury to give weight to the fact that he had "turned himself in, not on one crime but on four ... that the [police otherwise] would not have solved." The weight of defense counsel's closing, however, was devoted to explaining that it was difficult to find a reason why the jury should spare Williams' life.[2]

The jury found a probability of future dangerousness and unanimously fixed Williams' punishment at death. The trial judge concluded that such punishment was "proper" and "just" and imposed the death sentence. The

---

2. In defense counsel's words: "I will admit too that it is very difficult to ask you to show mercy to a man who maybe has not shown much mercy himself. I doubt very seriously that he thought much about mercy when he was in Mr. Stone's bedroom that night with him. I doubt very seriously that he had mercy very highly on his mind when he was walking along West Green and the incident with Alberta Stroud. I doubt very seriously that he had mercy on his mind when he took two cars that didn't belong to him. Admittedly it is very difficult to get us and ask that you give this man mercy when he has shown so little of it himself. But I would ask that you would."

Virginia Supreme Court affirmed the conviction and sentence. It rejected Williams' argument that when the trial judge imposed sentence, he failed to give mitigating weight to the fact that Williams had turned himself in.

State Habeas Corpus Proceedings

In 1988 Williams filed for state collateral relief in the Danville Circuit Court. The petition was subsequently amended, and the Circuit Court (the same judge who had presided over Williams' trial and sentencing) held an evidentiary hearing on Williams' claim that trial counsel had been ineffective. Based on the evidence adduced after two days of hearings, Judge Ingram found that Williams' conviction was valid, but that his trial attorneys had been ineffective during sentencing. Among the evidence reviewed that had not been presented at trial were documents prepared in connection with Williams' commitment when he was 11 years old that dramatically described mistreatment, abuse, and neglect during his early childhood, as well as testimony that he was "borderline mentally retarded," had suffered repeated head injuries, and might have mental impairments organic in origin. The habeas hearing also revealed that the same experts who had testified on the State's behalf at trial believed that Williams, if kept in a "structured environment," would not pose a future danger to society.

Counsel's failure to discover and present this and other significant mitigating evidence was "below the range expected of reasonable, professional competent assistance of counsel." Counsel's performance thus "did not measure up to the standard required under the holding of Strickland v. Washington, 466 U.S. 668 (1984), and [if it had,] there is a reasonable probability that the result of the sentencing phase would have been different." [Acting under the applicable state procedures,] Judge Ingram therefore recommended [to the Virginia Supreme Court] that Williams be granted a rehearing on the sentencing phase of his trial.

The Virginia Supreme Court did not accept that recommendation. Although it assumed, without deciding, that trial counsel had been ineffective, it disagreed with the trial judge's conclusion that Williams had suffered sufficient prejudice to warrant relief. [T]he court concluded that there was no reasonable possibility that the omitted evidence would have affected the jury's sentencing recommendation, and that Williams had failed to demonstrate that his sentencing proceeding was fundamentally unfair.

Federal Habeas Corpus Proceedings

Having exhausted his state remedies, Williams sought a federal writ of habeas corpus pursuant to 28 U.S.C. § 2254. After reviewing the state habeas hearing transcript and the state courts' findings of fact and conclusions of law, the federal trial judge agreed with the Virginia trial judge: The death sentence was constitutionally infirm.

[T]he judge ... identified five categories of mitigating evidence that counsel had failed to introduce,[4] and he rejected the argument that counsel's failure to conduct an adequate investigation had been a strategic decision to rely almost entirely on the fact that Williams had voluntarily confessed.

According to Williams' trial counsel's testimony before the state habeas court, counsel did not fail to seek Williams' juvenile and social services records because he thought they would be counterproductive, but because counsel erroneously believed that " 'state law didn't permit it.' " Counsel also acknowledged in the course of the hearings that information about Williams' childhood would have been important in mitigation. And counsel's failure to contact a potentially persuasive character witness was likewise not a conscious strategic choice, but simply a failure to return that witness' phone call offering his service. Finally, even if counsel neglected to conduct such an investigation at the time as part of a tactical decision, the District Judge found, tactics as a matter of reasonable performance could not justify the omissions.

Turning to the prejudice issue, the judge determined that there was " 'a reasonable probability that, but for counsel's unprofessional errors, the result of the proceeding would have been different.' *Strickland*, 466 U.S. at 694." He found that the Virginia Supreme Court had erroneously assumed that Lockhart v. Fretwell, 506 U.S. 364 (1993), had modified the *Strickland* standard for determining prejudice, and that it had made an important error of fact in discussing its finding of no prejudice.[5] ...

The Federal Court of Appeals reversed. ...[6] We granted certiorari, and now reverse.

---

4. "(i) Counsel did not introduce evidence of the Petitioner's background.... (ii) Counsel did not introduce evidence that Petitioner was abused by his father. (iii) Counsel did not introduce testimony from correctional officers who were willing to testify that defendant would not pose a danger while incarcerated. Nor did counsel offer prison commendations awarded to Williams for his help in breaking up a prison drug ring and for returning a guard's wallet. (iv) Several character witnesses were not called to testify.... [T]he testimony of Elliott, a respected CPA in the community, could have been quite important to the jury.... (v) Finally, counsel did not introduce evidence that Petitioner was borderline mentally retarded, though he was found competent to stand trial."

5. "Specifically, the Virginia Supreme Court found no prejudice, reasoning: 'The mitigation evidence that the prisoner says, in retrospect, his trial counsel should have discovered and offered barely would have altered the profile of this defendant that was presented to the jury. At most, this evidence would have shown that numerous people, mostly relatives, thought that defendant was nonviolent and could cope very well in a structured environment.' The Virginia Supreme Court ignored or overlooked the evidence of Williams' difficult childhood and abuse and his limited mental capacity. It is also unreasonable to characterize the additional evidence as coming from 'mostly relatives.' ... Bruce Elliott, a respected professional in the community, and several correctional officers offered to testify on Williams behalf."

6. Like the Virginia Supreme Court, the Court of Appeals assumed, without deciding, that the performance of trial counsel fell below an objective standard of reasonableness.

II

... The warden here contends that federal habeas corpus relief is prohibited by the amendment to 28 U.S.C. § 2254, enacted as a part of the Antiterrorism and Effective Death Penalty Act of 1996 (AEDPA). The relevant portion of that amendment provides:

> (d) An application for a writ of habeas corpus on behalf of a person in custody pursuant to the judgment of a State court shall not be granted with respect to any claim that was adjudicated on the merits in State court proceedings unless the adjudication of the claim—
>
>> (1) resulted in a decision that was contrary to, or involved an unreasonable application of, clearly established Federal law, as determined by the Supreme Court of the United States....

... The inquiry mandated by the amendment relates to the way in which a federal habeas court exercises its duty to decide constitutional questions; the amendment does not alter the underlying grant of jurisdiction in § 2254(a). When federal judges exercise their federal-question jurisdiction under the "judicial Power" of Article III of the Constitution, it is "emphatically the province and duty" of those judges to "say what the law is." Marbury v. Madison, 5 U.S. (1 Cranch) 137 (1803). At the core of this power is the federal courts' independent responsibility—independent from its coequal branches in the Federal Government, and independent from the separate authority of the several States—to interpret federal law. A construction of AEDPA that would require the federal courts to cede this authority to the courts of the States would be inconsistent with the practice that federal judges have traditionally followed in discharging their duties under Article III of the Constitution. If Congress had intended to require such an important change in the exercise of our jurisdiction, we believe it would have spoken with much greater clarity than is found in the text of AEDPA.

This basic premise informs our interpretation of both parts of § 2254(d)(1): first, the requirement that the determinations of state courts be tested only against "clearly established Federal law, as determined by the Supreme Court of the United States," and second, the prohibition on the issuance of the writ unless the state court's decision is "contrary to, or involved an unreasonable application of," that clearly established law. We address each part in turn.

The "clearly established law" requirement

In Teague v. Lane, 489 U.S. 288 (1989), we held that the petitioner was not entitled to federal habeas relief because he was relying on a rule of federal law that had not been announced until after his state conviction became final. The antiretroactivity rule recognized in *Teague*, which prohibits reliance on "new rules," is the functional equivalent of a statutory provision commanding exclusive reliance on "clearly established law." Because there is no reason to believe that Congress intended to require federal courts to ask both whether a rule sought on habeas is "new" under *Teague*—which remains the law—and also whether it is "clearly established" under AEDPA, it seems safe to assume that Congress had congruent concepts in mind. It is perfectly clear that AEDPA codifies *Teague* to the extent that *Teague* requires federal habeas courts to deny relief that is contingent upon a rule of law not clearly established at the time the state conviction became final.

Teague's core principles are therefore relevant to our construction of this requirement. Justice Harlan recognized the "inevitable difficulties" that come with "attempting 'to determine whether a particular decision has really announced a 'new' rule at all or whether it has simply applied a well-established constitutional principle to govern a case which is closely analogous to those which have been previously considered in the prior case law.'" Mackey v. United States, 401 U.S. 667, 695 (quoting Desist v. United States, 394 U.S. 244, 263 (1969)). But *Teague* established some guidance for making this determination, explaining that a federal habeas court operates within the bounds of comity and finality if it applies a rule "dictated by precedent existing at the time the defendant's conviction became final." *Teague*, 489 U.S., at 301 (emphasis deleted). A rule that "breaks new ground or imposes a new obligation on the States or the Federal Government," ibid., falls outside this universe of federal law.

To this, AEDPA has added, immediately following the "clearly established law" requirement, a clause limiting the area of relevant law to that "determined by the Supreme Court of the United States." 28 U.S.C. § 2254(d)(1). If this Court has not broken sufficient legal ground to establish an asked-for constitutional principle, the lower federal courts cannot themselves establish such a principle with clarity sufficient to satisfy the AEDPA bar. In this respect, we agree with the Seventh Circuit that this clause "extends the principle of *Teague* by limiting the source of doctrine on which a federal court may rely in addressing the application for a writ." Lindh v. Murphy, 96 F.3d 856, 869 (7th Cir.1996). As that court explained:

> This is a retrenchment from former practice, which allowed the United States courts of appeals to rely on their own jurisprudence in addition to that of the Supreme Court. The novelty in this portion § 2254(d)(1) is not the "contrary to" part but the reference to "Federal law, *as determined by the Supreme Court of the United States*" (emphasis added). This extends the principle of *Teague* by limiting the source of doctrine on which a federal court may rely in addressing the application for a writ. It does not, however, purport to limit the federal courts' independent interpretive authority with respect to federal questions.

A rule that fails to satisfy the foregoing criteria is barred by *Teague* from application on collateral review, and, similarly, is not available as a basis for relief in a habeas case to which AEDPA applies.

In the context of this case, we also note that, as our precedent interpreting *Teague* has demonstrated, rules of law may be sufficiently clear for habeas purposes even when they are expressed in terms of a generalized standard rather than as a bright-line rule. As Justice Kennedy has explained:

> If the rule in question is one which of necessity requires a case-by-case examination of the evidence, then we can tolerate a number of specific applications without saying that those applications themselves create a new rule.... Where the beginning point is a rule of this general application, a rule designed for the specific purpose of evaluating a myriad of factual contexts, it will be the infrequent case that yields a result so novel that it forges a new rule, one not dictated by precedent.

Wright v. West, 505 U.S. 277, 308–09 (1992) (opinion concurring in judgment). Moreover, the determination whether or not a rule is clearly established at the time a state court renders its final judgment of conviction is a question as to which the "federal courts must make an independent evaluation." Id., at 305 (O'Connor, J., concurring in judgment); accord id., at 307 (Kennedy, J., concurring).

It has been urged, in contrast, that we should read *Teague* and its progeny to encompass a broader principle of deference requiring federal courts to "validat[e] 'reasonable, good-faith interpretations' of the law" by state courts. The position has been bolstered with references to our statements elucidating the "new rule" inquiry as one turning on whether "reasonable jurists" would agree the rule was not clearly established. This presumption of deference was in essence the position taken by three Members of this Court in *Wright*, 505 U.S., at 290–91 (opinion of Thomas, J.) ("[A] federal habeas court 'must defer to the state court's decision rejecting the claim unless that decision is patently unreasonable'").

Teague, however, does not extend this far. The often repeated language that *Teague* endorses "reasonable, good-faith interpretations" by state courts is an explanation of policy, not a statement of law. The *Teague* cases reflect this Court's view that habeas corpus is not to be used as a second criminal trial, and federal courts are not to run roughshod over the considered findings and judgments of the state courts that conducted the original trial and heard the initial appeals. On the contrary, we have long insisted that federal habeas courts attend closely to those considered decisions, and give them full effect when their findings and judgments are consistent with federal law. But as Justice O'Connor explained in *Wright*, 505 U.S., at 305:

[T]he duty of the federal court in evaluating whether a rule is "new" is not the same as deference; ... *Teague* does not direct federal courts to spend less time or effort scrutinizing the existing federal law, on the ground that they can assume the state courts interpreted it properly.

[T]he maxim that federal courts should "give great weight to the considered conclusions of a coequal state judiciary" ... does not mean that we have held in the past that federal courts must presume the correctness of a state court's legal conclusions on habeas, or that a state court's incorrect legal determination has ever been allowed to stand because it was reasonable. We have always held that federal courts, even on habeas, have an independent obligation to say what the law is.

We are convinced that in the phrase, "clearly established law," Congress did not intend to modify that independent obligation.

The "contrary to, or an unreasonable application of," requirement

The message that Congress intended to convey by using the phrases, "contrary to" and "unreasonable application of" is not entirely clear. The prevailing view in the Circuits is that the former phrase requires de novo review of "pure" questions of law and the latter requires some sort of "reasonability" review of so-called mixed questions of law and fact.

We are not persuaded that the phrases define two mutually exclusive categories of questions. Most constitutional questions that arise in habeas corpus proceedings—and therefore most "decisions" to be made—require the federal judge to apply a rule of law to a set of facts, some of which may be disputed and some undisputed. For example, an erroneous conclusion that particular circumstances established the voluntariness of a confession, or that there exists a conflict of interest when one attorney represents multiple defendants, may well be described either as "contrary to" or as an "unreasonable application of" the governing rule of law. In constitutional adjudication, as in the common law, rules of law often develop incrementally as earlier decisions are applied to new factual situations. But rules that depend upon such elaboration are hardly less lawlike than those that establish a bright-line test.

Indeed, our pre-AEDPA efforts to distinguish questions of fact, questions of law, and "mixed questions," and to create an appropriate standard of habeas review for each, generated some not insubstantial differences of opinion as to which issues of law fell into which category of question, and as to which standard of review applied to each. We thus think the Fourth Circuit was correct when it attributed the lack of clarity in the statute, in part, to the overlapping meanings of the phrases "contrary to" and "unreasonable application of."

The statutory text likewise does not obviously prescribe a specific, recognizable standard of review for dealing with either phrase. Significantly, it does not use any term, such as "de novo" or "plain error," that would easily identify a familiar standard of review. Rather, the text is fairly read simply as a command that a federal court not issue the habeas writ unless the state court was wrong as a matter of law or unreasonable in its application of law in a given case. The suggestion that a wrong state-court "decision"—a legal judgment rendered "after consideration of *facts, and . . . law*," Black's Law Dictionary 407 (6th ed. 1990) (emphasis added)—may no longer be redressed through habeas (because it is unreachable under the "unreasonable application" phrase) is based on a mistaken insistence that the § 2254(d)(1) phrases have not only independent, but mutually exclusive, meanings. Whether or not a federal court can issue the writ "under [the] 'unreasonable application' clause," the statute is clear that habeas may issue under § 2254(d)(1) if a state court "decision" is "contrary to . . . clearly established Federal law." We thus anticipate that there will be a variety of cases, like this one, in which both phrases may be implicated.

Even though we cannot conclude that the phrases establish "a body of rigid rules," they do express a "mood" that the federal judiciary must respect. In this respect, it seems clear that Congress intended federal judges to attend with the utmost care to state-court decisions, including all of the reasons supporting their decisions, before concluding that those proceedings were infected by constitutional error sufficiently serious to warrant the issuance of the writ. Likewise, the statute in a separate provision provides for the habeas remedy when a state-court decision "was based on an unreasonable determination of the facts *in light of the evidence presented in the State court proceeding.*" 28 U.S.C. § 2254(d)(2) (1994 ed., Supp. III) (emphasis added). While this provision is not before us in this case, it provides relevant context for our interpretation of § 2254(d)(1); in this respect, it bolsters our conviction that federal habeas courts must make as the starting point of their analysis the state courts' determinations of fact, including that aspect of a "mixed question" that rests on a finding of fact. AEDPA plainly sought to ensure a level of "deference to the determinations of state courts," provided those determinations did not conflict with federal law or apply federal law in an unreasonable way. Congress wished to curb delays, to prevent "retrials" on federal habeas, and to give effect to state convictions to the extent possible under law. When federal courts are able to fulfill these goals within the bounds of the law, AEDPA instructs them to do so.

On the other hand, it is significant that the word "deference" does not appear in the text of the statute itself. Neither the legislative history, nor the statutory text, suggests any difference in the so-called "deference" depending on which of the two phrases is implicated.[13] Whatever "defer-

---

13. As Judge Easterbrook has noted, the statute surely does not require the kind of "deference" appropriate in other contexts: "It does not tell us to 'defer' to state deci-

ence" Congress had in mind with respect to both phrases, it surely is not a requirement that federal courts actually defer to a state-court application of the federal law that is, in the independent judgment of the federal court, in error. As Judge Easterbrook noted with respect to the phrase "contrary to":

> Section 2254(d) requires us to give state courts' opinions a respectful reading, and to listen carefully to their conclusions, but when the state court addresses a legal question, it is the law "as determined by the Supreme Court of the United States" that prevails.

Lindh, 96 F.3d, at 869.

Our disagreement with Justice O'Connor about the precise meaning of the phrase "contrary to," and the word "unreasonable," is, of course, important, but should affect only a narrow category of cases. The simplest and first definition of "contrary to" as a phrase is "in conflict with." Webster's Ninth New Collegiate Dictionary 285 (1983). In this sense, we think the phrase surely capacious enough to include a finding that the state-court "decision" is simply "erroneous" or wrong. (We hasten to add that even "diametrically different" from, or "opposite" to, an established federal law would seem to include "decisions" that are wrong in light of that law.) And there is nothing in the phrase "contrary to"—as Justice O'Connor appears to agree—that implies anything less than independent review by the federal courts. Moreover, state-court decisions that do not "conflict" with federal law will rarely be "unreasonable" under either her reading of the statute or ours. We all agree that state-court judgments must be upheld unless, after the closest examination of the state-court judgment, a federal court is firmly convinced that a federal constitutional right has been violated. Our difference is as to the cases in which, at first-blush, a state-court judgment seems entirely reasonable, but thorough analysis by a federal court produces a firm conviction that that judgment is infected by constitutional error. In our view, such an erroneous judgment is "unreasonable" within the meaning of the act even though that conclusion was not immediately apparent.

In sum, the statute directs federal courts to attend to every state-court judgment with utmost care, but it does not require them to defer to the opinion of every reasonable state-court judge on the content of federal law.

sions, as if the Constitution means one thing in Wisconsin and another in Indiana. Nor does it tell us to treat state courts the way we treat federal administrative agencies. Deference after the fashion of Chevron U.S.A. Inc. v. Natural Resources Defense Council, Inc., 467 U.S. 837 (1984), depends on delegation. Congress did not delegate interpretive or executive power to the state courts. They exercise powers under their domestic law, constrained by the Constitution of the United States. 'Deference' to the jurisdictions bound by those constraints is not sensible." Lindh v. Murphy, 96 F.3d 856, 868 (7th Cir.1996) (en banc).

If, after carefully weighing all the reasons for accepting a state court's judgment, a federal court is convinced that a prisoner's custody—or, as in this case, his sentence of death—violates the Constitution, that independent judgment should prevail. Otherwise the federal "law as determined by the Supreme Court of the United States" might be applied by the federal courts one way in Virginia and another way in California. In light of the well-recognized interest in ensuring that federal courts interpret federal law in a uniform way, we are convinced that Congress did not intend the statute to produce such a result.

III

In this case, Williams contends that he was denied his constitutionally guaranteed right to the effective assistance of counsel when his trial lawyers failed to investigate and to present substantial mitigating evidence to the sentencing jury. The threshold question under AEDPA is whether Williams seeks to apply a rule of law that was clearly established at the time his state-court conviction became final. That question is easily answered because the merits of his claim are squarely governed by our holding in Strickland v. Washington, 466 U.S. 668 (1984).

We explained in *Strickland* that a violation of the right on which Williams relies has two components:

> First, the defendant must show that counsel's performance was deficient. This requires showing that counsel made errors so serious that counsel was not functioning as the "counsel" guaranteed the defendant by the Sixth Amendment. Second, the defendant must show that the deficient performance prejudiced the defense. This requires showing that counsel's errors were so serious as to deprive the defendant of a fair trial, a trial whose result is reliable.

To establish ineffectiveness, a "defendant must show that counsel's representation fell below an objective standard of reasonableness." To establish prejudice he "must show that there is a reasonable probability that, but for counsel's unprofessional errors, the result of the proceeding would have been different. A reasonable probability is a probability sufficient to undermine confidence in the outcome."

It is past question that the rule set forth in *Strickland* qualifies as "clearly established Federal law, as determined by the Supreme Court of the United States." ... Williams is therefore entitled to relief if the Virginia Supreme Court's decision rejecting his ineffective-assistance claim was either "contrary to, or involved an unreasonable application of," that established law. It was both.

IV

The Virginia Supreme Court erred in holding that our decision in Lockhart v. Fretwell, 506 U.S. 364 (1993), modified or in some way supplanted the rule set down in *Strickland*. It is true that while the *Strickland* test provides sufficient guidance for resolving virtually all ineffective-assistance-of-counsel claims, there are situations in which the overriding focus on fundamental fairness may affect the analysis. Thus, on the one hand, as *Strickland* itself explained, there are a few situations in which prejudice may be presumed. And, on the other hand, there are also situations in which it would be unjust to characterize the likelihood of a different outcome as legitimate "prejudice." Even if a defendant's false testimony might have persuaded the jury to acquit him, it is not fundamentally unfair to conclude that he was not prejudiced by counsel's interference with his intended perjury. Nix v. Whiteside, 475 U.S. 157, 175–76 (1986).

Similarly, in *Lockhart*, we concluded that, given the overriding interest in fundamental fairness, the likelihood of a different outcome attributable to an incorrect interpretation of the law should be regarded as a potential "windfall" to the defendant rather than the legitimate "prejudice" contemplated by our opinion in *Strickland*. The death sentence that Arkansas had imposed on Bobby Ray Fretwell was based on an aggravating circumstance (murder committed for pecuniary gain) that duplicated an element of the underlying felony (murder in the course of a robbery). Shortly before the trial, the United States Court of Appeals for the Eighth Circuit had held that such "double counting" was impermissible, but Fretwell's lawyer (presumably because he was unaware of the [relevant] decision) failed to object to the use of the pecuniary gain aggravator. Before Fretwell's claim for federal habeas corpus relief reached this Court, the [Eighth Circuit] case was overruled. Accordingly, even though the Arkansas trial judge probably would have sustained a timely objection to the double counting, it had become clear that the State had a right to rely on the disputed aggravating circumstance. Because the ineffectiveness of Fretwell's counsel had not deprived him of any substantive or procedural right to which the law entitled him, we held that his claim did not satisfy the "prejudice" component of the *Strickland* test.

Cases such as *Nix* and *Lockhart* do not justify a departure from a straightforward application of *Strickland* when the ineffectiveness of counsel does deprive the defendant of a substantive or procedural right to which the law entitles him. In the instant case, it is undisputed that Williams had a right—indeed, a constitutionally protected right—to provide the jury with the mitigating evidence that his trial counsel either failed to discover or failed to offer.

Nevertheless, the Virginia Supreme Court read our decision in *Lockhart* to require a separate inquiry into fundamental fairness even when Williams is able to show that his lawyer was ineffective and that his ineffectiveness probably affected the outcome of the proceeding. . . . Unlike the Virginia Supreme Court, the state trial judge omitted any reference to *Lockhart* and simply relied on our opinion in *Strickland* as stating the correct standard for judging ineffective-assistance claims. . . . The trial judge analyzed the ineffective-assistance claim under the correct standard; the Virginia Supreme Court did not.

We are likewise persuaded that the Virginia trial judge correctly applied both components of that standard to Williams' ineffectiveness claim. Although he concluded that counsel competently handled the guilt phase of the trial, he found that their representation during the sentencing phase fell short of professional standards—a judgment barely disputed by the State in its brief to this Court. The record establishes that counsel did not begin to prepare for that phase of the proceeding until a week before the trial. They failed to conduct an investigation that would have uncovered extensive records graphically describing Williams' nightmarish childhood, not because of any strategic calculation but because they incorrectly thought that state law barred access to such records. Had they done so, the jury would have learned that Williams' parents had been imprisoned for the criminal neglect of Williams and his siblings,[19] that Williams had been severely and repeatedly beaten by his father, that he had been committed to the custody of the social services bureau for two years during his parents' incarceration (including one stint in an abusive foster home), and then, after his parents were released from prison, had been returned to his parents' custody.

Counsel failed to introduce available evidence that Williams was "borderline mentally retarded" and did not advance beyond sixth grade in school. They failed to seek prison records recording Williams' commendations for helping to crack a prison drug ring and for returning a guard's missing wallet, or the testimony of prison officials who described Williams as among the inmates "least likely to act in a violent, dangerous or provocative way." Counsel failed even to return the phone call of a certified public accountant who had offered to testify that he had visited Williams frequently when Williams was incarcerated as part of a prison ministry program, that Williams "seemed to thrive in a more regimented and structured environment," and that Williams was proud of the carpentry degree he earned while in prison.

Of course, not all of the additional evidence was favorable to Williams. The juvenile records revealed that he had been thrice committed to the juvenile system—for aiding and abetting larceny when he was 11 years old, for pulling a false fire alarm when he was 12, and for breaking and entering when he was 15. But as the Federal District Court correctly observed, the

---

19. Juvenile records contained the following description of his home: "The home was a complete wreck.... There were several places on the floor where someone had had a bowel movement. Urine was standing in several places in the bedrooms. There were dirty dishes scattered over the kitchen, and it was impossible to step any place on the kitchen floor where there was no trash.... The children were all dirty and none of them had on under-pants. Noah and Lula were so intoxicated, they could not find any clothes for the children, nor were they able to put the clothes on them.... The children had to be put in Winslow Hospital, as four of them, by that time, were definitely under the influence of whiskey."

failure to introduce the comparatively voluminous amount of evidence that did speak in Williams' favor was not justified by a tactical decision to focus on Williams' voluntary confession. Whether or not those omissions were sufficiently prejudicial to have affected the outcome of sentencing, they clearly demonstrate that trial counsel did not fulfill their obligation to conduct a thorough investigation of the defendant's background.

We are also persuaded, unlike the Virginia Supreme Court, that counsel's unprofessional service prejudiced Williams within the meaning of *Strickland*. After hearing the additional evidence developed in the postconviction proceedings, the very judge who presided at Williams' trial and who once determined that the death penalty was "just" and "appropriate," concluded that there existed "a reasonable probability that the result of the sentencing phase would have been different" if the jury had heard that evidence. . . .

The Virginia Supreme Court's own analysis of prejudice reaching the contrary conclusion was . . . unreasonable in at least two respects. First, as we have already explained, the State Supreme Court mischaracterized at best the appropriate rule, made clear by this Court in *Strickland*, for determining whether counsel's assistance was effective within the meaning of the Constitution. While it may also have conducted an "outcome determinative" analysis of its own, it is evident to us that the court's decision turned on its erroneous view that a "mere" difference in outcome is not sufficient to establish constitutionally ineffective assistance of counsel. Its analysis in this respect was thus not only "contrary to," but also, inasmuch as the Virginia Supreme Court relied on the inapplicable exception recognized in *Lockhart*, an "unreasonable application of" the clear law as established by this Court.

Second, the State Supreme Court's prejudice determination was unreasonable insofar as it failed to evaluate the totality of the available mitigation evidence—both that adduced at trial, and the evidence adduced in the habeas proceeding—in reweighing it against the evidence in aggravation. [T]he state court failed even to mention the sole argument in mitigation that trial counsel did advance—Williams turned himself in, alerting police to a crime they otherwise would never have discovered, expressing remorse for his actions, and cooperating with the police after that. While this, coupled with the prison records and guard testimony, may not have overcome a finding of future dangerousness, the graphic description of Williams' childhood, filled with abuse and privation, or the reality that he was "borderline mentally retarded," might well have influenced the jury's appraisal of his moral culpability. The circumstances recited in his several confessions are consistent with the view that in each case his violent behavior was a compulsive reaction rather than the product of cold-blooded premeditation. Mitigating evidence unrelated to dangerousness may alter the jury's selection of penalty, even if it does not undermine or rebut the prosecution's death-eligibility case. The Virginia Supreme Court did not entertain that possibility. It thus failed to accord appropriate weight to the body of mitigation evidence available to trial counsel.

V

In our judgment, the state trial judge was correct both in his recognition of the established legal standard for determining counsel's effectiveness, and in his conclusion that the entire postconviction record, viewed as a whole and cumulative of mitigation evidence presented originally, raised "a reasonable probability that the result of the sentencing proceeding would have been different" if competent counsel had presented and explained the significance of all the available evidence. It follows that the Virginia Supreme Court rendered a "decision that was contrary to, or involved an unreasonable application of, clearly established Federal law." Williams' constitutional right to the effective assistance of counsel as defined in Strickland v. Washington, 466 U.S. 668 (1984), was violated.

Accordingly, the judgment of the Court of Appeals is reversed, and the case is remanded for further proceedings consistent with this opinion.

It is so ordered.

■ JUSTICE O'CONNOR delivered the opinion of the Court with respect to Part II (except as to the footnote), concurred in part, and concurred in the judgment.*

... I agree ... that the Virginia Supreme Court's adjudication of Terry Williams' application for state habeas corpus relief ... "resulted in a decision that was contrary to, or involved an unreasonable application of, clearly established Federal law, as determined by the Supreme Court of the United States." ... I ... join Parts I, III, and IV of the Court's opinion. Because I disagree, however, with the interpretation of § 2254(d)(1) set forth in Part II of Justice Stevens' opinion, I write separately to explain my views.

I

Before 1996, this Court held that a federal court entertaining a state prisoner's application for habeas relief must exercise its independent judgment when deciding both questions of constitutional law and mixed constitutional questions (i.e., application of constitutional law to fact). In other words, a federal habeas court owed no deference to a state court's resolution of such questions of law or mixed questions. [O]ur precedents dictated that a federal court should grant a state prisoner's petition for habeas relief if that court were to conclude in its independent judgment that the relevant state court had erred on a question of constitutional law or on a mixed constitutional question.

---

*Justice Kennedy joins this opinion in its entirety. The Chief Justice and Justice Thomas join this opinion with respect to Part II. Justice Scalia joins this opinion with respect to Part II, except as to the footnote.

If today's case were governed by the federal habeas statute prior to Congress' enactment of AEDPA in 1996, I would agree with Justice Stevens that Williams' petition for habeas relief must be granted if we, in our independent judgment, were to conclude that his Sixth Amendment right to effective assistance of counsel was violated.

II

A

Williams' case is not governed by the pre–1996 version of the habeas statute. Because he filed his petition in December 1997, Williams' case is governed by the statute as amended by AEDPA. ... Accordingly, for Williams to obtain federal habeas relief, he must first demonstrate that his case satisfies the condition set by § 2254(d)(1). That provision modifies the role of federal habeas courts in reviewing petitions filed by state prisoners.

Justice Stevens' opinion in Part II essentially contends that § 2254(d)(1) does not alter the previously settled rule of independent review. Indeed, the opinion concludes its statutory inquiry with the somewhat empty finding that § 2254(d)(1) does no more than express a " 'mood' that the federal judiciary must respect." For Justice Stevens, the congressionally enacted "mood" has two important qualities. First, "federal courts [must] attend to every state-court judgment with utmost care" by "carefully weighing all the reasons for accepting a state court's judgment." Second, if a federal court undertakes that careful review and yet remains convinced that a prisoner's custody violates the Constitution, "that independent judgment should prevail." ...

Justice Stevens arrives at his erroneous interpretation by means of one critical misstep. He fails to give independent meaning to both the "contrary to" and "unreasonable application" clauses of the statute. ... By reading § 2254(d)(1) as one general restriction on the power of the federal habeas court, Justice Stevens manages to avoid confronting the specific meaning of the statute's "unreasonable application" clause and its ramifications for the independent-review rule. ... Section 2254(d)(1) defines two categories of cases in which a state prisoner may obtain federal habeas relief with respect to a claim adjudicated on the merits in state court. Under the statute, a federal court may grant a writ of habeas corpus if the relevant state-court decision was either (1) *"contrary to* ... clearly established Federal law, as determined by the Supreme Court of the United States," or (2) *"involved an unreasonable application of* ... clearly established Federal law, as determined by the Supreme Court of the United States." (Emphases added.)

The Court of Appeals for the Fourth Circuit properly accorded both the "contrary to" and "unreasonable application" clauses independent meaning. The Fourth Circuit's interpretation of § 2254(d)(1) in Williams' case relied, in turn, on that court's previous decision in Green v. French, 143 F.3d 865 (4th Cir.1998). ... With respect to the first of the two statutory clauses, the Fourth Circuit held in *Green* that a state-court decision can be "contrary to" this Court's clearly established precedent in two ways. First, a state-court decision is contrary to this Court's precedent if the state court arrives at a conclusion opposite to that reached by this Court on a question of law. Second, a state-court decision is also contrary to this Court's precedent if the state court confronts facts that are materially indistinguishable from a relevant Supreme Court precedent and arrives at a result opposite to ours.

The word "contrary" is commonly understood to mean "diametrically different," "opposite in character or nature," or "mutually opposed." Webster's Third New International Dictionary 495 (1976). The text of § 2254(d)(1) therefore suggests that the state court's decision must be substantially different from the relevant precedent of this Court. The Fourth Circuit's interpretation of the "contrary to" clause accurately reflects this textual meaning. A state-court decision will certainly be contrary to our clearly established precedent if the state court applies a rule that contradicts the governing law set forth in our cases. Take, for example, our decision in Strickland v. Washington, 466 U.S. 668 (1984). If a state court were to reject a prisoner's claim of ineffective assistance of counsel on the grounds that the prisoner had not established by a preponderance of the evidence that the result of his criminal proceeding would have been different, that decision would be "diametrically different," "opposite in character or nature," and "mutually opposed" to our clearly established precedent because we held in *Strickland* that the prisoner need only demonstrate a "reasonable probability that ... the result of the proceeding would have been different." A state-court decision will also be contrary to this Court's clearly established precedent if the state court confronts a set of facts that are materially indistinguishable from a decision of this Court and nevertheless arrives at a result different from our precedent. Accordingly, in either of these two scenarios, a federal court will be unconstrained by § 2254(d)(1) because the state-court decision falls within that provision's "contrary to" clause.

On the other hand, a run-of-the-mill state-court decision applying the correct legal rule from our cases to the facts of a prisoner's case would not fit comfortably within § 2254(d)(1)'s "contrary to" clause. Assume, for example, that a state-court decision on a prisoner's ineffective-assistance claim correctly identifies *Strickland* as the controlling legal authority and, applying that framework, rejects the prisoner's claim. Quite clearly, the state-court decision would be in accord with our decision in *Strickland* as to the legal prerequisites for establishing an ineffective-assistance claim, even assuming the federal court considering the prisoner's habeas application might reach a different result applying the *Strickland* framework itself. It is difficult, however, to describe such a run-of-the-mill state-court decision as "diametrically different" from, "opposite in character or nature" from, or "mutually opposed" to *Strickland*, our clearly established precedent. Although the state-court decision may be contrary to the federal court's conception of how *Strickland* ought to be applied in that particular case, the decision is not "mutually opposed" to *Strickland* itself.

Justice Stevens would instead construe § 2254(d)(1)'s "contrary to" clause to encompass such a routine state-court decision. That construction, however, saps the "unreasonable application" clause of any meaning. If a federal habeas court can, under the "contrary to" clause, issue the writ whenever it concludes that the state court's application of clearly established federal law was incorrect, the "unreasonable application" clause becomes a nullity. We must, however, if possible, give meaning to every clause of the statute. Justice Stevens not only makes no attempt to do so, but also construes the "contrary to" clause in a manner that ensures that the "unreasonable application" clause will have no independent meaning. We reject that expansive interpretation of the statute. Reading § 2254(d)(1)'s "contrary to" clause to permit a federal court to grant relief in cases where a state court's error is limited to the manner in which it applies Supreme Court precedent is suspect given the logical and natural fit of the neighboring "unreasonable application" clause to such cases.

The Fourth Circuit's interpretation of the "unreasonable application" clause of § 2254(d)(1) is generally correct. That court held in *Green* that a state-court decision can involve an "unreasonable application" of this Court's clearly established precedent in two ways. First, a state-court decision involves an unreasonable application of this Court's precedent if the state court identifies the correct governing legal rule from this Court's cases but unreasonably applies it to the facts of the particular state prisoner's case. Second, a state-court decision also involves an unreasonable application of this Court's precedent if the state court either unreasonably extends a legal principle from our precedent to a new context where it should not apply or unreasonably refuses to extend that principle to a new context where it should apply.

A state-court decision that correctly identifies the governing legal rule but applies it unreasonably to the facts of a particular prisoner's case certainly would qualify as a decision "involv[ing] an unreasonable application of . . . clearly established Federal law." . . . *

The Fourth Circuit also held in *Green* that state-court decisions that unreasonably extend a legal principle from our precedent to a new context where it should not apply (or unreasonably refuse to extend a legal principle to a new context where it should apply) should be analyzed under § 2254(d)(1)'s "unreasonable application" clause. Although that holding

---

* The legislative history of § 2254(d)(1) also supports this interpretation. See, e.g., 142 Cong. Rec. 7799 (1996) (remarks of Sen. Specter) ("[U]nder the bill deference will be owed to state courts' decisions on the application of federal law to the facts. Unless it is unreasonable, a state court's decision applying the law to the facts will be upheld"); 141 Cong. Rec. 14666 (1995) (remarks of Sen. Hatch) ("[W]e allow a federal court to overturn a state court decision only if it is contrary to clearly established federal law or if it involves an 'unreasonable application' of clearly established federal law to the facts").

may perhaps be correct, the classification does have some problems of precision. Just as it is sometimes difficult to distinguish a mixed question of law and fact from a question of fact, it will often be difficult to identify separately those state-court decisions that involve an unreasonable application of a legal principle (or an unreasonable failure to apply a legal principle) to a new context. Indeed, on the one hand, in some cases it will be hard to distinguish a decision involving an unreasonable extension of a legal principle from a decision involving an unreasonable application of law to facts. On the other hand, in many of the same cases it will also be difficult to distinguish a decision involving an unreasonable extension of a legal principle from a decision that "arrives at a conclusion opposite to that reached by this Court on a question of law." Today's case does not require us to decide how such "extension of legal principle" cases should be treated under § 2254(d)(1). For now it is sufficient to hold that when a state-court decision unreasonably applies the law of this Court to the facts of a prisoner's case, a federal court applying § 2254(d)(1) may conclude that the state-court decision falls within that provision's "unreasonable application" clause.

B

There remains the task of defining what exactly qualifies as an "unreasonable application" of law under § 2254(d)(1). The Fourth Circuit held in *Green* that a state-court decision involves an "unreasonable application of . . . clearly established Federal law" only if the state court has applied federal law "in a manner that reasonable jurists would all agree is unreasonable." The placement of this additional overlay on the "unreasonable application" clause was erroneous. It is difficult to fault the Fourth Circuit for using this language given the fact that we have employed nearly identical terminology to describe the related inquiry undertaken by federal courts in applying the nonretroactivity rule of *Teague*. For example, in Lambrix v. Singletary, 520 U.S. 518 (1997), we stated that a new rule is not dictated by precedent unless it would be "apparent to *all reasonable jurists*." (Emphasis added). In Graham v. Collins, 506 U.S. 461 (1993), another nonretroactivity case, we employed similar language, stating that we could not say "that *all reasonable jurists* would have deemed themselves compelled to accept Graham's claim in 1984." (Emphasis added.)

Defining an "unreasonable application" by reference to a "reasonable jurist," however, is of little assistance to the courts that must apply § 2254(d)(1) and, in fact, may be misleading. Stated simply, a federal habeas court making the "unreasonable application" inquiry should ask whether the state court's application of clearly established federal law was objectively unreasonable. The federal habeas court should not transform the inquiry into a subjective one by resting its determination instead on the simple fact that at least one of the Nation's jurists has applied the relevant federal law in the same manner the state court did in the habeas petitioner's case. The "all reasonable jurists" standard would tend to mislead federal habeas courts by focusing their attention on a subjective inquiry rather than on an objective one. . . .

The term "unreasonable" is no doubt difficult to define. That said, it is a common term in the legal world and, accordingly, federal judges are familiar with its meaning. For purposes of today's opinion, the most important point is that an unreasonable application of federal law is different from an incorrect application of federal law. . . . Congress specifically used the word "unreasonable," and not a term like "erroneous" or "incorrect." Under § 2254(d)(1)'s "unreasonable application" clause, then, a federal habeas court may not issue the writ simply because that court concludes in its independent judgment that the relevant state-court decision applied clearly established federal law erroneously or incorrectly. Rather, that application must also be unreasonable. . . .

Throughout this discussion the meaning of the phrase "clearly established Federal law, as determined by the Supreme Court of the United States" has been put to the side. That statutory phrase refers to the holdings, as opposed to the dicta, of this Court's decisions as of the time of the relevant state-court decision. In this respect, the "clearly established Federal law" phrase bears only a slight connection to our *Teague* jurisprudence. With one caveat, whatever would qualify as an old rule under our *Teague* jurisprudence will constitute "clearly established Federal law, as determined by the Supreme Court of the United States" under § 2254(d)(1). The one caveat, as the statutory language makes clear, is that § 2254(d)(1) restricts the source of clearly established law to this Court's jurisprudence.

In sum, § 2254(d)(1) places a new constraint on the power of a federal habeas court to grant a state prisoner's application for a writ of habeas corpus with respect to claims adjudicated on the merits in state court. Under § 2254(d)(1), the writ may issue only if one of the following two conditions is satisfied—the state-court adjudication resulted in a decision that (1) "was contrary to . . . clearly established Federal law, as determined by the Supreme Court of the United States," or (2) "involved an unreasonable application of . . . clearly established Federal law, as determined by the Supreme Court of the United States." Under the "contrary to" clause, a federal habeas court may grant the writ if the state court arrives at a conclusion opposite to that reached by this Court on a question of law or if the state court decides a case differently than this Court has on a set of materially indistinguishable facts. Under the "unreasonable application" clause, a federal habeas court may grant the writ if the state court identifies the correct governing legal principle from this Court's decisions but unreasonably applies that principle to the facts of the prisoner's case.

III

Although I disagree with Justice Stevens concerning the standard we must apply under § 2254(d)(1) in evaluating Terry Williams' claims on habeas, I agree with the Court that the Virginia Supreme Court's adjudication of Williams' claim of ineffective assistance of counsel resulted in a decision that was both contrary to and involved an unreasonable application of this Court's clearly established precedent. Specifically, I believe that the Court's discussion in Parts III and IV is correct and that it demonstrates the reasons that the Virginia Supreme Court's decision in Williams' case, even under the interpretation of § 2254(d)(1) I have set forth above, was both contrary to and involved an unreasonable application of our precedent.

First, I agree with the Court that our decision in *Strickland* undoubtedly qualifies as "clearly established Federal law, as determined by the Supreme Court of the United States," within the meaning of § 2254(d)(1). Second, I agree that the Virginia Supreme Court's decision was contrary to that clearly established federal law to the extent it held that our decision in Lockhart v. Fretwell, 506 U.S. 364 (1993), somehow modified or supplanted the rule set forth in *Strickland*. . . .

Third, I also agree with the Court that, to the extent the Virginia Supreme Court did apply *Strickland*, its application was unreasonable. As the Court correctly recounts, Williams' trial counsel failed to conduct investigation that would have uncovered substantial amounts of mitigation evidence. . . . The consequence of counsel's failure to conduct the requisite, diligent investigation into his client's troubling background and unique personal circumstances manifested itself during his generic, unapologetic closing argument, which provided the jury with no reasons to spare petitioner's life. . . . Based on its consideration of all of this evidence, the same trial judge that originally found Williams' death sentence "justified and warranted," concluded that trial counsel's deficient performance prejudiced Williams, and accordingly recommended that Williams be granted a new sentencing hearing. The Virginia Supreme Court's decision reveals an obvious failure to consider the totality of the omitted mitigation evidence. For that reason, and the remaining factors discussed in the Court's opinion, I believe that the Virginia Supreme Court's decision "involved an unreasonable application of . . . clearly established Federal law, as determined by the Supreme Court of the United States."

Accordingly, although I disagree with the interpretation of § 2254(d)(1) set forth in Part II of Justice Stevens' opinion, I join Parts I, III, and IV of the Court's opinion and concur in the judgment of reversal.

■ CHIEF JUSTICE REHNQUIST, with whom JUSTICE SCALIA and JUSTICE THOMAS join, concurring in part and dissenting in part.

I agree with the Court's interpretation of 28 U.S.C. § 2254(d)(1), see ante (opinion of O'Connor, J.), but disagree with its decision to grant habeas relief in this case.

There is "clearly established Federal law, as determined by [this Court]" that governs petitioner's claim of ineffective assistance of counsel:

Strickland v. Washington, 466 U.S. 668 (1984). Thus, we must determine whether the Virginia Supreme Court's adjudication was "contrary to" or an "unreasonable application of" *Strickland*.

Generally, in an ineffective-assistance-of-counsel case where the state court applies *Strickland*, federal habeas courts can proceed directly to "unreasonable application" review. But, according to the substance of petitioner's argument, this could be one of the rare cases where a state court applied the wrong Supreme Court precedent, and, consequently, reached an incorrect result. Petitioner argues, and the Court agrees, that the Virginia Supreme Court improperly held that Lockhart v. Fretwell, 506 U.S. 364 (1993), "modified or in some way supplanted" the rule set down in *Strickland*. I agree that such a holding would be improper. But the Virginia Supreme Court did not so hold as it did not rely on *Lockhart* to reach its decision.

Before delving into the evidence presented at the sentencing proceeding, the Virginia Supreme Court stated:

> We shall demonstrate that the criminal proceeding sentencing defendant to death was not fundamentally unfair or unreliable, and that the prisoner's assertions about the potential effects of the omitted proof do not establish a "reasonable probability" that the result of the proceeding would have been different, nor any probability sufficient to undermine confidence in the outcome. Therefore, any ineffective assistance of counsel did not result in actual prejudice to the accused.

Williams v. Warden, 254 Va. 16, 25, 487 S.E.2d 194, 199 (1997).

While the first part of this statement refers to *Lockhart*, the rest of the statement is straight out of *Strickland*. Indeed, after the initial allusion to *Lockhart*, the Virginia Supreme Court's analysis explicitly proceeds under *Strickland* alone. Because the Virginia Supreme Court did not rely on *Lockhart* to make its decision, and, instead, appropriately relied on *Strickland*, that court's adjudication was not "contrary to" this Court's clearly established precedent

The question then becomes whether the Virginia Supreme Court's adjudication resulted from an "unreasonable application of" *Strickland*. In my view, it did not.

I, like the Virginia Supreme Court and the Federal Court of Appeals below, will assume without deciding that counsel's performance fell below an objective standard of reasonableness. As to the prejudice inquiry, I agree with the Court of Appeals that evidence showing that petitioner presented a future danger to society was overwhelming. As that court stated:

> The murder of Mr. Stone was just one act in a crime spree that lasted most of Williams's life. Indeed, the jury heard evidence that, in the months following the murder of Mr. Stone, Williams savagely beat an elderly woman, stole two cars, set fire to a home,

stabbed a man during a robbery, set fire to the city jail, and confessed to having strong urges to choke other inmates and to break a fellow prisoner's jaw.

In *Strickland*, we said that both the performance and prejudice components of the ineffectiveness inquiry are mixed questions of law and fact. It is with this kind of a question that the "unreasonable application of" clause takes on meaning. While the determination of "prejudice" in the legal sense may be a question of law, the subsidiary inquiries are heavily factbound.

Here, there was strong evidence that petitioner would continue to be a danger to society, both in and out of prison. It was not, therefore, unreasonable for the Virginia Supreme Court to decide that a jury would not have been swayed by evidence demonstrating that petitioner had a terrible childhood and a low IQ. The potential mitigating evidence that may have countered the finding that petitioner was a future danger was testimony that petitioner was not dangerous while in detention. But, again, it is not unreasonable to assume that the jury would have viewed this mitigation as unconvincing upon hearing that petitioner set fire to his cell while awaiting trial for the murder at hand and has repeated visions of harming other inmates.

Accordingly, I would hold that habeas relief is barred by 28 U.S.C. § 2254(d).

NOTES ON THE 1996 LEGISLATION

1. Questions and Comments on *Terry Williams v. Taylor*. In her opinion stating the Court's interpretation of § 2254(d), Justice O'Connor describes two distinct types of cases. In the first, to be decided under the "contrary to" clause, "a federal habeas court may grant the writ if the state court arrives at a conclusion opposite to that reached by this Court on a question of law or if the state court decides a case differently than this Court has on a set of materially indistinguishable facts." In the second, to be decided under the "unreasonable application" clause, "a federal habeas court may grant the writ if the state court identifies the correct governing legal principle from this Court's decisions but unreasonably applies that principle to the facts of the prisoner's case."

Speaking for four Justices on this point, Justice Stevens saw but a single category:

> We are not persuaded that the phrases define two mutually exclusive categories of questions. Most constitutional questions that arise in habeas corpus proceedings—and therefore most "decisions" to be made—require the federal judge to apply a rule of law to a set of facts, some of which may be disputed and some undisputed. For example, an erroneous conclusion that particular circumstances established the voluntariness of a confession, or

that there exists a conflict of interest when one attorney represents multiple defendants, may well be described either as "contrary to" or as an "unreasonable application of "the governing rule of law.

Justice Stevens adds that the difference between his view and that of the Court "is, of course, important, but should affect only a narrow category of cases." What, exactly, are the "important" differences between the two opinions? Will they "affect only a narrow category of cases"? Quite apart from subtle (or "important") differences in how the interpretation of § 2254(d) is stated, at the end of the day how did the law change in 1996? Will the 1996 revision of § 2254(d) have a significant impact on federal habeas litigation?

Consider, in this respect, the division of the Court on the ultimate outcome in *Terry Williams*. Recall that three Justices (Thomas, joined by Rehnquist and Scalia) concluded in Wright v. West, 505 U.S. 277 (1992), that federal habeas courts " 'must defer to the state court's decision rejecting the claim unless that decision is patently unreasonable.' " The remainder of the Court adhered to the pre–1966 doctrine that questions of law and mixed questions of law and fact were to be decided de novo by federal habeas courts. After *Terry Williams*, can it be said that § 2254(d) codified the Thomas position in *Wright v. West*? Or does *Terry Williams* reflect, essentially, the same split among the Justices seen in *Wright v. West*?

Finally, what are the incentives for state-court decisionmaking established by § 2254(d)? Should a state supreme court ignore Court of Appeals decisions and focus only on "clearly established Federal law, as determined by the Supreme Court of the United States"? Should it refuse to recognize the implications of a line of Supreme Court decisions and focus only on what has been "clearly established" to date?

2. Bell v. Cone. The Court applied *Williams* in Bell v. Cone, ___ U.S. ___ (2002). The defendant was sentenced to death for the murder of an elderly couple. He sought federal habeas on the ground, previously presented to the state courts, that he was inadequately represented by counsel at the sentencing phase of his trial. He claimed both that the state court applied the wrong federal standard and that its application of the federal standard was unreasonable. Chief Justice Rehnquist wrote for the Court. He began by summarizing the rationale in *Williams*:

> As we stated in *Williams*, § 2254(d)(1)'s "contrary to" and "unreasonable application" clauses have independent meaning. A federal habeas court may issue the writ under the "contrary to" clause if the state court applies a rule different from the governing law set forth in our cases, or if it decides a case differently than we have done on a set of materially indistinguishable facts. The court may grant relief under the "unreasonable application" clause if the state court correctly identifies the governing legal principle from our decisions but unrea-

sonably applies it to the facts of the particular case. The focus of the latter inquiry is on whether the state court's application of clearly established federal law is objectively unreasonable, and we stressed in *Williams* that an unreasonable application is different from an incorrect one.

Over the dissent of Justice Stevens, the Court held first that the state courts had applied the correct federal standard. The state court decision did not violate the strictures of the "contrary to" clause. The question then was whether its application of the correct standard was unreasonable. On that point, the Court said:

> The remaining issue, then, is whether respondent can obtain relief on the ground that the state court's adjudication of his claim involved an "unreasonable application" of Strickland v. Washington, 466 U.S. 668 (1984). In *Strickland* we said that "[j]udicial scrutiny of a counsel's performance must be highly deferential" and that "every effort [must] be made to eliminate the distorting effects of hindsight, to reconstruct the circumstances of counsel's challenged conduct, and to evaluate the conduct from counsel's perspective at the time." Thus, even when a court is presented with an ineffective-assistance claim not subject to § 2254(d)(1) deference, a defendant must overcome the "presumption that, under the circumstances, the challenged action 'might be considered sound trial strategy.'"
>
> For respondent to succeed, however, he must do more than show that he would have satisfied *Strickland*'s test if his claim were being analyzed in the first instance, because under § 2254(d)(1), it is not enough to convince a federal habeas court that, in its independent judgment, the state-court decision applied *Strickland* incorrectly. Rather, he must show that the Tennessee Court of Appeals applied *Strickland* to the facts of his case in an objectively unreasonable manner. This, we conclude, he cannot do.

The Court supported this conclusion with an analysis of the lawyer's performance. There were no other dissents.

3. *Horn v. Banks.* Does *Teague* survive the enactment of the new federal habeas legislation? In Horn v. Banks, ___ U.S. ___ (2002), the Court held that it does. Federal habeas courts are required to apply a *Teague* analysis even though a state post-conviction court addresses the criminal defendant's claims on the merits and even though the state court's decision makes an "unreasonable" mistake in its application of federal law.

Banks had been convicted of murder and sentenced to death. The Supreme Court decided Mills v. Maryland, 486 U.S. 367 (1988), after his direct appeal had been denied. *Mills* held that a capital jury cannot be required unanimously to agree that a particular mitigating circumstance exists before they may consider that circumstance in their sentencing decision. Banks sought state post-conviction relief on the grounds that the jury instructions in his case violated the strictures of *Mills*. The Pennsylvania Supreme court disagreed, holding that the jury instructions were consistent with *Mills*. On federal habeas, the Circuit Court held that it did not have to address the applicability of *Teague* because the state courts themselves had applied *Mills* retroactively. It then applied § 2254(d), holding that the Pennsylvania Supreme Court's application of *Mills* was "unreasonable."

> The Supreme Court reversed in a unanimous per curiam opinion:

> While it is of course a necessary prerequisite to federal habeas relief that a prisoner satisfy the AEDPA standard of review set forth in 28 U.S.C. § 2254(d) ... , none of our post-AEDPA cases have suggested that a writ of habeas corpus should automatically issue if a prisoner satisfies the AEDPA standard, or that AEDPA relieves courts from the responsibility of addressing properly raised *Teague* arguments. To the contrary, if our post-AEDPA cases suggest anything about AEDPA's relationship to *Teague,* it is that the AEDPA and *Teague* inquiries are distinct. ...Thus, in addition to performing any analysis required by AEDPA, a federal court considering a habeas petition must conduct a threshold *Teague* analysis when the issue is properly raised by the state.

Since the state had properly raised *Teague* in both lower federal courts, the Supreme Court remanded for determination of whether *Mills* was to be retroactively applied in light of the *Teague* analysis.

4. Additional Ambiguities. [Here read Note 3, page 742. Add two new paragraphs at the end of the Note:]

> Notice that Justice O'Connor states in *Terry Williams* that the statutory phrase "clearly established Federal law, as determined by the Supreme Court of the United States" in § 2254(d) "refers to the holdings, as opposed to the dicta, of this Court's decisions *as of the time of the relevant state-court decision.*" [Emphasis added.] Does this mean, contrary to *Teague*, that there are no occasions when "new" Supreme Court decisions will be applied on federal habeas corpus?

> Consider the following hypothetical. Assume the state courts, following established Supreme Court precedent, uphold a criminal conviction because they conclude that the underlying conduct on which the conviction was based was not protected speech under the First Amendment. Assume also (a) that the relevant Supreme Court precedents are later overruled, meaning that the underlying conduct is now protected speech; and (b) that collateral attack is no longer available in the state courts. If the convicted defendant then seeks federal habeas, what result?

Page 741, add new footnote after second paragraph of Note 1:

a. For an extensive elaboration of this position and criticism of the result in *Lindh*, see James S. Liebman and William F. Ryan, "Some Effectual Power": The Quantity and Quality of Decisionmaking Required of Article III Courts, 98 Colum. L. Rev. 696 (1998). For a response to Liebman and Ryan, see Kent S. Scheidegger, Habeas Corpus, Relitigation, and the Legislative Power, 98 Colum. L. Rev. 888 (1998).

Page 742, add a footnote after the first question at the top of the page:

a. The early case law in the circuit courts is examined and an analysis of the appropriate standards of review is presented in Evan Tsen Lee, Section 2254(d) of the New Habeas Statute: An (Opinionated) User's Manual, 51 Vand. L. Rev. 103 (1998). See also Note, Rewriting the Great Writ: Standards of Review for Habeas Corpus under the New 28 U.S.C. § 2254, 110 Harv. L. Rev. 1868 (1997). Both authors disagree with Yackle's interpretation. Yackle has argued elsewhere that the new habeas provisions "are unlikely to have large-scale, systematic effects on the outcomes in habeas corpus ... cases." Mark Tushnet & Larry Yackle, Symbolic Statutes and Real Laws: The Pathologies of the Antiterrorism and Effective Death Penalty Act and the Prison Litigation Reform Act, 47 Duke L.J. 1 (1997).

Page 743, add a new Note:

4. Bibliography. A symposium in the Georgetown Law Journal entitled Congress and the Courts: Jurisdiction and Remedies contains six articles provoked in part by the 1996 habeas legislation: Vicki C. Jackson, Introduction: Congressional Control of Jurisdiction and the Future of the Federal Courts—Opposition, Agreement, and Hierarchy, 86 Geo. L.J. 2445 (1998); David Cole, Jurisdiction and Liberty: Habeas Corpus and Due Process as Limits on Congress's Control of Federal Jurisdiction, 86 Geo. L.J. 2481 (1998); John Harrison, Jurisdiction, Congressional Power, and Constitutional Remedies, 86 Geo. L.J. 2513 (1998); Lawrence G. Sager, *Klein*'s First Principle: A Proposed Solution, 86 Geo. L.J. 2525 (1998); Daniel J. Meltzer, Congress, Courts, and Constitutional Remedies, 86 Geo. L.J. 2537 (1998); Judith Resnick, The Federal Courts and Congress: Additional Sources, Alternative Texts, and Altered Aspirations, 86 Geo. L.J. 2589 (1998).

Page 754, add a footnote after the second sentence of the first full paragraph:

f. Suppose the ineffective assistance claim could have been presented to the state courts but was not. Does the failure properly to exhaust that claim mean that it cannot be asserted as cause for the procedural default of another claim? The Court answered "yes" in Edwards v. Carpenter, 529 U.S. 446 (2000). The habeas petitioner is required to establish "cause and prejudice" to excuse failure to raise the ineffective assistance claim in order for it to suffice as "cause" for the failure to raise the other claim. Joined by Justice Stevens, Justice Breyer dissented from this holding, concluding that it "unnecessarily adds to [the] complexity [of the Court's habeas jurisprudence]."—[Footnote by eds.]

Page 754, omit Note 6 and substitute the following:

6. Finality of Completed Sentences Used to Enhance a Current Sentence. Numerous state and federal laws permit sentences for criminal convictions to be enhanced based on previous criminal convictions. May the defendant collaterally attack the current sentence on the ground that a prior conviction was unconstitutionally obtained? The Court answered "no" in a pair of cases decided by five-to-four votes.

The first case, Daniels v. United States, 532 U.S. 374 (2001), was a § 2255 proceeding. The defendant claimed that his current federal sentence was invalid because it was based on prior state convictions obtained by guilty pleas that were not knowing and voluntary and, in one case, that was the result of ineffective assistance of counsel. The Court had held in Custis v. United States, 511 U.S. 485 (1994), that prior state convictions could not be collaterally attacked in the enhanced sentencing proceeding itself. This bar was extended in *Daniels*:

> If ... a prior conviction used to enhance a federal sentence is no longer open to direct or collateral attack in its own right because the defendant failed to pursue those remedies while they were available (or because the defendant did so unsuccessfully), then that defendant is without recourse. The presumption of validity that attached to the prior conviction at the time of sentencing is conclusive, and the defendant may not collaterally attack his prior conviction through a motion under § 2255.

In Lackawanna County District Attorney v. Coss, 532 U.S. 394 (2001), the Court extended *Daniels* to a habeas corpus petition filed by a state prisoner. In *Coss*, the defendant sought to attack a prior state conviction, for which the sentence had been fully served but which had been used to enhance his current state sentence, on the ground of ineffective assistance of counsel. The Court said "no," paraphrasing *Daniels*:

> [A]s in *Daniels*, we hold that once a state conviction is no longer open to direct or collateral attack in its own right because the defendant failed to pursue those remedies while they were available (or because the defendant did so unsuccessfully), the conviction may be regarded as conclusively valid. If that conviction is later used to enhance a criminal sentence, the defendant generally may not challenge the enhanced sentence through a petition under § 2254 on the ground that the prior conviction was unconstitutionally obtained.

In both cases the Court recognized one exception and the possibility of a second. The exception was based on Gideon v. Wainwright, 372 U.S. 335 (1963). If no counsel had been appointed in the proceedings resulting in the prior conviction, a collateral attack based on *Gideon* would be permissible. In addition, "there may be rare cases in which no channel of review was actually available to a defendant with respect to a prior conviction, due to no fault of his own." While neither of the cases before the Court presented this situation, the Court left open the possibility of collateral attack if such a case should arise.

Page 756, add a footnote at the end of Note 5:

h. The Court held in Trest v. Cain, 522 U.S. 87 (1997), that circuit courts are not *required* to raise a procedural default sua sponte that the parties did not raise or argue. Rather, procedural default is normally a defense that the state is obligated to raise and preserve. The Court declined to decide, however, whether circuit courts are *permitted* to rely on a procedural default that the state has waived or failed to raise.

Page 757, add at end of first paragraph of Note 8:

; Larry W. Yackle, The American Bar Association and Federal Habeas Corpus, 61 Law & Contemp. Probs. 171 (1998).

Page 763, omit the Notes on Procedural Foreclosure under the 1996 Legislation and substitute the following:

Lee v. Kemna

Supreme Court of the United States, 2002.
534 U.S. 362.

■ JUSTICE GINSBURG delivered the opinion of the Court.

Petitioner Remon Lee asserts that a Missouri trial court deprived him of due process when the court refused to grant an overnight continuance of his trial. Lee sought the continuance to locate subpoenaed, previously present, but suddenly missing witnesses key to his defense against felony charges. On direct review, the Missouri Court of Appeals disposed of the case on a state procedural ground. That court found the continuance motion defective under the State's rules. It therefore declined to consider the merits of Lee's plea that the trial court had denied him a fair opportunity to present a defense. Whether the state ground dispositive in the Missouri Court of Appeals is adequate to preclude federal habeas corpus review is the question we here consider and decide.

On the third day of his trial, Lee was convicted of first-degree murder and armed criminal action. His sole affirmative defense was an alibi; Lee maintained he was in California, staying with his family, when the Kansas City crimes for which he was indicted occurred. Lee's mother, stepfather, and sister voluntarily came to Missouri to testify on his behalf. They were sequestered in the courthouse at the start of the trial's third day. For reasons then unknown, they were not in the courthouse later in the day when defense counsel sought to present their testimony. Discovering their absence, defense counsel moved for a continuance until the next morning so that he could endeavor to locate the three witnesses and bring them back to court.

The trial judge denied the motion, stating that it looked to him as though the witnesses had "in effect abandoned the defendant" and that, for personal reasons, he would "not be able to be [in court the next day] to try the case." Furthermore, he had "another case set for trial" the next weekday. The trial resumed without pause, no alibi witnesses testified, and the jury found Lee guilty as charged.

Neither the trial judge nor the prosecutor identified any procedural flaw in the presentation or content of Lee's motion for a continuance. The Missouri Court of Appeals, however, held the denial of the motion proper because Lee's counsel had failed to comply with Missouri Supreme Court Rules not relied upon or even mentioned in the trial court: Rule 24.09, which requires that continuance motions be in written form, accompanied by an affidavit; and Rule 24.10, which sets out the showings a movant must make to gain a continuance grounded on the absence of witnesses.

We hold that the Missouri Rules, as injected into this case by the state appellate court, did not constitute a state ground adequate to bar federal habeas review. Caught in the midst of a murder trial and unalerted to any procedural defect in his presentation, defense counsel could hardly be expected to divert his attention from the proceedings rapidly unfolding in the courtroom and train, instead, on preparation of a written motion and affidavit. Furthermore, the trial court, at the time Lee moved for a continuance, had in clear view the information needed to rule intelligently on the merits of the motion. Beyond doubt, Rule 24.10 serves the State's important interest in regulating motions for a continuance–motions readily susceptible to use as a delaying tactic. But under the circumstances of this case, we hold that petitioner Lee, having substantially, if imperfectly, made the basic showings Rule 24.10 prescribes, qualifies for adjudication of his federal, due process claim. His asserted right to defend should not depend on a formal "ritual . . . [that] would further no perceivable state interest." Osborne v. Ohio, 495 U.S. 103, 124 (1990).

I

On August 27, 1992, Reginald Rhodes shot and killed Steven Shelby on a public street in Kansas City, Missouri. He then jumped into the passenger side of a waiting truck, which sped away. Rhodes pleaded guilty, and Remon Lee, the alleged getaway driver, was tried for first-degree murder and armed criminal action.

Lee's trial took place within the span of three days in February 1994. His planned alibi defense–that he was in California with his family at the time of the murder–surfaced at each stage of the proceedings. During voir dire on the first day of trial, Lee's court-appointed defense attorney informed prospective jurors that "[t]here will be a defense in this case, which is a defense of alibi." Later in the voir dire, defense counsel identified the three alibi witnesses as Lee's mother, Gladys Edwards, Lee's sister, Laura Lee, and Lee's stepfather, James Edwards, a minister.

The planned alibi defense figured prominently in counsels' opening statements on day two of Lee's trial. The prosecutor, at the close of her statement, said she expected an alibi defense from Lee and would present testimony to disprove it. Defense counsel, in his opening statement, described the alibi defense in detail, telling the jury that the evidence would show Lee was not in Kansas City, and therefore could not have engaged in crime there, in August 1992. Specifically, defense counsel said three close family members would testify that Lee came to visit them in Ventura, California, in July 1992 and stayed through the end of October. Lee's mother and stepfather would say they picked him up from the airport at the start of his visit and returned him there at the end. Lee's sister would testify that Lee resided with her and her four children during this time. All three would affirm that they saw Lee regularly throughout his unbroken sojourn.

During the prosecution case, two eyewitnesses to the shooting identified Lee as the driver. The first, Reginald Williams, admitted during cross-examination that he had told Lee's first defense counsel in a taped interview that Rhodes, not Lee, was the driver. Williams said he had given that response because he misunderstood the question and did not want to be "bothered" by the interviewer. The second eyewitness, William Sanders, was unable to pick Lee out of a photographic array on the day of the shooting; Sanders identified Lee as the driver for the first time 18 months after the murder.

Two other witnesses, Rhonda Shelby and Lynne Bryant, were called by the prosecutor. Each testified that she knew Lee and had seen him in Kansas City the night before the murder. Both said Lee was with Rhodes, who had asked where Steven Shelby (the murder victim) was. The State offered no physical evidence connecting Lee to the murder and did not suggest a motive.

The defense case began at 10:25 a.m. on the third and final day of trial. Two impeachment witnesses testified that morning. Just after noon, counsel met with the trial judge in chambers for a charge conference. At that meeting, the judge apparently agreed to give an alibi instruction submitted by Lee.[1]

At some point in the late morning or early afternoon, the alibi witnesses left the courthouse. Just after one o'clock, Lee took the stand outside the presence of the jury and, for the record, responded to his counsel's questions concerning his knowledge of the witnesses' unanticipated absence. Lee, under oath, stated that Gladys and James Edwards and Laura Lee had voluntarily traveled from California to testify on his behalf. He affirmed his counsel's representations that the three witnesses, then staying with Lee's uncle in Kansas City, had met with Lee's counsel and received subpoenas from him; he similarly affirmed that the witnesses had met with a Kansas City police officer, who interviewed them on behalf

---

1. That Lee had submitted an alibi instruction during the charge conference became apparent when the trial judge, delivering the charge, began to read the proposed instruction. He was interrupted by the prosecutor and defense counsel, who reminded him that the instruction was no longer necessary.

of the prosecutor. Lee said he had seen his sister, mother, and stepfather in the courthouse that morning at 8:30 and later during a recess.

On discovering the witnesses' absence, Lee could not call them at his uncle's house because there was no phone on the premises. He asked his girlfriend to try to find the witnesses, but she was unable to do so. Although Lee did not know the witnesses' whereabouts at that moment, he said he knew "in fact they didn't go back to California" because "they had some ministering ... to do" in Kansas City both Thursday and Friday evenings. He asked for "a couple hours' continuance [to] try to locate them, because it's very valuable to my case." Defense counsel subsequently moved for a continuance until the next morning, to gain time to enforce the subpoenas he had served on the witnesses. The trial judge responded that he could not hold court the next day because "my daughter is going to be in the hospital all day ... [s]o I've got to stay with her."

After a brief further exchange between court and counsel, the judge denied the continuance request. The judge observed:

"It looks to me as though the folks were here and then in effect abandoned the defendant. And that, of course, we can't–we can't blame that on the State. The State had absolutely nothing to do with that. That's–it's too bad. The Court will not be able to be here tomorrow to try the case."

Counsel then asked for a postponement until Monday (the next business day after the Friday the judge was to spend with his daughter in the hospital). The judge denied that request too, noting that he had another case set for trial that day.

In a final colloquy before the jury returned to the courtroom, defense counsel told the court he would be making a motion for judgment of acquittal. The judge asked, "You're going to give that to me ... orally and you'll supplement that with a written motion?" Counsel agreed.

When the jurors returned, defense counsel informed them that the three witnesses from California he had planned to call "were here and have gone"; further, counsel did not "know why they've gone." The defense then rested. In closing argument, Lee's counsel returned to the alibi defense he was unable to present. "I do apologize," he said, "I don't know what happened to my witnesses. They're not here. Couldn't put them on on the question of alibi." The prosecutor commented on the same gap: "Where are those alibi witnesses that [defense counsel] promised you from opening[?] They're not here."

After deliberating for three hours, the jury convicted Lee on both counts. He was subsequently sentenced to prison for life without possibility of parole.

The trial court later denied Lee's new trial motion, which Lee grounded, in part, on the denial of the continuance motion. Lee, at first pro se but later represented by appointed counsel, next filed a motion for state postconviction relief. Lee argued, inter alia, that the refusal to grant his request for an overnight continuance deprived him of his federal constitutional right to a defense.[3] In his postconviction motion, Lee asserted that the three witnesses had left the courthouse because "an unknown person," whom he later identified as an employee of the prosecutor's office, had told them "they were not needed to testify." The postconviction court denied the motion, stating that under Missouri law, an allegedly improper denial of a continuance fits within the category "trial error," a matter to be raised on direct appeal, not in a collateral challenge to a conviction.

Lee's direct appeal and his appeal from the denial of postconviction relief were consolidated before the Missouri Court of Appeals. There, Lee again urged that the trial court's refusal to continue the case overnight denied him due process and the right to put on a defense. In response, the State argued for the first time that Lee's continuance request had a fatal procedural flaw. In particular, the State contended that Lee's application failed to comply with Missouri Supreme Court Rule 24.10 (Rule 24.10), which lists the showings required in a continuance request based on the absence of witnesses.[4] By the State's reckoning, Lee's request did not show the materiality of the California witnesses' testimony or the grounds for believing that the witnesses could be found within a reasonable time; in addition, the prosecution urged, Lee failed to "testify that the witness[es'] absence was not due to his own procurement."

The Missouri Court of Appeals affirmed Lee's conviction and the denial of postconviction relief. The appellate court first noted that Lee's continuance motion was oral and therefore did not comply with Missouri Supreme Court Rule 24.09 (Rule 24.09), which provides that such applications shall

---

3. Missouri procedure at the time required Lee to file his postconviction motion in the sentencing court shortly after he filed his notice of direct appeal. See Mo. Sup.Ct. Rule 29.15(b) (1994) (requiring motion to be made within 30 days of filing of court transcript in appellate court considering direct appeal). The direct appeal was "suspended" while the trial court considered the postconviction motion. See Rule 29.15(*l*).

4. Rule 24.10 reads: ... "An application for a continuance on account of the absence of witnesses or their evidence shall show:

"(a) The facts showing the materiality of the evidence sought to be obtained and due diligence upon the part of the applicant to obtain such witness or testimony;

"(b) The name and residence of such witness, if known, or, if not known, the use of diligence to obtain the same, and also facts showing reasonable grounds for belief that the attendance or testimony of such witness will be procured within a reasonable time;

"(c) What particular facts the affiant believes the witness will prove, and that he knows of no other person whose evidence or attendance he could have procured at the trial, by whom he can prove or so fully prove the same facts;

"(d) That such witness is not absent by the connivance, consent, or procurement of the applicant, and such application is not made for vexation or delay, but in good faith for the purpose of obtaining a fair and impartial trial.

"If the court shall be of the opinion that the affidavit is insufficient it shall permit it to be amended."

be in written form, accompanied by an affidavit.[5] "Thus," the Court of Appeals said, "the trial court could have properly denied the motion for a failure to comply with Rule 24.09." Even assuming the adequacy of Lee's oral motion, the court continued, the application "was made without the factual showing required by Rule 24.10." The court did not say which components of Rule 24.10 were unsatisfied. "When a denial to grant a motion for continuance is based on a deficient application," the Court of Appeals next said, "it does not constitute an abuse of discretion." Lee's subsequent motions for rehearing and transfer to the Missouri Supreme Court were denied.

In January 1998, Lee, proceeding pro se, filed an application for writ of habeas corpus in the United States District Court for the Western District of Missouri. Lee once again challenged the denial of his continuance motion. He appended affidavits from the three witnesses, each of whom swore to Lee's alibi; sister, mother, and stepfather alike stated that they had left the courthouse while the trial was underway because a court officer told them their testimony would not be needed that day.[6] Lee maintained that the State had engineered the witnesses' departure; accordingly, he asserted that prosecutorial misconduct, not anything over which he had control, prompted the need for a continuance.

The District Court denied the writ. The witnesses' affidavits were not cognizable in federal habeas proceedings, the court held, because Lee could have offered them to the state courts but failed to do so. The Federal District Court went on to reject Lee's continuance claim, finding in the Missouri Court of Appeals' invocation of Rule 24.10 an adequate and independent state-law ground barring further review.

The Court of Appeals for the Eighth Circuit granted a certificate of appealability, limited to the question whether Lee's "due process rights were violated by the state trial court's failure to allow him a continuance," and affirmed the denial of Lee's habeas petition. Federal review of Lee's due process claim would be unavailable, the court correctly observed, if the

---

5. Rule 24.09 reads: ... "An application for a continuance shall be made by a written motion accompanied by the affidavit of the applicant or some other credible person setting forth the facts upon which the application is based, unless the adverse party consents that the application for continuance may be made orally."

6. The witnesses' accounts of their departure from the courthouse were as follows:

Laura Lee: "[T]hose people in Missouri told us we could leave because our testimony would not be needed until the next day."

Gladys Edwards: "[T]he officer of the court came and told us that the prosecutor stated that the state[']s case will again take up the remainder of that day. That [o]ur testimony will not be needed until the following day, that we could leave until the following day. He ... told [u]s not to worry, the Judge knows *[w]e came to testify,* they have [o]ur statements, and the trial will not be over until we testify. So at those instructions we left."

James Edwards: "[W]hile at the [c]ourthouse, we were told by an officer of the court that [o]ur testimony would not be needed until the following day, we were excused until then."

state court's rejection of that claim " 'rest[ed] . . . on a state law ground that is independent of the federal question and adequate to support the judgment,' regardless of 'whether the state law ground is substantive or procedural.' " "The Missouri Court of Appeals rejected Lee's claim because his motion for a continuance did not comply with [Rules] 24.09 and 24.10," the Eighth Circuit next stated. Thus, that court concluded, "the claim was procedurally defaulted." . . .

We granted Lee's pro se petition for a writ of certiorari and appointed counsel. We now vacate the Court of Appeals judgment.

II

This Court will not take up a question of federal law presented in a case "if the decision of [the state] court rests on a state law ground that is *independent* of the federal question and *adequate* to support the judgment." Coleman v. Thompson, 501 U.S. 722, 729 (1991) (emphases added). The rule applies with equal force whether the state-law ground is substantive or procedural. We first developed the independent and adequate state ground doctrine in cases on direct review from state courts, and later applied it as well "in deciding whether federal district courts should address the claims of state prisoners in habeas corpus actions." Ibid. "[T]he adequacy of state procedural bars to the assertion of federal questions," we have recognized, is not within the State's prerogative finally to decide; rather, adequacy "is itself a federal question." Douglas v. Alabama, 380 U.S. 415, 422 (1965).

Lee does not suggest that Rules 24.09 and 24.10, as brought to bear on this case by the Missouri Court of Appeals, depended in any way on federal law. Nor does he question the general applicability of the two codified Rules. He does maintain that both Rules–addressed initially to Missouri trial courts, but in his case invoked only at the appellate stage–are inadequate, under the extraordinary circumstances of this case, to close out his federal, fair-opportunity-to-defend claim. We now turn to that dispositive issue.

Ordinarily, violation of "firmly established and regularly followed" state rules–for example, those involved in this case–will be adequate to foreclose review of a federal claim. James v. Kentucky, 466 U.S. 341, 348 (1984). There are, however, exceptional cases in which exorbitant application of a generally sound rule renders the state ground inadequate to stop consideration of a federal question. See Davis v. Wechsler, 263 U.S. 22, 24 (1923) (Holmes, J.) ("Whatever springs the State may set for those who are endeavoring to assert rights that the State confers, the assertion of federal rights, when plainly and reasonably made, is not to be defeated under the name of local practice."). This case fits within that limited category.

Our analysis and conclusion are informed and controlled by Osborne v. Ohio, 495 U.S. 103 (1990). There, the Court considered Osborne's objections that his child pornography conviction violated due process because the trial judge had not required the government to prove two elements of the alleged crime: lewd exhibition and scienter. The Ohio Supreme Court held the constitutional objections procedurally barred because Osborne had failed to object contemporaneously to the judge's charge, which did not instruct the jury that it could convict only for conduct that satisfied both the scienter and the lewdness elements.

We agreed with the State that Osborne's failure to urge the trial court to instruct the jury on scienter qualified as an "adequate state-law ground [to] preven[t] us from reaching Osborne's due process contention on that point." Ohio law, which was not in doubt, required proof of scienter unless the applicable statute specified otherwise. The State's contemporaneous objection rule, we observed, "serves the State's important interest in ensuring that counsel do their part in preventing trial courts from providing juries with erroneous instructions."

"With respect to the trial court's failure to instruct on lewdness, however, we reach[ed] a different conclusion." Counsel for Osborne had made his position on that essential element clear in a motion to dismiss overruled just before trial, and the trial judge, "in no uncertain terms," had rejected counsel's argument. After a brief trial, the judge charged the jury in line with his ruling against Osborne on the pretrial motion to dismiss. Counsel's failure to object to the charge by reasserting the argument he had made unsuccessfully on the motion to dismiss, we held, did not deter our disposition of the constitutional question. "Given this sequence of events," we explained, it was proper to "reach Osborne's [second] due process claim," for Osborne's attorney had "pressed the issue of the State's failure of proof on lewdness before the trial court and ... nothing would be gained by requiring Osborne's lawyer to object a second time, specifically to the jury instructions." In other words, although we did not doubt the general applicability of the Ohio Rule of Criminal Procedure requiring contemporaneous objection to jury charges, we nevertheless concluded that, in this atypical instance, the Rule would serve "no perceivable state interest."

Our decision, we added in *Osborne*, followed from "the general principle that an objection which is ample and timely to bring the alleged federal error to the attention of the trial court and enable it to take appropriate corrective action is sufficient to serve legitimate state interests, and therefore sufficient to preserve the claim for review here." This general principle, and the unusual "sequence of events" before us–rapidly unfolding events that Lee and his counsel could not have foreseen, and for which they were not at all responsible–similarly guide our judgment in this case. ...

The asserted procedural oversights in Lee's case, his alleged failures fully to comply with Rules 24.09 and 24.10, were first raised more than two and a half years after Lee's trial. The two Rules, Missouri maintains, "work together to enhance the reliability of a *trial court's* determination of whether to delay a scheduled criminal trial due to the absence of a witness." Nevertheless, neither the prosecutor nor the trial judge so much as mentioned the Rules as a reason for denying Lee's continuance motion. If either prosecutor or judge considered supplementation of Lee's motion necessary, they likely would have alerted the defense at the appropriate time, and Lee would have had an opportunity to perfect his plea to hold the case over until the next day. Rule 24.10, we note, after listing the components of a continuance motion, contemplates subsequent perfection: "If the court shall be of the opinion that the affidavit is insufficient it shall permit it to be amended."

The State, once content that the continuance motion was ripe for trial court disposition on the merits, had a second thought on appeal. It raised Rule 24.10 as a new argument in its brief to the Missouri Court of Appeals; even then, the State did not object to the motion's oral form. The Missouri Court of Appeals, it seems, raised Rule 24.09's writing requirements ("a written motion accompanied by [an] affidavit") on its own motion.

Three considerations, in combination, lead us to conclude that this case falls within the small category of cases in which asserted state grounds are inadequate to block adjudication of a federal claim. First, when the trial judge denied Lee's motion, he stated a reason that could not have been countered by a perfect motion for continuance. The judge said he could not carry the trial over until the next day because he had to be with his daughter in the hospital; the judge further informed counsel that another scheduled trial prevented him from concluding Lee's case on the following business day. Although the judge hypothesized that the witnesses had "abandoned" Lee, he had not "a scintilla of evidence or a shred of information" on which to base this supposition, 213 F.3d, at 1040 (Bennett, C. J., dissenting).

Second, no published Missouri decision directs flawless compliance with Rules 24.09 and 24.10 in the unique circumstances this case presents—the sudden, unanticipated, and at the time unexplained disappearance of critical, subpoenaed witnesses on what became the trial's last day. Lee's predicament, from all that appears, was one Missouri courts had not confronted before. "[A]lthough [the rules themselves] may not [have been] novel, ... [their] application to the facts here was." Sullivan v. Little Hunting Park, Inc., 396 U.S. 229, 245 (1969) (Harlan, J., dissenting).

Third and most important, given "the realities of trial," Lee substantially complied with Missouri's key Rule. As to the "written motion" requirement, Missouri's brief in this Court asserted: "Nothing would have prevented counsel from drafting a brief motion and affidavit complying with Rul[e] 24.09 in longhand while seated in the courtroom." At oral argument, however, Missouri's counsel edged away from this position. Counsel stated: "I'm not going to stand on the formality ... of a writing or even the formality of an affidavit." This concession was well advised. Missouri does not rule out oral continuance motions; they are expressly authorized, upon consent of the adverse party, by Rule 24.09. And the written transcript of the brief trial court proceedings enabled an appellate court to comprehend the situation quickly. In sum, we are drawn to the conclusion reached by the Eighth Circuit dissenter: "[A]ny seasoned trial lawyer would agree" that insistence on a written continuance application, supported by an affidavit, "in the midst of trial upon the discovery that subpoenaed witnesses are suddenly absent, would be so bizarre as to inject an Alice-in-Wonderland quality into the proceedings." 213 F.3d, at 1047.

Regarding Rule 24.10, the only Rule raised on appeal by the prosecution, the Missouri Court of Appeals' decision was summary. Although that court did not specify the particular components of the Rule neglected by Lee, the State here stresses two: "Lee's counsel never mentioned during his oral motion for continuance the testimony he expected the missing witnesses to give"; further, he "gave the trial court no reason to believe that the missing witnesses could be located within a reasonable time."

These matters, however, were either covered by the oral continuance motion or otherwise conspicuously apparent on the record. The testimony that the alibi witnesses were expected to give had been previewed during voir dire at the outset of the three-day trial, then detailed in defense counsel's opening statement delivered just one day before the continuance motion. Two of the prosecution's witnesses testified in part to anticipate and rebut the alibi. An alibi instruction was apparently taken up at the charge conference held less than an hour before the trial court denied the continuance motion. When defense counsel moved for a continuance, the judge asked a question indicating his recognition that alibi witness Gladys Edwards was Lee's mother.

Given the repeated references to the anticipated alibi witness testimony each day of trial, it is inconceivable that anyone in the courtroom harbored a doubt about what the witnesses had traveled from California to Missouri to say on the stand or why their testimony was material, indeed indispensable, to the defense. It was also evident that no witness then in the Kansas City vicinity could effectively substitute for the family members with whom Lee allegedly stayed in Ventura, California. . . .

Moreover, Lee showed "reasonable grounds for belief" that the continuance would serve its purpose. He said he knew the witnesses had not left Kansas City because they were to "ministe[r]" there the next two evenings; he provided their local address; and he sought less than a day's continuance to enforce the subpoenas for their attendance.

Concerning his "diligence . . . to obtain" the alibi testimony, see Rule 24.10(a), Lee and his counsel showed: the witnesses had voluntarily traveled from California to appear at the trial; counsel had subpoenaed the witnesses when he interviewed them in Kansas City; the witnesses had telephoned counsel the evening before the third trial day and had agreed to come to court that next day; the witnesses in fact were in court at 8:30 in the morning waiting in a witness room; and Lee saw them during a recess. Countering "procurement" of the witnesses' absence by the defense, see

Rule 24.10(d), Lee affirmed that he did not know "why they left" or "where they went," and asked for just "a couple hours' continuance [to] try to locate them."

Rule 24.10, like other state and federal rules of its genre, serves a governmental interest of undoubted legitimacy. It is designed to arm trial judges with the information needed to rule reliably on a motion to delay a scheduled criminal trial. The Rule's essential requirements, however, were substantially met in this case. Few transcript pages need be read to reveal the information called for by Rule 24.10. "[N]othing would [have] be[en] gained by requiring" Lee's counsel to recapitulate in (a), (b), (c), (d) order the showings the Rule requires. See *Osborne,* 495 U.S., at 124; cf. Staub v. City of Baxley, 355 U.S. 313, 319–20 (1958) (failure to challenge "specific sections" of an ordinance not an adequate state ground barring review of federal claim when party challenged constitutionality of entire ordinance and all sections were "interdependent"). "Where it is inescapable that the defendant sought to invoke the substance of his federal right, the asserted state-law defect in form must be more evident than it is here." James v. Kentucky, 466 U.S. 341, 351 (1984).

... We chart no new course. We merely apply *Osborne's* sound reasoning and limited holding to the circumstances of this case. If the dissent's shrill prediction that today's decision will disrupt our federal system were accurate, we would have seen clear signals of such disruption in the eleven years since *Osborne*. The absence of even dim distress signals demonstrates both the tight contours of *Osborne* and the groundlessness of the dissent's frantic forecast of doom.

It may be questioned, moreover, whether the dissent, put to the test, would fully embrace the unyielding theory that it is never appropriate to evaluate the state interest in a procedural rule against the circumstances of a particular case. If that theory holds, it would matter not at all why the witnesses left. Even if the evidence would show beyond doubt that the witnesses left because a court functionary told them to go, saying their testimony would not be needed until the next day, see supra, n. 6, Lee would lose under the dissent's approach. And that result would be unaffected should it turn out that the functionary acted on the instigation of a prosecutor who knew the judge would be at the hospital with his daughter the next day. The particular application, never mind how egregious, would be ignored so long as the Rule, like the mine run of procedural rules, generally serves a legitimate state interest.

To summarize, there was in this case no reference whatever in the trial court to Rules 24.09 and 24.10, the purported procedural impediments the Missouri Court of Appeals later pressed. Nor is there any indication that formally perfect compliance with the Rules would have changed the trial court's decision. Furthermore, no published Missouri decision demands unmodified application of the Rules in the urgent situation Lee's case presented. Finally, the purpose of the Rules was served by Lee's submissions both immediately before and at the short trial. Under the special circumstances so combined, we conclude that no adequate state-law ground hinders consideration of Lee's federal claim.[17]

Because both the District Court and the Court of Appeals held Lee's due process claim procedurally barred, neither court addressed it on the merits. We remand the case for that purpose.

* * *

For the reasons stated, the judgment of the United States Court of Appeals for the Eighth Circuit is vacated, and the case is remanded for further proceedings consistent with this opinion.

It is so ordered.

■ JUSTICE KENNEDY, with whom JUSTICE SCALIA and JUSTICE THOMAS join, dissenting.

The Court's decision commits us to a new and, in my view, unwise course. Its contextual approach places unnecessary and unwarranted new responsibilities on state trial judges, injects troubling instability into the criminal justice system, and reaches the wrong result even under its own premises. These considerations prompt my respectful dissent.

I

The rule that an adequate state procedural ground can bar federal review of a constitutional claim has always been "about federalism," Coleman v. Thompson, 501 U.S. 722, 726 (1991), for it respects state rules of procedure while ensuring that they do not discriminate against federal rights. The doctrine originated in cases on direct review, where the existence of an independent and adequate state ground deprives this Court of jurisdiction. The rule applies with equal force, albeit for somewhat different reasons, when federal courts review the claims of state prisoners in habeas corpus proceedings, where ignoring procedural defaults would circumvent the jurisdictional limits of direct review and "undermine the State's interest in enforcing its laws."

Given these considerations of comity and federalism, a procedural ground will be deemed inadequate only when the state rule "force[s] resort to an arid ritual of meaningless form." Staub v. City of Baxley, 355 U.S. 313, 320 (1958). *Staub*'s formulation was imprecise, but the cases that followed clarified the two essential components of the adequate state ground inquiry: first, the defendant must have notice of the rule; and second, the State must have a legitimate interest in its enforcement.

---

17. In view of this disposition, we do not reach further questions raised by Lee, i.e., whether he has shown "cause" and "prejudice" to excuse any default, Wainwright v. Sykes, 433 U.S. 72, 90–91 (1977), or has made sufficient showing of "actual innocence" under Schlup v. Delo, 513 U.S. 298, 315 (1995), to warrant a hearing of the kind ordered in that case.

The Court need not determine whether the requirement of Missouri Supreme Court Rule 24.09 that all continuance motions be made in writing would withstand scrutiny under the second part of this test (or, for that matter, whether Lee had cause not to comply with it). Even if it could be assumed, for the sake of argument, that Rule 24.09 would not afford defendants a fair opportunity to raise a federal claim, the same cannot be said of Rule 24.10. The latter Rule simply requires a party requesting a continuance on account of missing witnesses to explain why it is needed, and the Rule serves an undoubted and important state interest in facilitating the orderly management of trials. Other States have similar requirements. The Court's explicit depreciation of Rule 24.10–and implicit depreciation of its many counterparts–is inconsistent with the respect due to state courts and state proceedings.

A

The initial step of the adequacy inquiry considers whether the State has put litigants on notice of the rule. The Court will disregard state procedures not firmly established and regularly followed. . . . As the majority acknowledges, Rule 24.10 is not in this category. . . . Rule 24.10 is codified and followed in regular practice.

Several of the considerations offered in support of today's decision, however, would seem to suggest that the Court believes Rule 24.10 was not firmly established or regularly followed at the time of Lee's trial. For example, the majority cites the lack of published decisions directing flawless compliance with the Rule in the unique circumstances this case presents. [T]he Court's underlying, quite novel argument ignores the nature of rulemaking. If the Court means what it says on this point, few procedural rules will give rise to an adequate state ground. Almost every case presents unique circumstances that cannot be foreseen and articulated by prior decisions, and general rules like Rule 24.10 are designed to eliminate second-guessing about the rule's applicability in special cases. Rule 24.10's plain language admits of no exception, and the Court cites no Missouri case establishing a judge-made exemption in any circumstances, much less circumstances close to these. Its applicability here was clear.

The Court also ventures into new territory by implying that the trial judge's failure to cite the Rule was meaningful and by noting that he did not give a reason for denying the continuance that could have been addressed by a motion complying with the Rule. If these considerations were significant, however, we would have relied upon them in previous cases where the trial court's denial of the defendant's motion on the merits was affirmed by the state appellate court because of an uncited procedural defect. [Our prior decisions have not] used this rationale to disregard a state procedural rule, and with good reason. To require trial judges, as a matter of federal law, to cite their precise grounds for decision would place onerous burdens on the state courts, and it is well settled that an appellate tribunal may affirm a trial court's judgment on any ground supported by the record. ...Notwithstanding the Court's guess about the judge's and prosecution's inner thoughts concerning the completeness of Lee's motion, the Missouri Court of Appeals tells us that Lee's failure to comply with the Rule is considered consequential as a matter of state law. If Lee had complied with Rule 24.10, the trial court might have granted the continuance or given a different reason for denying it. The trial court, in effect, is deemed to have relied on Rule 24.10 when it found Lee had not made a sufficient showing.

Lee was on notice of the applicability of Rule 24.10, and the Court appears to recognize as much. The consideration most important to the Court's analysis relates not to this initial question, but rather to the second part of the adequacy inquiry, which asks whether the rule serves a legitimate state interest. Here, too, in my respectful view, the Court errs.

B

A defendant's failure to comply with a firmly established and regularly followed rule has been deemed an inadequate state ground only when the State had no legitimate interest in the rule's enforcement. Osborne v. Ohio, 495 U.S. 103, 124 (1990). Most state procedures are supported by various legitimate interests, so established rules have been set aside only when they appeared to be calculated to discriminate against federal law, or, as one treatise puts it, they did not afford the defendant "a reasonable opportunity to assert federal rights." [Citation omitted.]

In light of this standard, the adequacy of Rule 24.10 has been demonstrated. Delays in criminal trials can be "a distinct reproach to the administration of justice," Powell v. Alabama, 287 U.S. 45, 59 (1932), and States have a strong interest in ensuring that continuances are granted only when necessary. Rule 24.10 anticipates that at certain points during a trial, important witnesses may not be available. In these circumstances, a continuance may be appropriate if the movant makes certain required representations demonstrating good cause to believe the continuance would make a real difference to the case.

The Court acknowledges, as it must, that Rule 24.10 does not discriminate against federal law or deny defendants a reasonable opportunity to assert their rights. Instead, the Rule "serves a governmental interest of undoubted legitimacy" in "arm[ing] trial judges with the information needed to rule reliably on a motion to delay a scheduled criminal trial." Nor is there any doubt Lee did not comply with the Rule, for the Missouri court's word on that state-law question is final. The Court's acceptance of these two premises should lead it to conclude that Lee's violation of the Rule was an adequate state ground for the Missouri court's decision.

Yet the Court deems Lee's default inadequate because, it says, to the extent feasible under the circumstances, he substantially complied with the Rule's essential requirements. These precise terms have not been used in the Court's adequacy jurisprudence before, and it is necessary to explore their implications. The argument is not that Missouri has no interest in enforcing compliance with the Rule in general, but rather that it had no interest in enforcing full compliance in this particular case. This is so, the Court holds, because the Rule's essential purposes were substantially served by other procedural devices, such as opening statement, voir dire, and Lee's testimony on the stand. These procedures, it is said, provided the court with the information the Rule requires the motion itself to contain. . . .

[This use of a] case-by-case approach is contrary to the principles of federalism underlying our habeas corpus jurisprudence. Procedural rules, like the substantive laws they implement, are the products of sovereignty and democratic processes. The States have weighty interests in enforcing rules that protect the integrity and uniformity of trials, even when "the reason for the rule does not clearly apply." *Staub v. City of Baxley,* 355 U.S., at 333 (Frankfurter, J., dissenting). Regardless of the particular facts in extraordinary cases, then, Missouri has a freestanding interest in Rule 24.10 as a rule.

By ignoring that interest, the majority's approach invites much mischief at criminal trials, and the burden imposed upon States and their courts will be heavy. All requirements of a rule are, in the rulemaker's view, essential to fulfill its purposes; imperfect compliance is thus, by definition, not compliance at all. Yet the State's sound judgment on these matters can now be overridden by a federal court, which may determine for itself, given its own understanding of the rule's purposes, whether a requirement was essential or compliance was substantial in the unique circumstances of any given case. Henceforth, each time a litigant does not comply with an established state procedure, the judge must inquire, even "in the midst of trial, . . . whether noncompliance should be excused because some alternative procedure might be deemed adequate in the particular situation." The trial courts, then the state appellate courts, and, in the end, the federal habeas courts in numerous instances must comb through the full transcript and trial record, searching for ways in which the defendant might have substantially complied with the essential requirements of an otherwise broken rule. . . .

[E]ven if it made sense to consider the adequacy of state rules on a case-by-case basis, the Court would be wrong to conclude that enforcement of Rule 24.10 would serve no purpose in this case. Erroneous disregard of state procedural rules will be common under the regime endorsed by the Court today, for its basic assumption–that the purposes of a particular state procedure can be served by use of a rather different one–ignores the realities of trial. The Court here sweeps aside as unnecessary a rule that would have produced the very predicate the trial court needed to grant the motion: an assurance that the defense witnesses were still prepared to offer material testimony.

The majority contends that Lee compensated for any inadequacies in his motion, even if through inadvertence, by various remarks and observations made during earlier parts of the trial. To reach this conclusion, the Court must construe counsel's statements with a pronounced liberality. Even if we could assume, however, that Lee and his lawyer provided all the required information at some point, we could not conclude that ... in the terms used by today's majority, ... "the Rule's essential requirements ... were substantially met." The most critical information the Rule requires– "[W]hat particular facts the affiant believes the witness will prove"–was revealed not at the time of the motion, but at earlier stages: voir dire, opening statements, and perhaps, the majority speculates, the charge conference. To say the essential requirements of Rule 24.10 were met, then, is to assume the requirement that representations be made at the time of the motion is not central to the Rule or its objectives.

This assumption ignores the State's interest in placing all relevant information before the trial court when the motion is made, rather than asking the judge to rely upon his or her memory of earlier statements. The assumption looks past the State's corresponding interest in facilitating appellate review by placing all information relevant to the continuance motion in a single place in the record. The assumption also ignores the plain fact that the posture of this case was far different when Lee made his continuance motion than it was at the outset of the trial. Even if the judge recalled the precise details of voir dire and opening statements (as the majority believes), the State's interest in requiring Lee to make the representations after the prosecution rested was no less pronounced.

As the very existence of rules like Rule 24.10 indicates, seasoned trial judges are likely to look upon continuance motions based on the absence of witnesses with a considerable degree of skepticism. This case was no different, for the trial judge suspected that the witnesses had abandoned Lee. The majority is simply wrong to suggest that no one in the courtroom harbored a doubt about what Lee's family members would have said if they had returned. On the contrary, in light of the witnesses' sudden disappearance, it is more likely that no one in the courtroom would have had any idea what to expect.

The Court fails to recognize that the trial judge was quite capable of distinguishing between counsel's brave promises to the jury at various stages of the trial and what counsel could in fact deliver when the continuance was sought. There is nothing unusual about lawyers using hyperbole in statements to the jury but then using careful and documented arguments when making representations to the court in support of requests for specific rulings. Trial judges must distinguish between the two on a daily basis. ...

[T]he whole course of these proceedings served to confirm what the trial judge told counsel at the outset of the case: "I don't have a lot of faith in what's said in opening statement." Opening statements can be imprecise, and are sometimes designed to force the opposition's hand or shape the jurors' perception of events. When the time came for presentation of the defense case, counsel faced significant obstacles in establishing the alibi he had promised before. Indeed, it is a fair inference to say the alibi defense had collapsed altogether. Two witnesses with no connection to the defendants or the crime identified Lee as the driver of the automobile used by the passenger-gunman. Any thought that difficulties with these eyewitnesses' identification might give Lee room to present his alibi defense was dispelled by two additional witnesses for the prosecution. Both had known Lee for a considerable period of time, so the chances of mistaken identity were minimal. Both saw him in Kansas City–not in California–on the night before the murder. He was not only in town, they testified, but also with the shooter and looking for the victim.

Faced with this and other evidence adduced by the prosecution, defense counsel elected to open not with the alibi witnesses whose testimony was supposed to be so critical, but rather with two witnesses who attempted to refute a collateral aspect of the testimony given by one of the prosecution's eyewitnesses. Only then did the defense call the alibi witnesses, who were to testify that Lee went to California to attend a birthday party in July 1992 and did not return to Kansas City until October. At this point the case was far different from what defense counsel might have hoped for at the opening.

When Lee's witnesses were then reported missing, the judge had ample reason to believe they had second thoughts about testifying. All three of Lee's family members had traveled from California to testify, but all three left without speaking to Lee or his lawyer. Two sets of witnesses, four persons in all, had just placed Lee in Kansas City; and the prosecution had said it had in reserve other witnesses prepared to rebut the alibi testimony. Lee had been sentenced to 80 years in Missouri prison for an unrelated armed assault and robbery, and any witness who was considering perjury would have had little inducement to take that risk–a risk that would have became more pronounced after the prosecution's witnesses had testified–if Lee would serve a long prison term in any event. The judge's skepticism seems even more justified when it is noted that six weeks later, during a hearing on Lee's motion for a new trial, counsel still did not explain where Lee's family members had gone or why they had left. It was not until 17 months later, in an amended motion for postconviction relief, that Lee first gave the Missouri courts an explanation for his family's disappearance.

Before any careful trial judge granted a continuance in these circumstances, he or she would want a representation that the movant believed the missing witnesses were still prepared to offer the alibi testimony. If Lee and his counsel had any reason to believe his witnesses had not abandoned him, this representation would not have been difficult to make, and the trial judge would have had reason to credit it. Yet defense counsel was careful at all stages to avoid making this precise representation. . . . When he moved for the continuance, Lee's counsel, consistent with his guarded approach, would not say the witnesses would still testify as advertised....

No one—not Lee, not his attorney—stood before the court and expressed a belief, as required by Rule 24.10, that the missing witnesses would still testify that Lee had been in California on the night of the murder. Without that assurance, the judge had little reason to believe the continuance would be of any use. In concluding that the purposes of Rule 24.10 were served by promises made in an opening statement, the majority has ignored one of the central purposes of the Rule.

In sum, Rule 24.10 served legitimate state interests, both as a general matter and as applied to the facts of this case. Lee's failure to comply was an adequate state ground, and the Court's contrary determination does not bode well for the adequacy doctrine or federalism.

II

A federal court could consider the merits of Lee's defaulted federal claim if he had shown cause for the default and prejudice therefrom, see Wainwright v. Sykes, 433 U.S. 72, 90–91 (1977), or made out a compelling case of actual innocence, see Schlup v. Delo, 513 U.S. 298, 314–15 (1995). He has done neither.

As to the first question, Lee says the sudden disappearance of his witnesses caused him to neglect Rule 24.10. In one sense, of course, he is right, for he would not have requested the continuance, much less failed to comply with Rule 24.10, if his witnesses had not left the courthouse. The argument, though, is unavailing. The cause component of the cause-and-prejudice analysis requires more than a but-for causal relationship between the cause and the default. Lee must also show, given the state of the trial when the motion was made, that an external factor "impeded counsel's efforts to comply with the State's procedural rule." Murray v. Carrier, 477 U.S. 478, 488 (1986). While the departure of his key witnesses may have taken him by surprise (and caused him not to comply with Rule 24.09's writing requirement), nothing about their quick exit stopped him from making a complete oral motion and explaining their absence, the substance of their anticipated testimony, and its materiality.

Nor has Lee shown that an evidentiary hearing is needed to determine whether "a constitutional violation has probably resulted in the conviction of one who is actually innocent." Id., at 496. To fall within this "narrow class of cases," McCleskey v. Zant, 499 U.S. 467, 494 (1991), Lee must demonstrate "that it is more likely than not that no reasonable juror would have convicted him in light of the new evidence." *Schlup v. Delo*, supra, at 332. Lee would offer the testimony of his mother, stepfather, and sister; but to this day, almost eight years after the trial, Lee has not produced a shred of tangible evidence corroborating their story that he had flown to California to attend a four-month long birthday party at the time of the murder. To acquit, the jury would have to overlook this problem, ignore the relatives' motive to concoct an alibi for their kin, and discount the prosecution's four eyewitnesses. Even with the relatives' testimony, a reasonable juror could vote to convict. . . .

Sound principles of federalism counsel against [the Court's] result. I would affirm the judgment of the Court of Appeals.

NOTES ON PROCEDURAL FORECLOSURE UNDER THE 1996 LEGISLATION

1. Effect of Prior Litigation of the Facts in State Court. Section 2254(e)(1) provides that:

> In a proceeding instituted by an application for a writ of habeas corpus by a person in custody pursuant to the judgment of a State court, a determination of a factual issue made by a State court shall be presumed to be correct. The applicant shall have the burden of rebutting the presumption of correctness by clear and convincing evidence.

This provision repudiates the *Townsend v. Sain* approach to relitigation of facts that have previously been litigated in state court.[a] Gone is the discretion of the federal habeas court to hold a hearing in any case "where the material facts are in dispute." Gone also is the requirement that a hearing be held in any case where the standard of a "full and fair hearing" in the state court has not been met. Instead, the findings of the state court "shall be presumed to be correct" and the federal habeas applicant has the burden of rebutting the presumption by the heightened standard of "clear and convincing evidence."

2. Effect of Failure to Litigate Claims in State Court. *Lee v. Kemna* relies on two propositions as to which it appears that the Court is unanimous.

The first is that a state procedural ground does not foreclose litigation of a claim on the merits in a federal habeas court if the state ground is, for whatever reason, *in*adequate. The Court disagrees in *Lee*, to be sure, about whether the state procedural ground advanced there was in fact inadequate, as well as about the appropriate scope of the adequacy inquiry. It does not seem to disagree, however, about the effect of a conclusion that the state ground is inadequate.

The second proposition is that an *adequate* state procedural ground does not foreclose federal litigation of the claim on the merits if the defendant can establish "cause and prejudice" under *Wainwright v. Sykes* or a compelling case of actual innocence under *Schlup v. Delo*. Application of the adequate and independent state ground doctrine is not the end of the inquiry. Even if the state courts refuse to hear a claim based on appropriate

---

[a] Larry W. Yackle disagrees. See Federal Evidentiary Hearings Under the New Habeas Corpus Statute, 6 B.U. Pub. Interest L.J. 135 (1996).

reliance on an adequate and independent state ground, the defendant has an opportunity–albeit an opportunity difficult to satisfy–to avoid procedural foreclosure of asserted federal claims.

Why two sets of inquiries? Why not require "cause and prejudice" in all instances where the state advances a procedural reason for refusing to hear a federal claim, whether or not the state ground is adequate? Or why not eliminate the "cause and prejudice" inquiry and permit federal habeas only when it can be demonstrated that a proffered state procedural ground is not "adequate and independent"? Would it be enough to recognize a "compelling case of actual innocence" as the only exception to the preclusive effect of an adequate and independent state ground?

Consider also the Court's disagreement in *Lee* about the scope and application of the adequate state ground doctrine. Who has the better of it?

3. *Michael Wayne Williams v. Taylor*: The meaning of § 2254(e)(2). Section 2254(e)(2) of the 1996 legislation provides as follows:

> If the applicant has failed to develop the factual basis of a claim in State court proceedings, the court shall not hold an evidentiary hearing on the claim unless the applicant shows that–
>
> (A) the claim relies on–
>
> (i) a new rule of constitutional law, made retroactive to cases on collateral review by the Supreme Court, that was previously unavailable; or
>
> (ii) a factual predicate that could not have been previously discovered through the exercise of due diligence; and
>
> (B) the facts underlying the claim would be sufficient to establish by clear and convincing evidence that but for constitutional error, no reasonable factfinder would have found the applicant guilty of the underlying offense.

Should Lee have been required to satisfy the terms of this statute in order for his federal claims to be heard?

The answer is found in the Court's unanimous decision in Michael Wayne Williams v. Taylor, 529 U.S. 420 (2000). Williams was sentenced to death following his conviction for multiple murders. His subsequent federal habeas petition made three claims: a *Brady* violation for failure by the prosecutor to disclose potentially favorable evidence; a claim that his trial was unfair because of the participation of a biased juror; and prosecutor misconduct for failure to disclose prior knowledge of the potential juror bias. None of the claims had been presented to the state courts.

The Court began its analysis by focusing on the word "failed" in the introductory clause of § 2254(e)(2):

> Section 2254(e)(2) begins with a conditional clause, "[i]f the applicant has failed to develop the factual basis of a claim in State court

proceedings," which directs attention to the prisoner's efforts in state court. We ask first whether the factual basis was indeed developed in state court, a question susceptible, in the normal course, of a simple yes or no answer. Here the answer is no.

The Commonwealth would have the analysis begin and end there. Under its no-fault reading of the statute, if there is no factual development in the state court, the federal habeas court may not inquire into the reasons for the default when determining whether the opening clause of § 2254(e)(2) applies. We do not agree with the Commonwealth's interpretation of the word "failed."

The word "failed," the Court held, contains a component of fault:

> To say a person has failed in a duty implies he did not take the necessary steps to fulfill it. He is, as a consequence, at fault and bears responsibility for the failure. In this sense, a person is not at fault when his diligent efforts to perform an act are thwarted, for example, by the conduct of another or by happenstance. Fault lies, in those circumstances, either with the person who interfered with the accomplishment of the act or with no one at all. We conclude Congress used the word "failed" in the sense just described. Had Congress intended a no-fault standard, it would have had no difficulty in making its intent plain. It would have had to do no more than use, in lieu of the phrase "has failed to," the phrase "did not."
>
> Under the opening clause of § 2254(e)(2), a failure to develop the factual basis of a claim is not established unless there is lack of diligence, or some greater fault, attributable to the prisoner or the prisoner's counsel.

The Court then talked about the relation between this standard and the "cause and prejudice" inquiry found in its prior decisions:

> Our interpretation of § 2254(e)(2)'s opening clause has support in Keeney v. Tamayo–Reyes, 504 U.S. 1 (1992), a case decided four years before AEDPA's enactment. . . . Section 2254(e)(2)'s initial inquiry into whether "the applicant has failed to develop the factual basis of a claim in State court proceedings" echoes *Keeney*'s language regarding "the state prisoner's failure to develop material facts in state court." In *Keeney*, the Court borrowed the cause and prejudice standard applied to procedurally defaulted claims, see Wainwright v. Sykes, 433 U.S. 72, 87–88 (1977), deciding there was no reason "to distinguish between failing to properly assert a federal claim in state court and failing in state court to properly develop such a claim." As is evident from the similarity between the Court's phrasing in *Keeney* and the opening clause of § 2254(e)(2), Congress intended to preserve at least one aspect of *Keeney*'s holding: prisoners who are at fault for the deficiency in the state-court record must satisfy a heightened standard to obtain an evidentiary hearing. To be sure, in requiring that prisoners who

have not been diligent satisfy § 2254(e)(2)'s provisions rather than show cause and prejudice, and in eliminating a freestanding "miscarriage of justice" exception, Congress raised the bar *Keeney* imposed on prisoners who were not diligent in state-court proceedings. Contrary to the Commonwealth's position, however, there is no basis in the text of § 2254(e)(2) to believe Congress used "fail" in a different sense than the Court did in *Keeney* or otherwise intended the statute's further, more stringent requirements to control the availability of an evidentiary hearing in a broader class of cases than were covered by *Keeney*'s cause and prejudice standard.

Section 2254(e)(2)(A)(ii) itself contains a due diligence standard. Is that inconsistent with the Court's interpretation of the introductory clause? The Court said "no":

> The Commonwealth argues a reading of "failed to develop" premised on fault empties § 2254(e)(2)(A)(ii) of its meaning. To treat the prisoner's lack of diligence in state court as a prerequisite for application of § 2254(e)(2), the Commonwealth contends, renders a nullity of the statute's own diligence provision requiring the prisoner to show "a factual predicate [of his claim] could not have been previously discovered through the exercise of due diligence." § 2254(e)(2)(A)(ii). We disagree.
>
> The Commonwealth misconceives the inquiry mandated by the opening clause of § 2254(e)(2). The question is not whether the facts could have been discovered but instead whether the prisoner was diligent in his efforts. The purpose of the fault component of "failed" is to ensure the prisoner undertakes his own diligent search for evidence. Diligence for purposes of the opening clause depends upon whether the prisoner made a reasonable attempt, in light of the information available at the time, to investigate and pursue claims in state court; it does not depend, as the Commonwealth would have it, upon whether those efforts could have been successful. Though lack of diligence will not bar an evidentiary hearing if efforts to discover the facts would have been in vain, see § 2254(e)(2)(A)(ii), and there is a convincing claim of innocence, see § 2254(e)(2)(B), only a prisoner who has neglected his rights in state court need satisfy these conditions. The statute's later reference to diligence pertains to cases in which the facts could not have been discovered, whether there was diligence or not. In this important respect § 2254(e)(2)(A)(ii) bears a close resemblance to (e)(2)(A)(i), which applies to a new rule that was not available at the time of the earlier proceedings. ...In these two parallel provisions Congress has given prisoners who fall within § 2254(e)(2)'s opening clause an opportunity to obtain an evidentiary hearing where the legal or factual basis of the claims did not exist at the time of state-court proceedings.

And finally, the Court said, its interpretation of the statute was consistent with principles of comity, finality, and federalism:

We are not persuaded by the Commonwealth's further argument that anything less than a no-fault understanding of the opening clause is contrary to AEDPA's purpose to further the principles of comity, finality, and federalism. There is no doubt Congress intended AEDPA to advance these doctrines. Federal habeas corpus principles must inform and shape the historic and still vital relation of mutual respect and common purpose existing between the States and the federal courts. In keeping this delicate balance we have been careful to limit the scope of federal intrusion into state criminal adjudications and to safeguard the States' interest in the integrity of their criminal and collateral proceedings. . . .

It is consistent with these principles to give effect to Congress' intent to avoid unneeded evidentiary hearings in federal habeas corpus, while recognizing the statute does not equate prisoners who exercise diligence in pursuing their claims with those who do not. Principles of exhaustion are premised upon recognition by Congress and the Court that state judiciaries have the duty and competence to vindicate rights secured by the Constitution in state criminal proceedings. Diligence will require in the usual case that the prisoner, at a minimum, seek an evidentiary hearing in state court in the manner prescribed by state law. . . . For state courts to have their rightful opportunity to adjudicate federal rights, the prisoner must be diligent in developing the record and presenting, if possible, all claims of constitutional error. If the prisoner fails to do so, himself or herself contributing to the absence of a full and fair adjudication in state court, § 2254(e)(2) prohibits an evidentiary hearing to develop the relevant claims in federal court, unless the statute's other stringent requirements are met. Federal courts sitting in habeas are not an alternative forum for trying facts and issues which a prisoner made insufficient effort to pursue in state proceedings. Yet comity is not served by saying a prisoner "has failed to develop the factual basis of a claim" where he was unable to develop his claim in state court despite diligent effort. In that circumstance, an evidentiary hearing is not barred by § 2254(e)(2).

The Court then applied these conclusions to the claims Williams sought to raise. The *Brady* claim, it held, was foreclosed because the defense lawyers could with ordinary diligence have discovered the situation in time to present it to the state courts. Since defense counsel "failed" to present the claim in state courts, and since the defendant admitted before the Supreme Court that he could not satisfy the provisions of § 2254(e)(2)(B), the 1966 legislation precluded federal habeas consideration of that claim.

The juror bias and prosecutor misconduct claims, however, were another matter. One of the jurors had been married for 17 years (with four children) to the prosecution's lead witness at trial. They had been divorced for 15 years at the time of trial. One of the prosecutors, moreover, had represented the juror in the uncontested divorce. None of these facts came to light in the judge's questioning of the juror prior to the trial, during the trial, or in subsequent state post-conviction proceedings. They were discovered by happenstance when the defendant's federal habeas counsel interviewed two other jurors who referred to the juror in question by the same last name as the lead prosecution witness. The Court examined the prior proceedings with care and concluded:

> [I]f the prisoner has made a reasonable effort to discover the claims to commence or continue state proceedings, § 2254(e)(2) will not bar him from developing them in federal court. ...[Here,] there was no basis for an [earlier] investigation into [the juror's] marriage history. Section 2254(e)(2) does not apply to petitioner's related claims of juror bias and prosecutorial misconduct.
>
> We further note the Commonwealth has not argued that petitioner could have sought relief in state court once he discovered the factual bases of these claims some time between appointment of federal habeas counsel on July 2, 1996, and the filing of his federal habeas petition on November 20, 1996. As an indigent, petitioner had 120 days following appointment of state habeas counsel to file a petition with the Virginia Supreme Court. Va.Code Ann. § 8.01–654.1 (1999). State habeas counsel was appointed on August 10, 1995, about a year before petitioner's investigator on federal habeas uncovered the information regarding [the juror and the prosecutor]. As state postconviction relief was no longer available at the time the facts came to light, it would have been futile for petitioner to return to the Virginia courts. In these circumstances, though the state courts did not have an opportunity to consider the new claims, petitioner cannot be said to have failed to develop them in state court by reason of having neglected to pursue remedies available under Virginia law.
>
> Our analysis should suffice to establish cause for any procedural default petitioner may have committed in not presenting these claims to the Virginia courts in the first instance. Questions regarding the standard for determining the prejudice that petitioner must establish to obtain relief on these claims can be addressed by the Court of Appeals or the District Court in the course of further proceedings. These courts, in light of cases such as Smith v. Phillips, 455 U.S. 209, 215 (1982) ("[T]he remedy for allegations of juror partiality is a hearing in which the defendant has the opportunity to prove actual bias"), will take due account of the District Court's earlier [finding that the juror] "... deliberately failed to tell the truth on voir dire."

4. Questions and Comments on *Michael Wayne Williams v. Taylor*. As the Court unanimously holds in *Michael Wayne Williams*, the *Sykes* "cause and prejudice" standard, as applied in *Keeney v. Tamayo-Reyes*, survives the enactment of § 2254(e)(2). And as the Court holds in *Lee*, the adequate and independent state ground doctrine can provide an independent basis for hearing a state claim without even considering the "cause and prejudice" standard.

The result is a three-tiered inquiry:

(1) If the state's reason for not hearing a federal claim is noncompliance with a state procedure that is either not adequate or not independent, the federal habeas court can hear the claim on the merits. This is the result in *Lee*.

(2) If the state's reason for not hearing the claim is adequate and independent, the limitations of § 2254(e)(2) do not apply if the federal habeas applicant's lawyers made a "reasonable effort" to discover available claims or otherwise were not at fault. Under *Williams*, this will satisfy the "cause" component of the *Wainwright v. Sykes* standard and afford the habeas applicant an opportunity to establish "prejudice." The limitations of § 2254(e)(2) do not apply to cases where the defendant's lawyers failed to raise a claim but exercised "due diligence" in their representation.[b]

(3) If all else fails, the habeas applicant can attempt to excuse the effect of failing to raise a claim in state court by satisfying the restrictive provisions of § 2254(e)(2)(A) and (B).

Consider the impact of this interpretation of § 2254(e)(2). If "cause and prejudice" cannot be established to excuse a procedural default in state court, then the restrictions of § 2254(e)(2)(A) and (B) will come into play. Are there likely to be many situations when "cause and prejudice" cannot be established but the standards of § 2254(e)(2)(A) and (B) could be? Suppose a federal habeas court believes that cause and prejudice cannot be shown, but that "a fundamental miscarriage of justice would result from failure to hold a federal evidentiary hearing." What is it to do then? Will all such cases fit into § 2254(e)(2)(A) and (B)? Must they? How are cases to be analyzed where, in the words of Murray v. Carrier, 477 U.S. 478, 496 (1986), "a constitutional violation has probably resulted in the conviction of one who is actually innocent"?

If "cause and prejudice" can be established, on the other hand, the applicant is entitled to a hearing. What happens then? Does the federal habeas court consider the constitutional claim de novo and grant the relief the state court should have granted if the claim had been properly raised? What else could it do? Can it consider Court of Appeals decisions, or is it limited by analogy to § 2254(d) to "clearly established Federal law, as

---

b. If Williams had sought to litigate the juror bias and prosecutor misconduct claims in state court after he became aware of them, the state courts would–as the Supreme Court points out–have held them time-barred. This would have constituted an adequate and independent state ground for refusing to hear the claims. But this would not have precluded the federal habeas courts from going forward because Williams could have established "cause" for his failure to litigate in state court and would be entitled to a hearing to establish "prejudice."

determined by the Supreme Court of the United States"? Can it extend the federal law even slightly beyond what had been "clearly established" at the time of trial?

Finally, the Supreme Court held in *Michael Wayne Williams* that the petitioner had established "cause" for two of his claims. How is he to show "prejudice" on remand? Is he to be afforded a hearing at which he "has the opportunity to show actual bias" by the juror? Or must he first establish "prejudice" in order to get such a hearing? If the former, does this mean that only "cause" need be shown in order to get a hearing? If the latter, how could the defendant show what it would take a hearing to demonstrate?

5. The New Legislation in Capital Cases. [Here read Note 3 on pages 764–65.]

Page 780, replace footnote b:

b. This includes discretionary review in the highest court of the state. But there is ambiguity about whether such review must be sought if the highest state court has made it clear that routine presentation of all possible claims is unwelcome because its function is to hear only questions of statewide importance. See O'Sullivan v. Boerckel, 526 U.S. 838 (1999). There is no requirement, however, that certiorari be sought in the United States Supreme Court after a decision by the highest court of the state. Fay v. Noia, 372 U.S. 391 (1963).

Page 780, substitute the following for the fourth paragraph of Note 2:

There are adverse consequences, moreover, if the habeas petitioner failed to raise an available claim in previous state litigation. In O'Sullivan v. Boerckel, 526 U.S. 838 (1999), for example, the Court enforced a procedural foreclosure on three of the petitioner's six habeas claims. The reason was that he could have raised these claims in his application for discretionary review in the state Supreme Court but did not do so. His failure properly to exhaust his available state remedies, in other words, led to procedural foreclosure of his unexhausted claims. See also Edwards v. Carpenter, 529 U.S. 446 (2000).

Page 783, substitute for footnote e:

e. In Carey v. Saffold, ___ U.S. ___ (2002), the Court held that state post-convictions proceedings were "pending," and therefore tolled the federal one-year statute of limitations, during the time between a lower state court's decision and the filing of a notice of appeal to a higher state court. It disagreed five to four, however, about the application of this standard to the particular California procedure before the Court.

As amended, § 2255 contains one-year limit on federal prisoners who seek collateral relief defined in terms similar to § 2244(d).

Page 786, add a footnote at the end of paragraph (b):

h. The Court held in Slack v. McDaniel, 529 U.S. 473 (2000), that "a habeas petition which is filed after an initial petition was dismissed without adjudication on the merits for failure to exhaust state remedies is not a 'second or successive' petition as that term is understood in the habeas corpus context. Federal courts do, however, retain broad powers to prevent duplicative or unnecessary litigation." Justice Scalia, joined by Justice Thomas, dissented from this part of the Court's holding. The initial habeas case was filed before the effective date of the 1996 legislation.

Page 786, add new Notes and Main Cases:

9. *Stewart v. Martinez–Villareal*. In Stewart v. Martinez–Villareal, 523 U.S. 637 (1998), the Court answered one of the questions about *Rose v. Lundy* posed above. If Lundy allowed his federal petition to be dismissed, returned to state court to litigate his unexhausted claims, lost in state court, and then presented all his claims in a new federal petition, he would not, it appears, be subject to the limitations of § 2244(b).

Martinez–Villareal was convicted of murder and sentenced to death. The state courts affirmed on direct appeal, and a series of state-court habeas petitions were denied. Martinez–Villareal then filed three successive petitions for federal habeas, all of which were denied because they contained claims on which state remedies had not been exhausted. He then filed a fourth federal habeas petition. This petition asserted, among other claims, that Martinez–Villareal was not competent to be executed. He relied on Ford v. Wainwright, 477 U.S. 399 (1986), which held that the death penalty could not be inflicted on a prisoner who was insane.

The District Court dismissed the *Ford* claim on the ground that it was premature (no date of execution had yet been set). It then granted habeas relief on one of the other claims, but the Court of Appeals reversed and reinstated the conviction. Both courts indicated that they did not mean to foreclose a later assertion of the *Ford* claim.

Soon thereafter the state set a date of execution. After a hearing in state court on Martinez–Villareal's mental condition, it was determined that he was fit to be executed. He then renewed his *Ford* claim in federal court. This presented two questions: whether court of appeals permission to file the claim was required because it was a "second or successive application" under 28 U.S.C. § 2244(b)(3)[h]; and whether the limits of 28 U.S.C. § 2244(b)(1) and (2)[i] were applicable. The Court of Appeals held

h. "(A) Before a second or successive application permitted by this section is filed in the district court, the applicant shall move in the appropriate court of appeals for an order authorizing the district court to consider the application. . . .

"(E) The grant or denial of an authorization by a court of appeals to file a second or successive application shall not be appealable and shall not be the subject of a petition for rehearing or for a writ of certiorari."

i. "(1) A claim presented in a second or successive habeas corpus application under section 2254 that was presented in a prior application shall be dismissed.

"(2) A claim presented in a second or successive habeas corpus application under section 2254 that was not presented in a prior application shall be dismissed unless—

"(A) the applicant shows that the claim relies on a new rule of constitutional law, made retroactive to cases on collateral review by the supreme court, that was previously unavailable; or

"(B)(i) the factual predicate for the claim could not have been discovered previously through the exercise of due diligence; and

(ii) the facts underlying the claim, if proven and viewed in light

that § 2244(b) did not apply to a petition that raised only a competency to be executed claim, and accordingly remanded the case to the District Court for resolution of the merits. The state at this point successfully sought certiorari to review the Court of Appeals' decision.

The Supreme Court first held that it had jurisdiction (in spite of § 2244(b)(3)(E)) because the Court of Appeals had held § 2244(b) inapplicable. Chief Justice Rehnquist then wrote for the Court:

> "The state contends that because respondent has already had one 'fully-litigated habeas petition, the plain meaning of § 2244(b) . . . requires his new petition to be treated as successive.' Under that reading of the statute, respondent is entitled to only one merits judgment of his federal habeas claims. Because respondent has already presented a petition to the District Court, and the District Court and Court of Appeals have acted on that petition, § 2244(b) must apply to any subsequent request for federal habeas relief. . . .
>
> "This may have been the second time that respondent has asked the federal courts to provide relief on his *Ford* claim, but this does not mean that there were two separate applications, the second of which was necessarily subject to § 2244(b). There was only one application for habeas relief, and the District Court ruled (or should have ruled) on each claim at the time it became ripe. Respondent was entitled to an adjudication of all of the claims presented in his earlier . . . application for federal habeas relief. The Court of Appeals was therefore correct in holding that respondent was not required to get authorization to file a 'second or successive' application before his *Ford* claim could be heard.
>
> "If the state's interpretation of 'second or successive' were correct, the implications for habeas practice would be far-reaching and seemingly perverse. [N]one of our cases expounding [the exhaustion] doctrine have ever suggested that a prisoner whose habeas petition was dismissed for failure to exhaust state remedies, and who then did exhaust those remedies and return to federal court, was by such action filing a successive petition. A court where such a petition was filed could adjudicate these claims under the same standard as would govern those made in any other first petition.
>
> "We believe that respondent's *Ford* claim here—previously dismissed as premature—should be treated in the same manner as the claim of a petitioner who returns to a federal habeas court

of the evidence as a whole, would be sufficient to establish by clear and convincing evidence that, but for constitutional error, no reasonable factfinder would have found the applicant guilty of the underlying offense."

after exhausting state remedies. True, the cases are not identical; respondent's *Ford* claim was dismissed as premature, not because he had not exhausted state remedies, but because his execution was not imminent and therefore his competency to be executed could not be determined at that time. But in both situations, the habeas petitioner does not receive an adjudication of his claim. To hold otherwise would mean that a dismissal of a first habeas petition for technical procedural reasons would bar the prisoner from ever obtaining federal habeas review."

Justices Thomas and Scalia dissented. They thought the plain language of § 2244(b) required dismissal of the petition.

10. Questions and Comments on *Martinez-Villareal*. In a footnote in his opinion in *Martinez-Villareal*, Chief Justice Rehnquist said that "[t]his case does not present the situation where a prisoner raises a *Ford* claim for the first time in a petition filed after the federal courts have already rejected the prisoner's initial habeas application. Therefore, we have no occasion to decide whether such a filing would be a 'second or successive application' within the meaning of [§ 2244(b)]."

What possible difference could this make? Does the Court's reading of the language of § 2244(b) turn on the fact that Martinez–Villareal had sought *Ford* relief at a time when it was not available to him? Does the footnote mean that careful lawyers will now raise *Ford* claims routinely in all first habeas petitions just in case their clients lose their sanity as the time of execution approaches?

From another perspective, how, indeed, does the Court read the language of § 2244(b) to justify its decision? Does the "plain meaning" of the statute support any other view but the dissent's?

Duncan v. Walker

Supreme Court of the United States, 2001.
533 U.S. 167.

■ JUSTICE O'CONNOR delivered the opinion of the Court.

Title 28 U.S.C. § 2244(d)(2) (1994 ed., Supp. V) provides: "The time during which a properly filed application for State post-conviction or other collateral review with respect to the pertinent judgment or claim is pending shall not be counted toward any period of limitation under this subsection." This case presents the question whether a federal habeas corpus petition is an "application for State post-conviction or other collateral review" within the meaning of this provision.

I

In 1992, several judgments of conviction for robbery were entered against respondent Sherman Walker in the New York state courts. The last of these convictions came in June 1992, when respondent pleaded guilty to robbery in the first degree in the New York Supreme Court, Queens County. Respondent was sentenced to 7 to 14 years in prison on this conviction.

Respondent unsuccessfully pursued a number of state remedies in connection with his convictions. It is unnecessary to describe all of these proceedings herein.... Respondent's last conviction became final in April 1996, prior to the April 24, 1996, effective date of the Antiterrorism and Effective Death Penalty Act of 1996 (AEDPA), 110 Stat. 1214.

In a single document dated April 10, 1996, respondent filed a complaint under 42 U.S.C. § 1983 and a petition for habeas corpus under 28 U.S.C. § 2254 in the United States District Court for the Eastern District of New York. On July 9, 1996, the District Court dismissed the complaint and petition without prejudice. With respect to the habeas petition, the District Court, citing § 2254(b), concluded that respondent had not adequately set forth his claim because it was not apparent that respondent had exhausted available state remedies....

On May 20, 1997, more than one year after AEDPA's effective date, respondent filed another federal habeas petition in the same District Court. It is undisputed that respondent had not returned to state court since the dismissal of his first federal habeas filing. On May 6, 1998, the District Court dismissed the petition as time barred....

The United States Court of Appeals for the Second Circuit reversed the District Court's judgment, reinstated the habeas petition, and remanded the case for further proceedings. The Court of Appeals noted at the outset that, because respondent's conviction had become final prior to AEDPA's effective date, he had until April 24, 1997, to file his federal habeas petition. The court also observed that the exclusion from the limitation period of the time during which respondent's first federal habeas petition was pending in the District Court would render the instant habeas petition timely.... We granted certiorari.... We now reverse.

II

Our task is to construe what Congress has enacted. We begin, as always, with the language of the statute. Respondent reads § 2244(d)(2) to apply the word "State" only to the term "post-conviction" and not to the phrase "other collateral." Under this view, a properly filed federal habeas petition tolls the limitation period. Petitioner contends that the word "State" applies to the entire phrase "post-conviction or other collateral review." Under this view, a properly filed federal habeas petition does not toll the limitation period.

We believe that petitioner's interpretation of § 2244(d)(2) is correct for several reasons. To begin with, Congress placed the word "State" before "post-conviction or other collateral review" without specifically naming any kind of "Federal" review. The essence of respondent's position is that Congress used the phrase "other collateral review" to incorporate federal habeas petitions into the class of applications for review that toll the limitation period. But a comparison of the text of § 2244(d)(2) with the language of other AEDPA provisions supplies strong evidence that, had Congress intended to include federal habeas petitions within the scope of § 2244(d)(2), Congress would have mentioned "Federal" review expressly. In several other portions of AEDPA, Congress specifically used both the words "State" and "Federal" to denote state and federal proceedings....

Section 2244(d)(2), by contrast, employs the word "State," but not the word "Federal," as a modifier for "review." ... We find no likely explanation for Congress' omission of the word "Federal" in § 2244(d)(2) other than that Congress did not intend properly filed applications for federal review to toll the limitation period. It would be anomalous, to say the least, for Congress to usher in federal review under the generic rubric of "other collateral review" in a statutory provision that refers expressly to "State" review, while denominating expressly both "State" and "Federal" proceedings in other parts of the same statute. The anomaly is underscored by the fact that the words "State" and "Federal" are likely to be of no small import when Congress drafts a statute that governs federal collateral review of state court judgments.

Further, were we to adopt respondent's construction of the statute, we would render the word "State" insignificant, if not wholly superfluous.... We are especially unwilling to do so when the term occupies so pivotal a place in the statutory scheme as does the word "State" in the federal habeas statute. But under respondent's rendition of § 2244(d)(2), Congress' inclusion of the word "State" has no operative effect on the scope of the provision. If the phrase "State post-conviction or other collateral review" is construed to encompass both state and federal collateral review, then the word "State" places no constraint on the class of applications for review that toll the limitation period. The clause instead would have precisely the same content were it to read "post-conviction or other collateral review."

The most that could then be made of the word "State" would be to say that Congress singled out applications for "State post-conviction" review as one example from the universe of applications for collateral review. Under this approach, however, the word "State" still does nothing to delimit the entire class of applications for review that toll the limitation period. A construction under which the word "State" does nothing more than further modify "post-conviction" relegates "State" to quite an insignificant role in the statutory provision. We believe that our duty to "give each word some operative effect" where possible requires more in this context....

Incarceration pursuant to a state criminal conviction may be by far the most common and most familiar basis for satisfaction of the "in custody" requirement in § 2254 cases. But there are other types of state court judgments pursuant to which a person may be held in custody within the meaning of the federal habeas statute. For example, federal habeas corpus review may be available to challenge the legality of a state court order of civil commitment or a state court order of civil contempt.... Congress also may have employed the construction "post-conviction or other collateral" in recognition of the diverse terminology that different States employ to represent the different forms of collateral review that are available after a conviction.... Congress may have refrained from exclusive reliance on the term "post-conviction" so as to leave no doubt that the tolling provision applies to all types of state collateral review available after a conviction and not just to those denominated "post-conviction" in the parlance of a particular jurisdiction....

Consideration of the competing constructions in light of AEDPA's purposes reinforces the conclusion that we draw from the text. Petitioner's interpretation of the statute is consistent with "AEDPA's purpose to further the principles of comity, finality, and federalism." Williams v. Taylor, 529 U.S. 420, 436 (2000). Specifically, under petitioner's construction, § 2244(d)(2) promotes the exhaustion of state remedies while respecting the interest in the finality of state court judgments. Under respondent's interpretation, however, the provision would do far less to encourage exhaustion prior to seeking federal habeas review and would hold greater potential to hinder finality....

The one-year limitation period of § 2244(d)(1) quite plainly serves the well-recognized interest in the finality of state court judgments. This provision reduces the potential for delay on the road to finality by restricting the time that a prospective federal habeas petitioner has in which to seek federal habeas review.

The tolling provision of § 2244(d)(2) balances the interests served by the exhaustion requirement and the limitation period. Section 2244(d)(2) promotes the exhaustion of state remedies by protecting a state prisoner's ability later to apply for federal habeas relief while state remedies are being pursued. At the same time, the provision limits the harm to the interest in finality by according tolling effect only to "properly filed application[s] for State post-conviction or other collateral review."

By tolling the limitation period for the pursuit of state remedies and not during the pendency of applications for federal review, § 2244(d)(2) provides a powerful incentive for litigants to exhaust all available state remedies before proceeding in the lower federal courts. But if the statute were construed so as to give applications for federal review the same tolling effect as applications for state collateral review, then § 2244(d)(2) would furnish little incentive for individuals to seek relief from the state courts before filing federal habeas petitions. The tolling provision instead would be indifferent between state and federal filings. While other statutory provisions, such as § 2254(b) itself, of course, would still provide individuals with good reason to exhaust, § 2244(d)(2) would be out of step with this design. At the same time, respondent's interpretation would further undermine the interest in finality by creating more potential for delay in the adjudication of federal-law claims.

A diminution of statutory incentives to proceed first in state court would also increase the risk of the very piecemeal litigation that the exhaustion requirement is designed to reduce. We have observed that "strict enforcement of the exhaustion requirement will encourage habeas petitioners to exhaust all of their claims in state court and to present the federal court with a single habeas petition." Rose v. Lundy, 455 U.S. 509, 520 (1982). But were we to adopt respondent's construction of § 2244(d)(2), we would dilute the efficacy of the exhaustion requirement in achieving this objective. Tolling the limitation period for a federal habeas petition that is dismissed without prejudice would thus create more opportunities for delay and piecemeal litigation without advancing the goals of comity and federalism that the exhaustion requirement serves. We do not believe that Congress designed the statute in this manner....

Respondent contends that petitioner's construction of the statute creates the potential for unfairness to litigants who file timely federal habeas petitions that are dismissed without prejudice after the limitation period has expired. But our sole task in this case is one of statutory construction, and upon examining the language and purpose of the statute, we are convinced that § 2244(d)(2) does not toll the limitation period during the pendency of a federal habeas petition.

We also note that, when the District Court dismissed respondent's first federal habeas petition without prejudice, respondent had more than nine months remaining in the limitation period in which to cure the defects that led to the dismissal. It is undisputed, however, that petitioner neither returned to state court nor filed a nondefective federal habeas petition before this time had elapsed. Respondent's May 1997 federal habeas petition also contained claims different from those presented in his April 1996 petition. In light of these facts, we have no occasion to address ... the question that Justice Stevens raises concerning the availability of equitable tolling.

We hold that an application for federal habeas corpus review is not an "application for State post-conviction or other collateral review" within the meaning of 28 U.S.C. § 2244(d)(2). Section 2244(d)(2) therefore did not toll the limitation period during the pendency of respondent's first federal habeas petition. The judgment of the Court of Appeals is reversed, and the case is remanded for further proceedings consistent with this opinion.

It is so ordered.

■ JUSTICE SOUTER, concurring.

Although I join the Court's opinion in full, I have joined Justice Stevens's separate opinion pointing out that nothing bars a district court from retaining jurisdiction pending complete exhaustion of state remedies, and that a claim for equitable tolling could present a serious issue on facts different from those before us.

■ JUSTICE STEVENS, with whom JUSTICE SOUTER joins, concurring in part and concurring in the judgment.

For substantially the reasons stated [in] the Court's opinion, I agree that the better reading of 28 U.S.C. § 2244(d)(2) (1994 ed., Supp. V) is that it encompasses only "State" applications for "post-conviction or other collateral review." Thus, as the Court holds, "an application for federal habeas corpus review is not an 'application for State post-conviction or other collateral review' within the meaning of 28 U.S.C. § 2244(d)(2)." I write separately to add two observations regarding the equitable powers of the federal courts, which are unaffected by today's decision construing a single provision of the Antiterrorism and Effective Death Penalty Act of 1996 (AEDPA), 110 Stat. 1214.

First, although the Court's pre-AEDPA decision in Rose v. Lundy, 455 U.S. 509, 522 (1982), prescribed the dismissal of federal habeas corpus petitions containing unexhausted claims, in our post-AEDPA world there is no reason why a district court should not retain jurisdiction over a meritorious claim and stay further proceedings pending the complete exhaustion of state remedies. Indeed, there is every reason to do so when AEDPA gives a district court the alternative of simply denying a petition containing unexhausted but nonmeritorious claims, see 28 U.S.C. § 2254(b)(2) (1994 ed., Supp. V), and when the failure to retain jurisdiction would foreclose federal review of a meritorious claim because of the lapse of AEDPA's one-year limitations period.

Second, despite the Court's suggestion that tolling the limitations period for a first federal habeas petition would undermine the "purposes" of AEDPA, neither the Court's narrow holding, nor anything in the text or legislative history of AEDPA, precludes a federal court from deeming the limitations period tolled for such a petition as a matter of equity. The Court's opinion does not address a federal court's ability to toll the limitations period apart from § 2244(d)(2). Furthermore, a federal court might very well conclude that tolling is appropriate based on the reasonable belief that Congress could not have intended to bar federal habeas review for petitioners who invoke the court's jurisdiction within the 1–year interval prescribed by AEDPA.

After all, federal habeas corpus has evolved as the product of both judicial doctrine and statutory law. [F]ederal courts may well conclude that Congress simply overlooked the class of petitioners whose timely filed habeas petitions remain pending in district court past the limitations period, only to be dismissed after the court belatedly realizes that one or more claims have not been exhausted. As a result, equitable considerations may make it appropriate for federal courts to fill in a perceived omission on the part of Congress by tolling AEDPA's statute of limitations for unexhausted federal habeas petitions. Today's ruling does not preclude that possibility, given the limited issue presented in this case and the Court's correspondingly limited holding.

I concur in the Court's holding on the understanding that it does not foreclose either of the above safeguards against the potential for injustice that a literal reading of § 2244(d)(2) might otherwise produce.

■ JUSTICE BREYER, with whom JUSTICE GINSBURG joins, dissenting.

The federal habeas corpus statute limits the period of time during which a state prisoner may file a federal habeas petition to one year, ordinarily running from the time the prisoner's conviction becomes final in the state courts. See 28 U.S.C. § 2244(d) (1994 ed., Supp. V). Section 2244(d)(2) tolls that one-year period while "a properly filed application for State post-conviction or other collateral review ... is pending." The question before us is whether this tolling provision applies to federal, as well as state, collateral review proceedings. Do the words "other collateral review" encompass federal habeas corpus proceedings? I believe that they do.

To understand my conclusion, one must understand why the legal issue before us is significant. Why would a state prisoner ever want federal habeas corpus proceedings to toll the federal habeas corpus limitations period? After all, the very point of tolling is to provide a state prisoner adequate time to file a federal habeas petition. If the petitioner has already filed that petition, what need is there for further tolling?

The answer to this question—and the problem that gives rise to the issue before us—is that a federal court may be required to dismiss a state prisoner's federal habeas petition, not on the merits, but because that prisoner has not exhausted his state collateral remedies for every claim presented in the federal petition. Such a dismissal means that a prisoner wishing to pursue the claim must return to state court, pursue his state remedies, and then, if he loses, again file a federal habeas petition in federal court. All this takes time. The statute tolls the one-year limitations period during the time the prisoner proceeds in the state courts. But unless the statute also tolls the limitations period during the time the defective petition was pending in federal court, the state prisoner may find, when he seeks to return to federal court, that he has run out of time.

This possibility is not purely theoretical. A Justice Department study indicates that 63% of all habeas petitions are dismissed, and 57% of those are dismissed for failure to exhaust state remedies. See U.S. Dept. of Justice, Office of Justice Programs, Bureau of Justice Statistics, Federal Habeas Corpus Review: Challenging State Court Criminal Convictions 17 (1995) (hereinafter Federal Habeas Corpus Review). And it can take courts a significant amount of time to dispose of even those petitions that are not addressed on the merits; on the average, district courts took 268 days to dismiss petitions on procedural grounds. *Id.*, at 23–24; see also *id.*, at 19 (of all habeas petitions, nearly half were pending in the district court for six months or longer; 10% were pending more than two years). Thus, if the words "other collateral review" do not include federal collateral review, a large group of federal habeas petitioners, seeking to return to federal court after subsequent state-court rejection of an unexhausted claim, may find their claims time barred. Moreover, because district courts vary substantially in the time they take to rule on habeas petitions, two identically situated prisoners can receive opposite results. If Prisoner *A* and Prisoner *B* file mixed petitions in different district courts six months before the federal limitations period expires, and the court takes three months to dismiss Prisoner *A*'s petition, but seven months to dismiss Prisoner *B*'s petition, Prisoner *A* will be able to return to federal court after exhausting state remedies, but Prisoner *B*—due to no fault of his own—may not.

On the other hand, if the words "other collateral review" include federal collateral review, state prisoners whose federal claims have been dismissed for nonexhaustion will simply add to the one-year limitations period the time they previously spent in both state and federal proceedings. Other things being equal, they will be able to return to federal court after pursuing the state remedies that remain available. And similarly situated prisoners will not suffer different outcomes simply because they file their petitions in different district courts.

The statute's language, read by itself, does not tell us whether the words "State post-conviction or other collateral review" include federal habeas proceedings. Rather, it is simply unclear whether Congress intended the word "State" to modify "post-conviction" review alone, or also to modify "other collateral review" (as the majority believes). Indeed, most naturally read, the statute refers to two distinct kinds of applications: (1) applications for "State post-conviction" review and (2) applications for "other collateral review," a broad category that, on its face, would include applications for federal habeas review. The majority's reading requires either an unusual intonation—"*State* post-conviction-or-other-collateral *review*"—or a slight rewrite of the language, by inserting the word "State" where it does not appear, between "other" and "collateral." Regardless, I believe that either reading is possible. The statute's words, by themselves, have no singular "plain meaning."

Neither do I believe that the various interpretive canons to which the majority appeals can solve the problem. [T]he majority attempts to ascertain Congress's intent by looking to the tolling provision's statutory neighbors. It points to other provisions where Congress explicitly used the words "State" and "Federal" together, expressing its intent to cover both kinds of proceedings. And it reasons that Congress's failure to do so here displays a different intent.

But other statutory neighbors show that, when Congress wished unambiguously to limit tolling to state proceedings, "it knew how to do so." Custis v. United States, 511 U.S. 485, 492 (1994).... In fact, the "argument from neighbors" shows only that Congress might have spoken more clearly than it did. It cannot prove the statutory point.

The majority also believes that only its interpretation gives effect to every word in the statute—in particular the word "State." It asks: If Congress meant to cover federal habeas review, why does the word "State" appear in the statute? Federal habeas proceedings are a form of post-conviction proceedings. So, had Congress meant to cover them, it would have just said "post-conviction and other collateral review."

But this argument proves too much, for one can ask with equal force: If Congress intended to exclude federal habeas proceedings, why does the word "post-conviction" appear in the statute? State post-conviction proceedings are a form of collateral review. So, had Congress meant to exclude federal collateral proceedings, it could have just said "State collateral review," thereby clearly indicating that the phrase applies only to state proceedings.

In fact, this kind of argument, viewed realistically, gets us nowhere. Congress probably picked out "State post-conviction" proceedings from the universe of collateral proceedings and mentioned it separately because State post-conviction proceedings are a salient example of collateral proceedings. But to understand this is not to understand whether the universe from which Congress picked "State post-conviction" proceedings as an example is the universe of *all* collateral proceedings, or the universe of *state* collateral proceedings. The statute simply does not say.

Indeed, the majority recognizes that neither the statute's language, nor the application of canons of construction, is sufficient to resolve the problem. It concedes that the phrase "other collateral review," if construed as "other [State] collateral review," would add little to the coverage that the words "State post-conviction ... review" would provide in its absence. The majority resolves this difficulty by noting that "other collateral review" could also include either review of state civil confinement proceedings or state post-conviction review to which a State refers by some other name, such as state "habeas" proceedings.

But it is difficult to believe that Congress had state civil proceedings in mind, given that other provisions within § 2244 indicate that Congress saw criminal proceedings as its basic subject matter. For instance, the exceptions to the bar against successive petitions in § 2244(d) seem to presume that the petition at issue challenges a criminal conviction. Nor does it seem likely that Congress would have expected federal courts applying the tolling provision to construe "post-conviction" review to exclude state "habeas" petitions challenging convictions. The statute in which the words "State post-conviction proceedings" appear is a *federal* statute, and federal courts would be likely to apply those words to whatever state proceedings in fact fall within this federal description, whatever different labels different States might choose to attach. It is simpler, more meaningful, and just as logical to assume that Congress meant the words "other collateral review" to cast a wider net—a net wide enough to include federal collateral proceedings such as those that precede a dismissal for nonexhaustion.

Faced with this statutory ambiguity, I would look to statutory purposes in order to reach a proper interpretation. And, while I agree that Congress sought to "further the principles of comity, finality, and federalism," I would also ask whether Congress would have intended to create the kind of "unexhausted petition" problem that I described at the outset. The answer is no. Congress enacted a statute that all agree gave state prisoners a full year (plus the duration of state collateral proceedings) to file a federal habeas corpus petition. Congress would not have intended to shorten that time dramatically, at random, and perhaps erase it altogether, "den[ying] the petitioner the protections of the Great Writ entirely," Lonchar v. Thomas, 517 U.S. 314, 324 (1996), simply because the technical nature of the habeas rules led a prisoner initially to file a petition in the wrong court.

The majority's argument assumes a congressional desire to strengthen the prisoners' incentive to file in state court first. But that is not likely to be the result of today's holding. After all, virtually every state prisoner already knows that he must first exhaust state-court remedies; and I imagine that virtually all of them now try to do so. The problem arises because the vast majority of federal habeas petitions are brought without legal representation. See Federal Habeas Corpus Review 14 (finding that 93% of habeas petitioners in study were *pro se*). Prisoners acting *pro se* will often not know whether a change in wording between state and federal petitions will be seen in federal court as a new claim or a better way of stating an old one; and they often will not understand whether new facts brought forward in the federal petition reflect a new claim or better support for an old one. Insofar as that is so, the Court's approach is likely to lead not to fewer improper federal petitions, but to increased confusion, as prisoners hesitate to change the language of state petitions or add facts, and to greater unfairness. And it will undercut one significant purpose of the provision before us—to grant state prisoners a fair and reasonable time to bring a first federal habeas corpus petition.

Nor is it likely that prisoners will deliberately seek to delay by repeatedly filing unexhausted petitions in federal court, as the Court suggests. First, prisoners not under a sentence of death (the vast majority of habeas petitioners) have no incentive to delay adjudication of their claims. Rather, "[t]he prisoner's principal interest ... is in obtaining speedy federal relief." *Rose v. Lundy,* 455 U.S., at 520. Second, the prisoner who chooses to go into federal court with unexhausted claims runs the risk that the district court will simply deny those claims on the merits, as it is permitted to do, before the prisoner has had the opportunity to develop a record in state court. Third, district courts have the power to prevent vexatious repeated filings by, for instance, ordering that a petition filed after a mixed petition is dismissed must contain only exhausted claims. Thus, the interest in reducing "piecemeal litigation" is not likely to be significantly furthered by the majority's holding.

Finally, the majority's construction of the statute will not necessarily promote comity. Federal courts, understanding that dismissal for nonexhaustion may mean the loss of any opportunity for federal habeas review, may tend to read ambiguous earlier state-court proceedings as having adequately exhausted a federal petition's current claims. For similar reasons, wherever possible, they may reach the merits of a federal petition's claims without sending the petitioner back to state court for exhaustion. To that extent, the majority's interpretation will result in a lesser, not a greater, respect for the state interests to which the majority refers. In addition, by creating pressure to expedite consideration of habeas petitions and to reach the merits of arguably exhausted claims, it will impose a heavier burden on the district courts. (While Justice Stevens' sound suggestions that district courts hold mixed petitions in abeyance and employ equitable tolling would properly ameliorate some of the unfairness of the majority's interpretation, they will also add to the burdens on the district courts in a way that simple tolling for federal habeas petitions would not.)

In two recent cases, we have assumed that Congress did not want to deprive state prisoners of first federal habeas corpus review, and we have interpreted statutory ambiguities accordingly. In Stewart v. Martinez-Villareal, 523 U.S. 637 (1998), we held that a federal habeas petition filed after the initial filing was dismissed as premature should not be deemed a "second or successive" petition barred by § 2244, lest "dismissal . . . for technical procedural reasons . . . bar the prisoner from ever obtaining federal habeas review." And in Slack v. McDaniel, 529 U.S. 473 (2000), we held that a federal habeas petition filed after dismissal of an initial filing for nonexhaustion should not be deemed a "second or successive petition," lest "the complete exhaustion rule" become a " 'trap' " for " 'the unwary *pro se* prisoner.' " Making the same assumption here, I would interpret the ambiguous provision before us to permit tolling for federal habeas petitions.

In both *Martinez-Villareal* and *Slack,* the Court discerned the purpose of an ambiguous statutory provision by assuming that (absent a contrary indication) congressional purpose would mirror that of most reasonable human beings knowledgeable about the area of the law in question. And the Court kept those purposes firmly and foremost in mind as it sought to understand the statute. Today it takes a different approach—an approach that looks primarily, though not exclusively, to linguistic canons to dispel the uncertainties caused by ambiguity. Where statutory language is ambiguous, I believe these priorities are misplaced. Language, dictionaries, and canons, unilluminated by purpose, can lead courts into blind alleys, producing rigid interpretations that can harm those whom the statute affects. If generalized, the approach, bit by bit, will divorce law from the needs, lives, and values of those whom it is meant to serve—a most unfortunate result for a people who live their lives by law's light. The Court was right in *Martinez-Villareal* and *Slack* to see purpose as key to the statute's meaning and to understand Congress as intending the same; it is wrong to reverse its interpretive priorities here.

With respect, I dissent.

Tyler v. Cain

Supreme Court of the United States, 2001.
533 U.S. 656.

■ JUSTICE THOMAS delivered the opinion of the Court.

Under Cage v. Louisiana, 498 U.S. 39 (1990) (per curiam), a jury instruction is unconstitutional if there is a reasonable likelihood that the jury understood the instruction to allow conviction without proof beyond a reasonable doubt.[1] In this case, we must decide whether this rule was "made retroactive to cases on collateral review by the Supreme Court." 28 U.S.C. § 2244(b)(2)(A) (1994 ed., Supp. V). We hold that it was not.

I

During a fight with his estranged girlfriend in March 1975, petitioner Melvin Tyler shot and killed their 20-day-old daughter. A jury found Tyler guilty of second-degree murder, and his conviction was affirmed on appeal. After sentencing, Tyler assiduously sought postconviction relief. By 1986, he had filed five state petitions, all of which were denied. He next filed a federal habeas petition, which was unsuccessful as well. After this Court's decision in *Cage*, Tyler continued his efforts. Because the jury instruction defining reasonable doubt at Tyler's trial was substantively identical to the instruction condemned in *Cage*, Tyler filed a sixth state postconviction petition, this time raising a *Cage* claim. The State District Court denied relief, and the Louisiana Supreme Court affirmed.

In early 1997, Tyler returned to federal court. Seeking to pursue his *Cage* claim, Tyler moved the United States Court of Appeals for the Fifth Circuit for permission to file a second habeas corpus application, as required by the Antiterrorism and Effective Death Penalty Act of 1996 (AEDPA), 110 Stat. 1214.[2] The Court of Appeals recognized that it could not grant the motion unless Tyler made "a prima facie showing," § 2244(b)(3)(C), that his "claim relies on a new rule of constitutional law,

---

1. In *Cage*, this Court observed that a reasonable juror "could have" interpreted the instruction at issue to permit a finding of guilt without the requisite proof. In Estelle v. McGuire, 502 U.S. 62, 72, and n. 4 (1991), however, this Court made clear that the proper inquiry is not whether the instruction "could have" been applied unconstitutionally, but whether there is a reasonable likelihood that the jury did so apply it. See also Victor v. Nebraska, 511 U.S. 1, 6 (1994) ("The constitutional question in the present cases ... is whether there is a reasonable likelihood that the jury understood the instructions to allow conviction based on proof insufficient to meet the [constitutional] standard").

2. AEDPA requires that, "[b]efore a second or successive application ... is filed in the district court, the applicant shall move in the appropriate court of appeals for an order authorizing the district court to consider the application." 28 U.S.C. § 2244(b)(3)(A) (1994 ed., Supp. V).

made retroactive to cases on collateral review by the Supreme Court, that was previously unavailable," § 2244(b)(2)(A). Finding that Tyler had made the requisite prima facie showing, the Court of Appeals granted the motion, thereby allowing Tyler to file a habeas petition in District Court.

The District Court proceeded to the merits of Tyler's claim and held that, although *Cage* should apply retroactively, Tyler was not entitled to collateral relief. Under AEDPA, a state prisoner can prevail only if the state court's decision "was contrary to, or involved an unreasonable application of, clearly established Federal law, as determined by the Supreme Court of the United States." § 2254(d)(1). Concluding that Tyler could not overcome this barrier, the District Court denied his petition.

The Court of Appeals affirmed. It stated, however, that the District Court erred by failing first to determine whether Tyler "satisfied AEDPA's successive habeas standard." AEDPA requires a district court to dismiss a claim in a second or successive application unless, as relevant here, the applicant "shows" that the "claim relies on a new rule of constitutional law, *made retroactive to cases on collateral review by the Supreme Court*, that was previously unavailable,"[3] § 2244(b)(2)(A) (emphasis added); § 2244(b)(4). Relying on Circuit precedent, the Court of Appeals concluded that Tyler did not meet this standard because he "could not show that any Supreme Court decision renders the *Cage* decision retroactively applicable to cases on collateral review."

The Courts of Appeals are divided on the question whether *Cage* was "made retroactive to cases on collateral review by the Supreme Court," as required by 28 U.S.C. § 2244(b)(2)(A). To resolve this conflict, we granted certiorari.

II

AEDPA greatly restricts the power of federal courts to award relief to state prisoners who file second or successive habeas corpus applications. If the prisoner asserts a claim that he has already presented in a previous federal habeas petition, the claim must be dismissed in all cases. § 2244(b)(1). And if the prisoner asserts a claim that was *not* presented in a previous petition, the claim must be dismissed unless it falls within one of two narrow exceptions. One of these exceptions is for claims predicated on newly discovered facts that call into question the accuracy of a guilty verdict. § 2244(b)(2)(B). The other is for certain claims relying on new rules of constitutional law. § 2244(b)(2)(A).

3. This requirement differs from the one that applicants must satisfy in order to obtain permission from a court of appeals to file a second or successive petition. As noted above, a court of appeals may authorize such a filing only if it determines that the applicant makes a "prima facie showing" that the application satisfies the statutory standard. § 2244(b)(3)(C). But to survive dismissal in district court, the applicant must actually "sho[w]" that the claim satisfies the standard.

It is the latter exception that concerns us today. Specifically, § 2244(b)(2)(A) covers claims that "rel[y] on a new rule of constitutional law, made retroactive to cases on collateral review by the Supreme Court, that was previously unavailable." This provision establishes three prerequisites to obtaining relief in a second or successive petition: First, the rule on which the claim relies must be a "new rule" of constitutional law; second, the rule must have been "made retroactive to cases on collateral review by the Supreme Court"; and third, the claim must have been "previously unavailable." In this case, the parties ask us to interpret only the second requirement; respondent does not dispute that *Cage* created a "new rule" that was "previously unavailable." Based on the plain meaning of the text read as a whole, we conclude that "made" means "held" and, thus, the requirement is satisfied only if this Court has held that the new rule is retroactively applicable to cases on collateral review.

A

As commonly defined, "made" has several alternative meanings, none of which is entirely free from ambiguity. See, e.g., Webster's Ninth New Collegiate Dictionary 718–19 (1991) (defining "to make" as "to cause to happen," "to cause to exist, occur or appear," "to lay out and construct," and "to cause to act in a certain way"). Out of context, it may thus be unclear which meaning should apply in § 2244(b)(2)(A), and how the term should be understood. We do not, however, construe the meaning of statutory terms in a vacuum. Rather, we interpret the words "in their context and with a view to their place in the overall statutory scheme." Davis v. Michigan Dept. of Treasury, 489 U.S. 803, 809 (1989). In § 2244(b)(2)(A), the word "made" falls within a clause that reads as follows: "[A] new rule of constitutional law, made retroactive to cases on collateral review *by the Supreme Court*." (Emphasis added.) Quite significantly, under this provision, the Supreme Court is the only entity that can "ma[k]e" a new rule retroactive. The new rule becomes retroactive, not by the decisions of the lower court or by the combined action of the Supreme Court and the lower courts, but simply by the action of the Supreme Court.

The only way the Supreme Court can, by itself, "lay out and construct" a rule's retroactive effect, or "cause" that effect "to exist, occur, or appear," is through a holding. The Supreme Court does not "ma[k]e" a rule retroactive when it merely establishes principles of retroactivity and leaves the application of those principles to lower courts. In such an event, any legal conclusion that is derived from the principles is developed by the lower court (or perhaps by a combination of courts), not by the Supreme Court.[4] We thus conclude that a new rule is not "made retroactive to cases on collateral review" unless the Supreme Court holds it to be retroactive.[5]

---

4. Similarly, the Supreme Court does not make a rule retroactive through dictum, which is not binding. Cf. Seminole Tribe of Fla. v. Florida, 517 U.S. 44, 67 (1996) (contrasting dictum with holdings, which include the final disposition of a case as well as the preceding determinations "*necessary* to that result" (emphasis added)).

5. Tyler argues that defining "made" to mean "held" would create an anomaly:

To be sure, the statute uses the word "made," not "held." But we have already stated, in a decision interpreting another provision of AEDPA, that Congress need not use the word "held" to require as much. In Williams v. Taylor, 529 U.S. 362 (2000), we concluded that the phrase "clearly established Federal law, as *determined* by the Supreme Court of the United States," § 2254(d)(1) (emphasis added), "refers to the holdings, as opposed to the dicta, of this Court's decisions." The provision did not use the word "held," but the effect was the same. Congress, needless to say, is permitted to use synonyms in a statute. And just as "determined" and "held" are synonyms in the context of § 2254(d)(1), "made" and "held" are synonyms in the context of § 2244(b)(2)(A).

We further note that our interpretation is necessary for the proper implementation of the collateral review structure created by AEDPA. Under the statute, before a state prisoner may file a second or successive habeas application, he "shall move in the appropriate court of appeals for an order authorizing the district court to consider the application." § 2244(b)(3)(A). The court of appeals must make a decision on the application within 30 days. § 2244(b)(3)(D). In this limited time, the court of appeals must determine whether the application "makes a prima facie showing that [it] satisfies the [second habeas standard]." § 2244(b)(3)(C). It is unlikely that a court of appeals could make such a determination in the allotted time if it had to do more than simply rely on Supreme Court holdings on retroactivity. The stringent time limit thus suggests that the courts of appeals do not have to engage in the difficult legal analysis that can be required to determine questions of retroactivity in the first instance.

B

Because "made" means "held" for purposes of § 2244(b)(1)(A), it is clear that the *Cage* rule has not been "made retroactive to cases on collateral review by the Supreme Court." *Cage* itself does not hold that it is retroactive. The only holding in *Cage* is that the particular jury instruction violated the Due Process Clause.

Tyler argues, however, that a subsequent case, Sullivan v. Louisiana, 508 U.S. 275 (1993), made the *Cage* rule retroactive. But *Sullivan* held only

When it is obvious that a rule should be retroactive, the courts of appeals will not be in conflict, and this Court will never decide to hear the case and will never make the rule retroactive. Thus, Tyler concludes, we should construe § 2244(b)(2)(A) to allow for retroactive application whenever the "principles" of our decisions, as interpreted by the courts of appeals, indicate that retroactivity is appropriate. This argument is flawed, however.

First, even if we disagreed with the legislative decision to establish stringent procedural requirements for retroactive application of new rules, we do not have license to question the decision on policy grounds. Second, the "anomalous" result that Tyler predicts is speculative at best, because AEDPA does not limit our discretion to grant certiorari to cases in which the courts of appeals have reached divergent results.

that a *Cage* error is structural—i.e., it is not amenable to harmless-error analysis and "will always invalidate the conviction." Conceding that the holding in *Sullivan* does not render *Cage* retroactive to cases on collateral review, Tyler contends that the reasoning in *Sullivan* makes clear that retroactive application is warranted by the principles of Teague v. Lane, 489 U.S. 288 (1989). Under *Teague*, a new rule can be retroactive to cases on collateral review if, and only if, it falls within one of two narrow exceptions to the general rule of nonretroactivity. The exception relevant here is for "watershed rules of criminal procedure implicating the fundamental fairness and accuracy of the criminal proceeding." Graham v. Collins, 506 U.S. 461, 478 (1993). To fall within this exception, a new rule must meet two requirements: Infringement of the rule must "seriously diminish the likelihood of obtaining an accurate conviction," and the rule must " 'alter our understanding of the *bedrock procedural elements*' essential to the fairness of a proceeding." Sawyer v. Smith, 497 U.S. 227, 242 (1990).

According to Tyler, the reasoning of *Sullivan* demonstrates that the *Cage* rule satisfies both prongs of this *Teague* exception. First, Tyler notes, *Sullivan* repeatedly emphasized that a *Cage* error fundamentally undermines the reliability of a trial's outcome. And second, Tyler contends, the central point of *Sullivan* is that a *Cage* error deprives a defendant of a bedrock element of procedural fairness: the right to have the jury make the determination of guilt beyond a reasonable doubt. Tyler's arguments fail to persuade, however. The most he can claim is that, based on the principles outlined in *Teague*, this Court *should* make *Cage* retroactive to cases on collateral review. What is clear, however, is that we have not "made" *Cage* retroactive to cases on collateral review.[6]

Justice Breyer observes that this Court can make a rule retroactive over the course of two cases. We do not disagree that, with the right combination of holdings, the Court could do this. But even so, the Court has not made *Cage* retroactive. Multiple cases can render a new rule retroactive only if the holdings in those cases necessarily dictate retroactivity of the new rule. The only holding in *Sullivan* is that a *Cage* error is structural error. There is no second case that held that all structural-error rules apply retroactively or that all structural-error rules fit within the second *Teague* exception. The standard for determining whether an error is structural is not coextensive with the second *Teague* exception,[7] and a

---

6. We also reject Tyler's attempt to find support in our disposition in Adams v. Evatt, 511 U.S. 1001 (1994). In *Adams*, we vacated an opinion of the Court of Appeals for the Fourth Circuit, which had held that *Cage* was not retroactive, and remanded for further consideration in light of *Sullivan*. Our order, however, was not a "final determination on the merits." Henry v. Rock Hill, 376 U.S. 776, 777 (per curiam). It simply indicated that, in light of "intervening developments," there was a "reasonable probability" that the Court of Appeals would reject a legal premise on which it relied and which may affect the outcome of the litigation. Lawrence v. Chater, 516 U.S. 163, 167 (1996) (per curiam).

7. As explained above, the second *Teague* exception is available only if the new rule

holding that a particular error is structural does not logically dictate the conclusion that the second *Teague* exception has been met.

III

Finally, Tyler suggests that, if *Cage* has not been made retroactive to cases on collateral review, we should make it retroactive today. We disagree. Because Tyler's habeas application was his second, the District Court was required to dismiss it unless Tyler showed that this Court already had made *Cage* retroactive. § 2244(b)(4) ("A district court shall dismiss any claim presented in a second or successive application that the court of appeals has authorized to be filed unless the applicant shows that the claim satisfies the requirements of this section"); § 2244(b)(2)(A) ("A claim presented in a second or successive habeas corpus application under section 2254 that was not presented in a prior application shall be dismissed unless . . . the applicant shows that the claim relies on a new rule of constitutional law, made retroactive to cases on collateral review by the Supreme Court, that was previously unavailable"). We cannot decide today whether *Cage* is retroactive to cases on collateral review, because that decision would not help Tyler in this case. Any statement on *Cage*'s retroactivity would be dictum, so we decline to comment further on the issue.

* * *

The judgment of the Court of Appeals is affirmed.

It is so ordered.

■ JUSTICE O'CONNOR, concurring.

I join the Court's opinion and write separately to explain more fully the circumstances in which a new rule is "made retroactive to cases on collateral review by the Supreme Court." 28 U.S.C. § 2244(b)(2)(A) (1994 ed., Supp. V).

It is only through the holdings of this Court, as opposed to this Court's dicta and as opposed to the decisions of any other court, that a new rule is "made retroactive . . . by the Supreme Court" within the meaning of

" ' "*alter[s]* our understanding of the bedrock procedural elements" ' essential to the fairness of a proceeding." Sawyer v. Smith, 497 U.S. 227, 242 (emphasis added). Classifying an error as structural does not necessarily alter our understanding of these bedrock procedural elements. Nor can it be said that all new rules relating to due process (or even the "fundamental requirements of due process," see [the dissent]) alter such understanding. See, e.g., *Sawyer*, supra, at 244 (holding that the rule in Caldwell v. Mississippi, 472 U.S. 320 (1985), did not fit within the second *Teague* exception even though it "added to an existing guarantee of due process protection against fundamental unfairness"); O'Dell v. Netherland, 521 U.S. 151, 167 (1997) (holding that the rule in Simmons v. South Carolina, 512 U.S. 154 (1994), which has been described as serving "one of the hallmarks of due process," id., at 175 (O'Connor, J, concurring in judgment), did not fit within the second *Teague* exception). On the contrary, the second *Teague* exception is reserved only for truly "watershed" rules. As we have recognized, it is unlikely that any of these watershed rules "ha[s] yet to emerge." *Sawyer*, supra, at 243.

§ 2244(b)(2)(A). The clearest instance, of course, in which we can be said to have "made" a new rule retroactive is where we expressly have held the new rule to be retroactive in a case on collateral review and applied the rule to that case. But, as the Court recognizes, a single case that expressly holds a rule to be retroactive is not a sine qua non for the satisfaction of this statutory provision. This Court instead may "ma[k]e" a new rule retroactive through multiple holdings that logically dictate the retroactivity of the new rule. To apply the syllogistic relationship described by Justice Breyer, if we hold in Case One that a particular type of rule applies retroactively to cases on collateral review and hold in Case Two that a given rule is of that particular type, then it necessarily follows that the given rule applies retroactively to cases on collateral review. In such circumstances, we can be said to have "made" the given rule retroactive to cases on collateral review.

The relationship between the conclusion that a new rule is retroactive and the holdings that "ma[k]e" this rule retroactive, however, must be strictly logical—i.e., the holdings must *dictate* the conclusion and not merely provide principles from which one *may* conclude that the rule applies retroactively. As the Court observes, "[t]he Supreme Court does not 'ma[k]e' a rule retroactive when it merely establishes principles of retroactivity and leaves the application of those principles to lower courts." The Court instead can be said to have "made" a rule retroactive within the meaning of § 2244(b)(2)(A) only where the Court's holdings logically permit no other conclusion than that the rule is retroactive.

It is relatively easy to demonstrate the required logical relationship with respect to the first exception articulated in Teague v. Lane, 489 U.S. 288 (1989). Under this exception, "a new rule should be applied retroactively if it places 'certain kinds of primary, private individual conduct beyond the power of the criminal law-making authority to proscribe.'" When the Court holds as a new rule in a subsequent case that a particular species of primary, private individual conduct is beyond the power of the criminal lawmaking authority to proscribe, it necessarily follows that this Court has "made" that new rule retroactive to cases on collateral review. The Court has done so through its holdings alone, without resort to dicta and without any application of principles by lower courts.

The matter is less straightforward with respect to the second *Teague* exception, which is reserved for "watershed rules of criminal procedure." A case announcing a new rule could conceivably hold that infringement of the rule "seriously diminish[es] the likelihood of obtaining an accurate conviction" and that the rule "'alter[s] our understanding of the *bedrock procedural elements* essential to the fairness of a proceeding'" without holding in so many words that the rule "applies retroactively" and without actually applying that rule retroactively to a case on collateral review. The "precise contours" of this *Teague* exception, of course, "may be difficult to discern," Saffle v. Parks, 494 U.S. 484, 495 (1990), and the judgment involved in our "ma[king]" a new rule retroactive under this exception is likely to be more subjective and self-conscious than is the case with *Teague*'s first exception. But the relevant inquiry is not whether the new rule comes within the *Teague* exception at all, but the more narrow and manageable inquiry of whether this Court's holdings, by strict logical necessity, "ma[k]e" the new rule retroactive within the meaning of § 2244(b)(2)(A). While such logical necessity does not obtain in this particular case, this Court could "ma[k]e" a new rule retroactive under *Teague*'s second exception in this manner.

■ JUSTICE BREYER, with whom JUSTICE STEVENS, JUSTICE SOUTER, and JUSTICE GINSBURG join, dissenting.

In Cage v. Louisiana, 498 U.S. 39 (1990) (per curiam), this Court held that a certain jury instruction violated the Constitution because it inaccurately defined "reasonable doubt," thereby permitting a jury to convict "based on a degree of proof below that required by the Due Process Clause." Here we must decide whether this Court has "made" *Cage* "retroactive to cases on collateral review." 28 U.S.C. § 2244(b)(2)(A) (1994 ed., Supp. V). I believe that it has.

The Court made *Cage* retroactive in two cases taken together. Case One is Teague v. Lane, 489 U.S. 288 (1989). That case, as the majority says, held (among other things) that a new rule is applicable retroactively to cases on collateral review if (1) infringement of the new rule will "seriously diminish the likelihood of obtaining an accurate conviction" and (2) the new rule " 'alter[s] our understanding of the bedrock procedural elements that must be found to vitiate the fairness of a particular conviction' " (emphasis deleted).

Case Two is Sullivan v. Louisiana, 508 U.S. 275 (1993). This Court decided *Sullivan* after several lower courts had held that *Cage*'s rule did not fall within the *Teague* "watershed" exception I have just mentioned. The question in *Sullivan* was whether a violation of the *Cage* rule could ever count as harmless error. The Court answered that question in the negative. In so concluding, the Court reasoned that an instruction that violated *Cage* by misdescribing the concept of reasonable doubt "vitiates *all* the jury's findings," and deprives a criminal defendant of a "basic protection ... without which a criminal trial cannot reliably serve its function." It renders the situation as if "there has been no jury verdict within the meaning of the Sixth Amendment."

To reason as the Court reasoned in *Sullivan is* to hold (in *Teague*'s language) (1) that infringement of the *Cage* rule "seriously diminish[es] the likelihood of obtaining an accurate conviction" and (2) that *Cage* "alter[s] our understanding of the bedrock procedural elements" that are essential to the fairness of a criminal trial (emphasis deleted). That is because an instruction that makes "*all* the jury's findings" untrustworthy must "diminish the likelihood of obtaining an accurate conviction." It is because a deprivation of a "basic protection" needed for a trial to "serve its function" is a deprivation of a "bedrock procedural elemen[t]." And it is because *Cage* significantly "alter[ed]" pre-existing law. That is what every Court of

Appeals to have considered the matter has concluded. [Citations omitted.] And I do not see how the majority can deny that this is so.

Consequently, *Sullivan*, in holding that a *Cage* violation can never be harmless because it leaves the defendant with no jury verdict known to the Sixth Amendment, also holds that *Cage* falls within *Teague*'s "watershed" exception. The matter is one of logic. If Case One holds that all men are mortal and Case Two holds that Socrates is a man, we do not need Case Three to hold that Socrates is mortal. It is also a matter of law. If Case One holds that a party's expectation measures damages for breach of contract and Case Two holds that Circumstances X, Y, and Z create a binding contract, we do not need Case Three to hold that in those same circumstances expectation damages are awarded for breach. Ordinarily, in law, to hold that a set of circumstances falls within a particular legal category is simultaneously to hold that, other things being equal, the normal legal characteristics of members of that category apply to those circumstances.

The majority says that *Sullivan*'s only "holding" is that *Cage* error is structural, and that this "holding" does not dictate the "watershed" nature of the *Cage* rule. But the majority fails to identify a meaningful difference between the definition of a watershed rule under *Teague* and the standard that we have articulated in the handful of instances in which we have held errors structural, namely, that structural errors deprive a defendant of a " 'basic protectio[n]' " without which a " 'trial cannot reliably serve its function as a vehicle for determination of guilt or innocence' " to the point where " 'no criminal punishment may be regarded as fundamentally fair.' " Arizona v. Fulminante, 499 U.S. 279, 310 (1991). In principle *Teague* also adds an element that "structural error" alone need not encompass, namely, the requirement that a violation of the rule must undermine accuracy. But that additional accuracy requirement poses no problem here, for our language in *Sullivan* could not have made clearer that *Cage* error seriously undermines the accuracy and reliability of a guilty verdict.

Of course, as the majority points out, identifying an error as structural need not "alter our understanding of th[e] fundamental procedural elements" that are essential to a fair trial. But this "altering" requirement is not a problem here. No one denies that *Cage*'s rule was a new one.... And our holding that such a misdescription of the burden of proof means that "there has been no jury verdict within the meaning of the Sixth Amendment," *Sullivan*, 508 U.S., at 280, certainly altered the understanding of the significance of such an error.

Insofar as the majority means to suggest that a rule may be sufficiently "new" that it does not apply retroactively but not "new enough" to qualify for the watershed exception, I note only that the cases establishing this exception suggest no such requirement. Rather than focus on the "degree of newness" of a new rule, these decisions emphasize that watershed rules are those that form part of the fundamental requirements of due process.

See *Teague*, 489 U.S., at 311–12; cf. O'Dell v. Netherland, 521 U.S. 151, 167 (1997) (holding that "narrow right of rebuttal" established by Simmons v. South Carolina, 512 U.S. 154 (1994), "has hardly alter[ed] our understanding of the *bedrock procedural elements* essential to the fairness of a proceeding"); Caspari v. Bohlen, 510 U.S. 383, 396 (1994) (holding that application of double jeopardy bar to successive noncapital sentencing would not be unfair and would enhance rather than hinder accuracy); Sawyer v. Smith, 497 U.S. 227, 242–44 (1990) (holding that rule which "provid[ed] an additional measure of protection" to existing prohibition on prosecutorial remarks that render a proceeding "fundamentally unfair" was not "an 'absolute prerequisite to fundamental fairness'" that would fall within the second *Teague* exception).

Nor does the majority explain why the reasoning that was necessary to our holding in *Sullivan* (and is therefore binding upon all courts) lacks enough legal force to "make" the *Cage* rule retroactive. Cf. Seminole Tribe of Fla. v. Florida, 517 U.S. 44, 67 (1996) ("We adhere ... not to mere obiter dicta, but rather to the well-established rationale upon which the Court based the results of its earlier decisions. When an opinion issues for the Court, it is not only the result but also those portions of the opinion necessary to that result by which we are bound"). In any event, technical issues about what constitutes a "holding" are beside the point. The statutory provision before us does not use the words "holding" or "held." It uses the word "made." It refers to instances in which the Supreme Court has "*made*" a rule of law "retroactive to cases on collateral review." 28 U.S.C. § 2244(b)(2)(A) (1994 ed., Supp. V) (emphasis added). And that is just what the Supreme Court, through *Teague* and *Sullivan*, has done with respect to the rule of *Cage*.

I agree with Justice O'Connor–as does a majority of the Court—when (in describing a *different Teague* exception) she says that "[w]hen the Court holds as a new rule in a subsequent case that a particular species of primary, private individual conduct is beyond the power of the criminal lawmaking authority to proscribe, it necessarily follows that this Court has 'made' that new rule retroactive to cases on collateral review." But I do not understand why a decision by this Court which makes it apparent that a rule is retroactive under *Teague*'s second exception will necessarily be "more subjective and self-conscious." Of course, it will sometimes be difficult to decide whether an earlier Supreme Court case has satisfied the watershed rule's requirements. But that is not so here. In *Sullivan*, this Court used language that unmistakably stated that a defective reasonable-doubt instruction undermines the accuracy of a trial and deprives the defendant of a bedrock element that is essential to the fairness of a criminal proceeding. That is sufficient to make *Teague*'s watershed exception applicable.

I would add two further points. First, nothing in the statute's purpose favors, let alone requires, the majority's conclusion. That purpose, as far as

I can surmise, is to bar successive petitions when lower courts, but not the Supreme Court, have held a rule not to be "new" under *Teague* because dictated by their own precedent or when lower courts have themselves adopted new rules and then determined that the *Teague* retroactivity factors apply. Here, consistent with such a purpose, the Supreme Court has previously spoken.

Second, the most likely consequence of the majority's holding is further procedural complexity. After today's opinion, the only way in which this Court can make a rule such as *Cage*'s retroactive is to repeat its *Sullivan* reasoning in a case triggered by a prisoner's filing a first habeas petition (a "second or successive" petition itself being barred by the provision here at issue) or in some other case that presents the issue in a posture that allows such language to have the status of a "holding." Then, after the Court takes the case and says that it meant what it previously said, prisoners could file "second or successive" petitions to take advantage of the now-clearly-made-applicable new rule. We will be required to restate the obvious, case by case, even when we have explicitly said, but not "held," that a new rule is retroactive.

Even this complex route will remain open only if the relevant statute of limitations is interpreted to permit its one-year filing period to run from the time that this Court has "made" a new rule retroactive, not from the time it initially recognized that new right. See 28 U.S.C. § 2244(d)(1)(C) (1994 ed., Supp. V) (limitations period runs from "the date on which the constitutional right asserted was initially recognized by the Supreme Court, if the right has been newly recognized by the Supreme Court and made retroactively applicable to cases on collateral review"). Otherwise, the Court's approach will generate not only complexity, along with its attendant risk of confusion, but also serious additional unfairness.

I do not understand the basis for the Court's approach. I fear its consequences. For these reasons, with respect, I dissent.

Page 808, add to the citations in Note 2:

Arleen Anderson, Responding to the Challenge of Actual Innocence Claims After *Herrera v. Collins*, 71 Temple L. Rev. 489 (1998) (proposing that it is "in the states' best interests to provide their own post-conviction procedures for reviewing claims of actual innocence"); Lissa Griffin, The Correction of Wrongful Convictions: A Comparative Perspective, 16 Am. U. Int'l L. Rev. 1241 (2001) (comparing the English and American approaches to the resolution of post-conviction claims of innocence).

Page 808, add after the Notes on *Herrera v. Collins*:

Bousley v. United States

Supreme Court of the United States, 1998.
523 U.S. 614.

■ CHIEF JUSTICE REHNQUIST delivered the opinion of the Court.

Petitioner pleaded guilty to "using" a firearm in violation of 18 U.S.C. § 924(c)(1) in 1990. Five years later we held in Bailey v. United States, 516

U.S. 137 (1995), that § 924(c)(1)'s "use" prong requires the government to show "active employment of the firearm." Petitioner meanwhile had sought collateral relief under 28 U.S.C. § 2255, claiming that his guilty plea was not knowing and intelligent because he was misinformed by the District Court as to the nature of the charged crime. We hold that, although this claim was procedurally defaulted, petitioner may be entitled to a hearing on the merits of it if he makes the necessary showing to relieve the default.

Following his arrest in March 1990, petitioner was charged with possession of methamphetamine with intent to distribute, in violation of 21 U.S.C. § 841(a)(1). A superseding indictment added the charge that he "knowingly and intentionally used ... firearms during and in relation to a drug trafficking crime," in violation of 18 U.S.C. § 924(c). Petitioner agreed to plead guilty to both charges while reserving the right to challenge the quantity of drugs used in calculating his sentence.

The District Court accepted petitioner's pleas, finding that he was "competent to enter [the] pleas, that [they were] voluntarily entered, and that there [was] a factual basis for them." Following a sentencing hearing, the District Court sentenced petitioner to 78 months' imprisonment on the drug count, a consecutive term of 60 months' imprisonment on the § 924(c) count, and four years of supervised release. Petitioner appealed his sentence, but did not challenge the validity of his plea. The Court of Appeals affirmed.

In June 1994, petitioner sought a writ of habeas corpus under 28 U.S.C. § 2241, challenging the factual basis for his guilty plea on the ground that neither the "evidence" nor the "plea allocution" showed a "connection between the firearms in the bedroom of the house, and the garage, where the drug trafficking occurred." A magistrate judge recommended that the petition be treated as a motion under 28 U.S.C. § 2255 and recommended dismissal, concluding that there was a factual basis for petitioner's guilty plea because the guns in petitioner's bedroom were in close proximity to drugs and were readily accessible. The District Court adopted the magistrate judge's Report and Recommendation and ordered that the petition be dismissed.

Petitioner appealed. While his appeal was pending, we held in *Bailey* that a conviction for use of a firearm under § 924(c)(1) requires the government to show "active employment of the firearm." As we explained, active employment includes uses such as "brandishing, displaying, bartering, striking with, and, most obviously, firing or attempting to fire" the weapon, but does not include mere possession of a firearm. Thus, a "defendant cannot be charged under § 924(c)(1) merely for storing a weapon near drugs or drug proceeds," or for "placement of a firearm to provide a sense of security or to embolden."

Following our decision in *Bailey*, the Court of Appeals appointed counsel to represent petitioner. Counsel argued that *Bailey* should be applied "retroactively," that petitioner's guilty plea was involuntary because he was misinformed about the elements of a § 924(c)(1) offense, that this claim was not waived by his guilty plea, and that his conviction should therefore be vacated. Nevertheless, the Court of Appeals affirmed the District Court's order of dismissal.

We then granted certiorari to resolve a split among the Circuits over the permissibility of post-*Bailey* collateral attacks on § 924(c)(1) convictions obtained pursuant to guilty pleas. Because the government disagreed with the Court of Appeals' analysis, we appointed amicus curiae to brief and argue the case in support of the judgment below.

A plea of guilty is constitutionally valid only to the extent it is "voluntary" and "intelligent." Brady v. United States, 397 U.S. 742, 748 (1970). We have long held that a plea does not qualify as intelligent unless a criminal defendant first receives "real notice of the true nature of the charge against him, the first and most universally recognized requirement of due process." Smith v. O'Grady, 312 U.S. 329, 334 (1941). Amicus contends that petitioner's plea was intelligently made because, prior to pleading guilty, he was provided with a copy of his indictment, which charged him with "using" a firearm. Such circumstances, standing alone, give rise to a presumption that the defendant was informed of the nature of the charge against him. Henderson v. Morgan, 426 U.S. 637, 647 (1976). Petitioner nonetheless maintains that his guilty plea was unintelligent because the District Court subsequently misinformed him as to the elements of a § 924(c)(1) offense. In other words, petitioner contends that the record reveals that neither he, nor his counsel, nor the court correctly understood the essential elements of the crime with which he was charged. Were this contention proven, petitioner's plea would be, contrary to the view expressed by the Court of Appeals, constitutionally invalid. . . .

Amicus urges us to apply the rule of Teague v. Lane, 489 U.S. 288 (1989), to petitioner's claim that his plea was not knowing and intelligent. In *Teague*, we held that "new constitutional rules of criminal procedure will not be applicable to those cases which have become final before the new rules are announced," unless the new rule "places 'certain kinds of primary, private individual conduct beyond the power of the criminal lawmaking authority to proscribe,'" or could be considered a "watershed rul[e] of criminal procedure." But we do not believe that *Teague* governs this case. The only constitutional claim made here is that petitioner's guilty plea was not knowing and intelligent. There is surely nothing new about this principle, enumerated as long ago as *Smith v. O'Grady*, supra. And because *Teague* by its terms applies only to procedural rules, we think it is inapplicable to the situation in which this Court decides the meaning of a criminal statute enacted by Congress.

This distinction between substance and procedure is an important one in the habeas context. The *Teague* doctrine is founded on the notion that one of the "principal functions of habeas corpus [is] 'to assure that no man has been incarcerated under a procedure which creates an impermissibly large risk that the innocent will be convicted.'" *Teague*, 489 U.S., at 312. Consequently, unless a new rule of criminal procedure is of such a nature that "without [it] the likelihood of an accurate conviction is seriously diminished," 489 U.S., at 313, there is no reason to apply the rule retroactively on habeas review. By contrast, decisions of this Court holding that a substantive federal criminal statute does not reach certain conduct, like decisions placing conduct "'beyond the power of the criminal lawmaking authority to proscribe,'" id., at 311, necessarily carry a significant risk that a defendant stands convicted of "an act that the law does not make criminal." Davis v. United States, 417 U.S. 333, 346 (1974). For under our federal system it is only Congress, and not the courts, which can make conduct criminal. United States v. Hudson & Goodwin, 11 U.S. (7 Cranch) 32 (1812). Accordingly, it would be inconsistent with the doctrinal underpinnings of habeas review to preclude petitioner from relying on our decision in *Bailey* in support of his claim that his guilty plea was constitutionally invalid.

Though petitioner's claim is not *Teague*-barred, there are nonetheless significant procedural hurdles to its consideration on the merits. We have strictly limited the circumstances under which a guilty plea may be attacked on collateral review. "It is well settled that a voluntary and intelligent plea of guilty made by an accused person, who has been advised by competent counsel, may not be collaterally attacked." Mabry v. Johnson, 467 U.S. 504, 508 (1984). And even the voluntariness and intelligence of a guilty plea can be attacked on collateral review only if first challenged on direct review. Habeas review is an extraordinary remedy and "'will not be allowed to do service for an appeal.'" Reed v. Farley, 512 U.S. 339, 354 (1994). Indeed, "the concern with finality served by the limitation on collateral attack has special force with respect to convictions based on guilty pleas." United States v. Timmreck, 441 U.S. 780, 784 (1979). In this case, petitioner contested his sentence on appeal, but did not challenge the validity of his plea. In failing to do so, petitioner procedurally defaulted the claim he now presses on us.

In an effort to avoid this conclusion, petitioner contends that his claim falls within an exception to the procedural default rule for claims that could not be presented without further factual development. In Waley v. Johnston, 316 U.S. 101 (1942) (per curiam), we held that there was such an exception for a claim that a plea of guilty had been coerced by threats made by a government agent, when the facts were "dehors the record and their effect on the judgment was not open to consideration and review on appeal." Petitioner's claim, however, differs significantly from that advanced in *Waley*. He is not arguing that his guilty plea was involuntary because it was coerced, but rather that it was not intelligent because the information provided him by the District Court at his plea colloquy was erroneous. This type of claim can be fully and completely addressed on direct review based on the record created at the plea colloquy.

Where a defendant has procedurally defaulted a claim by failing to raise it on direct review, the claim may be raised in habeas only if the defendant can first demonstrate either "cause" and actual "prejudice," Murray v. Carrier, 477 U.S. 478, 485 (1986); Wainwright v. Sykes, 433 U.S. 72, 87 (1977), or that he is "actually innocent," *Murray*, 477 U.S., at 496; Smith v. Murray, 477 U.S. 527, 537 (1986).

Petitioner offers two explanations for his default in an attempt to demonstrate cause. First, he argues that "the legal basis for his claim was not reasonably available to counsel" at the time his plea was entered. This argument is without merit. While we have held that a claim that "is so novel that its legal basis is not reasonably available to counsel" may constitute cause for a procedural default, Reed v. Ross, 468 U.S. 1, 16 (1984), petitioner's claim does not qualify as such. The argument that it was error for the District Court to misinform petitioner as to the statutory elements of § 924(c)(1) was most surely not a novel one. Indeed, at the time of petitioner's plea, the Federal Reporters were replete with cases involving challenges to the notion that "use" is synonymous with mere "possession."[2] Petitioner also contends that his default should be excused because, "before *Bailey*, any attempt to attack [his] guilty plea would have been futile." This argument too is unavailing. As we clearly stated in Engle v. Isaac, 456 U.S. 107, 130 (1982), "futility cannot constitute cause if it means simply that a claim was 'unacceptable to that particular court at that particular time.'" Therefore, petitioner is unable to establish cause for his default.

Petitioner's claim may still be reviewed in this collateral proceeding if he can establish that the constitutional error in his plea colloquy "has probably resulted in the conviction of one who is actually innocent." *Murray v. Carrier*, 477 U.S., at 496. To establish actual innocence, petitioner must demonstrate that, "'in light of all the evidence,'" "it is more likely than not that no reasonable juror would have convicted him." Schlup v. Delo, 513 U.S. 298, 327–28 (1995). The District Court failed to address petitioner's actual innocence, perhaps because petitioner failed to raise it initially in his § 2255 motion. However, the government does not contend that petitioner waived this claim by failing to raise it below. Accordingly, we believe it appropriate to remand this case to permit petitioner to attempt to make a showing of actual innocence.

---

2. Even were we to conclude that petitioner's counsel was unaware at the time that petitioner's plea colloquy was constitutionally deficient, "[w]here the basis of a ... claim is available, and other defense counsel have perceived and litigated that claim, the demands of comity and finality counsel against labeling alleged unawareness of the objection as cause for a procedural default." Engle v. Isaac, 456 U.S. 107, 134 (1982).

It is important to note in this regard that "actual innocence" means factual innocence, not mere legal insufficiency. See Sawyer v. Whitley, 505 U.S. 333, 339 (1992). In other words, the government is not limited to the existing record to rebut any showing that petitioner might make. Rather, on remand, the government should be permitted to present any admissible evidence of petitioner's guilt even if that evidence was not presented during petitioner's plea colloquy and would not normally have been offered before our decision in *Bailey*.[3] In cases where the government has forgone more serious charges in the course of plea bargaining, petitioner's showing of actual innocence must also extend to those charges.

In this case, the government maintains that petitioner must demonstrate that he is actually innocent of both "using" and "carrying" a firearm in violation of § 924(c)(1). But petitioner's indictment charged him only with "using" firearms in violation of § 924(c)(1). And there is no record evidence that the government elected not to charge petitioner with "carrying" a firearm in exchange for his plea of guilty. Accordingly, petitioner need demonstrate no more than that he did not "use" a firearm as that term is defined in *Bailey*.

If, on remand, petitioner can make that showing, he will then be entitled to have his defaulted claim of an unintelligent plea considered on its merits. The judgment of the Court of Appeals is therefore reversed, and the case is remanded for further proceedings consistent with this opinion.

It is so ordered.

■ JUSTICE STEVENS, concurring in part and dissenting in part.

While I agree with the Court's central holding and with its conclusion that none of its judge-made rules foreclose petitioner's collateral attack on his conviction under 18 U.S.C. § 924(c), I believe there is a flaw in its analysis that will affect the proceedings on remand. Given the fact that the record now establishes that the plea of guilty to the § 924(c) charge was constitutionally invalid, petitioner remains presumptively innocent of that offense. Accordingly, unless he again pleads guilty, the burden is on the government to prove his unlawful use of a firearm.

I

This case does not raise any question concerning the possible retroactive application of a new rule of law, cf. Teague v. Lane, 489 U.S. 288 (1989), because our decision in Bailey v. United States, 516 U.S. 137 (1995), did not change the law. It merely explained what § 924(c) had meant ever since the statute was enacted. The fact that a number of Courts of Appeals

---

3. Justice Scalia contends that this factual innocence inquiry will be unduly complicated by the absence of a trial transcript in the guilty plea context. We think his concerns are overstated. In the federal system, where this case arose, guilty pleas must be accompanied by proffers, recorded verbatim on the record, demonstrating a factual basis for the plea. See Fed. Rules Crim. Proc. 11(f), (g).

had construed the statute differently is of no greater legal significance than the fact that 42 U.S.C. § 1981 had been consistently misconstrued prior to our decision in Patterson v. McLean Credit Union, 491 U.S. 164 (1989). Our comment on the significance of the pre-*Patterson* jurisprudence applies equally to the pre-*Bailey* cases construing § 924(c):

> "*Patterson* did not overrule any prior decision of this Court; rather, it held and therefore established that the prior decisions of the Courts of Appeals which read § 1981 to cover discriminatory contract termination were incorrect. They were not wrong according to some abstract standard of interpretive validity, but by the rules that necessarily govern our hierarchical federal court system. It is this Court's responsibility to say what a statute means, and once the Court has spoken, it is the duty of other courts to respect that understanding of the governing rule of law. A judicial construction of a statute is an authoritative statement of what the statute meant before as well as after the decision of the case giving rise to that construction." Rivers v. Roadway Express, Inc., 511 U.S. 298, 312–13 (1994).

Thus in 1990 when petitioner was advised by the trial judge, by his own lawyer, and by the prosecutor that mere possession of a firearm would support a conviction under § 924(c), he received critically incorrect legal advice. The fact that all of his advisers acted in good-faith reliance on existing precedent does not mitigate the impact of that erroneous advice. Its consequences for petitioner were just as severe, and just as unfair, as if the court and counsel had knowingly conspired to deceive him in order to induce him to plead guilty to a crime that he did not commit. Our cases make it perfectly clear that a guilty plea based on such misinformation is constitutionally invalid. Smith v. O'Grady, 312 U.S. 329, 334 (1941); Henderson v. Morgan, 426 U.S. 637, 644–45 (1976). Petitioner's conviction and punishment on the § 924(c) charge "are for an act that the law does not make criminal. There can be no room for doubt that such a circumstance 'inherently results in a complete miscarriage of justice' and 'present[s] exceptional circumstances' that justify collateral relief under [28 U.S.C.] § 2255." Davis v. United States, 417 U.S. 333, 346–47 (1974).

II

The government charges petitioner with "procedural default" because he did not challenge his guilty plea on direct appeal. The Court accepts this argument and therefore places the burden on petitioner to demonstrate either "cause and prejudice" or "actual innocence." Yet the Court cites no authority for its conclusion that "even the voluntariness and intelligence of a guilty plea can be attacked on collateral review only if first challenged on direct review."[1] Moreover, the primary case upon which the government

---

1. The Court does cite Reed v. Farley, 512 U.S. 339, 354 (1994), for the general proposition that habeas review "'will not be allowed to do service for an appeal.'" *Reed* is

relies, *United States v. Timmreck*, 441 U.S. 780 (1979), actually supports the contrary proposition: that a constitutionally invalid guilty plea may be set aside on collateral attack whether or not it was challenged on appeal.

Several years before we decided *Timmreck*, the Court had held that it is reversible error for a trial judge to accept a guilty plea without following the procedures dictated by Rule 11 of the Federal Rules of Criminal Procedure. *McCarthy v. United States*, 394 U.S. 459 (1969). The question in *Timmreck* was whether such an error was sufficiently serious to support a collateral attack under 28 U.S.C. § 2255. Because the error was neither jurisdictional nor constitutional, we held that collateral relief was unavailable. If we had thought that the failure to challenge the constitutionality of a guilty plea on direct appeal amounted to procedural default, there would have been no need in *Timmreck* to rely on the critical difference between reversible error and the more fundamental kind of error that can be corrected on collateral review. The opinion makes it clear that an ordinary Rule 11 violation must be challenged on appeal; the only criterion for collateral review that it mentions is that the error must be jurisdictional or constitutional. . . .

The Court has never held that the constitutionality of a guilty plea cannot be attacked collaterally unless it is first challenged on direct review. Moreover, as the facts of this case demonstrate, such a holding would be unwise and would defeat the very purpose of collateral review. A layman who justifiably relied on incorrect advice from the court and counsel in deciding to plead guilty to a crime that he did not commit will ordinarily continue to assume that such advice was accurate during the time for taking an appeal. The injustice of his conviction is not mitigated by the passage of time. His plea should be treated as a nullity and the conviction based on such a plea should be voided.

Because the record in this case already unambiguously demonstrates that petitioner's plea to the § 924(c) charge is invalid as a matter of constitutional law, I would remand with directions to vacate his § 924(c) conviction and allow him to plead anew.

■ JUSTICE SCALIA, with whom JUSTICE THOMAS joins, dissenting.

I agree with the Court that petitioner has not demonstrated "cause" for failing to challenge the validity of his guilty plea on direct review. I disagree, however, that a defendant who has pleaded guilty can be given the opportunity to avoid the consequences of his inexcusable procedural default by having the courts inquire into whether " 'it is more likely than

---

inapposite, however, as it involved neither a constitutional violation nor a guilty plea. In *Reed*, the Court rejected a state prisoner's statutory claim brought under 28 U.S.C. § 2254 on the grounds that the prisoner had neither made a timely objection nor suffered prejudice. . . .

not that no reasonable juror would have convicted him' " of the offense to which he pleaded guilty.

No criminal-law system can function without rules of procedure conjoined with a rule of finality. Evidence not introduced, or objections not made, at the appropriate time cannot be brought forward to reopen the conviction after judgment has been rendered. In the United States, we have developed generous exceptions to the rule of finality, one of which permits reopening, via habeas corpus, when the petitioner shows "cause" excusing the procedural default, and "actual prejudice" resulting from the alleged error. We have gone even beyond that generous exception in a certain class of cases: cases that have actually gone to trial. There we have held that, "even in the absence of a showing of cause for the procedural default," habeas corpus will be granted "where a constitutional violation has probably resulted in the conviction of one who is actually innocent." Schlup v. Delo, 513 U.S. 298, 321 (1995). In every one of our cases that has considered the possibility of applying this so-called actual-innocence exception, a defendant had asked a habeas court to adjudicate a successive or procedurally defaulted constitutional claim after his conviction by a jury. [Citations omitted.]

There are good reasons for this limitation: First and foremost, it is feasible to make an accurate assessment of "actual innocence" when a trial has been had. In *Schlup*, for example, we said that to sustain an "actual innocence" claim the petitioner must "show that it is more likely than not that no reasonable juror would have convicted him *in the light of the new evidence.*" 513 U.S., at 327 (emphasis added). That "new evidence" was to be evaluated, of course, along with the "old evidence," consisting of the transcript of the trial. The habeas court was to "make its determination concerning the petitioner's innocence in light of all the evidence, including that alleged to have been illegally admitted (but with due regard to any unreliability of it) and evidence tenably claimed to have been wrongly excluded or to have become available only after the trial." *Schlup*, supra, at 328. As the Court's opinion today makes clear, the government is permitted to supplement the trial record with any additional evidence of guilt, but the court begins with (and ordinarily ends with) a complete trial transcript to rely upon. But how is the court to determine "actual innocence" upon our remand in the present case, where conviction was based upon an admission of guilt? Presumably the defendant will introduce evidence (perhaps nothing more than his own testimony) showing that he did not "use" a firearm in committing the crime to which he pleaded guilty, and the government, eight years after the fact, will have to find and produce witnesses saying that he did. This seems to me not to remedy a miscarriage of justice, but to produce one.*

---

* The Court believes these concerns are overstated because, in the federal system, the court must be satisfied that there is a factual basis for the plea. This displays a sad lack of solicitude for state courts, which handle the overwhelming majority of criminal cases. But

Secondly, the Court has given as one of its justifications for the supergenerous miscarriage-of-justice exception to inexcusable default, "the fact that habeas corpus petitions that advance a substantial claim of actual innocence are extremely rare." *Schlup,* supra, at 321. That may be true enough of petitions challenging jury convictions; it assuredly will not be true of petitions challenging the "voluntariness" of guilty pleas. I put "voluntariness" in quotation marks, because we are not dealing here with only coerced confessions, which may indeed be rare enough. The present case is here because, in Henderson v. Morgan, 426 U.S. 637, 644–46 (1976), this Court held that where neither the indictment, defense counsel, nor the trial court explained to the defendant that intent to kill was an element of second-degree murder, his plea to that offense was "involuntary." A plea, the Court explained, can "not be voluntary in the sense that it constitute[s] an intelligent admission that he committed the offense unless the defendant receive[s] 'real notice of the true nature of the charge against him, the first and most universally recognized requirement of due process.'" Of course the word "voluntary" had never been used (by precise speakers, at least) in that sense—in the sense of "intelligent"—and what the *Henderson* line of cases did was, by sleight-of-tongue, to obliterate the distinction between involuntary confessions and misinformed or even uninformed confessions. Once all those categories have been lumped together, the cases within them are not at all rare, but indeed exceedingly numerous.

It is well established that "when this Court construes a statute, it is explaining its understanding of what the statute has meant continuously since the date when it became law." Rivers v. Roadway Express, Inc., 511 U.S. 298, 313, n. 12 (1994). Thus, every time this Court resolves a Circuit split regarding the elements of a crime defined in a federal statute, most if not all defendants who pleaded guilty in those Circuits on the losing end of

even in the federal system, the "factual basis" requirement will typically be of no use. Consider the factual basis for the guilty plea in the present case, as set forth in the plea agreement:

> "The parties ... agree that, on or about March 19, 1990, ... the defendant knowingly used firearms during and in relation to a drug-trafficking offense.... The following firearms were found in the defendant's bedroom near the 6.9 grams of methamphetamine: a loaded Walther PBK .380 caliber handgun, serial number A016494; and a loaded .22 caliber Advantage Arms 4–shot revolver. The defendant admits ownership and possession of these two guns. This conduct constituted a violation of Title 18, United States Code, Section 924(c). Three other firearms were found in the two briefcases containing the bulk of the methamphetamine: a loaded .22 caliber North American Arms handgun, serial number C7854; a loaded .45 caliber Colt Model 1911 semiautomatic handgun, serial number 244682; an unloaded Ruger .357 caliber revolver, serial number 151–36099. The defendant denies knowledge of these guns."

Of course "knowingly used" in this statement presumably means "knowingly used" in the erroneous sense that prompts this litigation. And that will almost always be the situation where the "involuntariness" of the plea is a consequence of subsequently clarified uncertainty in the law: the factual basis will not include a fact which, by hypothesis, the court and the parties think irrelevant.

the split will have confessed "involuntarily," having been advised by the Court, or by their counsel, that the law was what (as it turns out) it was not—or even (since this would suffice for application of *Henderson*) merely not having been advised that the law was what (as it turns out) it was. Indeed the latter basis for "involuntariness" (mere lack of "real notice of the charge against him," *Henderson*, supra, at 665) might be available even to those defendants pleading guilty in the Circuits on the winning side of the split. Thus, our decision in Bailey v. United States, 516 U.S. 137 (1995), has generated a flood of 28 U.S.C. § 2255 habeas petitions, each asserting actual innocence of "using" a firearm in violation of 18 U.S.C. § 924(c). This term, we will resolve a Circuit split over the meaning of another element ("carry" a firearm) in the same statute. And we will also resolve Circuit splits over the requisite elements of five other federal criminal statutes.

To the undeniable fact that the claim of "actual innocence" is much more likely to be available in guilty-plea cases than in jury-trial cases, there must be added the further undeniable fact that guilty-plea cases are very much more numerous than jury-trial cases. Last year, 51,647 of the 55,648 defendants convicted and sentenced in federal court (or nearly 93 per cent) pleaded guilty. Administrative Office of the United States Courts, L. Mecham, Judicial Business of the United States Courts: 1997 Report of the Director 214.

When all these factors are taken into account, it could not be clearer that the premise for our adoption in *Schlup* of the super-generous "miscarriage of justice" exception to normal finality rules—viz., that the cases in which defendants seek to invoke the exception would be "extremely rare"—is simply not true when the exception is extended to guilty pleas. To the contrary, the cases will be extremely frequent, placing upon the criminal-justice system a burden it will be unable to bear—especially in light of the fact, discussed earlier, that on remand the habeas trial court will not have any trial record on the basis of which to make the "actual innocence" determination.

Not only does the disposition agreed upon today overload the criminal-justice system; it makes relief available where equity demands that relief be denied. When a defendant pleads guilty, he waives his right to have a jury make the requisite findings of guilt—typically in exchange for a lighter sentence or reduced charges. Thus, defendants plead guilty to charges that have not been proven—that perhaps could not be proven—in order to avoid conviction on charges of which they are "actually guilty," which carry a harsher penalty. Under today's holding, a defendant who is the "wheelman" in a bank robbery in which a person is shot and killed, and who pleads guilty in state court to the offense of voluntary manslaughter in order to avoid trial on felony-murder charges, is entitled to federal habeas review of his contention that his guilty plea was "involuntary" because he was not advised that intent-to-kill was an element of the manslaughter offense, and that he was "actually innocent" of manslaughter because he had no intent to kill. In such a case, it is excusing the petitioner from his procedural default, not holding him to it, that would be the miscarriage of justice.

The Court evidently seeks to avoid this absurd consequence by prescribing that the defendant's "showing of actual innocence must also extend" to any charge the government has "forgone." This is not even a fully satisfactory solution in theory, since it assumes that the "forgone" charge is identifiable. If, as is often the case, the bargaining occurred before the charge was filed ("charge-bargaining" instead of "plea-bargaining"), it will almost surely not be identifiable. And of course in practical terms, the solution is no solution at all. To avoid the patent inequity, the government will be called upon to refute, without any factual record to rely upon, not only the defendant's testimony of his innocence on the charge of conviction, but his testimony of innocence on the "forgone" charge as well—and as to the second, even the finding of "factual basis" required in federal courts will not exist. But even if rebuttal evidence existed, it is a bizarre waste of judicial resources to require mini-trials on charges made in dusty indictments (or indeed, if they could be identified, on charges never made), just to determine whether the defendant can litigate a procedurally defaulted challenge to a guilty plea on a different offense. Rube Goldberg would envy the scheme the Court has created.

* * *

It would be marvelously inspiring to be able to boast that we have a criminal-justice system in which a claim of "actual innocence" will always be heard, no matter how late it is brought forward, and no matter how much the failure to bring it forward at the proper time is the defendant's own fault. But of course we do not have such a system, and no society unwilling to devote unlimited resources to repetitive criminal litigation ever could. The "actual innocence" exception this Court has invoked to overcome inexcusable procedural default in cases decided by a jury "seeks to balance the societal interests in finality, comity, and conservation of scarce judicial resources with the individual interest in justice that arises in the extraordinary case." *Schlup*, 513 U.S., at 324. Since the balance struck there simply does not obtain in the guilty-plea context, today's decision is not a logical extension of *Schlup*, and it is a grave mistake. For these reasons, I respectfully dissent.

CHAPTER VIII

STATE SOVEREIGN IMMUNITY AND THE 11TH AMENDMENT

Page 825, add at the end of Note 5:

See also David J. Bederman, Admiralty and the Eleventh Amendment, 72 Notre Dame L. Rev. 935 (1997) (arguing that both text and history of the 11th amendment confirm its inapplicability in admiralty); Erwin Chemerinsky, Against Sovereign Immunity, 53 Stan. L. Rev. 1201 (2001) (criticizing recent expansions of state sovereign immunity); Alfred Hill, In Defense of Our Law of Sovereign Immunity, 42 B.C.L. Rev. 485 (2001) (a detailed rebuttal of academic criticism of the constitutionalization of sovereign immunity); Mark Strasser, *Hans, Ayers*, and Eleventh Amendment Jurisprudence: On Justification, Rationalization, and Sovereign Immunity, 10 Geo. Mason L. Rev. 251 (2001) (examining *Hans* in historical context and concluding that although it made sense at that time, it does not justify modern Eleventh Amendment jurisprudence).

An important recent article offers a new synthesis of 11th amendment history. See James E. Pfander, History and State Suability: An "Explanatory" Account of the Eleventh Amendment, 83 Corn. L. Rev. 1269 (1998). Pfander focuses on the substantial debts that states had incurred in fighting the Revolutionary War and finds that the framers of the Constitution adopted a "temporal compromise": "they imposed federal limits on future state fiscal policy, but left the states free to manage existing obligations as they saw fit...." What was so deeply shocking about *Chisholm*, says Pfander, was not so much that it allowed suits against states as that it allowed federal courts "to entertain suits to enforce obligations that the states had incurred under the Articles of Confederation." Pfander concludes that this historical understanding "strong[ly] supports" revisionist attacks on *Hans*.

Also of importance on these issues is Ann Woolhandler, The Common Law Origins of Constitutionally Compelled Remedies, 107 Yale L.J. 77 (1997). Following a comprehensive examination of the history, she concludes that *Ex parte Young* "did not fundamentally alter the role of the federal courts so much as [it] gradually changed the [label] under which litigants continued to do what they had done in the past." She finds a "historically settled consensus that the federal courts should administer a federalized set of rights and remedies for federal constitutional rights."

For a genuinely original idea about the Eleventh Amendment, see Caleb Nelson, Sovereign Immunity as a Doctrine of Personal Jurisdiction, 115 Harv. L. Rev. 1561 (2002). Nelson argues that in the 1780s, the concept of sovereign immunity traveled in the orbit of *personal* jurisdiction rather than *subject-matter* jurisdiction. Unconsenting states were thought to enjoy exemptions from compulsory process. When *Chisholm v. Georgia* held that Article III overrode those exemptions, the Eleventh Amendment responded by giving states a different kind of protection: it carved cases like *Chisholm* out of the federal courts' subject-matter jurisdiction. According to Nelson, this "subject matter jurisdiction" immunity does not extend beyond the Amendment's terms. But if *Chisholm* was wrong about the original meaning of Article III (as the modern Supreme Court has concluded), then states should continue to enjoy the original "personal jurisdiction" immunity, even in situations that the Eleventh Amendment does not cover. Understanding this "two-track system" of jurisdictional immunities, Nelson argues, resolves a number of apparent contradictions in current doctrine and points the way toward a clearer justification for according states some kind of jurisdictional protection even when the Eleventh Amendment does not in terms apply.

Finally, for an article that examines the role of officer suits under 42 U.S.C. § 1983 as an alternative to suits against states, see John C. Jeffries, Jr., In Praise of the Eleventh Amendment and Section 1983, 84 Va. L. Rev. 49 (1998).

Page 847, add to footnote b:

However, a state that has consented to suit in its own courts and removes such a suit to federal court has thereby waived its 11th amendment immunity. Lapides v. Board of Regents of the University System of Georgia, ___ U.S. ___ (2002).

Page 879, delete the existing NOTES ON *SEMINOLE TRIBE* and replace with the following:

NOTE ON *SEMINOLE TRIBE*

Scholarly reaction to *Seminole Tribe* has been swift and varied. Many scholars linked *Seminole Tribe* to United States v. Lopez, 514 U.S. 549 (1995), and the revival of limits on congressional power under the commerce clause. See, e.g., Herbert Hovenkamp, Judicial Restraint and Constitutional Federalism: The Supreme Court's *Lopez* and *Seminole Tribe* Decisions, 96 Colum. L. Rev. 2213 (1996); Henry Paul Monaghan, The Sovereign Immunity "Exception," 110 Harv. L. Rev. 102 (1995); John C. Yoo, The Judicial Safeguards of Federalism, 70 Southern Cal. L. Rev. 1311 (1997). Monaghan viewed *Seminole Tribe* as perhaps reflecting "a visceral feeling among the majority on the Court that the role of the states in our federal structure has been so diminished as to become unintelligible."

Additional commentary appears in William A. Fletcher, The Eleventh Amendment: Unfinished Business, 75 Notre Dame L. Rev. 843 (2000) (arguing for *Union Gas* and against *Seminole Tribe* on the ground that state sovereign immunity from private suit is less justified when a state engages in commercial activity than when it exercises sovereign functions); Daniel J. Meltzer, The *Seminole* Decision and State Sovereign Immunity, 1996 Sup. Ct. Rev. 1 (exploring *Seminole Tribe*'s impact on 11th amendment doctrine); Carlos Manuel Vázquez, What Is Eleventh Amendment Immunity?, 106 Yale L.J. 1683 (1997) (analyzing *Seminole Tribe* as it bears on competing conceptions of the 11th amendment); Kit Kinports, Implied Waiver After *Seminole Tribe*, 82 Minn. L. Rev. 793 (1998) (pointing out that while Congress exercising article I power may not unilaterally abrogate 11th amendment immunity, it can use the conditional grant of federal funds to solicit state waivers); Wayne L. Baker, *Seminole* Speaks to Sovereign Immunity and *Ex Parte Young*, 71 St. John's L. Rev. 739 (1997) (concluding that Congress could easily evade *Seminole Tribe* by creating a private right of action against state officials); Katherine F. Nelson, Resolving Native American Land Claims and the Eleventh Amendment: Changing the Balance of Power, 39 Villanova L. Rev. 525 (1994) (a pre-*Seminole Tribe* consideration of 11th amendment problems in the particular context of Native American claims against states).

Page 880, add after *Seminole Tribe*:

SECTION 2A: THE 1999 DECISIONS

Alden v. Maine

Supreme Court of the United States, 1999.
527 U.S. 706.

■ JUSTICE KENNEDY delivered the opinion of the Court.

In 1992, petitioners, a group of probation officers, filed suit against their employer, the state of Maine, in the United States District Court for the District of Maine. The officers alleged the state had violated the overtime provisions of the Fair Labor Standards Act of 1938 (FLSA), 29 U.S.C. § 201 et seq., and sought compensation and liquidated damages. While the suit was pending, this Court decided Seminole Tribe v. Florida, 517 U.S. 44 (1996), which made it clear that Congress lacks power under article I to abrogate the states' sovereign immunity from suits commenced or prosecuted in the federal courts. Upon consideration of *Seminole Tribe*, the District Court dismissed petitioners' action, and the Court of Appeals affirmed. Petitioners then filed the same action in state court. The state trial court dismissed the suit on the basis of sovereign immunity, and the Maine Supreme Judicial Court affirmed. . . .

We hold that the powers delegated to Congress under article I of the United States Constitution do not include the power to subject nonconsenting states to private suits for damages in state courts. . . .

I

The 11th amendment makes explicit reference to the states' immunity from suits "commenced or prosecuted against one of the United States by Citizens of another State, or by Citizens or Subjects of any Foreign State." We have, as a result, sometimes referred to the states' immunity from suit as "11th amendment immunity." The phrase is convenient shorthand but something of a misnomer, for the sovereign immunity of the states neither derives from nor is limited by the terms of the 11th amendment. Rather, as the Constitution's structure, and its history, and the authoritative interpretations by this Court make clear, the states' immunity from suit is a fundamental aspect of the sovereignty which the states enjoyed before the ratification of the Constitution, and which they retain today (either literally or by virtue of their admission into the Union upon an equal footing with the other states) except as altered by the plan of the Convention or certain constitutional amendments.

A

. . . The federal system established by our Constitution preserves the sovereign status of the states in two ways. First, it reserves to them a substantial portion of the nation's primary sovereignty, together with the dignity and essential attributes inhering in that status. . . . Second, even as to matters within the competence of the national government, the constitutional design secures the founding generation's rejection of "the concept of a central government that would act upon and through the states" in favor of "a system in which the state and federal governments would exercise concurrent authority over the people—who were, in Hamilton's words, 'the only proper objects of government.' " Printz v. United States, 521 U.S. 898, 919 (1997) (quoting The Federalist No. 15, at 109). . . .

The states thus retain "a residuary and inviolable sovereignty." The Federalist No. 39, at 245. They are not relegated to the role of mere provinces or political corporations, but retain the dignity, though not the full authority, of sovereignty.

B

The generation that designed and adopted our federal system considered immunity from private suits central to sovereign dignity. When the Constitution was ratified, it was well established in English law that the Crown could not be sued without consent in its own courts. . . . Although the American people had rejected other aspects of English political theory, the doctrine that a sovereign could not be sued without its consent was universal in the states when the Constitution was drafted and ratified. See

Chisholm v. Georgia, 2 U.S. (2 Dall.) 419, 434–35 (1793) (Iredell, J., dissenting). . . .

The leading advocates of the Constitution assured the people in no uncertain terms that the Constitution would not strip the states of sovereign immunity. One assurance was contained in The Federalist No. 81, written by Alexander Hamilton:

> "It is inherent in the nature of sovereignty not to be amenable to the suit of an individual *without its consent*. This is the general sense, and the general practice of mankind; and the exemption, as one of the attributes of sovereignty, is now enjoyed by the government of every state in the Union. Unless therefore, there is a surrender of this immunity in the plan of the convention, it will remain with the states, and the danger intimated must be merely ideal. . . . There is no color to pretend that the state governments would, by the adoption of that plan, be divested of the privilege of paying their own debts in their own way, free from every constraint but that which flows from the obligations of good faith. The contracts between a nation and individuals are only binding on the conscience of the sovereign, and have no pretensions to a compulsive force. They confer no right of action independent of the sovereign will. To what purpose would it be to authorize suits against states for the debts they owe? How could recoveries be enforced? It is evident that it could not be done without waging war against the contracting state; and to ascribe to the federal courts, by mere implication, and in destruction of the preexisting right of the state governments, a power which would involve such a consequence, would be altogether forced and unwarrantable." Id. at 487–88 (emphasis in original).

At the Virginia ratifying convention, James Madison echoed this theme:

> "Its jurisdiction in controversies between a state and citizens of another state is much objected to, and perhaps without reason. It is not in the power of individuals to call any state into court. . . .
>
> ". . . It appears to me that this [clause] can have no operation but this—to give a citizen a right to be heard in the federal courts, and if a state should condescend to be a party, this court may take cognizance of it." 3 J. Elliot, Debates on the Federal Constitution 533 (2d ed. 1854) (hereinafter Elliot's Debates).

When Madison's explanation was questioned, John Marshall provided immediate support:

> "With respect to disputes between a state and the citizens of another state, its jurisdiction has been decried with unusual vehemence. I hope no gentleman will think that a state will be called at the bar of the federal court. Is there no such case at present? Are

there not many cases in which the legislature of Virginia is a party, and yet the state is not sued? It is not rational to suppose, that the sovereign power shall be dragged before a court. The intent is, to enable states to recover claims of individuals residing in other states. I contend this construction is warranted by the words. But, say they, there will be partiality in it if a state cannot be defendant. . . . It is necessary to be so, and cannot be avoided. I see a difficulty in making a state defendant, which does not prevent its being plaintiff." Id., at 555.

. . . Despite the persuasive assurances of the Constitution's leading advocates . . . , this Court held, just five years after the Constitution was adopted, that article III authorized a private citizen of another state to sue the state of Georgia without its consent. Chisholm v. Georgia, 2 U.S. (2 Dall.) 419 (1793). . . .

It might be argued that the *Chisholm* decision was a correct interpretation of the constitutional design and that the 11th amendment represented a deviation from the original understanding. This, however, seems unsupportable. First, despite the opinion of Justice Iredell, the majority failed to address either the practice or the understanding that prevailed in the states at the time the Constitution was adopted. Second, even a casual reading of the opinions suggests the majority suspected the decision would be unpopular and surprising. Finally, two members of the majority acknowledged that the United States might well remain immune from suit despite article III's grant of jurisdiction over "Controversies to which the United States shall be a Party," see id. at 469 (Cushing, J.); id. at 478 (Jay, C.J.), and, invoking the example of actions to collect debts incurred before the Constitution was adopted, one raised the possibility of "exceptions," suggesting the rule of the case might not "extend to all the demands, and to every kind of action," see id. at 479 (Jay, C.J.). These concessions undercut the crucial premise that either the Constitution's literal text or the principal of popular sovereignty necessarily overrode widespread practice and opinion.

The text and history of the 11th amendment also suggest that Congress acted not to change but to restore the original constitutional design. Although earlier drafts of the amendment had been phrased as express limits on the judicial power granted in article III, see, e.g., 3 Annals of Congress 651–52 (1793) ("The Judicial Power of the United States shall not extend to any suits in law or equity, commenced or prosecuted against one of the United States . . ."), the adopted text addressed the proper interpretation of that provision of the original Constitution, see U.S. Const., amdt. 11 ("The Judicial Power of the United States shall not be construed to extend to any suit in law or equity, commenced or prosecuted against one of the United States . . ."). By its terms, then, the 11th amendment did not redefine the federal judicial power but instead overruled the Court. . . .

The text reflects the historical context and the congressional objective in endorsing the amendment for ratification. Congress chose not to enact language codifying the traditional understanding of sovereign immunity but rather to address the specific provisions of the Constitution that had raised concerns during the ratification debates and formed the basis of the *Chisholm* decision. Given the outraged reaction to *Chisholm* ..., it is doubtful that if Congress meant to write a new immunity into the Constitution it would have limited that immunity to the narrow text of the 11th amendment:

> "Can we suppose that, when the 11th amendment was adopted, it was understood to be left open for citizens of a state to sue their own state in federal courts, whilst the idea of suits by citizens of other states, or of foreign states, was indignantly repelled? Suppose that Congress, when proposing the 11th amendment, had appended to it a proviso that nothing therein contained should prevent a state from being sued by its own citizens in cases arising under the Constitution or laws of the United States, can we imagine that it would have been adopted by the states? The supposition that it would is almost an absurdity on its face." Hans v. Louisiana, 134 U.S. 1, 14–15 (1890).

The more natural inference is that the Constitution was understood, in light of its history and structure, to preserve the states' traditional immunity from private suits. As the amendment clarified the only provisions of the Constitution that anyone had suggested might support a contrary understanding, there was no reason to draft with a broader brush. ...

Although the dissent attempts to rewrite history to reflect a different original understanding, its evidence is unpersuasive.... The views voiced during the ratification debates by Edmund Randolph and James Wilson, when reiterated by the same individuals in their respective capacities as advocate and Justice in *Chisholm*, were decisively rejected by the 11th amendment.... In short, the scanty and equivocal evidence offered by the dissent establishes no more than what is evident from the decision in *Chisholm*—that some members of the founding generation disagreed with Hamilton, Madison, Marshall, [and] Iredell.... The events leading to the adoption of the 11th amendment, however, make clear that the individuals who believed the Constitution stripped the states of their immunity from suit were at most a small minority.

Not only do the ratification debates and the events leading to the adoption of the 11th amendment reveal the original understanding of the states' constitutional immunity from suit, they also underscore the importance of sovereign immunity to the founding generation. Simply put, "[t]he Constitution never would have been ratified if the states and their courts were to be stripped of their sovereign authority except as expressly provided by the Constitution itself." Atascadero State Hospital v. Scanlon, 473 U.S. 234, 239, n. 2 (1985).

C

The Court has been consistent in interpreting the adoption of the 11th amendment as conclusive evidence "that the decision in *Chisholm* was contrary to the well-understood meaning of the Constitution," *Seminole Tribe*, 517 U.S. at 69.... Following this approach, the Court has upheld states' assertions of sovereign immunity in various contexts falling outside the literal text of the 11th amendment. In *Hans v. Louisiana*, supra, the Court held that sovereign immunity barred a citizen from suing his own state under the federal-question head of jurisdiction. The Court was unmoved by the petitioner's argument that the 11th amendment, by its terms, applied only to suits brought by citizens of other states.... Later decisions rejected similar requests to conform the principle of sovereign immunity to the strict language of the 11th amendment in holding that nonconsenting states are immune from suits brought by federal corporations, Smith v. Reeves, 178 U.S. 436 (1900), foreign nations, Principality of Monaco v. Mississippi, 292 U.S. 313 (1934), or Indian tribes, Blatchford v. Native Village of Noatak, 501 U.S. 775 (1991), and in concluding that sovereign immunity is a defense to suits in admiralty, though the text of the 11th amendment addresses only suits "in law or equity," Ex parte New York, 256 U.S. 490 (1921).

These holdings reflect a settled doctrinal understanding, consistent with the views of the leading advocates of the Constitution's ratification, that sovereign immunity derives not from the 11th amendment but from the structure of the original Constitution itself. The 11th amendment confirmed rather than established sovereign immunity as a constitutional principle; it follows that the scope of the states' immunity from suit is demarcated not by the text of the amendment alone but by fundamental postulates implicit in the constitutional design. As we explained in *Principality of Monaco*:

> "Manifestly, we cannot rest with a mere literal application of the words of § 2 of article III, or assume that the letter of the 11th amendment exhausts the restrictions upon suits against nonconsenting states. Behind the words of the constitutional provisions are postulates which limit and control. There is the essential postulate that the controversies, as contemplated, shall be found to be of a justiciable character. There is also the postulate that states of the Union, still possessing attributes of sovereignty, shall be immune from suits, without their consent, save where there has been 'a surrender of this immunity in the plan of the convention.' " 292 U.S. at 322–23 (quoting The Federalist No. 81, at 487) (footnote omitted)....

II

In this case we must determine whether Congress has the power, under article I, to subject nonconsenting states to private suits in their own courts. ...

A

Petitioners contend the text of the Constitution and our recent sovereign immunity decisions establish that the states were required to relinquish this portion of their sovereignty. We turn first to these sources.

1

Article I, § 8 grants Congress broad power to enact legislation in several enumerated areas of national concern. The supremacy clause, furthermore, provides:

> "This Constitution, and the Laws of the United States which shall be made in Pursuance thereof ..., shall be the supreme Law of the Land; and the Judges in every State shall be bound thereby, any Thing in the Constitution or Laws of any state to the Contrary notwithstanding." U.S. Const., art. VI.

It is contended that, by virtue of these provisions, where Congress enacts legislation subjecting the states to suit, the legislation by necessity overrides the sovereign immunity of the states.

As is evident from its text, however, the supremacy clause enshrines as "the supreme Law of the Land" only those federal acts that accord with the constitutional design. Appeal to the supremacy clause alone merely raises the question whether a law is a valid exercise of the national power. . . .

The Constitution, by delegating to Congress the power to establish the supreme law of the land when acting within its enumerated powers, does not foreclose a state from asserting immunity to claims arising under federal law merely because that law derives not from the state itself but from the national power. A contrary view could not be reconciled with *Hans v. Louisiana*, supra, which sustained Louisiana's immunity in a private suit arising under the Constitution itself ... or with numerous other decisions to the same effect. We reject any contention that substantive federal law by its own force necessarily overrides the sovereign immunity of the states. When a state asserts its immunity to suit, the question is not the primacy of federal law but the implementation of the law in a manner consistent with the constitutional sovereignty of the states.

Nor can we conclude that the specific article I powers delegated to Congress necessarily include, by virtue of the necessary and proper clause or otherwise, the incidental authority to subject the states to private suits as a means of achieving objectives otherwise within the scope of the enumerated powers. Although some of our decisions had endorsed this contention, they have since been overruled, see *Seminole Tribe*, supra, at 63–67, 72; College Savings Bank v. Florida Prepaid Postsecondary Ed. Expense Bd., 527 U.S. 666, 680 (1999).

The cases we have cited, of course, came at last to the conclusion that neither the supremacy clause nor the enumerated powers of Congress confer authority to abrogate the states' immunity from suit in federal court. The logic of the decisions, however, does not turn on the forum in which the suits were prosecuted but extends to state-court suits as well.

The dissenting opinion seeks to reopen these precedents, contending that state sovereign immunity must derive either from the common law (in which case the dissent contends it is defeasible by statute) or from natural law (in which case the dissent believes it cannot bar a federal claim). As should be obvious to all, this is a false dichotomy. The text and the structure of the Constitution protect various rights and principles. Many of these, such as the right to trial by jury and the prohibition on unreasonable searches and seizures, derive from the common law. The common-law lineage of these rights does not mean they are defeasible by statute or remain mere common-law rights, however. They are, rather, constitutional rights, and form the fundamental law of the land. . . .

Despite the dissent's assertion to the contrary, the fact that a right is not defeasible by statute means only that it is protected by the Constitution, not that it derives from natural law. Whether the dissent's attribution of our reasoning and conclusions to natural law results from analytical confusion or rhetorical device, it is simply inaccurate. We do not contend the founders could not have stripped the states of sovereign immunity and granted Congress power to subject them to private suit but only that they did not do so. By the same token, the contours of sovereign immunity are determined by the founders' understanding, not by the principles or limitations derived from natural law.

The dissent has offered no evidence that the founders believed sovereign immunity extended only to cases where the sovereign was the source of the right asserted. No such limitation existed on sovereign immunity in England, where sovereign immunity was predicated on a different theory altogether. It is doubtful whether the King was regarded, in any meaningful sense, as the font of the traditions and customs which formed the substance of the common law, yet he could not be sued on a common-law claim in his own courts. And it strains credibility to imagine that the King could have been sued in his own court on, say, a French cause of action. . . .

2

There are isolated statements in some of our cases suggesting that the 11th amendment is inapplicable in state courts. See Hilton v. South Carolina Public Railways Comm'n, 502 U.S. 197, 204–05 (1991); Will v. Michigan Dept. of State Police, 491 U.S. 58, 63 (1989); *Atascadero State Hospital v. Scanlon*, supra, 473 U.S. at 239–40, n. 2; Maine v. Thiboutot, 448 U.S. 1, 9 n. 7 (1980); Nevada v. Hall, 440 U.S. 410, 418–21 (1979). . . . Two of the cases discussing state-court immunity may be dismissed out of hand. The footnote digressions in *Atascadero State Hospital* and *Thiboutot* were irrelevant to either opinion's holding or rationale. The discussion in *Will* was also unnecessary to the decision; our holding that 42 U.S.C.

§ 1983 did not create a cause of action against the states rendered it unnecessary to determine the scope of the states' constitutional immunity from suit in their own courts. Our opinions in *Hilton* and *Hall*, however, require closer attention, for in those cases we sustained suits against states in state courts.

In *Hilton* we held that an injured employee of a state-owned railroad could sue his employer (an arm of the state) in state court under the Federal Employers' Liability Act (FELA), 45 U.S.C. §§ 51–60. Our decision was "controlled and informed" by stare decisis. A generation earlier we had held that because the FELA made clear that all who operated railroads would be subject to suit by injured workers, states that chose to enter the railroad business after the statute's enactment impliedly waived their sovereign immunity from such suits. See Parden v. Terminal R. Co., 377 U.S. 184 (1964). Some states had excluded railroad workers from the coverage of their workers' compensation statutes on the assumption that FELA provided adequate protection for those workers. Closing the courts to FELA suits against state employers would have dislodged settled expectations and required an extensive legislative response.

There is language in *Hilton* which gives some support to the position of petitioners here but our decision did not squarely address, much less resolve, the question of Congress' power to abrogate states' immunity from suit in their own courts. The respondent in *Hilton*, the South Carolina Public Railways Commission, neither contested Congress' constitutional authority to subject it to suits for money damages nor raised sovereign immunity as an affirmative defense. Nor was the state's litigation strategy surprising. *Hilton* was litigated and decided in the wake of Pennsylvania v. Union Gas, 491 U.S. 1 (1989), and before this Court's decisions in New York v. United States, 505 U.S. 144 (1992), *Printz*, and *Seminole Tribe*. At that time it may have appeared to the state that Congress' power to abrogate its immunity from suit in any court was not limited by the Constitution at all, so long as Congress made its intent sufficiently clear.

Furthermore, our decision in *Parden* was based on concepts of waiver and consent. Although later decisions have undermined the basis of *Parden*'s reasoning, see, e.g., *College Savings Bank*, supra, at 680 (overruling *Parden*'s theory of constructive waiver), we have not questioned the general proposition that a state may waive its sovereign immunity and consent to suit.

Hilton, then, must be read in light of the doctrinal basis of *Parden*, the issues presented and argued by the parties, and the substantial reliance interests drawn into question by the litigation. When so read, we believe the decision is best understood not as recognizing a congressional power to subject nonconsenting states to private suits in their own courts, nor even as endorsing the constructive waiver theory of *Parden*, but as simply adhering, as a matter of stare decisis and presumed historical fact, to the narrow proposition that certain states had consented to be sued by injured workers covered by the FELA, at least in their own courts.

In *Hall* we considered whether California could subject Nevada to suit in California's courts and determined the Constitution did not bar it from doing so. We noted that "the doctrine of sovereign immunity is an amalgam of two quite different concepts, one applicable to suits in the sovereign's own courts and the other to suits in the courts of another sovereign." 440 U.S., at 414.... Since we determined the Constitution did not reflect an agreement between the states to respect the sovereign immunity of one another, California was free to determine whether it would respect Nevada's sovereignty as a matter of comity.

Our opinion in *Hall* did distinguish a state's immunity from suit in federal court from its immunity in the courts of other states; it did not, however, address or consider any differences between a state's sovereign immunity in federal court and in its own courts. Our reluctance to find an implied constitutional limit on the power of the states cannot be construed, furthermore, to support an analogous reluctance to find implied constitutional limits on the power of the federal government. The Constitution, after all, treats the powers of the states differently from the powers of the federal government. As we explained in *Hall*:

> "In view of the 10th amendment's reminder that powers not delegated to the federal government nor prohibited to the states are reserved to the states or to the people, the existence of express limitations on state sovereignty may equally imply that caution should be exercised before concluding that unstated limitations on state power were intended by the framers." Id. at 425 (footnote omitted).

The federal government, by contrast, "can claim no powers which are not granted to it by the constitution, and the powers actually granted must be such as are expressly given, or given by necessary implication." Martin v. Hunter's Lessee, 14 U.S. (1 Wheat.) 304, 326 (1816).

Our decision in *Hall* thus does not support the argument urged by petitioners here. The decision addressed neither Congress' power to subject states to private suits nor the states' immunity from suit in their own courts. In fact, the distinction drawn between a sovereign's immunity in its own courts and its immunity in the courts of another sovereign, as well as the reasoning on which this distinction was based, are consistent with, and even support, the proposition urged by the respondent here—that the Constitution reserves to the states a constitutional immunity from private suits in their own courts which cannot be abrogated by Congress.

Petitioners seek support in two additional decisions. In Reich v. Collins, 513 U.S. 106. 108 (1994), we held that, despite its immunity from suit in federal court, a state which holds out what plainly appears to be "a clear and certain" postdeprivation remedy for taxes collected in violation of federal law may not declare, after disputed taxes have been paid in reliance on this remedy, that the remedy does not in fact exist. This case arose in the context of tax-refund litigation, where a state may deprive a taxpayer of all other means of challenging the validity of its tax laws by holding out what appears to be a "clear and certain" postdeprivation remedy. In this context, due process requires the state to provide the remedy it has promised. The obligation arises from the Constitution itself; *Reich* does not speak to the power of Congress to subject states to suits in their own courts.

In Howlett v. Rose, 496 U.S. 356 (1990), we held that a state court could not refuse to hear a § 1983 suit against a school board on the basis of sovereign immunity. The school board was not an arm of the state, however, so it could not assert any constitutional defense of sovereign immunity to which the state would have been entitled. See Mt. Healthy City Bd. of Ed. v. Doyle, 429 U.S. 274, 280 (1977). In *Howlett*, then, the only question was "whether a state-law defense of 'sovereign immunity' is available to a school board otherwise subject to suit in a Florida court even though such a defense would not be available if the action had been brought in a federal forum." 496 U.S. at 358–59. The decision did not address the question of Congress' power to compel a state court to entertain an action against a nonconsenting state.

B

Whether Congress has authority under article I to abrogate a state's immunity from suit in its own courts is, then, a question of first impression. In determining whether there is "compelling evidence" that this derogation of the states' sovereignty is "inherent in the constitutional compact," *Blatchford*, supra, 501 U.S. at 781, we continue our discussion of history, practice, precedent, and the structure of the Constitution.

1

We look first to evidence of the original understanding of the Constitution. Petitioners contend that because the ratification debates and the events surrounding the adoption of the 11th amendment focused on the states' immunity from suit in federal courts, the historical record gives no instruction as to the founding generation's intent to preserve the states' immunity from suit in their own courts.

We believe, however, that the founders' silence is best explained by the simple fact that no one, not even the Constitution's most ardent opponents, suggested the document might strip the states of the immunity. In light of the overriding concern regarding the states' war-time debts, together with the well known creativity, foresight, and vivid imagination of the Constitution's opponents, the silence is most instructive. It suggests the sovereign's right to assert immunity from suit in its own courts was a principle so well established that no one conceived it would be altered by the new Constitution. . . .

In light of the language of the Constitution and the historical context, it is quite apparent why neither the ratification debates nor the language of the 11th amendment addressed the states' immunity from suit in their own courts. The concerns voiced at the ratifying conventions, the furor raised by *Chisholm*, and the speed and unanimity with which the amendment was adopted, moreover, underscore the jealous care with which the founding generation sought to preserve the sovereign immunity of the states. To read this history as permitting the inference that the Constitution stripped the states of immunity in their own courts and allowed Congress to subject them to suit there would turn on its head the concern of the founding generation—that article III might be used to circumvent state-court immunity. In light of the historical record it is difficult to conceive that the Constitution would have been adopted if it had been understood to strip the states of immunity from suit in their own courts and cede to the federal government a power to subject nonconsenting states to private suits in these fora.

2

Our historical analysis is supported by early congressional practice, which provides "contemporaneous and weighty evidence of the Constitution's meaning." *Printz*, 521 U.S. at 905 (internal quotation marks omitted). Although early Congresses enacted various statutes authorizing federal suits in state court, we have discovered no instance in which they purported to authorize suits against nonconsenting states in these fora. . . .

Not only were statutes purporting to authorize private suits against nonconsenting states in state courts not enacted by early Congresses, statutes purporting to authorize such suits in any forum are all but absent from our historical experience. The first statute we confronted that even arguably purported to subject the states to private actions was the FELA. See *Parden*, supra. The provisions of the FLSA at issue here, which were enacted in the aftermath of *Parden*, are among the first statutory enactments purporting in express terms to subject nonconsenting states to private suits. Although similar statutes have multiplied in the last generation, "they are of such recent vintage that they are no more probative than the [FLSA] of a constitutional tradition that lends meaning to the text. Their persuasive force is far outweighed by almost two centuries of apparent congressional avoidance of the practice." *Printz*, 521 U.S. at 918.

Even the recent statutes, moreover, do not provide evidence of an understanding that Congress has a greater power to subject states to suit in their own courts than in federal courts. On the contrary, the statutes purport to create causes of actions against the states which are enforceable in federal, as well as state, court. To the extent recent practice thus departs from longstanding tradition, it reflects not so much an understanding that the states have surrendered their immunity from suit in their own courts as the erroneous view, perhaps inspired by *Parden* and *Union Gas*, that Congress may subject nonconsenting states to private suits in any forum.

3

The theory and reasoning of our earlier cases suggest the states do retain a constitutional immunity from suit in their own courts. We have often described the states immunity in sweeping terms, without reference to whether the suit was prosecuted in state or federal court [citing cases]. We have said on many occasions, furthermore, that the states retain their immunity from private suits prosecuted in their own courts [citing cases]. We have also relied on the states' immunity in their own courts as a premise in our 11th amendment rulings.

In particular, the exception to our sovereign immunity doctrine recognized in Ex parte Young, 209 U.S. 123 (1908), is based in part on the premise that sovereign immunity bars relief against states and their officers in both state and federal courts, and that certain suits for declaratory or injunctive relief against state officers must therefore be permitted if the Constitution is to remain the supreme law of the land. ... Had we not understood the states to retain a constitutional immunity from suit in their own courts, the need for the *Ex parte Young* rule would have been less pressing, and the rule would not have formed so essential a part of our sovereign immunity doctrine. See Idaho v. Coeur d'Alene Tribe of Idaho, 521 U.S. 261, 270–71 (1997) (principal opinion).

As it is settled doctrine that neither substantive federal law nor attempted congressional abrogation under article I bars a state from raising a constitutional defense of sovereign immunity in federal court, our decisions suggesting that the states retain an analogous constitutional immunity from private suits in their own courts support the conclusion that Congress lacks the article I power to subject the states to private suits in those fora.

4

Our final consideration is whether a congressional power to subject nonconsenting states to private suits in their own courts is consistent with the structure of the Constitution. We look both to the essential principles of federalism and to the special role of the state courts in the constitutional design.

Although the Constitution grants broad powers to Congress, our federalism requires that Congress treat the states in a manner consistent with their status as residuary sovereigns and joint participants in the governance of the nation. ... Petitioners contend that immunity from suit in federal court suffices to preserve the dignity of the states. Private suits against nonconsenting states, however, present "the indignity of subjecting a state to the coercive process of judicial tribunals at the instance of private parties," In re Ayers, 123 U.S. 443, 505 (1887), regardless of the forum. Not only must a state defend or default but also it must face the prospect of being thrust, by federal fiat and against its will, into the disfavored status of a debtor, subject to the power of private citizens to levy on its treasury or perhaps even government buildings or property which the state administers on the public's behalf.

In some ways, of course, a congressional power to authorize private suits against nonconsenting states in their own courts would be even more offensive to state sovereignty than a power to authorize the suits in a federal forum. Although the immunity of one sovereign in the courts of another has often depended in part on comity or agreement, the immunity of a sovereign in its own courts has always been understood to be within the sole control of the sovereign itself. See generally *Hall*, 440 U.S. at 414–18. A power to press a state's own courts into federal service to coerce the other branches of the state, furthermore, is the power first to turn the state against itself and ultimately to commandeer the entire political machinery of the state against its will and at the behest of individuals. Such plenary federal control of state governmental processes denigrates the separate sovereignty of the states.

It is unquestioned that the federal government retains its own immunity from suit not only in state tribunals but also in its own courts. In light of our constitutional system recognizing the essential sovereignty of the states, we are reluctant to conclude that the states are not entitled to a reciprocal privilege.

Underlying constitutional form are considerations of great substance. Private suits against nonconsenting states—especially suits for money damages—may threaten the financial integrity of the states. It is indisputable that, at the time of the founding, many of the states could have been forced into insolvency but for their immunity from private suits for money damages. Even today, an unlimited congressional power to authorize suits in state court to levy upon the treasuries of the states for compensatory damages, attorney's fees, and even punitive damages could create staggering burdens, giving Congress a power and a leverage over the states that is not contemplated by our constitutional design. The potential national power would pose a severe and notorious danger to the states and their resources. . . .

A general federal power to authorize private suits for money damages would place unwarranted strain on the states' ability to govern in accordance with the will of their citizens. Today, as at the time of the founding, the allocation of scarce resources among competing needs and interests lies at the heart of the political process. While the judgment creditor of the state may have a legitimate claim for compensation, other important needs and worthwhile ends compete for access to the public fisc. Since all cannot be satisfied in full, it is inevitable that difficult decisions involving the most sensitive and political of judgments must be made. If the principle of representative government is to be preserved to the states, the balance between competing interests must be reached after deliberation by the political process established by the citizens of the state, not by judicial decree mandated by the federal government and invoked by the private citizen. ... When the federal government asserts authority over a state's most fundamental political processes, it strikes at the heart of the political accountability so essential to our liberty and republican form of government.

The asserted authority would blur not only the distinct responsibilities of the state and national governments but also the separate duties of the judicial and political branches of the state governments.... A state is entitled to order the processes of its own governance, assigning to the political branches, rather than the courts, the responsibility for directing the payment of debts. If Congress could displace a state's allocation of governmental power and responsibility, the judicial branch of the state, whose legitimacy derives from fidelity to the law, would be compelled to assume a role not only foreign to its experience but beyond its competence as defined by the very constitution from which its existence derives.

Congress cannot abrogate the states' sovereign immunity in federal court; were the rule to be different here, the national government would wield greater power in the state courts than in its own judicial instrumentalities.

The resulting anomaly cannot be explained by reference to the special role of the state courts in the constitutional design. Although Congress may not require the legislative or executive branches of the states to enact or administer federal regulatory programs, see *Printz*, supra, at 935; *New York*, 505 U.S. at 188, it may require state courts of "adequate and appropriate" jurisdiction, Testa v. Katt, 330 U.S. 386, 394 (1947), "to enforce federal prescriptions, insofar as those prescriptions relate to matters appropriate for the judicial power," *Printz*, supra, at 907. It would be an unprecedented step, however, to infer from the fact that Congress may declare federal law binding and enforceable in state courts the further principle that Congress' authority to pursue federal objectives through the state judiciaries exceeds not only its power to press other branches of the state into its service but even its control over the federal courts themselves. The conclusion would imply that Congress may in some cases act only through instrumentalities of the states. Yet, as Chief Justice Marshall explained, "[n]o trace is to be found in the constitution of an intention to create a dependence of the government of the union on those of the states, for the execution of the great powers assigned to it. Its means are adequate to its ends; and on those means alone was it expected to rely for the accomplishment of its ends." McCulloch v. Maryland, 17 U.S. (4 Wheat.) 316, 424 (1819). ...

We have recognized that Congress may require state courts to hear only "matters appropriate for the judicial power," *Printz*, 521 U.S. at 907.

Our sovereign immunity precedents establish that suits against nonconsenting states are not "properly susceptible of litigation in courts," *Hans*, 134 U.S. at 12, and, as a result, that "the 'entire judicial power granted by the Constitution' does not embrace authority to entertain such suits in the absence of the state's consent." *Principality of Monaco*, 292 U.S. at 329 (quoting *Ex parte New York*, 256 U.S. at 497). We are aware of no constitutional precept that would admit of a congressional power to require state courts to entertain federal suits which are not within the judicial power of the United States and could not be heard in federal courts. . . .

In light of history, practice, precedent, and the structure of the Constitution, we hold that the states retain immunity from private suit in their own courts, an immunity beyond the congressional power to abrogate by article I legislation.

III

The constitutional privilege of a state to assert its sovereign immunity in its own courts does not confer upon the state a concomitant right to disregard the Constitution or valid federal law. The states and their officers are bound by obligations imposed by the Constitution and by federal statutes that comport with the constitutional design. We are unwilling to assume the states will refuse to honor the Constitution or obey the binding laws of the United States. The good faith of the states thus provides an important assurance that "this Constitution, and the Laws of the United States which shall be made in Pursuance thereof . . . shall be the supreme Law of the Land." U.S. Const., art. VI.

Sovereign immunity, moreover, does not bar all judicial review of state compliance with the Constitution and valid federal law. Rather, certain limits are implicit in the constitutional principle of state sovereign immunity.

The first of these limits is that sovereign immunity bars suits only in the absence of consent. Many states, on their own initiative, have enacted statutes consenting to a wide variety of suits. . . . Nor, subject to constitutional limitations, does the federal government lack the authority or means to seek the states' voluntary consent to private suits. Cf. *South Dakota v. Dole*, 483 U.S. 203 (1987).

The states have consented, moreover, to some suits pursuant to the plan of the convention or to subsequent constitutional amendments. In ratifying the Constitution, the states consented to suits brought by other states or by the federal government. *Principality of Monaco*, supra, at 328–29 (collecting cases). . . . We have held also that in adopting the 14th amendment, the people required the states to surrender a portion of the sovereignty that had been preserved to them by the original Constitution, so that Congress may authorize private suits against nonconsenting states pursuant to its § 5 enforcement power. *Fitzpatrick v. Bitzer*, 427 U.S. 445 (1976). . . .

The second important limit to the principle of sovereign immunity is that it bars suits against states but not lesser entities. The immunity does not extend to suits prosecuted against a municipal corporation or other governmental entity which is not an arm of the state. See, e.g., Lincoln County v. Luning, 133 U.S. 529 (1890). Nor does sovereign immunity bar all suits against state officers. Some suits against state officers are barred by the rule that sovereign immunity is not limited to suits which name the state as a party if the suits are, in fact, against the state. The rule, however, does not bar certain actions against state officers for injunctive or declaratory relief. Compare *Ex parte Young*, supra, and *In re Ayers*, supra, with *Coeur d'Alene Tribe of Idaho*, supra, *Seminole Tribe*, supra, and Edelman v. Jordan, 415 U.S. 651 (1974). Even a suit for money damages may be prosecuted against a state officer in his individual capacity for unconstitutional or wrongful conduct fairly attributable to the officer himself, so long as the relief is sought not from the state treasury but from the officer personally. Scheuer v. Rhodes, 416 U.S. 232, 237–38 (1974).

The principle of sovereign immunity as reflected in our jurisprudence strikes the proper balance between the supremacy of federal law and the separate sovereignty of the states. Established rules provide ample means to correct ongoing violations of law and to vindicate the interests which animate the supremacy clause. That we have, during the first 210 years of our constitutional history, found it unnecessary to decide the question presented here suggests a federal power to subject nonconsenting states to private suits in their own courts is unnecessary to uphold the Constitution and valid federal statutes as the supreme law.

IV

The sole remaining question is whether Maine has waived its immunity. ... The state of Maine ... adheres to the general rule that "a specific authority conferred by an enactment of the legislature is requisite if the sovereign is to be taken as having shed the protective mantle of immunity," Cushing v. Cohen, 420 A.2d 919, 923 (Me.1980). Petitioners have not attempted to establish a waiver of immunity under this standard. Although petitioners contend the state has discriminated against federal rights by claiming sovereign immunity from this FLSA suit, there is no evidence that the state has manipulated its immunity in a systematic fashion to discriminate against federal causes of action. To the extent Maine has chosen to consent to certain classes of suits while maintaining its immunity from others, it has done no more than exercise a privilege of sovereignty concomitant to its constitutional immunity from suit. The state, we conclude, has not consented to suit.

V

This case at one level concerns the formal structure of federalism, but in a Constitution as resilient as ours form mirrors substance. Congress has vast power but not all power. When Congress legislates in matters affecting the states, it may not treat these sovereign entities as mere prefectures or corporations. Congress must accord states the esteem due to them as joint participants in a federal system, one beginning with the premise of sovereignty in both the central government and the separate states. Congress has ample means to ensure compliance with valid federal laws, but it must respect the sovereignty of the states.

In apparent attempt to disparage a conclusion with which it disagrees, the dissent attributes our reasoning to natural law. We seek to discover, however, only what the framers and those who ratified the Constitution sought to accomplish when they created a federal system. We appeal to no higher authority than the charter which they wrote and adopted. Theirs was the unique insight that freedom is enhanced by the creation of two governments, not one. We need not attach a label to our dissenting colleagues' insistence that the constitutional structure adopted by the founders must yield to the politics of the moment. Although the Constitution begins with the principle that sovereignty rests with the people, it does not follow that the national government becomes the ultimate, preferred mechanism for expressing the people's will. The states exist as a refutation of that concept. In choosing to ordain and establish the Constitution, the people insisted upon a federal structure for the very purpose of rejecting the idea that the will of the people in all instances is expressed by the central power, the one most remote from their control. The framers of the Constitution did not share our dissenting colleagues' belief that the Congress may circumvent the federal design by regulating the states directly when it pleases to do so, including by a proxy in which individual citizens are authorized to levy upon the state treasuries absent the states' consent to jurisdiction.

The case before us depends upon these principles. The state of Maine has not questioned Congress' power to prescribe substantive rules of federal law to which it must comply. Despite an initial good-faith disagreement about the requirements of the FLSA, it is conceded by all that the state has altered its conduct so that its compliance with federal law cannot now be questioned. The Solicitor General of the United States has appeared before this Court, however, and asserted that the federal interest in compensating the states' employees for alleged past violations of federal law is so compelling that the sovereign state of Maine must be stripped of its immunity and subjected to suit in its own courts by its own employees. Yet, despite specific statutory authorization, see 29 U.S.C. § 216(c), the United States apparently found the same interests insufficient to justify sending even a single attorney to Maine to prosecute this litigation. The difference between a suit by the United States on behalf of the employees and a suit by the employees implicates a rule that the national government must itself deem the case of sufficient importance to take action against the state; and history, precedent, and the structure of the Constitution make clear that, under the plan of the convention, the states have consented to suits of the first kind but not of the second. The judgment of the Supreme Judicial Court of Maine is

Affirmed.

■ JUSTICE SOUTER, with whom JUSTICE STEVENS, JUSTICE GINSBURG, and JUSTICE BREYER join, dissenting. . . .

Today's issue arises naturally in the aftermath of the decision in Seminole Tribe of Fla. v. Florida, 517 U.S. 44 (1996). The Court holds that the Constitution bars an individual suit against a state to enforce a federal statutory right under the Fair Labor Standards Act of 1938 (FLSA), 29 U.S.C. § 201 et seq., when brought in the state's courts over its objection. In thus complementing its earlier decision, the Court of course confronts the fact that the state forum renders the 11th amendment beside the point, and it has responded by discerning a simpler and more straightforward theory of state sovereign immunity than it found in *Seminole Tribe*: a state's sovereign immunity from all individual suits is a "fundamental aspect" of state sovereignty "confirmed" by the 10th amendment. As a consequence, *Seminole Tribe*'s contorted reliance on the 11th amendment and its background was presumably unnecessary; the 10th would have done the work with an economy that the majority in *Seminole Tribe* would have welcomed. . . .

The sequence of the Court's positions prompts a suspicion of error, and skepticism is confirmed by scrutiny of the Court's efforts to justify its holding. There is no evidence that the 10th amendment constitutionalized a concept of sovereign immunity as inherent in the notion of statehood, and no evidence that any concept of inherent sovereign immunity was understood historically to apply when the sovereign sued was not the font of the law. Nor does the Court fare any better with its subsidiary lines of reasoning, that the state-court action is barred by the scheme of American federalism, a result supposedly confirmed by a history largely devoid of precursors to the action considered here. The Court's federalism ignores the accepted authority of Congress to bind states under the FLSA and to provide for enforcement of federal rights in state court. The Court's history simply disparages the capacity of the Constitution to order relationships in a republic that has changed since the founding.

On each point the Court has raised it is mistaken, and I respectfully dissent from its judgment.

I

The Court rests its decision principally on the claim that immunity from suit was "a fundamental aspect of the sovereignty which the states enjoyed before the ratification of the Constitution," an aspect which the Court understands to have survived the ratification of the Constitution in 1788 and to have been "confirmed" and given constitutional status by the adoption of the 10th amendment in 1791. If the Court truly means by "sovereign immunity" what that term meant at common law, its argument would be insupportable. While sovereign immunity entered many new state legal systems as a part of the common law selectively received from England, it was not understood to be indefeasible or to have been given any such status by the new national Constitution, which did not mention it. Had the question been posed, state sovereign immunity could not have been thought to shield a state from suit under federal law on a subject committed to national jurisdiction by article I of the Constitution. Congress exercising its conceded article I power may unquestionably abrogate such immunity. I set out this position at length in my dissent in *Seminole Tribe* and will not repeat it here.

The Court does not, however, offer today's holding as a mere corollary to its reasoning in *Seminole Tribe*, substituting the 10th amendment for the 11th as the occasion demands, and it is fair to read its references to a "fundamental aspect" of state sovereignty as referring not to a prerogative inherited from the Crown, but to a conception necessarily implied by statehood itself. The conception is thus not one of common law so much as of natural law, a universally applicable proposition discoverable by reason. This, I take it, is the sense in which the Court so emphatically relies on Alexander Hamilton's reference in The Federalist No. 81 to the states' sovereign immunity from suit as an "inherent" right, a characterization that does not require, but is at least open to, a natural law reading.

I understand the Court to rely on the Hamiltonian formulation with the object of suggesting that its conception of sovereign immunity as a "fundamental aspect" of sovereignty was a substantially popular, if not the dominant, view in the periods of Revolution and Confederation. There is, after all, nothing else in the Court's opinion that would suggest a basis for saying that the ratification of the 10th amendment gave this "fundamental aspect" its constitutional status and protection against any legislative tampering by Congress. The Court's principal rationale for today's result, then, turns on history: was the natural law conception of sovereign immunity as inherent in any notion of an independent state widely held in the United States in the period preceding the ratification of 1788 (or the adoption of the 10th amendment in 1791)?

The answer is certainly no. There is almost no evidence that the generation of the framers thought sovereign immunity was fundamental in the sense of being unalterable. . . . Some framers thought sovereign immunity was an obsolete royal prerogative inapplicable in a republic; some thought sovereign immunity was a common-law power defeasible, like other common-law rights, by statute; and perhaps a few thought, in keeping with a natural law view distinct from the common-law conception, that immunity was inherent in a sovereign because the body that made a law could not logically be bound by it. Natural law thinking on the part of a doubtful few will not, however, support the Court's position.

A

The American Colonies did not enjoy sovereign immunity, that being a privilege understood in English law to be reserved for the Crown alone....

B

Starting in the mid–1760's, ideas about sovereignty in colonial America began to shift as Americans argued that, lacking a voice in Parliament, they had not in any express way consented to being taxed. The story of the subsequent development of conceptions of sovereignty is complex and uneven; here, it is enough to say that by the time independence was declared in 1776, the locus of sovereignty was still an open question, except that almost by definition, advocates of independence denied that sovereignty with respect to the American Colonies remained with the King in Parliament.

As the concept of sovereignty was unsettled, so was that of sovereign immunity. Some states appear to have understood themselves to be without immunity from suit in their own courts upon independence. Other new states understood themselves to be inheritors of the Crown's common-law sovereign immunity and so enacted statutes authorizing legal remedies against the state parallel to those available in England. . . .

Around the time of the Constitutional convention, then, there existed among the states some diversity of practice with respect to sovereign immunity; but despite a tendency among the state constitutions to announce and declare certain inalienable and natural rights of men and even of the collective people of a state, no state declared that sovereign immunity was one of those rights. To the extent that states were thought to possess immunity, it was perceived as a prerogative of the sovereign under common law. And where sovereign immunity was recognized as barring suit, provisions for recovery from the state were in order, just as they had been at common law in England.

C

At the Constitutional Convention, the notion of sovereign immunity, whether as natural law or as common law, was not an immediate subject of debate, and the sovereignty of a state in its own courts seems not to have been mentioned. This comes as no surprise, for although the Constitution required state courts to apply federal law, the framers did not consider the possibility that federal law might bind states, say, in their relations with their employees. In the subsequent ratification debates, however, the issue of jurisdiction over a state did emerge in the question whether states might be sued on their debts in federal court, and on this point, too, a variety of views emerged and the diversity of sovereign immunity conceptions displayed itself.

The only arguable support for the Court's absolutist view that I have found among the leading participants in the debate surrounding ratification was the one already mentioned, that of Alexander Hamilton in The Federalist No. 81, where he described the sovereign immunity of the states in language suggesting principles associated with natural law....

In the Virginia ratifying convention, Madison ... maintained that "it is not in the power of individuals to call any state into court," 3 J. Elliot, The Debates in the Several State Conventions on the Adoption of the Federal Constitution 533 (2d ed. 1836) (hereinafter Elliot's Debates), and thought that the phrase "in which a State shall be a Party" in article III, § 2, must be interpreted in light of that general principle, so that "the only operation it can have, is that, if a state should wish to bring a suit against a citizen, it must be brought before the federal court." Ibid. n15. John Marshall argued along the same lines against the possibility of federal jurisdiction over private suits against states, and he invoked the immunity of a state in its own courts in support of his argument....

There was no unanimity among the Virginians either on state-or federal-court immunity, however, for Edmund Randolph anticipated the position he would later espouse as plaintiff's counsel in Chisholm v. Georgia, 2 U.S. (2 Dall.) 419 (1793)....

At the farthest extreme from Hamilton, James Wilson made several comments in the Pennsylvania convention that suggested his hostility to any idea of state sovereign immunity. ... Wilson laid out his view that sovereignty was in fact not located in the states at all: "Upon what principle is it contended that the sovereign power resides in the state governments? The honorable gentleman has said truly, that there can be no subordinate sovereignty. Now, if there cannot, my position is, that the sovereignty resides in the people; they have not parted with it; they have only dispensed such portions of the power as were conceived necessary for the public welfare." 2 Elliot's Debates at 443. While this statement did not specifically address sovereign immunity, it expressed the major premise of what would later become Justice Wilson's position in *Chisholm*: that because the people, and not the states, are sovereign, sovereign immunity has no applicability to the states.

From a canvass of this spectrum of opinion expressed at the ratifying conventions, one thing is certain. No one was espousing an indefeasible, natural law view of sovereign immunity. The controversy over the enforceability of state debts subject to state law produced emphatic support for sovereign immunity from eminences as great as Madison and Marshall, but neither of them indicated adherence to any immunity conception outside the common law.

D

At the close of the ratification debates, the issue of the sovereign immunity of the states under article III had not been definitively resolved, and in some instances the indeterminacy led the ratification conventions to respond in ways that point to the range of thinking about the doctrine.

Several state ratifying conventions proposed amendments and issued declarations that would have exempted states from subjection to suit in federal court. [T]he state ratifying conventions' felt need for clarification on the question of state suability demonstrates that uncertainty surrounded the matter even at the moment of ratification. This uncertainty set the stage for the divergent views expressed in *Chisholm*.

E

If the natural law conception of sovereign immunity as an inherent characteristic of sovereignty enjoyed by the states had been broadly accepted at the time of the founding, one would expect to find it reflected somewhere in the five opinions delivered by the Court in *Chisholm v. Georgia*, supra. Yet that view did not appear in any of them. And since a bare two years before *Chisholm*, the Bill of Rights had been added to the original Constitution, if the 10th amendment had been understood to give federal constitutional status to state sovereign immunity so as to endue it with the equivalent of the natural law conception, one would be certain to find such a development mentioned somewhere in the *Chisholm* writings. In fact, however, not one of the opinions espoused the natural law view, and not one of them so much as mentioned the 10th amendment. Not even Justice Iredell, who alone among the Justices thought that a state could not be sued in federal court, echoed Hamilton or hinted at a constitutionally immutable immunity doctrine....

[I]n *Chisholm* two Justices (Jay and Wilson), both of whom had been present at the Constitutional Convention, took a position suggesting that states should not enjoy sovereign immunity (however conceived) even in their own courts; one (Cushing) was essentially silent on the issue of sovereign immunity in state court; one (Blair) took a cautious position affirming the pragmatic view that sovereign immunity was a continuing common law doctrine and that states would permit suit against themselves as of right; and one (Iredell) expressly thought that state sovereign immunity at common-law rightly belonged to the sovereign states. Not a single Justice suggested that sovereign immunity was an inherent and indefeasible right of statehood....

The Court, citing Hans v. Louisiana, 134 U.S. 1 (1890), says that the 11th amendment "overruled" *Chisholm*, but the animadversion is beside the point. The significance of *Chisholm* is its indication that in 1788 and 1791 it was not generally assumed (indeed, hardly assumed at all) that a state's sovereign immunity from suit in its own courts was an inherent, and not merely a common-law, advantage. On the contrary, the testimony of five eminent legal minds of the day confirmed that virtually everyone who understood immunity to be legitimate saw it as a common-law prerogative (from which it follows that it was subject to abrogation by Congress as to a matter within Congress's article I authority).

The Court does no better with its trio of arguments to undercut *Chisholm*'s legitimacy: that the *Chisholm* majority "failed to address either the practice or the understanding that prevailed in the states at the time the Constitution was adopted"; that "the majority suspected the decision would be unpopular and surprising"; and that "two members of the majority acknowledged that the United States might well remain immune from suit despite" article III. These three claims do not, of course, go to the question whether state sovereign immunity was understood to be "fundamental" or "inherent," but in any case, none of them is convincing. ...

Nor can the Court make good on its claim that the enactment of the 11th amendment retrospectively reestablished the view that had already been established at the time of the framing (though eluding the perception of all but one member of the Supreme Court).... There was nothing "established" about the position espoused by Georgia in the effort to repudiate its debts, and the Court's implausible suggestion to the contrary merely echoes the brio of its remark in *Seminole Tribe* that *Chisholm* was "contrary to the well-understood meaning of the Constitution." 517 U.S. at 69. The fact that *Chisholm* was no conceptual aberration is apparent from the ratification debates and the several state requests to rewrite article III. There was no received view either of the role this sovereign immunity would play in the circumstances of the case or of a conceptual foundation for immunity doctrine at odds with *Chisholm*'s reading of article III. As an author on whom the Court relies, has it, "there was no unanimity among the framers that immunity would exist," D. Currie, The Constitution in the Supreme Court: The First Century 19 (1985). ...

II

The Court's rationale for today's holding based on a conception of sovereign immunity as somehow fundamental to sovereignty or inherent in statehood fails for the lack of any substantial support for such a conception in the thinking of the founding era. The Court cannot be counted out yet, however, for it has a second line of argument looking not to a clause-based reception of the natural law conception or even to its recognition as a "background principle," see *Seminole Tribe*, 517 U.S. at 72, but to a structural basis in the Constitution's creation of a federal system. Immunity, the Court says, "inheres in the system of federalism established by the Constitution," its "contours [being] determined by the founders' understanding, not by the principles or limitations derived from natural law." Again, "we look both to the essential principles of federalism and to the special role of the state courts in the constitutional design." That is, the Court believes that the federal constitutional structure itself necessitates recognition of some degree of state autonomy broad enough to include sovereign immunity from suit in a state's own courts, regardless of the federal source of the claim asserted against the state. If one were to read the Court's federal structure rationale in isolation from the preceding portions of the opinion, it would appear that the Court's position on state sovereign immunity might have been rested entirely on federalism alone. If it had been, however, I would still be in dissent, for the Court's argument that state court sovereign immunity on federal questions is inherent in the very concept of federal structure is demonstrably mistaken.

A

[T]he general scheme of delegated sovereignty as between the two component governments of the federal system was clear, and was succinctly stated by Chief Justice Marshall: "In America, the powers of sovereignty are divided between the government of the union, and those of the states. They are each sovereign, with respect to the objects committed to it, and neither sovereign with respect to the objects committed to the other." McCulloch v. Maryland, 17 U.S. (4 Wheat.) 316, 410 (1819).

Hence the flaw in the Court's appeal to federalism. The state of Maine is not sovereign with respect to the national objective of the FLSA.[1] It is not the authority that promulgated the FLSA, on which the right of action in this case depends. That authority is the United States acting through the Congress, whose legislative power under article I of the Constitution to extend FLSA coverage to state employees has already been decided, see Garcia v. San Antonio Metropolitan Transit Authority, 469 U.S. 528 (1985), and is not contested here.

Nor can it be argued that because the state of Maine creates its own court system, it has authority to decide what sorts of claims may be entertained there, and thus in effect to control the right of action in this case. Maine has created state courts of general jurisdiction; once it has done so, the supremacy clause of the Constitution, which requires state courts to enforce federal law and state-court judges to be bound by it, requires the Maine courts to entertain this federal cause of action. Maine has advanced no " 'valid excuse,' " Howlett v. Rose, 496 U.S. 356, 369 (1990) (quoting Douglas v. New York, N. H. & H. R. Co., 279 U.S. 377, 387–88 (1929)), for its courts' refusal to hear federal-law claims in which Maine is a defendant, and sovereign immunity cannot be that excuse, simply because the state is not sovereign with respect to the subject of the claim against it. The Court's insistence that the federal structure bars Congress from making states susceptible to suit in their own courts is, then, plain mistake.[2]

---

1. It is therefore sheer circularity for the Court to talk of the "anomaly" that would arise if a state could be sued on federal law in its own courts, when it may not be sued under federal law in federal court, *Seminole Tribe*, supra. The short and sufficient answer is that the anomaly is the Court's own creation: the 11th amendment was never intended to bar federal-question suits against the states in federal court. The anomaly is that *Seminole Tribe*, an opinion purportedly grounded in the 11th amendment, should now be used as a lever to argue for state sovereign immunity in state courts, to which the 11th amendment by its terms does not apply.

2. Perhaps as a corollary to its view of sovereign immunity as to some degree indefeasible because "fundamental," the Court

B

It is symptomatic of the weakness of the structural notion proffered by the Court that it seeks to buttress the argument by relying on "the dignity and respect afforded a state, which the immunity is designed to protect" (quoting Idaho v. Coeur d'Alene Tribe of Idaho, 521 U.S. 261, 268 (1997)).... It would be hard to imagine anything more inimical to the republican conception, which rests on the understanding of its citizens precisely that the government is not above them, but of them, its actions being governed by law just like their own. Whatever justification there may be for an American government's immunity from private suit, it is not dignity.

It is equally puzzling to hear the Court say that "federal power to authorize private suits for money damages would place unwarranted strain on the states' ability to govern in accordance with the will of their citizens." So long as the citizens' will, expressed through state legislation, does not violate valid federal law, the strain will not be felt; and to the extent that state action does violate federal law, the will of the citizens of the United States already trumps that of the citizens of the state: the strain then is not only expected, but necessarily intended.

Least of all does the Court persuade by observing that "other important needs" than that of the "judgment creditor" compete for public money. The "judgment creditor" in question is not a dunning bill-collector, but a citizen whose federal rights have been violated, and a constitutional structure that stints on enforcing federal rights out of an abundance of delicacy toward the states has substituted politesse in place of respect for the rule of law.

III

If neither theory nor structure can supply the basis for the Court's conceptions of sovereign immunity and federalism, then perhaps history might. The Court apparently believes that because state courts have not historically entertained commerce clause-based federal-law claims against the states, such an innovation carries a presumption of unconstitutionality. At the outset, it has to be noted that this approach assumes a more cohesive record than history affords. In Hilton v. South Carolina Public Railways Comm'n, 502 U.S. 197 (1991) (Kennedy, J.), a case the Court labors mightily to distinguish, we held that a state-owned railroad could be

frets that the "power to press a state's own courts into federal service to coerce the other branches of the state ... is the power first to turn the state against itself and ultimately to commandeer the entire political machinery of the state against its will and at the behest of individuals." But this is to forget that the doctrine of separation of powers prevails in our Republic. When the state judiciary enforces federal law against state officials, as the supremacy clause requires it to do, it is not turning against the state's executive any more than we turn against the federal executive when we apply federal law to the United States: it is simply upholding the rule of law. There is no "commandeering" of the state's resources where the state is asked to do no more than enforce federal law.

sued in state court under the Federal Employers' Liability Act, 45 U.S.C. §§ 51–60, notwithstanding the lack of an express congressional statement, because "'the 11th amendment does not apply in state courts.'" *Hilton*, supra, at 205 (quoting Will v. Michigan Dept. of State Police, 491 U.S. 58, 63–64 (1989)). But even if the record were less unkempt, the problem with arguing from historical practice in this case is that past practice, even if unbroken, provides no basis for demanding preservation when the conditions on which the practice depended have changed in a constitutionally relevant way.

It was at one time, though perhaps not from the framing, believed that "Congress' authority to regulate the states under the commerce clause" was limited by "certain underlying elements of political sovereignty ... deemed essential to the states' 'separate and independent existence.'" See *Garcia*, 469 U.S. at 547–58 (quoting Lane County v. Oregon, 74 U.S. (7 Wall.) 71, 76 (1869)). On this belief, the preordained balance between state and federal sovereignty was understood to trump the terms of article I and preclude Congress from subjecting states to federal law on certain subjects. . . .

Today, however, in light of *Garcia*, supra (overruling National League of Cities v. Usery, 426 U.S. 833 (1976)), the law is settled that federal legislation enacted under the commerce clause may bind the states without having to satisfy a test of undue incursion into state sovereignty. . . . Because the commerce power is no longer thought to be circumscribed, the dearth of prior private federal claims entertained against the states in state courts does not tell us anything, and reflects nothing but an earlier and less expansive application of the commerce power.

Least of all is it to the point for the Court to suggest that because the framers would be surprised to find states subjected to a federal-law suit in their own courts under the commerce power, the suit must be prohibited by the Constitution. . . . If the framers would be surprised to see states subjected to suit in their own courts under the commerce power, they would be astonished by the reach of Congress under the commerce clause generally. The proliferation of government, state and federal, would amaze the framers, and the administrative state with its reams of regulations would leave them rubbing their eyes. But the framers' surprise at, say, the FLSA, or the Federal Communications Commission, or the Federal Reserve Board is no threat to the constitutionality of any one of them, for a very fundamental reason:

> "When we are dealing with words that also are a constituent act, like the Constitution of the United States, we must realize that they have called into life a being the development of which could not have been foreseen completely by the most gifted of its begetters. It was enough for them to realize or to hope that they had created an organism; it has taken a century and has cost their successors much sweat and blood to prove that they created a

nation. The case before us must be considered in the light of our whole experience and not merely in that of what was said a hundred years ago." Missouri v. Holland, 252 U.S. 416, 433 (1920) (Holmes, J.). . . .

IV

A

[T]here is much irony in the Court's profession that it grounds its opinion on a deeply rooted historical tradition of sovereign immunity, when the Court abandons a principle nearly as inveterate, and much closer to the hearts of the framers: that where there is a right, there must be a remedy. . . . Blackstone considered it "a general and indisputable rule, that where there is a legal right, there is also a legal remedy, by suit or action at law, whenever that right is invaded." 3 Blackstone * 23. The generation of the framers thought the principle so crucial that several states put it into their constitutions. And when Chief Justice Marshall asked about Marbury, "[i]f he has a right, and that right has been violated, do the laws of his country afford him a remedy?," Marbury v. Madison, 5 U.S. (1 Cranch) 137, 162 (1803), the question was rhetorical, and the answer clear:

> "The very essence of civil liberty certainly consists in the right of every individual to claim the protection of the laws, whenever he receives an injury. One of the first duties of government is to afford that protection. In Great Britain the king himself is sued in the respectful form of a petition, and he never fails to comply with the judgment of his court." Id. at 163.

Yet today the Court has no qualms about saying frankly that the federal right to damages afforded by Congress under the FLSA cannot create a concomitant private remedy. . . . It will not do for the Court to respond that a remedy was never available where the right in question was against the sovereign. A state is not the sovereign when a federal claim is pressed against it, and even the English sovereign opened itself to recovery and, unlike Maine, provided the remedy to complement the right. . . . Far from defaulting on debt to eyes-open creditors, Maine is simply withholding damages from private citizens to whom they appear to be due. . . . Why the state of Maine has not rendered this case unnecessary by paying damages to petitioners under the FLSA of its own free will remains unclear to me. The Court says that "it is conceded by all that the state has altered its conduct so that its compliance with federal law cannot now be questioned." But the ambiguous qualifier "now" allows the Court to avoid the fact that whatever its forward-looking compliance, the state still has not paid damages to petitioners; had it done so, the case before us would be moot.

V

[I]f the present majority had a defensible position one could at least accept its decision with an expectation of stability ahead. As it is, any such expectation would be naive. The resemblance of today's state sovereign immunity to the *Lochner* era's industrial due process is striking. The Court began this century by imputing immutable constitutional status to a conception of economic self-reliance that was never true to industrial life and grew insistently fictional with the years, and the Court has chosen to close the century by conferring like status on a conception of state sovereign immunity that is true neither to history nor to the structure of the Constitution. I expect the Court's late essay into immunity doctrine will prove the equal of its earlier experiment in laissez-faire, the one being as unrealistic as the other, as indefensible, and probably as fleeting.[a]

College Savings Bank v. Florida Prepaid Postsecondary Education Expense Board

Supreme Court of the United States, 1999.
527 U.S. 666.

■ JUSTICE SCALIA delivered the opinion of the Court.

The Trademark Remedy Clarification Act (TRCA), 106 Stat. 3567, subjects the states to suits brought under § 43(a) of the Trademark Act of 1946 (Lanham Act) for false and misleading advertising, 15 U.S.C. § 1125(a). The question presented in this case is whether that provision is effective to permit suit against a state for its alleged misrepresentation of its own product—either because the TRCA effects a constitutionally permissible abrogation of state sovereign immunity, or because the TRCA operates as an invitation to waiver of such immunity which is automatically accepted by a state's engaging in the activities regulated by the Lanham Act.

I

[W]e have recognized only two circumstances in which an individual may sue a state. First, Congress may authorize such a suit in the exercise of its power to enforce the 14th amendment—an amendment enacted after the 11th amendment and specifically designed to alter the federal-state balance. Fitzpatrick v. Bitzer, 427 U.S. 445 (1976). Second, a state may waive its sovereign immunity by consenting to suit. Clark v. Barnard, 108 U.S. 436, 447–48 (1883). This case turns on whether either of these two circumstances is present.

II

Section 43(a) of the Lanham Act, 15 U.S.C. § 1125(a), enacted in 1946, created a private right of action against "any person" who uses false

---

a. For a predictive analysis of *Alden* that anticipated the Court's result and much of its reasoning, see Richard H. Seamon, The Sovereign Immunity of States in Their Own Courts, 37 Brandeis L.J. 319 (1998–99). [Footnote by eds.]

descriptions or makes false representations in commerce. The TRCA amends § 43(a) by defining "any person" to include "any State, instrumentality of a State or employee of a State or instrumentality of a State acting in his or her official capacity." § 3(c), 106 Stat. 3568. The TRCA further amends the Lanham Act to provide that such state entities "shall not be immune, under the 11th amendment of the Constitution of the United States or under any other doctrine of sovereign immunity, from suit in federal court by any person, including any governmental or nongovernmental entity for any violation under this act," and that remedies shall be available against such state entities "to the same extent as such remedies are available ... in a suit against" a nonstate entity. § 3(b) (codified in 15 U.S.C. § 1122).

Petitioner College Savings Bank is a New Jersey chartered bank located in Princeton, New Jersey. Since 1987, it has marketed and sold CollegeSure certificates of deposit designed to finance the costs of college education. College Savings holds a patent upon the methodology of administering its CollegeSure certificates. Respondent Florida Prepaid Postsecondary Education Expense Board (Florida Prepaid) is an arm of the state of Florida. Since 1988, it has administered a tuition prepayment program designed to provide individuals with sufficient funds to cover future college expenses. College Savings brought a patent infringement action against Florida Prepaid in United States District Court in New Jersey. That action is the subject of today's decision in Florida Prepaid Postsecondary Ed. Expense Bd. v. College Savings Bank, 527 U.S. 666 (1999). In addition, and in the same court, College Savings filed the instant action alleging that Florida Prepaid violated § 43(a) of the Lanham Act by making misstatements about its own tuition savings plans in its brochures and annual reports.

Florida Prepaid moved to dismiss this action on the ground that it was barred by sovereign immunity. ... The United States intervened to defend the constitutionality of the TRCA. ... The District Court ... granted Florida Prepaid's motion to dismiss. The Court of Appeals affirmed. We granted certiorari.

III

We turn first to the contention that Florida's sovereign immunity was validly abrogated. Our decision three terms ago in Seminole Tribe of Fla. v. Florida, 517 U.S. 44 (1996), held that the power "to regulate Commerce" conferred by article I of the Constitution gives Congress no authority to abrogate state sovereign immunity. As authority for the abrogation in the present case, petitioner relies upon § 5 of the 14th amendment, which we held in *Fitzpatrick v. Bitzer*, supra, and reaffirmed in *Seminole Tribe*, 517 U.S. at 72–73, could be used for that purpose.

Section 1 of the 14th amendment provides that no state shall "deprive any person of ... property ... without due process of law." Section 5 provides that "the Congress shall have power to enforce, by appropriate legislation, the provisions of this article." We made clear in City of Boerne v. Flores, 521 U.S. 507, 516–29 (1997), that the term "enforce" is to be taken seriously—that the object of valid § 5 legislation must be the carefully delimited remediation or prevention of constitutional violations. Petitioner claims that, with respect to § 43(a) of the Lanham Act, Congress enacted the TRCA to remedy and prevent state deprivations without due process of two species of "property" rights: (1) a right to be free from a business competitor's false advertising about its own product, and (2) a more generalized right to be secure in one's business interests. Neither of these qualifies as a property right protected by the due process clause.

As to the first: The hallmark of a protected property interest is the right to exclude others. That is "one of the most essential sticks in the bundle of rights that are commonly characterized as property." Kaiser Aetna v. United States, 444 U.S. 164, 176 (1979). That is why the right that we all possess to use the public lands is not the "property" right of anyone—hence the sardonic maxim, explaining what economists call the "tragedy of the commons," res publica, res nullius. The Lanham Act may well contain provisions that protect constitutionally cognizable property interests—notably, its provisions dealing with infringement of trademarks, which are the "property" of the owner because he can exclude others from using them. The Lanham Act's false-advertising provisions, however, bear no relationship to any right to exclude; and Florida Prepaid's alleged misrepresentations concerning its own products intruded upon no interest over which petitioner had exclusive dominion. . . .

Petitioner argues that the common-law tort of unfair competition "by definition" protects property interests and thus the TRCA "by definition" is designed to remedy and prevent deprivations of such interests in the false-advertising context. Even as a logical matter, that does not follow, since not everything which *protects* property interests is designed to remedy or prevent *deprivations* of those property interests. A municipal ordinance prohibiting billboards in residential areas protects the property interests of homeowners, although erecting billboards would ordinarily not deprive them of property. To sweep within the 14th amendment the elusive property interests that are "by definition" protected by unfair-competition law would violate our frequent admonition that the due process clause is not merely a "font of tort law." Paul v. Davis, 424 U.S. 693, 701 (1976).

Petitioners second assertion of a property interest rests upon an argument similar to the one just discussed, and suffers from the same flaw. Petitioner argues that businesses are "property" within the meaning of the due process clause, and that Congress legislates under § 5 when it passes a law that prevents state interference with business (which false advertising does). The assets of a business (including its good will) unquestionably are property, and any state taking of those assets is unquestionably a "deprivation" under the 14th amendment. But business in the sense of *the activity of doing business*, or *the activity of making a profit* is not property in the ordinary sense—and it is only *that*, and not any business asset, which is impinged upon by a competitors' false advertising.

Finding that there is no deprivation of property at issue here, we need not pursue the follow-on question that *City of Boerne* would otherwise require us to resolve: whether the prophylactic measure taken under purported authority of § 5 (viz., prohibition of states' sovereign-immunity claims, which are not in themselves a violation of the 14th amendment) was genuinely necessary to prevent violation of the 14th amendment. We turn next to the question whether Florida's sovereign immunity, though not abrogated, was voluntarily waived.

IV

We have long recognized that a state's sovereign immunity is "a personal privilege which it may waive at pleasure." *Clark v. Barnard*, 108 U.S. at 447. The decision to waive that immunity, however, "is altogether voluntary on the part of the sovereignty." Beers v. Arkansas, 61 U.S. (20 How.) 527 (1858). Accordingly, our "test for determining whether a state has waived its immunity from federal-court jurisdiction is a stringent one." Atascadero State Hospital v. Scanlon, 473 U.S. 234, 241 (1985). Generally, we will find a waiver either if the state voluntarily invokes our jurisdiction or else if the state makes a "clear declaration" that it intends to submit itself to our jurisdiction. Thus, a state does not consent to suit in federal court merely by consenting to suit in the courts of its own creation. Smith v. Reeves, 178 U.S. 436, 441–45 (1900). Nor does it consent to suit in federal court merely by stating its intention to "sue and be sued," Florida Dept. of Health and Rehabilitative Servs. v. Florida Nursing Home Assn., 450 U.S. 147, 149–50 (1981) (per curiam), or even by authorizing suits against it "in any court of competent jurisdiction," Kennecott Copper Corp. v. State Tax Comm'n, 327 U.S. 573, 577–79 (1946). We have even held that a state may, absent any contractual commitment to the contrary, alter the conditions of its waiver and apply those changes to a pending suit. *Beers v. Arkansas*, supra.

There is no suggestion here that respondent Florida Prepaid expressly consented to being sued in federal court. ... Rather, petitioner College Savings and the United States both maintain that Florida Prepaid has "impliedly" or "constructively" waived its immunity from Lanham Act suit. They do so on the authority of Parden v. Terminal R. Co. of Ala. Docks Dept., 377 U.S. 184 (1964)—an elliptical opinion that stands at the nadir of our waiver (and, for that matter, sovereign immunity) jurisprudence. In *Parden*, we permitted employees of a railroad owned and operated by Alabama to bring an action under the Federal Employers' Liability Act (FELA) against their employer. Despite the absence of any provision in the statute specifically referring to the states, we held that the act authorized suits against the states by virtue of its general provision subjecting to suit "every common carrier by railroad . . . engaging in commerce between . . . the several States," 45 U.S.C. § 51. We further held that Alabama had waived its immunity from FELA suit even though Alabama law expressly disavowed any such waiver:

> "By enacting the [FELA] Congress conditioned the right to operate a railroad in interstate commerce upon amenability to suit in federal court as provided by the act; by thereafter operating a railroad in interstate commerce, Alabama must be taken to have accepted that condition and thus to have consented to suit." 377 U.S. at 192. . . .

Only nine years later, in Employees of Dept. of Public Health and Welfare of Mo. v. Department of Public Health and Welfare of Mo., 411 U.S. 279 (1973), we began to retreat from *Parden*. That case held—in an opinion written by one of the *Parden* dissenters over the solitary dissent of *Parden*'s author—that the state of Missouri was immune from a suit brought under the Fair Labor Standards Act by employees of its state health facilities. Although the statute specifically covered the state hospitals in question and such coverage was unquestionably enforceable in federal court by the United States, we did not think that the statute expressed with clarity Congress's intention to supersede the states' immunity from suits brought by individuals. We "put to one side" the *Parden* case, which we characterized as involving "dramatic circumstances" and "a rather isolated state activity," unlike the provision of the Fair Labor Standards Act in question that applied to a broad class of state employees. . . . We also distinguished the railroad in *Parden* on the ground that it was "operated for profit" "in the area where private persons and corporations normally ran the enterprise." 411 U.S. at 284. . . .

Several terms later, in Welch v. Texas Dept. of Highways and Public Transp., 483 U.S. 468 (1987), although we expressly avoided addressing the constitutionality of Congress's conditioning a state's engaging in commerce-clause activity upon the state's waiver of sovereign immunity, we said there was "no doubt that *Parden*'s discussion of congressional intent to negate 11th amendment immunity is no longer good law," and overruled *Parden* "to the extent [it] is inconsistent with the requirement that an abrogation of 11th amendment immunity by Congress must be expressed in unmistakably clear language," 483 U.S. at 478, and n.8.

College Savings and the United States [contend that a] *Parden*-style waiver of immunity, they say, is still possible after *Employees* and *Welch* so long as the following two conditions are satisfied: First, Congress must provide unambiguously that the state will be subject to suit if it engages in certain specified conduct governed by federal regulation. Second, the state must voluntarily elect to engage in the federally regulated conduct that subjects it to suit. In this latter regard, their argument goes, a state is never deemed to have constructively waived its sovereign immunity by engaging in activities that it cannot realistically choose to abandon, such as the operation of a police force; but constructive waiver is appropriate where a state runs an enterprise for profit, operates in a field traditionally occupied by private persons or corporations, engages in activities sufficiently removed from "core [state] functions" or otherwise acts as a "market participant" in interstate commerce. On this theory, Florida Prepaid constructively waived its immunity from suit by engaging in the voluntary and nonessential activity of selling and advertising a for-profit educational investment vehicle in interstate commerce after being put on notice by the clear language of the TRCA that it would be subject to Lanham Act liability for doing so.

We think that the constructive-waiver experiment of *Parden* was ill conceived, and see no merit in attempting to salvage any remnant of it. . . . *Parden* broke sharply with prior cases, and is fundamentally incompatible with later ones. We have never applied the holding of *Parden* to another statute, and in fact have narrowed the case in every subsequent opinion in which it has been under consideration. In short, *Parden* stands as an anomaly in the jurisprudence of sovereign immunity, and indeed in the jurisprudence of constitutional law. Today, we drop the other shoe: Whatever may remain of our decision in *Parden* is expressly overruled.

To begin with, we cannot square *Parden* with our cases requiring that a state's express waiver of sovereign immunity be unequivocal. . . . There is a fundamental difference between a state's expressing unequivocally that it waives its immunity, and Congress's expressing unequivocally its intention that if the state takes certain action it shall be deemed to have waived that immunity. . . .

Indeed, *Parden*-style waivers are simply unheard of in the context of *other* constitutionally protected privileges. As we said in Edelman v. Jordan, 415 U.S. 651, 673 (1974), "constructive consent is not a doctrine commonly associated with the surrender of constitutional rights." . . .

Given how anomalous it is to speak of the "constructive waiver" of a constitutionally protected privilege, it is not surprising that the very cornerstone of the *Parden* opinion was the notion that state sovereign immunity is not constitutionally grounded. . . . Our more recent decision in *Seminole Tribe* expressly repudiates that proposition, and in formally overruling *Parden* we do no more than make explicit what that case implied.

Recognizing a congressional power to exact constructive waivers of sovereign immunity through the exercise of article I powers would also, as a practical matter, permit Congress to circumvent the antiabrogation holding of *Seminole Tribe*. Forced waiver and abrogation are not even different sides of the same coin—they are the same side of the same coin. . . . There is little more than a verbal distinction between saying that Congress can make Florida liable to private parties for false or misleading advertising in interstate commerce of its prepaid tuition program, and saying the same thing but adding at the end "if Florida chooses to engage in such advertising." . . .

Nor do we think that the constitutionally grounded principle of state sovereign immunity is any less robust where, as here, the asserted basis for constructive waiver is conduct that the state realistically could choose to abandon, that is undertaken for profit, that is traditionally performed by private citizens and corporations, and that otherwise resembles the behavior of "market participants." Permitting abrogation or constructive waiver of the constitutional right only when these conditions exist would of course limit the evil—but it is hard to say that that limitation has any more support in text or tradition than, say, limiting abrogation or constructive waiver to the last Friday of the month. Since sovereign immunity itself was not traditionally limited by these factors, and since they have no bearing upon the voluntariness of the waiver, there is no principled reason why they should enter into our waiver analysis. . . .

The "market participant" cases from our dormant-commerce-clause jurisprudence, relied upon by the United States, are inapposite. Those cases hold that, where a state acts as a participant in the private market, it may prefer the goods or services of its own citizens, even though it could not do so while acting as a market regulator. . . . The "market participant" exception to judicially created dormant-commerce-clause restrictions makes sense because the evil addressed by those restrictions—the prospect that states will use custom duties, exclusionary trade regulations, and other exercises of governmental power (as opposed to the expenditure of state resources) to favor their own citizens—is entirely absent where the states are buying and selling in the market. In contrast, a suit by an individual against an unconsenting state is the very evil at which the 11th amendment is directed—and it exists whether or not the state is acting for profit, in a traditionally "private" enterprise, and as a "market participant." In the sovereign-immunity context, moreover, "evenhandness" between individuals and states is not to be expected: "The constitutional role of the states sets them apart from other employers and defendants." *Welch*, 483 U.S. at 477. . . .

V

The principal thrust of Justice Breyer's dissent is an attack upon the very legitimacy of state sovereign immunity itself. In this regard, Justice Breyer and the other dissenters proclaim that they are "not *yet* ready" (emphasis added), to adhere to the still-warm precedent of *Seminole Tribe* and to the 110-year-old decision in *Hans* that supports it. Accordingly, Justice Breyer reiterates (but only in outline form, thankfully) the now-fashionable revisionist accounts of the 11th amendment set forth in other opinions in a degree of repetitive detail that has despoiled our northern woods. Compare post with *Atascadero*, 473 U.S. at 258–302 (Brennan, J., dissenting); *Welch*, 483 U.S. at 504–16 (Brennan, J., dissenting); *Seminole*

Tribe, 517 U.S. at 76–99 (Stevens, J., dissenting); id. at 100–85 (Souter, J., dissenting). But see *Alden v. Maine*, 527 U.S. 706, 760 (1999) (Souter, J., dissenting). The arguments recited in these sources have been soundly refuted, and the position for which they have been marshaled has been rejected by constitutional tradition and precedent as clear and conclusive, and almost as venerable, as that which consigns debate over whether *Marbury v. Madison* was wrongly decided to forums more other-worldly than ours. On this score, we think nothing further need be said except two minor observations peculiar to this case.

First, Justice Breyer and the other dissenters have adopted a decidedly perverse theory of stare decisis. While finding themselves entirely unconstrained by a venerable precedent such as *Hans*, imbedded within our legal system for over a century, at the same time they cling desperately to an anomalous and severely undermined decision (*Parden*) from the 1960's. Surely this approach to stare decisis is exactly backwards—unless, of course, one wishes to use it as a weapon rather than a guide, in which case any old approach will do. Second, while we stress that the following observation has no bearing upon our resolution of this case, we find it puzzling that Justice Breyer would choose this occasion to criticize our sovereign-immunity jurisprudence as being ungrounded in constitutional text, since the present lawsuit that he would allow to go forward—having apparently been commenced against a state (Florida) by a citizen of another state—seems to fall four square within the literal text of the 11th amendment....

As for the more diffuse treatment of the subject of federalism contained in the last portion of Justice Breyer's opinion: It is alarming to learn that so many members of this Court subscribe to a theory of federalism that rejects "the details of any particular federalist doctrine"—which it says can and should "change to reflect the nation's changing needs"—and that puts forward as the only "unchanging goal" of federalism worth mentioning "the protection of liberty," which it believes is most directly achieved by "promoting the sharing among citizens of governmental decision-making authority," which in turn demands (we finally come to the point) "necessary legislative flexibility" for the people's representatives in Congress. ... Legislative flexibility on the part of Congress will be the touchstone of federalism when the capacity to support combustion becomes the acid test of a fire extinguisher. Congressional flexibility is desirable, of course—but only within the *bounds of federal power* established by the Constitution. Beyond those bounds (the theory of our Constitution goes), it is a menace. Our opinion today has sought to discern what the bounds are; the dissent denies them any permanent place. ...

Concluding, for the foregoing reasons, that the sovereign immunity of the state of Florida was neither validly abrogated by the Trademark Remedy Clarification Act, nor voluntarily waived by the state's activities in interstate commerce, we hold that the federal courts are without jurisdiction to entertain this suit against an arm of the state of Florida. The judgment of the Third Circuit dismissing the action is affirmed.

■ JUSTICE STEVENS, dissenting. . . .

The procedural posture of this case requires the Court to assume that Florida Prepaid is an "arm of the state" of Florida because its activities relate to the state's educational programs. But the validity of that assumption is doubtful if the Court's jurisprudence in this area is to be based primarily on present-day assumptions about the status of the doctrine of sovereign immunity in the 18th century. Sovereigns did not then play the kind of role in the commercial marketplace that they do today. In future cases, it may therefore be appropriate to limit the coverage of state sovereign immunity by treating the commercial enterprises of the states like the commercial activities of foreign sovereigns under the Foreign Sovereign Immunities Act of 1976. . . .

■ JUSTICE BREYER, with whom JUSTICE STEVENS, JUSTICE SOUTER, and JUSTICE GINSBURG join, dissenting.

The Court holds that Congress, in the exercise of its commerce power, cannot require a state to waive its immunity from suit in federal court even where the state engages in activity from which it might readily withdraw, such as federally regulated commercial activity. This Court has previously held to the contrary. Parden v. Terminal R. Co. of Ala. State Docks Dept., 377 U.S. 184 (1964). I would not abandon that precedent.

I

Thirty-five years ago this Court unanimously subscribed to the holding that the Court today overrules. Justice White, writing for four members of the Court who dissented on a different issue, succinctly described that holding as follows:

> "It is within the power of Congress to condition a state's permit to engage in the interstate transportation business on a waiver of the state's sovereign immunity from suits arising out of such business. Congress might well determine that allowing regulable conduct such as the operation of a railroad to be undertaken by a body legally immune from liability directly resulting from these operations is so inimical to the purposes of its regulation that the state must be put to the option of either foregoing participation in the conduct or consenting to legal responsibility for injury caused thereby." 377 U.S. at 198 (opinion of White, J., joined by Douglas, Harlan, and Stewart, JJ.). . . .

Far from being anomalous, *Parden*'s holding finds support in reason and precedent. When a state engages in ordinary commercial ventures, it acts like a private person, outside the area of its "core" responsibilities, and in a way unlikely to prove essential to the fulfillment of a basic governmental obligation. A Congress that decides to regulate those state commercial activities rather than to exempt the state likely believes that an exemption, by treating the state differently from identically situated private persons, would threaten the objectives of a federal regulatory program aimed primarily at private conduct. And a Congress that includes the state not only within its substantive regulatory rules but also (expressly) within a related system of private remedies likely believes that a remedial exemption would similarly threaten that program. It thereby avoids an enforcement gap which, when allied with the pressures of a competitive marketplace, could place the state's regulated private competitors at a significant disadvantage.

These considerations make Congress' need to possess the power to condition entry into the market upon a waiver of sovereign immunity (as "necessary and proper" to the exercise of its commerce power) unusually strong, for to deny Congress that power would deny Congress the power effectively to regulate *private* conduct. At the same time they make a state's need to exercise sovereign immunity unusually weak, for the state is unlikely to *have to* supply what private firms already supply, nor may it fairly demand special treatment, even to protect the public purse, when it does so. Neither can one easily imagine what the Constitution's founders would have thought about the assertion of sovereign immunity in this special context. These considerations, differing in kind or degree from those that would support a general congressional "abrogation" power, indicate that *Parden*'s holding is sound, irrespective of this Court's decisions in Seminole Tribe of Fla. v. Florida, 517 U.S. 44 (1996), and Alden v. Maine, 527 U.S. 706 (1999). . . .

The majority is . . . wrong to say that this Court has "narrowed" *Parden* in its "subsequent opinions," at least in any way relevant to today's decision. *Parden* considered two separate issues: (1) Does Congress have the *power* to require a state to waive its immunity? (2) How *clearly* must Congress speak when it does so? The Court has narrowed *Parden* only in respect to the second issue, not the first; but today we are concerned only with the first. The Court in Employees of Dept. of Public Health and Welfare of Mo. v. Department of Public Health and Welfare of Mo., 411 U.S. 279 (1973), for example, discussed whether Congress *had, or had not*, "lifted" sovereign immunity, not whether it *could, or could not*, have done so. . . . In short, except for those in today's majority, no member of this Court had ever questioned the holding of *Parden* that the Court today discards because it cannot find "merit in attempting to salvage any remnant of it."

Parden had never been questioned because, *Seminole Tribe* or not, it still makes sense. The line the Court today rejects has been drawn by this Court to place states outside the ordinary dormant commerce clause rules when they act as "market participants." And Congress has drawn this same line in the related context of foreign state sovereign immunity. 28 U.S.C. § 1605(a)(2). . . . Indeed, given the widely accepted view among modern nations that when a state engages in ordinary commercial activity sovereign immunity has no significant role to play, it is today's holding, not *Parden*, that creates the legal "anomaly."

II

I resist all the more strongly the Court's extension of *Seminole Tribe* in this case because, although I accept this Court's pre-*Seminole Tribe* sovereign immunity decisions, I am not yet ready to adhere to the proposition of law set forth in *Seminole Tribe*. In my view, Congress does possess the authority to abrogate a state's sovereign immunity where "necessary and proper" to the exercise of an article I power. My reasons include those that Justices Stevens and Souter already have described in detail [in their *Seminole Tribe* dissents]. . . .

By interpreting the Constitution as rendering immutable this one common-law doctrine (sovereign immunity), *Seminole Tribe* threatens the nation's ability to enact economic legislation needed for the future in much the way that Lochner v. New York, 198 U.S. 45 (1905), threatened the nation's ability to enact social legislation over 90 years ago. . . . The similarity to *Lochner* lies in the risk that *Seminole Tribe* and the Court's subsequent cases will deprive Congress of necessary legislative flexibility. Their rules will make it more difficult for Congress to create, for example, a decentralized system of individual private remedies, say a private remedial system needed to protect intellectual property, including computer-related educational materials, irrespective of the need for, or importance of, such a system in a 21st century advanced economy. Yet . . . Congress needs this kind of flexibility if it is to achieve one of federalism's basic objectives.

That basic objective should not be confused with the details of any particular federalist doctrine, for the contours of federalist doctrine have changed over the course of our nation's history. Thomas Jefferson's purchase of Louisiana, for example, reshaped the great debate about the need for a broad, rather than a literal, interpretation of federal powers; the Civil War effectively ended the claim of a state's right to "nullify" a federal law; the Second New Deal, and its ultimate judicial ratification, showed that federal and state legislative authority were not mutually exclusive; this Court's "civil rights" decisions clarified the protection against state infringement that the 14th amendment offers to basic human liberty. In each instance the content of specific federalist doctrines had to change to reflect the nation's changing needs (territorial expansion, the end of slavery, the Great Depression, and desegregation).

But those changing doctrines reflect at least one unchanging goal: the protection of liberty. Federalism helps to protect liberty not simply in our modern sense of helping the individual remain free of restraints imposed by a distant government, but more directly by promoting the sharing among citizens of governmental decisionmaking authority. . . .

In today's world, legislative flexibility is necessary if we are to protect this kind of liberty. Modern commerce and the technology upon which it rests needs large markets and seeks government large enough to secure trading rules that permit industry to compete in the global market place, to prevent pollution that crosses borders, and to assure adequate protection of health and safety by discouraging a regulatory "race to the bottom." Yet local control over local decisions remains necessary. Uniform regulatory decisions about, for example, chemical waste disposal, pesticides, or food labeling, will directly affect daily life in every locality. But they may reflect differing views among localities about the relative importance of the wage levels or environmental preferences that underlie them. Local control can take account of such concerns and help to maintain a sense of community despite global forces that threaten it. Federalism matters to ordinary citizens seeking to maintain a degree of control, a sense of community, in an increasingly interrelated and complex world.

Courts can remain sensitive to these needs when they interpret statutes and apply constitutional provisions, for example, the dormant commerce clause. But courts cannot easily draw the proper basic lines of authority. The proper local/national/international balance is often highly context specific. And judicial rules that would allocate power are often far too broad. Legislatures, however, can write laws that more specifically embody that balance. Specific regulatory schemes, for example, can draw lines that leave certain local authority untouched, or that involve states, local communities, or citizens directly through the grant of funds, powers, rights, or privileges. Depending upon context, Congress may encourage or require interaction among citizens working at various levels of government. That is why the modern substantive federalist problem demands a flexible, context-specific legislative response (and it does not help to constitutionalize an ahistoric view of sovereign immunity that, by freezing its remedial limitations, tends to place the state beyond the reach of law).

I recognize the possibility that Congress may achieve its objectives in other ways. Ex parte Young, 209 U.S. 123 (1908), is still available, though effective only where damages remedies are not important. Congress, too, might create a federal damages-collecting "enforcement" bureaucracy charged with responsibilities that Congress would prefer to place in the hands of states or private citizens. Or perhaps Congress will be able to achieve the results it seeks (including decentralization) by embodying the necessary state "waivers" in federal funding programs—in which case, the Court's decisions simply impose upon Congress the burden of rewriting legislation, for no apparent reason.

But none of these alternatives is satisfactory. Unfortunately, *Seminole Tribe*, and today's related decisions, separate one formal strand from the federalist skein—a strand that has been understood as anti-Republican since the time of Cicero—and they elevate that strand to the level of an immutable constitutional principle more akin to the thought of James I than of James Madison. They do so when the role sovereign immunity once played in helping to assure the states that their political independence would remain even after joining the union no longer holds center stage. They do so when a federal court's ability to enforce its judgment against a state is no longer a major concern. And they do so without adequate legal support grounded in either history or practical need. To the contrary, by making that doctrine immune from congressional article I modification, the Court makes it more difficult for Congress to decentralize governmental decisionmaking and to provide individual citizens, or local communities, with a variety of enforcement powers. By diminishing congressional flexibility to do so, the Court makes it somewhat more difficult to satisfy modern federalism's more important liberty-protecting needs. In this sense, it is counterproductive.

III

I do not know whether the state has engaged in false advertising or unfair competition as College Savings Bank alleges. But this case was dismissed at the threshold. Congress has clearly said that College Savings Bank may bring a Lanham Act suit in these circumstances. For the reasons set forth in this opinion, I believe Congress has the constitutional power so to provide. I would therefore reverse the judgment of the Court of Appeals.

Florida Prepaid Postsecondary Education Expense Board v. College Savings Bank

Supreme Court of the United States, 1999.
527 U.S. 627.

■ CHIEF JUSTICE REHNQUIST delivered the opinion of the Court.

In 1992, Congress amended the patent laws and expressly abrogated the states' sovereign immunity from claims of patent infringement. Respondent College Savings then sued the state of Florida for patent infringement, and the Court of Appeals held that Congress had validly abrogated the state's sovereign immunity from infringement suits pursuant to its authority under § 5 of the 14th amendment. We hold that, under City of Boerne v. Flores, 521 U.S. 507 (1997), the statute cannot be sustained as legislation enacted to enforce the guarantees of the 14th amendment's due process clause, and accordingly reverse the decision of the Court of Appeals.

I

Since 1987, respondent College Savings Bank, a New Jersey chartered savings bank located in Princeton, New Jersey, has marketed and sold certificates of deposit known as the CollegeSure CD, which are essentially annuity contracts for financing future college expenses. College Savings obtained a patent for its financing methodology, designed to guarantee investors sufficient funds to cover the costs of tuition for colleges. Petitioner Florida Prepaid Postsecondary Education Expenses Board (Florida Prepaid) is an entity created by the state of Florida that administers similar tuition prepayment contracts available to Florida residents and their children. College Savings claims that, in the course of administering its tuition prepayment program, Florida Prepaid directly and indirectly infringed College Savings' patent.

College Savings brought an infringement action under 35 U.S.C. § 271(a) against Florida Prepaid in the United States District Court for the District of New Jersey in November 1994. By the time College Savings filed its suit, Congress had already passed the Patent and Plant Variety Protection Remedy Clarification Act (Patent Remedy Act), 35 U.S.C. §§ 271(h), 296(a), ... to "clarify that States, instrumentalities of States, and officers and employees of States acting in their official capacity, are subject to suit in Federal court by any person for infringement of patents and plant variety protections." Pub. L. 102–560, preamble. ... Section 296(a) addresses the sovereign immunity issue ... specifically:

> "Any state, any instrumentality of a state, and any officer or employee of a state or instrumentality of a state acting in his official capacity, shall not be immune, under the 11th amendment of the Constitution of the United States or under any other doctrine of sovereign immunity, from suit in federal court by any person ... for infringement of a patent under section 271, or for any other violation under this title." ...

After this Court decided Seminole Tribe of Fla. v. Florida, 517 U.S. 44 (1996), Florida Prepaid moved to dismiss the action on the grounds of sovereign immunity. Florida Prepaid argued that the Patent Remedy Act was an unconstitutional attempt by Congress to use its article I powers to abrogate state sovereign immunity. College Savings responded that Congress had properly exercised its power pursuant to § 5 of the 14th amendment to enforce the guarantees of the due process clause in § 1 of the amendment. The United States intervened to defend the constitutionality of the statute. Agreeing with College Savings, the District Court denied Florida Prepaid's motion to dismiss, and the Federal Circuit affirmed. ...

II

... College Savings and the United States ... contend that Congress' enactment of the Patent Remedy Act validly abrogated the states' sovereign immunity. To determine the merits of this proposition, we must answer two questions: "first, whether Congress has 'unequivocally expressed its intent to abrogate the immunity,' ... and second, whether Congress has acted 'pursuant to a valid exercise of power.'" *Seminole Tribe*, supra, at 55. We agree with the parties and the Federal Circuit that in enacting the Patent Remedy Act, Congress has made its intention to abrogate the states' immunity " 'unmistakably clear in the language of the statute.' " *Dellmuth v. Muth*, 491 U.S. 223, 228 (1989). . . .

Whether Congress had the power to compel states to surrender their sovereign immunity for these purposes, however, is another matter. Congress justified the Patent Remedy Act under three sources of constitutional authority: the patent clause, art. I, § 8, cl. 8; the interstate commerce clause, art. I, § 8, cl. 3; and § 5 of the 14th amendment. . . . *Seminole Tribe* makes clear that Congress may not abrogate state sovereign immunity pursuant to its article I powers; hence the Patent Remedy Act cannot be sustained under either the commerce clause or the patent clause. . . .

Instead, College Savings and the United States argue that the Federal Circuit properly concluded that Congress enacted the Patent Remedy Act to secure the 14th amendment's protections against deprivations of property without due process of law. The 14th amendment provides in relevant part:

> "Section 1. . . . No State shall . . . deprive any person of life, liberty, or property, without due process of law. . . .
>
> Section 5. The Congress shall have power to enforce, by appropriate legislation, the provisions of this article."

. . . We have held that "the 'provisions of this article,' to which § 5 refers, include the due process clause of the 14th amendment." *City of Boerne v. Flores*, 521 U.S. at 519.

But the legislation must nonetheless be "appropriate" under § 5 as that term was construed in *City of Boerne*. . . . There, this Court held that the Religious Freedom Restoration Act of 1993 (RFRA), 42 U.S.C. § 2000bb et seq., exceeded Congress' authority under § 5 of the 14th amendment, insofar as RFRA was made applicable to the states. . . .

We thus held that for Congress to invoke § 5, it must identify conduct transgressing the 14th amendment's substantive provisions, and must tailor its legislative scheme to remedying or preventing such conduct. . . .

Can the Patent Remedy Act be viewed as remedial or preventive legislation aimed at securing the protections of the 14th amendment for patent owners? Following *City of Boerne*, we must first identify the 14th amendment "evil" or "wrong" that Congress intended to remedy, guided by the principle that the propriety of any § 5 legislation "must be judged with reference to the historical experience . . . it reflects." The underlying conduct at issue here is state infringement of patents and the use of sovereign immunity to deny patent owners compensation for the invasion of their patent rights. It is this conduct then—unremedied patent infringement by the states—that must give rise to the 14th amendment violation that Congress sought to redress in the Patent Remedy Act.

In enacting the Patent Remedy Act, however, Congress identified no pattern of patent infringement by the states, let alone a pattern of constitutional violations. . . . Though patents may be considered "property" for purposes of our analysis, the legislative record still provides little support for the proposition that Congress sought to remedy a 14th amendment violation in enacting the Patent Remedy Act. ... This Court has ... held that "in procedural due process claims, the deprivation by state action of a constitutionally protected interest ... is not in itself unconstitutional; what is unconstitutional is the deprivation of such an interest without due process of law." Zinermon v. Burch, 494 U.S. 113, 125 (1990) (emphasis deleted).

Thus, under the plain terms of the clause and the clear import of our precedent, a state's infringement of a patent, though interfering with a patent owner's right to exclude others, does not by itself violate the Constitution. Instead, only where the state provides no remedy, or only inadequate remedies, to injured patent owners for its infringement of their patent could a deprivation of property without due process result. See Parratt v. Taylor, 451 U.S. 527, 539–31 (1981).

Congress, however, barely considered the availability of state remedies for patent infringement and hence whether the states' conduct might have amounted to a constitutional violation under the 14th amendment. It did hear a limited amount of testimony to the effect that the remedies available in some states were uncertain.

The primary point made by these witnesses, however, was not that state remedies were constitutionally inadequate, but rather that they were less convenient than federal remedies, and might undermine the uniformity of patent law.

Congress itself said nothing about the existence or adequacy of state remedies in the statute or in the Senate Report, and made only a few fleeting references to state remedies in the House Report, essentially repeating the testimony of the witnesses. ...

The legislative record thus suggests that the Patent Remedy Act does not respond to a history of "widespread and persisting deprivation of constitutional rights" of the sort Congress has faced in enacting proper prophylactic § 5 legislation. *City of Boerne*, 521 U.S. at 526. Instead, Congress appears to have enacted this legislation in response to a handful of instances of state patent infringement that do not necessarily violate the Constitution. Though the lack of support in the legislative record is not determinative, identifying the targeted constitutional wrong or evil is still a critical part of our § 5 calculus because "strong measures appropriate to address one harm may be an unwarranted response to another, lesser one," id. at 530. Here, the record at best offers scant support for Congress' conclusion that states were depriving patent owners of property without due process of law by pleading sovereign immunity in federal-court patent actions.

Because of this lack, the provisions of the Patent Remedy Act are "so out of proportion to a supposed remedial or preventive object that [they] cannot be understood as responsive to, or designed to prevent, unconstitutional behavior." Id. at 532. . . .

The historical record and the scope of coverage therefore make it clear that the Patent Remedy Act cannot be sustained under § 5 of the 14th amendment. The examples of states avoiding liability for patent infringement by pleading sovereign immunity in a federal-court patent action are scarce enough, but any plausible argument that such action on the part of the state deprived patentees of property and left them without a remedy under state law is scarcer still. The statute's apparent and more basic aims were to provide a uniform remedy for patent infringement and to place states on the same footing as private parties under that regime. These are proper article I concerns, but that article does not give Congress the power to enact such legislation after *Seminole Tribe*.

The judgment of the Court of Appeals is reversed, and the case is remanded for proceedings consistent with this opinion.

It is so ordered.

■ JUSTICE STEVENS, with whom JUSTICE SOUTER, JUSTICE GINSBURG, and JUSTICE BREYER join, dissenting.

The Constitution vests Congress with plenary authority over patents and copyrights . . . This Court's recent decision in City of Boerne v. Flores, 521 U.S. 507 (1997), amply supports congressional authority to enact the Patent Remedy Act . . . . Before discussing *City of Boerne*, however, I shall comment briefly on the principle that undergirds all aspects of our patent system: national uniformity.

I

. . . Sound reasons support both Congress' authority over patents and its subsequent decision in 1800 to vest exclusive jurisdiction over patent infringement litigation in the federal courts. The substantive rules of law that are applied in patent infringement cases are entirely federal. . . . There is, accordingly, a strong federal interest in an interpretation of the patent statutes that is both uniform and faithful to the constitutional goals of stimulating invention and rewarding the disclosure of novel and useful advances in technology. Federal interests are threatened, not only by inadequate protection for patentees, but also when overprotection may have an adverse impact on a competitive economy. Therefore, consistency, uniformity, and familiarity with the extensive and relevant body of patent jurisprudence are matters of overriding significance in this area of the law. . . .

II

Our recent decision in *City of Boerne* sets out the general test for determining whether Congress has enacted "appropriate" legislation pursuant to § 5 of the 14th amendment. "There must be a congruence and proportionality between the injury to be prevented or remedied and the means adopted to that end." The first step of the inquiry, then, is to determine what injury Congress sought to prevent or remedy with the relevant legislation.

As the Court recognizes, Congress' authority under § 5 of the 14th amendment extends to enforcing the due process clause of that amendment. Congress decided, and I agree, that the Patent Remedy Act was a proper exercise of this power.

The Court acknowledges, as it must, that patents are property. . . . The question presented by this case . . . is whether the Patent Remedy Act, which clarified Congress' intent to subject state infringers to suit in federal court, may be applied to willful infringement.

As I read the Court's opinion, its negative answer to that question . . . relies entirely on perceived deficiencies in the evidence reviewed by Congress before it enacted the clarifying amendment. "In enacting the Patent Remedy Act . . . Congress identified no pattern of patent infringement by the states, let alone a pattern of constitutional violations."

It is quite unfair for the Court to strike down Congress' act based on an absence of findings supporting a requirement this Court had not yet articulated. The legislative history of the Patent Remedy Act makes it abundantly clear that Congress was attempting to hurdle the then-most-recent barrier this Court had erected in the 11th amendment course—the "clear statement" rule of Atascadero State Hospital v. Scanlon, 473 U.S. 234 (1985).

Nevertheless, Congress did hear testimony about inadequate state remedies for patent infringement when considering the Patent Remedy Act. . . . Congress heard other general testimony that state remedies would likely be insufficient to compensate inventors whose patents had been infringed. . . . In addition, Congress found that state infringement of patents was likely to increase. . . .

It is true that, when considering the Patent Remedy Act, Congress did not review the remedies available in each state for patent infringements and surmise what kind of recovery a plaintiff might obtain in a tort suit in all 50 jurisdictions. But, it is particularly ironic that the Court should view this fact as support for its holding. Given that Congress had long ago preempted state jurisdiction over patent infringement cases, it was surely reasonable for Congress to assume that such remedies simply did not exist. Furthermore, it is well known that not all states have waived their sovereign immunity from suit, and among those states that have, the contours of this waiver vary widely.

Even if such remedies might be available in theory, it would have been "appropriate" for Congress to conclude that they would not guarantee patentees due process in infringement actions against state defendants. State judges have never had the exposure to patent litigation that federal judges have experienced for decades, and, unlike infringement actions brought in federal district courts, their decisions would not be reviewable in the Court of Appeals for the Federal Circuit. Surely this Court would not undertake the task of reviewing every state court decision that arguably misapplied patent law. And even if 28 U.S.C. § 1338 is amended or construed to permit state courts to entertain infringement actions when a state is named as a defendant, given the Court's opinion in Alden v. Maine, 527 U.S. 706 (1999), it is by no means clear that state courts could be required to hear these cases at all. . . .

III

In my view, Congress had sufficient evidence of due process violations, whether actual or potential, to meet the requirement we expressed in *City of Boerne* that Congress can act under § 5 only to "remedy or prevent unconstitutional actions." See 521 U.S. at 519. The Court's opinion today threatens to read Congress' power to pass prophylactic legislation out of § 5 altogether; its holding is unsupported by *City of Boerne* and in fact conflicts with our reasoning in that case. . . .

By enacting [the Religious Freedom Restoration Act], Congress sought to change the meaning of the free exercise clause of the first amendment as it had been interpreted by this Court, rather than to remedy or to prevent violations of the clause as we had interpreted it. . . . The Patent Remedy Act, however, was passed to prevent future violations of due process, based on the substantiated fear that states would be unable or unwilling to provide adequate remedies for their own violations of patent-holders' rights. . . .

City of Boerne also identified a "proportionality" component to "appropriate" legislation under § 5. Our opinion expressly recognized that "preventive rules are sometimes appropriate" if there is "a congruence between the means used and the ends to be achieved. . . . Strong measures appropriate to address one harm may be an unwarranted response to another, lesser one." . . .

Again, the contrast between RFRA and the act at issue in this case could not be more stark. The sole purpose of this amendment is to abrogate the states' sovereign immunity as a defense to a charge of patent infringement. It has no impact whatsoever on any substantive rule of state law, but merely effectuates settled federal policy to confine patent infringement litigation to federal judges. There is precise congruence between "the means used" (abrogation of sovereign immunity in this narrow category of cases) and "the ends to be achieved" (elimination of the risk that the defense of sovereign immunity will deprive some patentees of property without due process of law).

That congruence is equally precise whether infringement of patents by state actors is rare or frequent. If they are indeed unusual, the statute will operate only in those rare cases. But if such infringements are common, or should become common as state activities in the commercial arena increase, the impact of the statute will likewise expand in precise harmony with the growth of the problem that Congress anticipated and sought to prevent. In either event the statute will have no impact on the states' enforcement of their own laws. None of the concerns that underlay our decision in *City of Boerne* are even remotely implicated in this case. ...

IV

For these reasons, I am convinced that the 1992 act should be upheld even if full respect is given to the Court's recent cases cloaking the states with increasing protection from congressional legislation. I do, however, note my continuing dissent from the Court's aggressive sovereign immunity jurisprudence; today, this Court once again demonstrates itself to be the champion of states' rights. In this case, it seeks to guarantee rights the states themselves did not express any particular desire in possessing: during Congress' hearings on the Patent Remedy Act, although invited to do so, the states chose not to testify in opposition to the abrogation of their immunity.

The statute that the Court invalidates today was only one of several "clear statements" that Congress enacted in response to the decision in *Atascadero State Hospital*, supra. In each of those clarifications Congress was fully justified in assuming that it had ample authority to abrogate sovereign immunity defenses to federal claims, an authority that the Court squarely upheld in Pennsylvania v. Union Gas Co., 491 U.S. 1 (1989). It was that *holding*—not just the "plurality opinion"—that was overruled in Seminole Tribe of Fla. v. Florida, 517 U.S. 44 (1996). The full reach of that case's dramatic expansion of the judge-made doctrine of sovereign immunity is unpredictable; its dimensions are defined only by the present majority's perception of constitutional penumbras rather than constitutional text. Until this expansive and judicially crafted protection of states' rights runs its course, I shall continue to register my agreement with the views expressed in the *Seminole* dissents and in the scholarly commentary on that case.

I respectfully dissent.[a]

---

[a]. For early analysis of the effect of *Seminole Tribe* on federal remedies for misappropriation of intellectual property, see Christina Bohannon and Thomas F. Cotter, When the State Steals Ideas: Is the Abrogation of State Sovereign Immunity from Federal Infringement Claims Constitutional in Light of *Seminole Tribe*?, 67 Fordham L. Rev. 1435 (1999) (correctly anticipating that federal attempts to authorize private infringement actions against states exceeds federal § 5 power); Paul J. Heald and Michael L. Wells, Remedies for the Misappropriation of Intellectual Property by State and Municipal Governments Before and After *Seminole Tribe*: The Eleventh Amendment and Other Immunity Doctrines, 55 W. & L.L. Rev. 849 (1998) (concluding, notwithstanding the doctrinal complexity, that federal law will provide remedies for most violations of intellectual property rights). [Footnote by eds.]

NOTES ON THE 1999 DECISIONS

1. ***Kimel v. Florida Board of Regents.*** The *College Savings Bank* cases were followed in Kimel v. Florida Board of Regents, 528 U.S. 62 (2000), which held that Congress could not constitutionally authorize damage actions against states for violation of the Age Discrimination in Employment Act. As originally passed in 1967, that statute covered only private employers. A 1974 enactment, however, extended the statute to public agencies, including states. A majority of the Supreme Court, excepting only Justices Thomas and Kennedy, found the requisite "clear statement" to authorize damage actions against states. In an opinion by Justice O'Connor, joined by Chief Justice Rehnquist and by Justices Scalia, Kennedy, and Thomas, the Court then held that the Age Discrimination in Employment Act, although undoubtedly within Congress's article I power, was not "appropriate legislation" under § 5 of the 14th amendment. The Court reasoned that since age discrimination generally did not violate equal protection (unless irrational), legislation to prohibit age discrimination in employment could not be justified as an attempt as "responsive to, or designed to prevent, unconstitutional behavior." City of Boerne v. Flores, 521 U.S. 507, 532 (1997). Justices Stevens, Souter, Ginsburg, and Breyer dissented on grounds of continued disagreement with *Seminole Tribe* and reiterated their view that article I power sufficed to override state sovereign immunity against private suits.

2. Bibliography. For an interesting reaction to *Alden* and the *Florida Prepaid* cases, see Ann Woolhandler, Old Property, New Property, and Sovereign Immunity, 75 Notre Dame L. Rev. 919 (2000). Woolhandler provides a historical defense of these decisions, arguing that due process requires damages remedies (either against states or state officers) for deprivations of "old property" but not necessarily for deprivations of "new property." "Old property" is shorthand for traditional property interests, while "new property" refers to "statutorily created expectations of compliance with federal law." While all "property" might be entitled to some due process protection, only traditional property interests necessarily trigger a constitutional right to compensation. On this view, the Supreme Court's decisions upholding state sovereign immunity against claims for violations of "new property" rights can be defended. For criticism of Woolhandler's approach, see Vicki C. Jackson, Principle and Compromise in Constitutional Adjudication: The Eleventh Amendment and State Sovereign Immunity, 75 Notre Dame L. Rev. 953 (2000).

For additional analysis of *Alden* in the same issue of the Notre Dame Law Review, see James E. Pfander, Once More Unto the Breach: Eleventh Amendment Scholarship and the Court, 75 Notre Dame L. Rev. 817 (2000) (introducing a symposium on state sovereign immunity and exploring the implications of *Alden* for Eleventh Amendment scholarship); Carlos Manuel Vázquez, Eleventh Amendment Schizophrenia, 75 Notre Dame L. Rev. 859 (2000) (exploring the "schizophrenia" of saying on the one hand that state sovereign immunity from private suits is constitutionally fundamental and beyond Congressional control and allowing on the other hand unlimited federal enforcement actions against states, as well as private suits against state officers); Daniel J. Meltzer, State Sovereign Immunity: Five Authors in Search of a Theory, 75 Notre Dame L. Rev. 1011 (2000) (criticizing the Court's efforts to promote federalism by limiting the enforcement of valid federal laws against states rather than by restricting the reach of federal legislative authority as "fail[ing] to promote any coherent conception of states' rights or state autonomy while harming legitimate national objectives"); John E. Nowak, The Gang of Five & the Second Coming of an Anti–Reconstruction Supreme Court, 75 Notre Dame L. Rev. 1091 (2000) (comparing recent decisions to those that dismantled or curtailed Reconstruction-era legislation); Suzanna Sherry, States Are People Too, 75 Notre Dame L. Rev. 1121 (2000) (criticizing analogies between state sovereign immunity and individuals rights); Daniel A. Farber, Pledging a New Allegiance: An Essay on Sovereignty and the New Federalism, 75 Notre Dame L. Rev. 1133 (2000) (examining *Alden* as reflecting a "new federalism" credo of state sovereignty); John V. Orth, History and the Eleventh Amendment, 75 Notre Dame L. Rev. 1147 (2000) (examining the use of history to justify various positions on state sovereign immunity); Jay Tidmarsh, A Dialogic Defense of *Alden*, 75 Notre Dame L. Rev. 1161 (2000) (defending the result in *Alden* as "within the range of permissible constitutional choice").

For other interesting reactions to these cases, see Pamela S. Karlan, The Irony of Immunity: The Eleventh Amendment, Irreparable Injury, and Section 1983, 53 Stan. L. Rev. 1311 (2001) (pointing out that precluding money damages for the victims of violations of federal statutes creates "irreparable injury" that would justify injunctive relief and suggesting that injunctions against state agencies are potentially broader and more intrusive than damage actions); Carlos Manuel Vázquez, Sovereign Immunity, Due Process, and the *Alden* Trilogy, 109 Yale L.J. 1927 (2000) (suggesting that *Florida Prepaid v. College Savings Bank* may have undermined *Alden* by interpreting due process to require that states provide remedies when they intentionally deprive persons of (at least some forms of) liberty or property in violation of federal law); Jonathan R. Siegel, Congress's Power to Authorize Suits Against States, 68 Geo. Wash. L. Rev. 44 (1999) (arguing that Congress could avoid the restrictions of Seminole Tribe and Alden by authorizing the federal government to espouse claims by private parties in suits against states).

Also see Christina Bohannan & Thomas F. Cotter, When the State Steals Ideas: Is the Abrogation of State Sovereign Immunity from Federal Infringement Claims Constitutional in Light of *Seminole Tribe*?, 67 Fordham L. Rev. 1435 (1999) (a predictive analysis of the issues presented in the *Florida Prepaid* decisions); Judith Olans Brown & Peter D. Enrich, Nostalgic Federalism, 28 Hastings Const. L. Q. 1 (2002) (criticizing *Kimel*); Melissa Hart, Conflating Scope of Right with Standard of Review: the

Supreme Court's "Strict Scrutiny" of Congressional Efforts to Enforce the Fourteenth Amendment, 46 Vill. L. Rev. 1091 (2001) (criticizing *Kimel*); Paul J. Heald & Michael L. Wells, Remedies for the Misappropriation of Intellectual Property by State and Municipal Governments Before and After *Seminole Tribe*: The Eleventh Amendment and Other Immunity Doctrines, 55 W. & L. L. Rev. 849 (1998) (analyzing federal remedies for violations of intellectual property rights before the *Florida Prepaid* cases); Calvin Massey, Federalism and the Rehnquist Court, 53 Hastings L. J. 431 (2002) (examining six main facets of the Court's approach to federalism).

Alden and related decisions continue to generate enormous commentary, most of which is highly critical. For a selection of recent articles, see Daan Braveman, Enforcement of Federal Rights Against States: *Alden* and Federalism Non–Sense, 49 Am. U. L. Rev. 611 (2000) (identifying various strands of federalism and condemning *Alden* and related decisions as "anachronistic and ill-designed to protect national interests"); Erwin Chemerinsky, The Hypocrisy of *Alden v. Maine*: Judicial Review, Sovereign Immunity, and the Rehnquist Court, 33 Loy. L. Rev. 1283 (2000) (condemning the Court's preference for state power over individual rights as "simply an unacceptable value choice in the American system of government"); Melvin R. Durchslag, Accommodation by Declaration, 33 Loy. L. Rev. 1375 (2000) (examining *Alden* and finding a "general distrust of federal legislative power coupled with a reborn faith in state government bound together with a constitutional ribbon that we call federalism"); Michael Wells, Available State Remedies: and the Fourteenth Amendment: Comments on *Florida Prepaid v. College Savings Bank*, 33 Loy. L. Rev. 1665 (2000) (focusing on the question of how one determines whether state remedies for violations of federal rights are "available and adequate"); James G. Wilson, The Eleventh Amendment Cases: Going "Too Far" with Judicial Neofederalism 33 Loy. L. Rev. 1687 (2000) (criticizing the Court's recent Eleventh Amendment decisions as "some of its worst in decades"); Daniel J. Meltzer, Overcoming Immunity: The Case of Federal Regulation of Intellectual Property, 53 Stan. L. Rev. 1331 (2001) (outlining strategies for enforcement of federal intellectual property statutes in light of Eleventh Amendment decisions); Vicki C. Jackson, Holistic Interpretation: *Fitzpatrick v. Bitzer* and Our Bifurcated Constitution, 53 Stan. L. Rev. 1259 (2001) (suggesting that the Fourteenth Amendment should be construed to have broadened the original grants of federal legislative power under Article I, with consequent expansion of Congress's ability to override state sovereign immunity); William J. Rich, Privileges or Immunities: The Missing Link in Establishing Congressional Power to Abrogate State Eleventh Amendment Immunity, 28 Hastings C.L.Q. 235 (2001) (arguing that the Privileges and Immunities Clause of the Fourteenth Amendment establishes Congress's power to override state sovereign immunity in protection of rights validly granted under federal law); Louise Weinberg, Of Sovereignty and Union: The Legends of *Alden*, 76 Notre Dame L. Rev. 1113 (2001) (extensively criticizing *Alden* and related decisions as intellectually unsupportable and misguided); Mark Strasser, *Chisholm*, the Eleventh Amendment, and Sovereign Immunity: On *Alden*'s Return to Confederation Principles, 28 Fla. St. L. Rev. 605 (2001) (arguing that the *Alden*'s understanding of state sovereign immunity against federal claims is "precisely what the Framers were attempting to displace when arguing for the ratification of the Constitution").

For rare expressions of qualified support for the Court's decisions, see Ernest A. Young, State Sovereign Immunity and the Future of Federalism, 1999 Sup. Ct. Rev. 1 (offering "a critique of the Court's state sovereign immunity decisions from a perspective that is highly sympathetic to states' rights and interests"); Roderick M. Hills, Jr., The Eleventh Amendment as Curb on Bureaucratic Power, 53 Stan. L. Rev. 1225 (2001) (suggesting that a ban on damages liability and a consequent reliance on injunctions might have the salutary effect of allowing state legislatures to exert better control over state agencies).

Additionally, there are several recent articles that examine the impact of the Court's state sovereign immunity decisions on specific areas of economic regulation or property rights. See, e.g., William A. Araiza, *Alden v. Maine* and the Web of Environmental Law, 33 Loy. L. Rev. 1513 (2000); Robert G. Bone, From Property to Contract: The Eleventh Amendment and University—Private Sector Intellectual Property Relationships, 33 Loy. L. Rev. 1467 (2000); Peter S. Menell, Economic Implications of State Sovereign Immunity from Infringement of Federal Intellectual Property Rights, 33 Loy. L. Rev. 1399 (2000).

Board of Trustees of the University of Alabama v. Garrett

Supreme Court of the United States, 2001.
531 U.S. 356.

■ CHIEF JUSTICE REHNQUIST delivered the opinion of the Court.

We decide here whether employees of the State of Alabama may recover money damages by reason of the State's failure to comply with the provisions of Title I of the Americans with Disabilities Act of 1990 (ADA or Act), 42 U.S.C. §§ 12111–12117.[1] We hold that such suits are barred by the Eleventh Amendment.

1. Respondents' complaints in the United States District Court alleged violations of both Title I and Title II of the ADA.... Though the briefs of the parties discuss both sections in their constitutional arguments, no party has briefed the question whether Title II of the ADA, dealing with the "services, programs, or activities of a public entity," 42 U.S.C. § 12132, is available for claims of employment discrimination when Title I of the ADA expressly deals with that subject. We are not disposed to decide the constitutional issue whether Title II, which has somewhat different remedial provisions from Title I, is appropriate legislation under § 5 of the Fourteenth Amendment when the parties have not favored us with briefing on the statutory question. To the extent the Court granted

The ADA prohibits certain employers, including the States, from "discriminating against a qualified individual with a disability because of the disability of such individual in regard to job application procedures, the hiring, advancement, or discharge of employees, employee compensation, job training, and other terms, conditions, and privileges of employment." §§ 12112(a), 12111(2), (5), (7). To this end, the Act requires employers to "make reasonable accommodations to the known physical or mental limitations of an otherwise qualified individual with a disability who is an applicant or employee, unless [the employer] can demonstrate that the accommodation would impose an undue hardship on the operation of the [employer's] business." § 12112(b)(5)(A).

"Reasonable accommodation" may include—

> (A) making existing facilities used by employees readily accessible to and usable by individuals with disabilities; and (B) job restructuring, part-time or modified work schedules, reassignment to a vacant position, acquisition or modification of equipment or devices, appropriate adjustment or modifications of examinations, training materials or policies, the provision of qualified readers or interpreters, and other similar accommodations for individuals with disabilities. § 12111(9).

The Act also prohibits employers from "utilizing standards, criteria, or methods of administration . . . that have the effect of discrimination on the basis of disability." § 12112(b)(3)(A).

The Act defines "disability" to include "(A) a physical or mental impairment that substantially limits one or more of the major life activities of such individual; (B) a record of such an impairment; or (C) being regarded as having such an impairment." § 12102(2). A disabled individual is otherwise "qualified" if he or she, "with or without reasonable accommodation, can perform the essential functions of the employment position that such individual holds or desires." § 12111(8).

Respondent Patricia Garrett, a registered nurse, was employed as the Director of Nursing, OB/Gyn/Neonatal Services, for the University of Alabama in Birmingham Hospital. In 1994, Garrett was diagnosed with breast cancer and subsequently underwent a lumpectomy, radiation treatment, and chemotherapy. Garrett's treatments required her to take substantial leave from work. Upon returning to work in July 1995, Garrett's supervisor informed Garrett that she would have to give up her Director position. Garrett then applied for and received a transfer to another, lower paying position as a nurse manager.

Respondent Milton Ash worked as a security officer for the Alabama Department of Youth Services (Department). Upon commencing this em-

---

certiorari on the question whether respondents may sue their state employers for damages under Title II of the ADA, see this Court's Rule 24.1(a), that portion of the writ is dismissed as improvidently granted.

ployment, Ash informed the Department that he suffered from chronic asthma and that his doctor recommended he avoid carbon monoxide and cigarette smoke, and Ash requested that the Department modify his duties to minimize his exposure to these substances. Ash was later diagnosed with sleep apnea and requested, again pursuant to his doctor's recommendation, that he be reassigned to daytime shifts to accommodate his condition. Ultimately, the Department granted none of the requested relief. Shortly after Ash filed a discrimination claim with the Equal Employment Opportunity Commission, he noticed that his performance evaluations were lower than those he had received on previous occasions.

Garrett and Ash filed separate lawsuits in the District Court, both seeking money damages under the ADA. Petitioners moved for summary judgment, claiming that the ADA exceeds Congress' authority to abrogate the State's Eleventh Amendment immunity. In a single opinion disposing of both cases, the District Court agreed with petitioners' position and granted their motions for summary judgment. The cases were consolidated on appeal to the Eleventh Circuit. The Court of Appeals reversed [holding] that the ADA validly abrogates the States' Eleventh Amendment immunity.

We granted certiorari to resolve a split among the Courts of Appeals on the question whether an individual may sue a State for money damages in federal court under the ADA.

I

... We have recognized ... that Congress may abrogate the States' Eleventh Amendment immunity when it both unequivocally intends to do so and "acts pursuant to a valid grant of constitutional authority." Kimel v. Florida Bd. of Regents, 528 U.S. 62, 73 (2000). The first of these requirements is not in dispute here. See 42 U.S.C. § 12202 ("A State shall not be immune under the eleventh amendment to the Constitution of the United States from an action in [a] Federal or State court of competent jurisdiction for a violation of this chapter"). The question, then, is whether Congress acted within its constitutional authority by subjecting the States to suits in federal court for money damages under the ADA.

Congress may not, of course, base its abrogation of the States' Eleventh Amendment immunity upon the powers enumerated in Article I. See Kimel, supra, at 79 ("Under our firmly established precedent then, if the [Age Discrimination in Employment Act of 1967] rests solely on Congress' Article I commerce power, the private petitioners in today's cases cannot maintain their suits against their state employers"). In Fitzpatrick v. Bitzer, 427 U.S. 445 (1976), however, we held that "the Eleventh Amendment, and the principle of state sovereignty which it embodies, are necessarily limited by the enforcement provisions of § 5 of the Fourteenth Amendment." Id. at 456 (internal citation omitted). As a result, we concluded, Congress may subject nonconsenting States to suit in federal court when it does so pursuant to a valid exercise of its § 5 power. Our cases have adhered to this proposition. Accordingly, the ADA can apply to the States only to the extent that the statute is appropriate § 5 legislation.[3]

Section 1 of the Fourteenth Amendment provides, in relevant part:

> No State shall make or enforce any law which shall abridge the privileges or immunities of citizens of the United States; nor shall any State deprive any person of life, liberty, or property, without due process of law; nor deny to any person within its jurisdiction the equal protection of the laws.

Section 5 of the Fourteenth Amendment grants Congress the power to enforce the substantive guarantees contained in § 1 by enacting "appropriate legislation." See City of Boerne v. Flores, 521 U.S. 507, 536 (1997). Congress is not limited to mere legislative repetition of this Court's constitutional jurisprudence. "Rather, Congress' power 'to enforce' the Amendment includes the authority both to remedy and to deter violation of rights guaranteed thereunder by prohibiting a somewhat broader swath of conduct, including that which is not itself forbidden by the Amendment's text." *Kimel*, supra, at 81; *City of Boerne*, supra, at 536.

City of Boerne also confirmed, however, the long-settled principle that it is the responsibility of this Court, not Congress, to define the substance of constitutional guarantees. Accordingly, § 5 legislation reaching beyond the scope of § 1's actual guarantees must exhibit "congruence and proportionality between the injury to be prevented or remedied and the means adopted to that end." Id. at 520.

II

The first step in applying these now familiar principles is to identify with some precision the scope of the constitutional right at issue. Here, that inquiry requires us to examine the limitations § 1 of the Fourteenth Amendment places upon States' treatment of the disabled. As we did last Term in *Kimel*, see 528 U.S. at 83, we look to our prior decisions under the Equal Protection Clause dealing with this issue.

In Cleburne v. Cleburne Living Center, Inc., 473 U.S. 432 (1985), we considered an equal protection challenge to a city ordinance requiring a special use permit for the operation of a group home for the mentally retarded. The specific question before us was whether the Court of Appeals had erred by holding that mental retardation qualified as a "quasi-suspect" classification under our equal protection jurisprudence. We answered that question in the affirmative, concluding instead that such legislation incurs only the minimum "rational-basis" review applicable to general social and economic legislation.[4] In a statement that today seems quite prescient, we explained that

---

3. It is clear that Congress intended to invoke § 5 as one of its bases for enacting the ADA. See 42 U.S.C. § 12101(b)(4).

4. Applying the basic principles of rationality review, *Cleburne* struck down the city ordinance in question. The Court's reasoning was that the city's purported justifica-

if the large and amorphous class of the mentally retarded were deemed quasi-suspect for the reasons given by the Court of Appeals, it would be difficult to find a principled way to distinguish a variety of other groups who have perhaps immutable disabilities setting them off from others, who cannot themselves mandate the desired legislative responses, and who can claim some degree of prejudice from at least part of the public at large. One need mention in this respect only the aging, the disabled, the mentally ill, and the infirm. We are reluctant to set out on that course, and we decline to do so.

Under rational-basis review, where a group possesses "distinguishing characteristics relevant to interests the State has the authority to implement," a State's decision to act on the basis of those differences does not give rise to a constitutional violation. Id. at 441. "Such a classification cannot run afoul of the Equal Protection Clause if there is a rational relationship between the disparity of treatment and some legitimate governmental purpose." Heller v. Doe, 509 U.S. 312, 320 (1993). Moreover, the State need not articulate its reasoning at the moment a particular decision is made. Rather, the burden is upon the challenging party to negative "'any reasonably conceivable state of facts that could provide a rational basis for the classification.'" Heller, supra, at 320 (quoting FCC v. Beach Communications, Inc., 508 U.S. 307, 313 (1993)).

Justice Breyer suggests that *Cleburne* stands for the broad proposition that state decisionmaking reflecting "negative attitudes" or "fear" necessarily runs afoul of the Fourteenth Amendment. Although such biases may often accompany irrational (and therefore unconstitutional) discrimination, their presence alone does not a constitutional violation make. As we noted in *Cleburne*: "Mere negative attitudes, or fear, *unsubstantiated by factors which are properly cognizable* in a zoning proceeding, are not permissible bases for treating a home for the mentally retarded differently...." Id. at 448 (emphasis added). This language, read in context, simply states the unremarkable and widely acknowledged tenet of this Court's equal protection jurisprudence that state action subject to rational-basis scrutiny does not violate the Fourteenth Amendment when it "rationally furthers the purpose identified by the State." Massachusetts Bd. of Retirement v. Murgia, 427 U.S. 307, 314 (1976) (per curiam).

Thus, the result of *Cleburne* is that States are not required by the Fourteenth Amendment to make special accommodations for the disabled, so long as their actions towards such individuals are rational. They could quite hardheadedly—and perhaps hardheartedly—hold to job-qualification

tions for the ordinance made no sense in light of how the city treated other groups similarly situated in relevant respects. Although the group home for the mentally retarded was required to obtained a special use permit, apartment houses, other multiple-family dwellings, retirement homes, nursing homes, sanitariums, hospitals, boarding houses, fraternity and sorority houses, and dormitories were not subject to the ordinance.

requirements which do not make allowance for the disabled. If special accommodations for the disabled are to be required, they have to come from positive law and not through the Equal Protection Clause.[5]

III

Once we have determined the metes and bounds of the constitutional right in question, we examine whether Congress identified a history and pattern of unconstitutional employment discrimination by the States against the disabled. Just as § 1 of the Fourteenth Amendment applies only to actions committed "under color of state law," Congress' § 5 authority is appropriately exercised only in response to state transgressions. The legislative record of the ADA, however, simply fails to show that Congress did in fact identify a pattern of irrational state discrimination in employment against the disabled.

Respondents contend that the inquiry as to unconstitutional discrimination should extend not only to States themselves, but to units of local governments, such as cities and counties. All of these, they say, are "state actors" for purposes of the Fourteenth Amendment. This is quite true, but the Eleventh Amendment does not extend its immunity to units of local government. See Lincoln County v. Luning, 133 U.S. 529, 530 (1890). These entities are subject to private claims for damages under the ADA without Congress' ever having to rely on § 5 of the Fourteenth Amendment to render them so. It would make no sense to consider constitutional violations on their part, as well as by the States themselves, when only the States are the beneficiaries of the Eleventh Amendment.

Congress made a general finding in the ADA that "historically, society has tended to isolate and segregate individuals with disabilities, and, despite some improvements, such forms of discrimination against individuals with disabilities continue to be a serious and pervasive social problem." 42 U.S.C. § 12101(a)(2). The record assembled by Congress includes many instances to support such a finding. But the great majority of these incidents do not deal with the activities of States.

Respondents in their brief cite half a dozen examples from the record that did involve States. A department head at the University of North Carolina refused to hire an applicant for the position of health administrator because he was blind; similarly, a student at a state university in South Dakota was denied an opportunity to practice teach because the dean at that time was convinced that blind people could not teach in public schools. A microfilmer at the Kansas Department of Transportation was fired because he had epilepsy; deaf workers at the University of Oklahoma were paid a lower salary than those who could hear. The Indiana State Person-

---

5. It is worth noting that by the time that Congress enacted the ADA in 1990, every State in the Union had enacted such measures....

nel Office informed a woman with a concealed disability that she should not disclose it if she wished to obtain employment.[6]

Several of these incidents undoubtedly evidence an unwillingness on the part of state officials to make the sort of accommodations for the disabled required by the ADA. Whether they were irrational under our decision in *Cleburne* is more debatable, particularly when the incident is described out of context. But even if it were to be determined that each incident upon fuller examination showed unconstitutional action on the part of the State, these incidents taken together fall far short of even suggesting the pattern of unconstitutional discrimination on which § 5 legislation must be based. See *Kimel*, 528 U.S. at 89–91; *City of Boerne*, 521 U.S. at 530–31. Congress, in enacting the ADA, found that "some 43,000,-000 Americans have one or more physical or mental disabilities." 42 U.S.C. § 12101(a)(1). In 1990, the States alone employed more than 4.5 million people. U.S. Dept. of Commerce, Bureau of Census, Statistical Abstract of the United States 338 (119th ed. 1999) (Table 534). It is telling, we think, that given these large numbers, Congress assembled only such minimal evidence of unconstitutional state discrimination in employment against the disabled.

Justice Breyer maintains that Congress applied Title I of the ADA to the States in response to a host of incidents representing unconstitutional state discrimination in employment against persons with disabilities. A close review of the relevant materials, however, undercuts that conclusion. Justice Breyer's Appendix C consists not of legislative findings, but of unexamined, anecdotal accounts of "adverse, disparate treatment by state officials." Of course, as we have already explained, "adverse, disparate treatment" often does not amount to a constitutional violation where rational-basis scrutiny applies. These accounts, moreover, were submitted not directly to Congress but to the Task Force on the Rights and Empowerment of Americans with Disabilities, which made no findings on the subject of state discrimination in employment.[7] See the Task Force's Report entitled From ADA to Empowerment (Oct. 12, 1990). And, had Congress truly understood this information as reflecting a pattern of unconstitutional behavior by the States, one would expect some mention of that conclusion in the Act's legislative findings. There is none. See 42 U.S.C. § 12101.

---

6. The record does show that some States, adopting the tenets of the eugenics movement of the early part of this century, required extreme measures such as sterilization of persons suffering from hereditary mental disease. These laws were upheld against constitutional attack 70 years ago in Buck v. Bell, 274 U.S. 200 (1927). But there is no indication that any State had persisted in requiring such harsh measures as of 1990 when the ADA was adopted.

7. Only a small fraction of the anecdotes Justice Breyer identifies in his Appendix C relate to state discrimination against the disabled in employment.... The overwhelming majority of these accounts pertain to alleged discrimination by the States in the provision of public services and public accommodations, which areas are addressed in Titles II and III of the ADA.

Although Justice Breyer would infer from Congress' general conclusions regarding societal discrimination against the disabled that the States had likewise participated in such action, the House and Senate committee reports on the ADA flatly contradict this assertion. After describing the evidence presented to the Senate Committee on Labor and Human Resources and its subcommittee (including the Task Force Report upon which the dissent relies), the Committee's report reached, among others, the following conclusion: "Discrimination still persists in such critical areas as *employment in the private sector*, public accommodations, public services, transportation, and telecommunications." S. Rep. No. 101–116, p. 6 (1989) (emphasis added). The House Committee on Education and Labor, addressing the ADA's employment provisions, reached the same conclusion: "After extensive review and analysis over a number of Congressional sessions, . . . there exists a compelling need to establish a clear and comprehensive Federal prohibition of discrimination on the basis of disability in the areas of *employment in the private sector*, public accommodations, public services, transportation, and telecommunications." H. R. Rep. No. 101–485, pt. 2 p. 28 (1990) (emphasis added). Thus, not only is the inference Justice Breyer draws unwarranted, but there is also strong evidence that Congress' failure to mention States in its legislative findings addressing discrimination in employment reflects that body's judgment that no pattern of unconstitutional state action had been documented.

Even were it possible to squeeze out of these examples a pattern of unconstitutional discrimination by the States, the rights and remedies created by the ADA against the States would raise the same sort of concerns as to congruence and proportionality as were found in *City of Boerne*, supra. For example, whereas it would be entirely rational (and therefore constitutional) for a state employer to conserve scarce financial resources by hiring employees who are able to use existing facilities, the ADA requires employers to "make existing facilities used by employees readily accessible to and usable by individuals with disabilities." 42 U.S.C. §§ 12112(5)(B), 12111(9). The ADA does except employers from the "reasonable accommodation" requirement where the employer "can demonstrate that the accommodation would impose an undue hardship on the operation of the business of such covered entity." § 12112(b)(5)(A). However, even with this exception, the accommodation duty far exceeds what is constitutionally required in that it makes unlawful a range of alternate responses that would be reasonable but would fall short of imposing an "undue burden" upon the employer. The Act also makes it the employer's duty to prove that it would suffer such a burden, instead of requiring (as the Constitution does) that the complaining party negate reasonable bases for the employer's decision.

The ADA also forbids "utilizing standards, criteria, or methods of administration" that disparately impact the disabled, without regard to whether such conduct has a rational basis. § 12112(b)(3)(A). Although disparate impact may be relevant evidence of racial discrimination, see

Washington v. Davis, 426 U.S. 229, 239 (1976), such evidence alone is insufficient even where the Fourteenth Amendment subjects state action to strict scrutiny.

The ADA's constitutional shortcomings are apparent when the Act is compared to Congress' efforts in the Voting Rights Act of 1965 to respond to a serious pattern of constitutional violations. In South Carolina v. Katzenbach, 383 U.S. 301 (1966), we considered whether the Voting Rights Act was "appropriate" legislation to enforce the Fifteenth Amendment's protection against racial discrimination in voting. Concluding that it was a valid exercise of Congress' enforcement power under § 2 of the Fifteenth Amendment, we noted that "before enacting the measure, Congress explored with great care the problem of racial discrimination in voting."

In that Act, Congress documented a marked pattern of unconstitutional action by the States. State officials, Congress found, routinely applied voting tests in order to exclude African-American citizens from registering to vote. Congress also determined that litigation had proved ineffective and that there persisted an otherwise inexplicable 50-percentage-point gap in the registration of white and African-American voters in some States. Congress' response was to promulgate in the Voting Rights Act a detailed but limited remedial scheme designed to guarantee meaningful enforcement of the Fifteenth Amendment in those areas of the Nation where abundant evidence of States' systematic denial of those rights was identified.

The contrast between this kind of evidence, and the evidence that Congress considered in the present case, is stark. Congressional enactment of the ADA represents its judgment that there should be a "comprehensive national mandate for the elimination of discrimination against individuals with disabilities." 42 U.S.C. § 12101(b)(1). Congress is the final authority as to desirable public policy, but in order to authorize private individuals to recover money damages against the States, there must be a pattern of discrimination by the States which violates the Fourteenth Amendment, and the remedy imposed by Congress must be congruent and proportional to the targeted violation. Those requirements are not met here, and to uphold the Act's application to the States would allow Congress to rewrite the Fourteenth Amendment law laid down by this Court in *Cleburne*.[9] Section 5 does not so broadly enlarge congressional authority. The judgment of the Court of Appeals is therefore

Reversed.

■ JUSTICE KENNEDY, with whom JUSTICE O'CONNOR joins, concurring.

---

9. Our holding here that Congress did not validly abrogate the States' sovereign immunity from suit by private individuals for money damages under Title I does not mean that persons with disabilities have no federal recourse against discrimination. Title I of the ADA still prescribes standards applicable to the States. Those standards can be enforced by the United States in actions for money damages, as well as by private individuals in actions for injunctive relief under Ex parte Young, 209 U.S. 123 (1908). In addition, state laws protecting the rights of persons with disabilities in employment and other aspects of life provide independent avenues of redress.

Prejudice, we are beginning to understand, rises not from malice or hostile animus alone. It may result as well from insensitivity caused by simple want of careful, rational reflection or from some instinctive mechanism to guard against people who appear to be different in some respects from ourselves. Quite apart from any historical documentation, knowledge of our own human instincts teaches that persons who find it difficult to perform routine functions by reason of some mental or physical impairment might at first seem unsettling to us, unless we are guided by the better angels of our nature. There can be little doubt, then, that persons with mental or physical impairments are confronted with prejudice which can stem from indifference or insecurity as well as from malicious ill will.

One of the undoubted achievements of statutes designed to assist those with impairments is that citizens have an incentive, flowing from a legal duty, to develop a better understanding, a more decent perspective, for accepting persons with impairments or disabilities into the larger society. The law works this way because the law can be a teacher. So I do not doubt that the Americans with Disabilities Act of 1990 will be a milestone on the path to a more decent, tolerant, progressive society.

It is a question of quite a different order, however, to say that the States in their official capacities, the States as governmental entities, must be held in violation of the Constitution on the assumption that they embody the misconceived or malicious perceptions of some of their citizens.... The failure of a State to revise policies now seen as incorrect under a new understanding of proper policy does not always constitute the purposeful and intentional action required to make out a violation of the Equal Protection Clause. See Washington v. Davis, 426 U.S. 229 (1976).

For the reasons explained by the Court, an equal protection violation has not been shown with respect to the several States in this case. If the States had been transgressing the Fourteenth Amendment by their mistreatment or lack of concern for those with impairments, one would have expected to find in decisions of the courts of the States and also the courts of the United States extensive litigation and discussion of the constitutional violations. This confirming judicial documentation does not exist....

It must be noted, moreover, that what is in question is not whether the Congress, acting pursuant to a power granted to it by the Constitution, can compel the States to act. What is involved is only the question whether the States can be subjected to liability in suits brought not by the Federal Government (to which the States have consented, see Alden v. Maine, 527 U.S. 706, 755 (1999)), but by private persons seeking to collect moneys from the state treasury without the consent of the State. The predicate for money damages against an unconsenting State in suits brought by private persons must be a federal statute enacted upon the documentation of patterns of constitutional violations committed by the State in its official capacity. That predicate, for reasons discussed here and in the decision of the Court, has not been established. With these observations, I join the Court's opinion.

■ JUSTICE BREYER, with whom JUSTICE STEVENS, JUSTICE SOUTER, and JUSTICE GINSBURG join, dissenting.

Reviewing the congressional record as if it were an administrative agency record, the Court holds the statutory provision before us, 42 U.S.C. § 12202, unconstitutional. The Court concludes that Congress assembled insufficient evidence of unconstitutional discrimination that Congress improperly attempted to "re-write" the law we established in Cleburne v. Cleburne Living Center, Inc., 473 U.S. 432 (1985), and that the law is not sufficiently tailored to address unconstitutional discrimination.

Section 5, however, grants Congress the "power to enforce, by appropriate legislation" the Fourteenth Amendment's equal protection guarantee. As the Court recognizes, state discrimination in employment against persons with disabilities might " 'run afoul of the Equal Protection Clause' " where there is no " 'rational relationship between the disparity of treatment and some legitimate governmental purpose' " (quoting Heller v. Doe, 509 U.S. 312, 320 (1993)). In my view, Congress reasonably could have concluded that the remedy before us constitutes an "appropriate" way to enforce this basic equal protection requirement. And that is all the Constitution requires.

I

The Court says that its primary problem with this statutory provision is one of legislative evidence. It says that "Congress assembled only ... minimal evidence of unconstitutional state discrimination in employment." In fact, Congress compiled a vast legislative record documenting " 'massive, society-wide discrimination' " against persons with disabilities. S. Rep. No. 101–116, pp. 8–9 (1989) (quoting testimony of Justin Dart, chairperson of the Task Force on the Rights and Empowerment of Americans with Disabilities). In addition to the information presented at 13 congressional hearings and its own prior experience gathered over 40 years during which it contemplated and enacted considerable similar legislation, Congress created a special task force to assess the need for comprehensive legislation. That task force held hearings in every State, attended by more than 30,000 people, including thousands who had experienced discrimination first hand. See From ADA to Empowerment, Task Force on the Rights and Empowerment of Americans with Disabilities, 16 (Oct. 12, 1990) (hereinafter Task Force Report). The task force hearings, Congress' own hearings, and an analysis of "census data, national polls, and other studies" led Congress to conclude that "people with disabilities, as a group, occupy an inferior status in our society, and are severely disadvantaged socially, vocationally, economically, and educationally." 42 U.S.C. § 12101(a)(6). As to employment,

Congress found that "two-thirds of all disabled Americans between the age of 16 and 64 [were] not working at all," even though a large majority wanted to, and were able to, work productively. S. Rep. No. 101–116, at 9. And Congress found that this discrimination flowed in significant part from "stereotypic assumptions" as well as "purposeful unequal treatment." 42 U.S.C. § 12101(a)(7).

The powerful evidence of discriminatory treatment throughout society in general, including discrimination by private persons and local governments, implicates state governments as well, for state agencies form part of that same larger society. There is no particular reason to believe that they are immune from the "stereotypic assumptions" and pattern of "purposeful unequal treatment" that Congress found prevalent. The Court claims that it "makes no sense" to take into consideration constitutional violations committed by local governments. But the substantive obligation that the Equal Protection Clause creates applies to state and local governmental entities alike. Local governments often work closely with, and under the supervision of, state officials, and in general, state and local government employers are similarly situated....

In any event, there is no need to rest solely upon evidence of discrimination by local governments or general societal discrimination. There are roughly 300 examples of discrimination by state governments themselves in the legislative record. See, e.g., Appendix C, infra. I fail to see how this evidence "falls far short of even suggesting the pattern of unconstitutional discrimination on which § 5 legislation must be based."

The congressionally appointed task force collected numerous specific examples, provided by persons with disabilities themselves, of adverse, disparate treatment by state officials. They reveal, not what the Court describes as "half a dozen" instances of discrimination, but hundreds of instances of adverse treatment at the hands of state officials—instances in which a person with a disability found it impossible to obtain a state job, to retain state employment, to use the public transportation that was readily available to others in order to get to work, or to obtain a public education, which is often a prerequisite to obtaining employment. State-imposed barriers also frequently made it difficult or impossible for people to vote, to enter a public building, to access important government services, such as calling for emergency assistance, and to find a place to live due to a pattern of irrational zoning decisions similar to the discrimination that we held unconstitutional in *Cleburne*, 473 U.S. at 448. See Appendix C.

As the Court notes, those who presented instances of discrimination rarely provided additional, independent evidence sufficient to prove in court that, in each instance, the discrimination they suffered lacked justification from a judicial standpoint. Perhaps this explains the Court's view that there is "minimal evidence of unconstitutional state discrimination." But a legislature is not a court of law. And Congress, unlike courts, must, and does, routinely draw general conclusions—for example, of likely motive or of likely relationship to legitimate need—from anecdotal and opinion-based evidence of this kind, particularly when the evidence lacks strong refutation. In reviewing § 5 legislation, we have never required the sort of extensive investigation of each piece of evidence that the Court appears to contemplate. Cf. Katzenbach v. Morgan, 384 U.S. 641, 652–56 (1966) (asking whether Congress' likely conclusions were reasonable, not whether there was adequate evidentiary support in the record). Nor has the Court traditionally required Congress to make findings as to state discrimination, or to break down the record evidence, category by category. Cf. *Morgan*, supra, at 654 (considering what Congress "might" have concluded).

Regardless, Congress expressly found substantial unjustified discrimination against persons with disabilities. 42 U.S.C. § 12101(9) (finding a pattern of "*unnecessary* discrimination and prejudice" that "costs the United States billions of dollars in *unnecessary* expenses resulting from dependency and nonproductivity" (emphasis added)). Moreover, it found that such discrimination typically reflects "stereotypic assumptions" or "purposeful unequal treatment." 42 U.S.C. § 12101(7). In making these findings, Congress followed our decision in *Cleburne*, which established that not only discrimination against persons with disabilities that rests upon "a bare . . . desire to harm a politically unpopular group," 473 U.S. at 447 (quoting Department of Agriculture v. Moreno, 413 U.S. 528, 534 (1973) (omission in *Cleburne*)), violates the Fourteenth Amendment, but also discrimination that rests solely upon "negative attitudes," "fear," 473 U.S. at 448, or "irrational prejudice," id. at 450. Adverse treatment that rests upon such motives is unjustified discrimination in *Cleburne*'s terms.

The evidence in the legislative record bears out Congress' finding that the adverse treatment of persons with disabilities was often arbitrary or invidious in this sense, and thus unjustified. For example, one study that was before Congress revealed that "most . . . governmental agencies in [one State] discriminated in hiring against job applicants for an average period of five years after treatment for cancer," based in part on coworkers' misguided belief that "cancer is contagious." 2 Leg. Hist. 1619–20 (testimony of Arlene B. Mayerson). A school inexplicably refused to exempt a deaf teacher, who taught at a school for the deaf, from a "listening skills" requirement. Government's Lodging 1503. A State refused to hire a blind employee as director of an agency for the blind—even though he was the most qualified applicant. Id. at 974. Certain state agencies apparently had general policies against hiring or promoting persons with disabilities. Id. at 1159, 1577. A zoo turned away children with Downs Syndrome "because [the zookeeper] feared they would upset the chimpanzees." S. Rep. No. 101-116, at 7. There were reports of numerous zoning decisions based upon "negative attitudes" or "fear," *Cleburne*, supra, at 448, such as a zoning board that denied a permit for an obviously pretextual reason after hearing arguments that a facility would house " 'deviants' " who needed " 'room to roam,' " Government's Lodging 1068. A complete listing of the hundreds of examples of discrimination by state and local governments that were submitted to the task force is set forth in Appendix C. Congress could have reasonably believed that these examples represented signs of a widespread problem of unconstitutional discrimination.

II

The Court's failure to find sufficient evidentiary support may well rest upon its decision to hold Congress to a strict, judicially created evidentiary standard, particularly in respect to lack of justification. Justice Kennedy's empirical conclusion—which rejects that of Congress—rests heavily upon his failure to find "extensive litigation and discussion of constitutional violations, in *the courts* of the United States'" (emphasis added). And the Court itself points out that, when economic or social legislation is challenged in court as irrational, hence unconstitutional, the "burden is upon the challenging party to negative any reasonably conceivable state of facts that could provide a rational basis for the classification." Or as Justice Brandeis, writing for the Court, put the matter many years ago, "if any state of facts reasonably can be conceived that would sustain" challenged legislation, then "there is a presumption of the existence of that state of facts, and one who assails the classification must carry the burden of showing ... that the action is arbitrary.'" Pacific States Box & Basket Co. v. White, 296 U.S. 176, 185 (1935) (quoting Borden's Farm Products Co. v. Baldwin, 293 U.S. 194, 209 (1934)). Imposing this special "burden" upon Congress, the Court fails to find in the legislative record sufficient indication that Congress has "negatived" the presumption that state action is rationally related to a legitimate objective.

The problem with the Court's approach is that neither the "burden of proof" that favors States nor any other rule of restraint applicable to *judges* applies to *Congress* when it exercises its § 5 power. "Limitations stemming from the nature of the judicial process ... have no application to Congress." Oregon v. Mitchell, 400 U.S. 112, 248 (1970) (Brennan, White, and Marshall, JJ., concurring in part and dissenting in part). Rational-basis review—with its presumptions favoring constitutionality—is "a paradigm of *judicial* restraint." FCC v. Beach Communications, Inc., 508 U.S. 307, 314 (1993) (emphasis added). And the Congress of the United States is not a lower court.

Indeed, the Court in *Cleburne* drew this very institutional distinction. We emphasized that "courts have been very reluctant, as they should be in our federal system and with our respect for the separation of powers, to closely scrutinize legislative choices." Our invocation of judicial deference and respect for Congress was based on the fact that "[§]5 of the [Fourteenth] Amendment empowers *Congress* to enforce [the equal protection] mandate." (emphasis added). Indeed, we made clear that the absence of a contrary congressional finding was critical to our decision to apply mere rational-basis review to disability discrimination claims—a "congressional direction" to apply a more stringent standard would have been "controlling." See also Washington v. Davis, 426 U.S. 229, 248 (1976) (refusing to invalidate a law based on the Equal Protection Clause because a disparate impact standard "should await legislative prescription"). In short, the Court's claim that "to uphold the Act's application to the States would allow Congress to rewrite the Fourteenth Amendment law laid down by this Court in *Cleburne*," is repudiated by *Cleburne* itself.

There is simply no reason to require Congress, seeking to determine facts relevant to the exercise of its § 5 authority, to adopt rules or presumptions that reflect a court's institutional limitations. Unlike courts, Congress can readily gather facts from across the Nation, assess the magnitude of a problem, and more easily find an appropriate remedy. Cf. *Cleburne*, supra, at 442–43 (addressing the problems of the "large and diversified group" of persons with disabilities "is a difficult and often a technical matter, very much a task for legislators guided by qualified professionals and not by the perhaps ill-informed opinions of the judiciary"). Unlike courts, Congress directly reflects public attitudes and beliefs, enabling Congress better to understand where, and to what extent, refusals to accommodate a disability amount to behavior that is callous or unreasonable to the point of lacking constitutional justification. Unlike judges, Members of Congress can directly obtain information from constituents who have first-hand experience with discrimination and related issues.

Moreover, unlike judges, Members of Congress are elected. When the Court has applied the majority's burden of proof rule, it has explained that we, i.e., the courts, do not " 'sit as a superlegislature to judge the wisdom or desirability of legislative policy determinations.' " Heller, 509 U.S. at 319 (quoting New Orleans v. Dukes, 427 U.S. 297, 303 (1976) (per curiam)). To apply a rule designed to restrict courts as if it restricted Congress' legislative power is to stand the underlying principle—a principle of judicial restraint—on its head. But without the use of this burden of proof rule or some other unusually stringent standard of review, it is difficult to see how the Court can find the legislative record here inadequate. Read with a reasonably favorable eye, the record indicates that state governments subjected those with disabilities to seriously adverse, disparate treatment. And Congress could have found, in a significant number of instances, that this treatment violated the substantive principles of justification—shorn of their judicial-restraint-related presumptions—that this Court recognized in *Cleburne*.

III

The Court argues in the alternative that the statute's damage remedy is not "congruent" with and "proportional" to the equal protection problem that Congress found (citing City of Boerne v. Flores, 521 U.S. 507, 520 (1997)). The Court suggests that the Act's "reasonable accommodation" requirement, 42 U.S.C. § 12112(b)(5)(A), and disparate impact standard, § 12112(b)(3)(A), "far exceed what is constitutionally required." But we have upheld disparate impact standards in contexts where they were not "constitutionally required." E.g., Griggs v. Duke Power Co., 401 U.S. 424, 432 (1971).

And what is wrong with a remedy that, in response to unreasonable employer behavior, requires an employer to make accommodations that are reasonable? Of course, what is "reasonable" in the statutory sense and what is "unreasonable" in the constitutional sense might differ. In other words, the requirement may exceed what is necessary to avoid a constitutional violation. But it is just that power—the power to require more than the minimum—that § 5 grants to Congress, as this Court has repeatedly confirmed. As long ago as 1880, the Court wrote that § 5 "brought within the domain of congressional power" whatever "tends to enforce submission" to its "prohibitions" and "to secure to all persons ... the equal protection of the laws." Ex parte Virginia, 100 U.S. 339, 346 (1880). More recently, the Court added that § 5's "draftsmen sought to grant to Congress, by a specific provision applicable to the Fourteenth Amendment, the same broad powers expressed in the Necessary and Proper Clause, Art. I, § 8, cl. 18." *Morgan*, 384 U.S. at 650.

In keeping with these principles, the Court has said that "it is not for us to review the congressional resolution of the various conflicting considerations—the risk or pervasiveness of the discrimination in governmental services..., the adequacy or availability of alternative remedies, and the nature and significance of the state interests that would be affected." 384 U.S. at 653. "It is enough that we be able to perceive a basis upon which the Congress might resolve the conflict as it did." Ibid. See also South Carolina v. Katzenbach, 383 U.S. 301, 324 (1966) (interpreting the similarly worded enforcement Clause of the Fifteenth Amendment to permit Congress to use "any rational means to effectuate the constitutional prohibition"). Nothing in the words "reasonable accommodation" suggests that the requirement has no "tendency to enforce" the Equal Protection Clause, that it is an irrational way to achieve the objective, that it would fall outside the scope of the Necessary and Proper Clause, or that it somehow otherwise exceeds the bounds of the "appropriate."

The Court's more recent cases have professed to follow the longstanding principle of deference to Congress. See Kimel v. Florida Bd. of Regents, 528 U.S. 62, 81 (2000) ("Congress' § 5 power is not confined to the enactment of legislation that merely parrots the precise wording of the Fourteenth Amendment." Rather, Congress can prohibit a "somewhat broader swath of conduct, including that which is not itself forbidden by the Amendment's text"); Florida Prepaid Postsecondary Ed. Expense Bd. v. College Savings Bank, 527 U.S. 627, 639 (1999) ("'Congress must have wide latitude'"); *City of Boerne*, 521 U.S. at 536 (Congress' "conclusions are entitled to much deference"). And even today, the Court purports to apply, not to depart from, these standards. But the Court's analysis and ultimate conclusion deprive its declarations of practical significance. The Court "sounds the word of promise to the ear but breaks it to the hope."

IV

The Court's harsh review of Congress' use of its § 5 power is reminiscent of the similar (now-discredited) limitation that it once imposed upon Congress' Commerce Clause power. Compare Carter v. Carter Coal Co., 298 U.S. 238 (1936), with United States v. Darby, 312 U.S. 100 (1941) (rejecting *Carter Coal*'s rationale). I could understand the legal basis for such review were we judging a statute that discriminated against those of a particular race or gender or a statute that threatened a basic constitutionally protected liberty such as free speech. The legislation before us, however, does not discriminate against anyone, nor does it pose any threat to basic liberty. And it is difficult to understand why the Court, which applies "minimum 'rational-basis' review" to statutes that *burden* persons with disabilities, subjects to far stricter scrutiny a statute that seeks to *help* those same individuals.

I recognize nonetheless that this statute imposes a burden upon States in that it removes their Eleventh Amendment protection from suit, thereby subjecting them to potential monetary liability. Rules for interpreting § 5 that would provide States with special protection, however, run counter to the very object of the Fourteenth Amendment. By its terms, that Amendment prohibits *States* from denying their citizens equal protection of the laws. Hence "principles of federalism that might otherwise be an obstacle to congressional authority are necessarily overridden by the power to enforce the Civil War Amendments 'by appropriate legislation.' Those Amendments were specifically designed as an expansion of federal power and an intrusion on state sovereignty." City of Rome v. United States, 446 U.S. 156, 179 (1980). See also Fitzpatrick v. Bitzer, 427 U.S. 445, 456 (1976). And, ironically, the greater the obstacle the Eleventh Amendment poses to the creation by Congress of the kind of remedy at issue here—the decentralized remedy of private damage actions—the more Congress, seeking to cure important national problems, such as the problem of disability discrimination before us, will have to rely on more uniform remedies, such as federal standards and court injunctions, 42 U.S.C. § 12188(a)(2), which are sometimes draconian and typically more intrusive. For these reasons, I doubt that today's decision serves any constitutionally based federalism interest.

The Court, through its evidentiary demands, its non-deferential review, and its failure to distinguish between judicial and legislative constitutional competencies, improperly invades a power that the Constitution assigns to Congress. Its decision saps § 5 of independent force, effectively "confining the legislative power ... to the insignificant role of abrogating only those state laws that the judicial branch [is] prepared to adjudge unconstitutional." *Morgan*, 384 U.S. at 648–49. Whether the Commerce

Clause does or does not enable Congress to enact this provision, in my view, § 5 gives Congress the necessary authority. For the reasons stated, I respectfully dissent.[a]

> **a.** Appendix C, to which both the majority and dissenting opinions refer, consists of a long list of brief entries referenced to page numbers in the report of the Task Force on the Rights and Empowerment of Americans with Disabilities. The entries are grouped by state. The first three entries under the first state, Alabama, are typical of the whole:
>
> 00002 discrimination against the mentally ill in city zoning process
>
> 00003 inaccessible exercise equipment at University of Alabama
>
> 00004 school failed to train teachers how to work with students with learning disabilities.
>
> [Footnote by eds.]

NOTE ON *FEDERAL MARITIME COMMISSION v. SOUTH CAROLINA STATE PORTS AUTHORITY*

The latest round in the Eleventh Amendment wars is Federal Maritime Commission v. South Carolina State Ports Authority, ___ U.S. ___ (2002), in which the Court extended 11th amendment protection to federal agency adjudication.

A federal statute authorizes the Federal Maritime Commission to protect maritime terminal users against discrimination by maritime terminal operators. The Commission hears complaints through an adjudicative process that begins with an administrative law judge. If the complainant prevails, the Commission can issue an order to the terminal operator to "cease and desist" discrimination and to pay "reparations" for past acts. Commission orders, however, can be enforced only through court order.

In this case, the South Carolina State Ports Authority repeatedly refused to allow Charleston port facilities to be used by a cruise ship operator that offered gambling in international waters. When the operator filed a complaint with the Federal Maritime Commission, the state responded that it was entitled to 11th amendment immunity against agency adjudication. The Fourth Circuit agreed, saying that "the proceeding 'walks, talks, and squawks very much like a lawsuit' and that '[i]ts placement within the Executive Branch cannot blind us to the fact that the proceeding is truly an adjudication.'" By the usual vote of five to four, the Supreme Court affirmed. Speaking through Justice Thomas, the Court said that the fact that the Commission's orders were not self-executing did not convert agency adjudication into direct enforcement against a state by the federal government: "The Attorney General's decision to bring an enforcement action against a State after the conclusion of the Commission's proceedings ... does not retroactively convert [agency] adjudication initiated and pursued by a private party into one initiated and pursued by the Federal Government." On this understanding, agency adjudication was barred.

Justice Breyer, joined by Justices Stevens, Souter, and Ginsburg, dissented. Breyer argued that even if the Court's prior 11th amendment decisions were correct, which he did not concede, they should not be extended to agency adjudication: "The Commission, but not a private party, may assess a penalty against the State for noncompliance [with the federal statute], and only a court acting at the Commission's request can compel compliance with a penalty order. In sum, no one can legally compel the State's obedience to [the federal statute] without a court order, and in no case would a court issue such an order ... absent the request of a federal agency or other federal instrumentality." Breyer therefore saw agency adjudication as analogous to direct enforcement actions against states by the federal government, to which the 11th amendment has no application.

Page 880, add at the beginning of Section 3, immediately before *Idaho v. Coeur d'Alene Tribe*:

INTRODUCTORY NOTE ON *COEUR D'ALENE TRIBE*

Of all the oddities in 11th amendment jurisprudence, none is stranger than *Seminole Tribe*'s treatment of *Ex parte Young*. For nearly a century, *Ex parte Young* has allowed prospective relief against states by resort to the fiction of suing a state officer. The *Seminole Tribe* Court purported not to question *Ex parte Young* but only to hold that Congress intended to preclude that option in the Indian Gaming Regulatory Act. Since prospective enforcement against state officers, as *Young* allows, would have implemented precisely the intention manifest in the statute, the Court's insistence that Congress actually intended to forbid this solution struck some as "singularly unpersuasive," Daniel J. Meltzer, The *Seminole* Decision and State Sovereign Immunity, 1996 Sup. Ct. Rev. 1, 43, and other, less polite observers as "wilfully perverse." John C. Jeffries, Jr., In Praise of the Eleventh Amendment and Section 1983, 84 Va. L. Rev. 47, 52 n.19 (1998).

So long as *Ex parte Young* remains generally intact, the practical significance of *Seminole Tribe* for questions of injunctive relief will be limited. Indeed, from all that appears, Congress could overrule *Seminole Tribe* simply by clarifying its intention to allow—or more accurately not to disallow—officer suits. On the other hand, *Seminole Tribe* and its progeny would mean a great deal if they portended any general limitation on *Ex parte Young*. That possibility was raised in the next main case.[a]

[a] For commentary on the relation of *Seminole Tribe* and *Ex Parte Young*, see Vicki L. Jackson, *Seminole Tribe*, the Eleventh Amendment, and the Potential Evisceration of *Ex Parte Young*, 72 N.Y.U. L. Rev. 495 (1997) (emphasizing the dangers of curtailing officer suits); David P. Currie, Response: *Ex Parte Young* After *Seminole Tribe*, 72 N.Y.U. L. Rev. 547 (1997) (offering a more optimistic response); Laura S. Fitzgerald, Beyond *Marbury*: Jurisdictional Self–Dealing in *Seminole Tribe*, 52 Vand. L. Rev. 407 (1999) (arguing that the Court has assumed a unilateral power to control its own jurisdiction in suits against states).

Page 888, add at the conclusion of Section 3:

NOTE ON *VERIZON MARYLAND, INC. v. PUBLIC SERVICE COMMISSION*

The suggestion that *Seminole Tribe* and *Coeur d'Alene Tribe* portended some general limitation on *Ex parte Young* was rejected in Verizon Maryland, Inc. v. Public Service Commission of Maryland, ___ U.S. ___ (2002). The suit arose about of a dispute between Verizon (formerly Bell Atlantic) and competitor MCI WorldCom. As the incumbent local telephone service provider in Maryland, Verizon was required by the Telecommunications Act of 1996 to negotiate "reciprocal compensation arrangements" for carrying the local calls of other providers. Such arrangements must be submitted to state authorities for approval. Verizon refused to compensate MCI WorldCom for calls made to local access numbers of internet service providers, claiming that such calls were not "local traffic." The Maryland Public Service Commission agreed with WorldCom's complaint and required compensation. Subsequently, the Federal Communications Commission issued a contrary ruling. The Maryland Public Service Commission then ruled that the agreement between Verizon and WorldCom survived as a matter of state law and that Verizon had to continue payments. Verizon sued in federal court, seeking injunctive and declaratory relief against the Commission and against its individual members, who were named in their official capacities, and against various competitors. The state defendants invoked the 11th amendment.

The Supreme Court found jurisdiction under 28 U.S.C. § 1331 and unanimously (with Justice O'Connor not participating) reaffirmed the availability of *Ex parte Young*. Speaking through Justice Scalia, the Court said:

> In determining whether the doctrine of *Ex parte Young* avoids an Eleventh Amendment bar to suit, a court need only conduct a 'straightforward inquiry into whether [the] complaint alleges an ongoing violation of federal law and seeks relief properly characterized as prospective. Idaho v. Coeur d'Alene Tribe, 521 U.S. 261, 296 (1997) (O'Connor, joined by Scalia and Thomas, concurring in part and concurring in judgment); see also id at 298–99 (Souter, dissenting, joined by Stevens, Ginsburg, and Breyer). Here Verizon sought injunctive and declaratory relief, alleging that the Commission's order requiring payment of reciprocal compensation was pre-empted by the 1996 Act and an FCC ruling. The prayer for injunctive relief—that state officials be restrained from enforcing an order in contravention of controlling federal law—clearly satisfies our 'straightforward inquiry.'
> ... As for Verizon's prayer for declaratory relief: That, to be sure, seeks a declaration of the *past*, as well as the *future*, ineffectiveness of the Commission's action, so that the past liability of private parties may be affected. But no past liability of the State, or of any of its

commissions, is at issue. ... Insofar as the exposure of the State is concerned, the prayer for declaratory relief adds nothing to the prayer for injunction.

This altogether standard account of the doctrine of *Ex parte Young* suggests that *Seminole Tribe* and *Coeur d'Alene Tribe* may be, for different reasons, exceptional.

Page 903, add a footnote at the end of the first full paragraph:

d. For an argument that the current remedies available to taxpayers who pay unconstitutional state taxes are inadequate and a proposal that Congress should enact legislation to correct the problem, see John F. Coverdale, Remedies for Unconstitutional State Taxes, 32 Conn. L. Rev. 73 (1999).

CHAPTER IX

42 U.S.C. § 1983

Page 919, add at the end of footnote g:

For recent investigation and reinterpretation of the history of § 1983, see David Achtenberg, A "Milder Measure of Villainy": The Unknown History of 42 U.S.C. § 1983 and the Meaning of "Under Color of" Law, 1999 Utah L. Rev. 1 (concluding that history "should dispel the remarkably persistent myth that the Forty–Second Congress never intended the provision to cover constitutional wrongs unless those wrongs were actually authorized by state law").

Page 937, add a new Note:

6a. *Crawford–El v. Britton.* At issue in Crawford–El v. Britton, 523 U.S. 574 (1998), was whether *Harlow*-inspired protections against discovery and trial should apply where improper motivation is alleged, not to overcome the defense of qualified immunity, but to establish the underlying constitutional violation. Examples are claims of racial discrimination, which require proof of discriminatory animus, and first amendment retaliation, which require proof of a retaliatory purpose.

Casually, almost as an aside, and apparently without dissent, the Court resolved the ambiguity in *Harlow* against any opportunity to overcome qualified immunity by proof of malice. After quoting *Harlow*'s statement that "bare allegations of malice should not suffice to subject government officials either to the costs of trial or to the burdens of broad-reaching discovery," the *Crawford–El* Court announced:

> "Under that standard, a defense of qualified immunity may not be rebutted by evidence that the defendant's conduct was malicious or otherwise improperly motivated. Evidence concerning the defendant's subjective intent is simply irrelevant to that defense."

On the question whether *Harlow* required analogous restrictions on proof of improper motivation where required by the underlying constitutional claim, the *Crawford–El* Court was a bit murky. At issue was the D.C. Circuit's ruling that a plaintiff alleging a constitutional violation requiring proof of improper motive had to prove that motive by clear and convincing evidence. By a vote of five to four, the Supreme Court disapproved that requirement. Speaking through Justice Stevens, the Court said that any *Harlow*-like adjustment in pleading, discovery, or summary judgment practice should come from the legislature, not the courts. Later in its opinion, however, the Court suggested several ways in which trial judges could constrain discovery and trial based on "bare allegations" of improper motivation. One such mechanism was to "insist that the plaintiff 'put forward specific, nonconclusory factual allegations' that establish improper motive causing cognizable injury in order to survive a prediscovery motion for dismissal or summary judgment," citing Siegert v. Gilley, 500 U.S. 226, 236 (1991) (Kennedy, J., concurring in the judgment). This remark raises the possibility that heightened *proof* may not be required in unconstitutional-motive cases but that heightened *pleading* may be. Apparently, another Supreme Court decision will required to resolve that question.

Page 940, add at the end of Note 7:

For additional criticism of the Supreme Court's immunity decisions, see Sheldon Nahmod, The Restructuring of Narrative and Empathy in Section 1983 Cases, 72 Chi.–Kent L. Rev. 819 (1997). Nahmod examines immunity decisions "from the perspective of narrative empathy" and concludes that the Court has "instruct[ed] the decision-maker, the judge (and *not* the jury), to empathize with the defendant ..., thus forcing § 1983 plaintiffs to bear their own losses even when their constitutional rights are violated."

For analysis of qualified immunity through the lens of the familiar distinction between rules and standards, see Alan K. Chen, The Ultimate Standard: Qualified Immunity in the Age of Constitutional Balancing Tests, 81 Iowa L. Rev. 261 (1995), which concludes that the "ultimate standard" of qualified immunity doctrine should be replaced by a more rule-oriented approach.

For analysis of qualified immunity from the perspective of a comparison with the criminal law, see Barbara E. Armacost, Qualified Immunity: Ignorance Excused, 51 Vand. L. Rev. 583 (1998). She examines qualified immunity in a variety of contexts and concludes that, "[t]he recognition that qualified immunity is about notice and that notice functions as a surrogate for fault—in much the same way that fair notice in criminal law acts as a proxy for fault—helps to explain the courts' analyses in constitutional damages cases."

Finally, for criticism of the Court's one-size-fits-all approach to qualified immunity and an argument that constitutional tort liability should take account of the presence or absence of alternative remedies, see John C. Jeffries, Jr., Disaggregating Constitutional Torts, 110 Yale L.J. 259 (2000). And for criticism of qualified immunity and of the whole scheme of officer liability, see Cornelia T.L. Pillard, Taking Fiction Seriously: The Strange Results of Public Officials' Individual Liability Under *Bivens*, 88 Geo. L.J. 65 (1999).

Page 941, add a new Note:

7a. Unnecessary Merits Adjudication? As *Anderson v. Creighton* suggests, and subsequent decisions make plain, there is an unusual sequence of decision in qualified immunity cases. First, a court determines whether a constitutional right was violated. If so, the court then decides whether the defendant's conduct was nevertheless protected by qualified immunity. Under this procedure, courts adjudicate constitutional claims on the merits even when the merits do not affect the outcome of damages actions.

A good example is Wilson v. Layne, 526 U.S. 603 (1999). Plaintiffs claimed that their fourth amendment rights had been violated when police invited *Washington Post* reporters to accompany them on a lawful search. The Court ruled first that such media "ride-alongs" violated the fourth amendment. The Court then found that, since the unconstitutionality of such actions was not clearly established at the time they were taken the defendants were protected by qualified immunity. Note that the second conclusion rendered the first unnecessary. Given that the law was not clearly established, the defendants would prevail against a claim for money damages whether or not their conduct violated the Constitution. Yet, the Court requires that the merits of constitutional tort claims be decided before consideration of qualified immunity. Why?

An answer to this question is attempted in John C. Jeffries, Jr., The Right–Remedy Gap in Constitutional Law, 109 Yale L.J. 87 (1999), which argues that the limitation of money damages by the law of qualified immunity is a two-edged sword. On the one hand, qualified immunity reduces the incentives for government officers to comply with existing constitutional requirements, whatever they may be. On the other hand, qualified immunity facilitates the growth and development of constitutional law by reducing the cost of innovation. New rules apply to future cases but do not trigger damages liability for past failure to comply with the new standards. The result, Jeffries argues, is not only to reduce the cost of constitutional innovation, but also to tilt constitutional adjudication from reparation toward reform, as societal resources are continually shifted away from cash compensation for past injury and toward the prevention of future harm. Obviously, this concern for the growth and direction of constitutional law would be entirely defeated if the existence of qualified immunity precluded adjudication of the merits.

For argument in a similar vein, see John M.M. Greabe, *Mirabile Dictum!*: The Case for "Unnecessary" Constitutional Ruling in Civil Rights Damages Actions, 74 Notre Dame L. Rev. 403 (1999) (arguing against "merits by-pass" and in favor of "not-strictly-necessary" constitutional adjudication).

Page 949, add a footnote at the end of Note 3:

b. The applicability to governments of general deterrence theory is challenged in Daryl Levinson, In Making Government Pay: Markets, Politics, and the Allocation of Constitutional Costs, 67 U. Chi. L. Rev. 345 (2000). Levinson argues that government officers do not necessarily respond to liability rules in the same way as private actors. "Because government actors respond to political, not market, incentives, we should not assume that government will internalize social costs just because it is forced to make a budgetary outlay." Moreover, even if government officers do respond to the prospect of money damages, deterrence will still fail if constitutional violations create benefits for a majority of citizens that outweigh the costs imposed on a few. Levinson's arguments suggest a profound skepticism about the utility of money damages in enforcing constitutional rights.

These ideas are examined in a symposium in the Georgia Law Review. Included is a Foreword by Thomas A Eaton, 35 Ga. L. Rev. 837 (2001), and an Afterword by Marshall Shapo, id., at 931. Articles in the symposium include: Myriam E. Gilles, In Defense of Making Government Pay: The Deterrent Effect of Constitutional Tort Remedies, 35 Ga. L. Rev. 845 (2001); Brian J. Serr, Turning Section 1983's Protection of Civil Rights Into an Attractive Nuisance: Extra-Textual Barriers in Municipal Liability Under *Monell*, 35 Ga. L. Rev. 881 (2001); Bernard P. Dauenhauer & Michael L. Wells, Corrective Justice and Constitutional Torts, 35 Ga. L. Rev. 903 (20001). For another response to Levinson, see Mark R. Brown, Deterring Bully Government: A Sovereign Dilemma, 76 Tulane L. Rev. 149 (2001) (using game theory to argue that government can be deterred by the prospect of damages liability).

Page 954, add the following at the end of Section 2:

Congress recently amended §§ 1983 and 1988 to overrule *Pulliam*. Section 1983 now provides that the person acting under color of state law "shall be liable to the party injured in an action at law, suit in equity, or other proper proceeding for redress, *except that in any action brought against a judicial officer for an act or omission taken in such officer's judicial capacity, injunctive relief shall not be granted unless a declaratory decree was violated or declaratory relief was unavailable.*" (Emphasis added.) Section 1988(b) now provides that the court may allow "a reasonable attorney's fee as part of the costs, *except that in any action brought against a judicial officer for an act or omission taken in such officer's judicial capacity, such officer shall not be held liable for any costs, including attorney's fees, unless such action was clearly in excess of such officer's jurisdiction.*" (Emphasis added.) Is anything left of *Pulliam* after this?

Page 1015, add at the end of footnote a:

For an elaborate criticism this aspect of *Swint* and an argument in favor of a properly circumscribed doctrine of pendent appellate jurisdiction applicable to all categories of interlocutory review, see Joan Steinman, The Scope of Appellate Jurisdiction: Pendent Appellate Jurisdiction Before and After *Swint*, 49 Hastings L.J. 1337 (1998).

Page 1017, add at the end of Note 2:

In addition, two recent symposia address issues of municipal liability from a variety of perspectives. Volume 48 of the DePaul Law Review published a symposium on Municipal Liability in Civil Rights Litigation, with contents as follows: Susan Bandes, Introduction: The Emperor's New Clothes, 48 DePaul L. Rev. 619 (1999); Jack M. Beermann, Municipal Responsibility for Constitutional Torts, id. at 627; Michael J. Gerhardt, Institutional Analysis of Municipal Liability Under Section 1983, id. at 669; Karen M. Blum, Municipal Liability: Derivative or Direct? Statutory or Constitutional? Distinguishing the *Canton* Case from the *Collins* Case, id. at 687; David F. Hamilton, The Importance and Overuse of Policy and Custom Claims: A View from One Trench, id. at 723; G. Flint Taylor, A Litigator's View of Discovery and Proof in Police Misconduct Policy and

Practice Cases, id. at 747. Volume 31 of the Urban Lawyer published a symposium on Reconsidering *Monell*'s Limitation on Municipal Liability for Civil Rights Violations, with an introduction by David M. Gelfand, 31 Urb. Law. 395 (1999) and the following articles: Robert J. Kaczorowski, Reflections on *Monell*'s Analysis of the Legislative History of Section 1983, id. at 407; Barbara Kritchevsky, Reexamining *Monell*: Basing Section 1983 Municipal Liability Doctrine on the Statutory Language, id. at 437; Robert E. Manley, Effective But Messy, *Monell* Should Endure, id. at 481; Oscar G. Chase and Arlo Monell Chase, *Monell*: The Story Behind the Landmark, id. at 491; Ronald Turner, Employer Liability for Supervisory Hostile Environment Sexual Harassment: Comparing Title VII's and Section 1983's Regulatory Regimes, id. at 503; Laura Oren, If *Monell* Were Reconsidered: Sexual Abuse and the Scope-of-Employment Doctrine in the Common Law, id. at 527.

Finally, for an interesting recent article that calls for renewed attention to "custom" as a basis of municipal liability, see Myriam E. Gilles, Breaking the Code of Silence: Rediscovering "Custom" in Section 1983 Municipal Liability, 80 B.U. L. Rev. 17 (2000). Gilles focuses particularly on the "police code of silence" as a "custom" that "causes" constitutional violations.

Page 1035, add at the beginning of footnote a:

For a recent reinterpretation of *Paul*, see Barbara E. Armacost, Race and Reputation: The Real Legacy of *Paul v. Davis*, 85 Va. L. Rev. 569 (1999) (arguing that much of the "scholarly hand-wringing" is misdirected, because most of the claims excluded from due process by *Paul* are redirected to other constitutional "homes").

Page 1040, add a new Note:

6. *County of Sacramento v. Lewis.* In other contexts as well, the availability of damages under § 1983 prompts special attention to the definition of the underlying right. At issue in County of Sacramento v. Lewis, 523 U.S. 833 (1998), was police liability for causing death in a high-speed automobile chase. The Supreme Court adopted a restrictive standard that effectively bars federal liability in such cases.

Sheriff's deputies encountered two boys on a motorcycle approaching at high speed. The deputies ordered the motorcycle to stop, but the boys evaded the patrol cars and drove away. Although the boys were suspected of nothing more serious than failure to stop, a deputy gave chase, following the motorcycle as close as 100 feet and reaching speeds as fast as 100 miles per hour. When the motorcycle tipped over, Philip Lewis, a 16-year-old boy who had been riding the motorcycle as a passenger, fell into the path of the patrol car and was killed. Lewis's parents sued the deputy and the county, alleging a violation of the boy's substantive due process right to life. Faced with these facts, the Ninth Circuit ruled that liability would be established on proof of "deliberate indifference to, or reckless disregard for, a person's right to life," but the Supreme Court disagreed.

Speaking through Justice Souter, the Court held that the proper standard for substantive due process analysis was not "deliberate indifference" but whether the deputy had been guilty of an abuse of power which "shocks the conscience." In the specific context of a high-speed automobile chase to apprehend suspected offenders, that standard required proof of an intent to harm the suspects. Justice Scalia, with whom Justice Thomas joined, objected to the Court's resuscitation of the "ne plus ultra, the Napoleon Brandy, the Mahatma Ghandi, the Celophane [citing Cole Porter] of subjectivity, th' ol' 'shocks the conscience' test," but agreed as to the result. Justice Stevens also concurred in the judgment on the ground that, because of uncertainty as to the legal standard, the defendant was entitled to qualified immunity. There was no dissent.

Page 1085, substitute the following for the existing footnote e:

e. For other decisions denying a damages remedy under § 1983, see Suter v. Artist M., 503 U.S. 347 (1992), and Blessing v. Freestone, 520 U.S. 329 (1997). In *Suter* the Court voted seven-two against § 1983 enforcement of the Adoption Assistance and Child Welfare Act of 1980, 42 U.S.C. §§ 620–28, 670–79a. The statute offers federal reimbursement for certain state expenses in the area of adoption and foster care, provided that the state has in place an approved plan, including "reasonable efforts" to prevent removal of children from their homes and to facilitate reunification of families. The Court that the statute did not confer on its beneficiaries a private right enforceable under § 1983. Justices Blackmun and Stevens dissented.

In *Blessing v. Freestone*, the Court reached a similar conclusion with respect to Title IV-D of the Social Security Act, concerning child support. The statute requires states to achieve "substantial compliance" with federal mandates on establishing paternity, locating absent parents, obtaining child support, and collecting overdue payments. Five mothers in Arizona of children eligible to receive child support sued after federal audits revealed pervasive deficiencies in complying with the federal requirements. The Supreme Court ruled, however, that the plaintiffs had failed to identify with the necessary specificity any individually enforceable rights created by federal law. The "substantial compliance" language was interpreted as merely providing a "yardstick" for enforcement by the Secretary of Health and Human Services of the very broad statutory mandates.

Page 1090, add a new Note:

11. *Gonzaga University v. Doe*: The Interaction of Section 1983 and Implied Rights of Action. The Supreme Court sought to align the tests for determining when there is an implied right of action and when § 1983 provides an express remedy in Gonzaga University v. Doe, ___ U.S. ___ (2002). The case concerned the Family Educational Rights and Privacy Act of 1974 (FERPA), 20 U.S.C. § 1232g, which prohibits federal funding of schools that permit the release of students' records without written consent. Doe alleged that Gonzaga, a private university in Washington state, violated FERPA by revealing allegations of sexual misconduct by an employee to state officials involved in teacher certification. The employee sued in state court under § 1983, and the state courts agreed that Gonzaga had acted under color of state law in helping the state officials. A jury awarded both compensatory and punitive damages, and the Washington Supreme Court upheld the verdict.

The United States Supreme Court reversed. Chief Justice Rehnquist began by noting that FERPA was enacted under Congress's spending clause power—that is, Congress required privacy of personal information as a condition of receiving federal funds, rather than as a direct legislative command. In Pennhurst State School and Hospital v. Halderman, 451 U.S. 1 (1981), the Court had held that federal funding provisions create individually enforceable rights only when Congress manifests an "unambiguous" intent to create them. Otherwise, the Court stated, the remedy "for state noncompliance with federally imposed conditions is not a private cause of action for noncompliance but rather action by the Federal Government to terminate funds to the State."

The Court recognized that prior decisions had caused "uncertainty" in the lower courts. Some decisions allowed plaintiffs to enforce statutory rights under § 1983 so long as they fell "within the general zone of interest that the statute is intended to protect; something less than what is required for a statute to create rights enforceable directly from the statute itself under an implied private right of action. Fueling this uncertainty is the notion that our implied private right of action cases have no bearing on the standards for discerning whether a statute creates rights enforceable by § 1983." In *Gonzaga University*, the Court rejected this approach:

> We now reject the notion that our cases permit anything short of an unambiguously conferred right to support a cause of action brought under § 1983. Section 1983 provides a remedy only for the deprivation of "rights, privileges, or immunities secured by the Constitution and laws" of the United States. Accordingly, only "rights," not "benefits" or "interests," may be enforced under that section. This being so, we further reject the notion that our implied right of action cases are separate and distinct from our § 1983 cases. To the contrary, our implied right of action cases should guide the determination of whether a statute confers rights enforceable under § 1983.
>
> We have recognized that whether a statutory violation may be enforced through § 1983 "is a different inquiry than that involved in determining whether a private right of action can be implied from a particular statute." Wilder v. Virginia Hospital Association, 496 U.S. 498, 508, n. 9 (1990). But the inquiries overlap in one meaningful respect—in either case we must first determine whether Congress intended to create a federal right. Thus we have held that "the question whether Congress . . . intended to create a private right of action [is] definitively answered in the negative" where "a statute by its terms grants no private rights to any identifiable class." Touche Ross & Co. v. Redington, 442 U.S. 560, 576 (1979). For a statute to create such private rights, its text must be "phrased in terms of the persons benefited." Cannon v. University of Chicago, 441 U.S. 677, 692, n. 13 (1979). . . . But even where a statute is phrased in such explicit rights-creating terms, a plaintiff suing under an implied right

of action still must show that the statute manifests an intent "to create not just a private right but also a private remedy." Alexander v. Sandoval, 532 U.S. 275, 286 (2001).

Plaintiffs suing under § 1983 do not have the burden of showing an intent to create a private remedy because § 1983 generally supplies a remedy for the vindication of rights secured by federal statutes. Once a plaintiff demonstrates that a statute confers an individual right, the right is presumptively enforceable by § 1983. But the initial inquiry—determining whether a statute confers any right at all—is no different from the initial inquiry in an implied right of action case, the express purpose of which is to determine whether or not a statute "confers rights on a particular class of persons." California v. Sierra Club, 451 U.S. 287, 294 (1981). . . .

A court's role in discerning whether personal rights exist in the § 1983 context should therefore not differ from its role in discerning whether personal rights exist in the implied right of action context. . . . Both inquiries simply require a determination as to whether or not Congress intended to confer individual rights upon a class of beneficiaries. . . . Accordingly, where the text and structure of a statute provide no indication that Congress intends to create new individual rights, there is no basis for a private suit, whether under § 1983 or under an implied right of action.

The Court found that FERPA did not contain the kind of rights-creating language that could support a § 1983 claim. It did not contain "individually focused terminology"—for example, that "no person shall be subjected to" violations of FERPA. Instead, FERPA had an "aggregate focus," referring to institutional policies and requiring that funds recipients "comply substantially." The conclusion that FERPA's nondisclosure provisions do not confer enforceable rights was "buttressed by the mechanism that Congress chose to provide for enforcing those provisions." The Court noted Congress' express direction to the Secretary of Education to "deal with violations" and the extensive administrative complaint structure the Secretary had created and found that "[t]hese administrative procedures squarely distinguish this case from Wright v. Roanoke Redevelopment and Housing Authority, 479 U.S. 418 (1987), and *Wilder*, supra, where an aggrieved individual lacked any federal review mechanism." Finally, the Court pointed to statutory language providing that "except for the conduct of hearings, none of the functions of the Secretary under this section shall be carried out in any of the regional offices" of the Department of Education. 20 U.S.C. § 1232g(g). The legislative history showed that Congress had provided for "centralized review" because of concern that "regionalizing the enforcement of [FERPA] may lead to multiple interpretations. . . ." 120 Cong. Rec. 39863 (1974) (joint statement). "It is implausible," the Court concluded, "to presume that the same Congress nonetheless intended private suits to be brought before thousands of federal-and state-court judges, which could only result in the sort of 'multiple interpretations' the Act explicitly sought to avoid."

Justice Breyer, joined by Justice Souter, concurred in the judgment. They agreed that congressional intent was the key issue in determining whether an individual could bring suit under § 1983, and that FERPA manifested no such intent, but would not have adopted a presumption that Congress intended to create a right only if the text or structure of a statute showed an "unambiguous" intent.

Justice Stevens, joined by Justice Ginsburg, dissented. He argued that the FERPA did contain rights-creating language. He also disagreed with what he saw as the Court's "needlessly borrowing from cases involving implied rights of action":

> [O]ur implied right of action cases "reflect a concern, grounded in separation of powers, that Congress rather than the courts controls the availability of remedies for violations of statutes." *Wilder*, 496 U.S. 498 at 509, n. 9. However, imposing the implied right of action framework upon the § 1983 inquiry is not necessary: The separation-of-powers concerns present in the implied right of action context "are not present in a § 1983 case," because Congress expressly authorized private suits in § 1983 itself. *Wilder*, 496 U.S. 498 at 509, n. 9.

Page 1126, add a footnote at the end of *City of Burlington v. Dague*:

a. The impact of *Dague* is assessed in Julie Davies, Federal Civil Rights Practice in the 1990's: The Dichotomy Between Reality and Practice, 48 Hastings L.J. 197 (1997). Davies reports that the reactions of civil rights lawyers are surprisingly mixed. Plaintiffs' lawyers generally agreed that *Dague* had lowered their leverage in settlement negotiations, but many viewed the loss of multipliers as relatively insignificant. Several "stated that under the lodestar formulation, they are paid at a high hourly rate, and that courts have adjusted for the lack of a multiplier by awarding them a greater percentage of the hours billed." Davies finds, however, that the lack of fee enhancement does affect lawyers bringing class actions, especially in cases requiring expert witnesses.

For a sophisticated economic analysis of the question of multipliers, see Peter H. Huang, A New Options Theory for Risk Multipliers of Attorney's Fees in Federal Civil Rights Litigation, 73 N.Y.U. L. Rev. 1943 (1998) (arguing on the basis of options theory that fee enhancement should be allowed but that multipliers should be set at "less than the initial reciprocal of the probability of the plaintiff prevailing in the lawsuit").

CHAPTER X

REMEDIAL INTERACTIONS

Page 1183, add at the end of the first full paragraph:

For a more recent article building on the work of Ronan Degnan and Stephen Burbank, see Howard M. Erichson, Interjurisdictional Preclusion, 96 Mich. L. Rev. 945 (1998).

APPENDIX B

SELECTED FEDERAL STATUTES

Page B–33, replace the text of 42 U.S.C. § 1983 with the following:

§ 1983. Civil action for deprivation of rights

Every person who, under color of any statute, ordinance, regulation, custom, or usage, of any State or Territory or the District of Columbia, subjects, or causes to be subjected, any citizen of the United States or other person within the jurisdiction thereof to the deprivation of any rights, privileges, or immunities secured by the Constitution and laws, shall be liable to the party injured in an action at law, suit in equity, or other proper proceeding for redress, except that in any action brought against a judicial officer for an act or omission taken in such officer's judicial capacity, injunctive relief shall not be granted unless a declaratory decree was violated or declaratory relief was unavailable. For the purposes of this section, any Act of Congress applicable exclusively to the District of Columbia shall be considered to be a statute of the District of Columbia.

Page B–35, replace the text of § 1988(b) with the following:

(b) Attorney's fees

In any action or proceeding to enforce a provision of sections 1981, 1981a, 1982, 1983, 1985, and 1986 of this title, title IX of Public Law 92–318, the Religious Freedom Restoration Act of 1993, title VI of the Civil Rights Act of 1964, or section 40302 of the Violence Against Women Act of 1994, or section 13981 of this title, the court, in its discretion, may allow the prevailing party, other than the United States, a reasonable attorney's fee as part of the costs, except that in any action brought against a judicial officer for an act or omission taken in such officer's judicial capacity, such officer shall not be held liable for any costs, including attorney's fees, unless such action was clearly in excess of such officer's jurisdiction.

*

APPENDIX C

JUDICIAL REVIEW

Page C–10, add to footnote d:

See also John Harrison, The Constitutional Origins and Implications of Judicial Review, 84 Va. L. Rev. 333 (1998) (providing a closely reasoned and persuasive derivation of *Marbury*'s conclusion from the text of the Constitution).

†